Britain, America and A
Propaganda 1945–53

In the Cold War battle for hearts and minds Britain was the first country to formulate a coordinated global response to communist propaganda. In January 1948, the British government launched a new propaganda policy designed to 'oppose the inroads of communism by taking the offensive against it'. A small section in the Foreign Office, the innocuously titled Information Research Department (IRD), was established to collate information on communist policy, tactics and propaganda, and coordinate the discreet dissemination of counter-propaganda to opinion formers at home and abroad.

This book demonstrates that propaganda was a primary concern of the postwar Governments of Clement Attlee and Winston Churchill, and traces the implementation of Britain's new propaganda policy at all levels from the Prime Minister to British diplomats in the field. It reveals the formidable array of opinion formers mobilised to support the IRD's anti-communist campaign including intellectuals, politicians, churchmen, and the BBC, and encompasses British anti-communist activities within NATO and in various Cold War confrontations in South-East Asia, the Middle East and behind the Iron Curtain. It also reveals for the first time the extent of Britain's involvement with US anti-communist propaganda activities such as Radio Free Europe.

Andrew Defty was awarded his PhD by the University of Salford in 2002. He is a graduate of Salford's MA in Intelligence and International Relations, and has lectured on intelligence, US–UK relations and the Cold War. This is his first book. He has published articles in the journal *Intelligence and National Security* and is editor of the newsletter of the Security and Intelligence Studies Group (SISG).

Cass series: Studies in intelligence
Series editors: Christopher Andrew and Richard J. Aldrich

Also in the Intelligence Series

British Military Intelligence in the Palestine Campaign 1914–1918
Yigal Sheffy

British Military Intelligence in the Crimean War, 1854–1856
Stephen M. Harris

Signals Intelligence in World War II
Edited by David Alvarez

Knowing Your Friends
Intelligence inside alliances and coalitions from 1914 to the Cold War
Edited by Martin S. Alexander

Eternal Vigilance
50 years of the CIA
Edited by Rhodri Jeffreys-Jones and Christopher Andrew

Nothing Sacred
Nazi espionage against the Vatican, 1939–1945
David Alvarez and Revd. Robert A. Graham

Intelligence Investigations
How ultra changed history
Ralph Bennett

Intelligence Analysis and Assessment
Edited by David Charters, A. Stuart Farson and Glenn P. Hastedt

TET 1968
Understanding the surprise
Ronnie E. Ford

Intelligence and Imperial Defence
British intelligence and the defence of the Indian empire 1904–1924
Richard J. Popplewell

Espionage
Past, present, future?
Edited by Wesley K. Wark

The Australian Security Intelligence Organization
An unofficial history
Frank Cain

Policing Politics
Security intelligence and the liberal democratic state
Peter Gill

From Information to Intrigue
Studies in secret service based on the Swedish experience 1939–45
C.G. McKay

Dieppe Revisited
A documentary investigation
John Campbell

More Instructions from the Centre
Andrew Gordievsky

Controlling Intelligence
Edited by Glenn P. Hastedt

Spy Fiction, Spy Films and Real Intelligence
Edited by Wesley K. Wark

Security and Intelligence in a Changing World
New perspectives for the 1990s
Edited by A. Stuart Farson, David Stafford and Wesley K. Wark

A Don at War
Sir David Hunt K.C.M.G., O.B.E. (reprint)

Intelligence and Military Operations
Edited by Michael I. Handel

Leaders and Intelligence
Edited by Michael I. Handel

War, Strategy and Intelligence
Michael I. Handel

Strategic and Operational Deception in the Second World War
Edited by Michael I. Handel

Codebreaker in the Far East
Alan Stripp

Intelligence for Peace
Edited by Hesi Carmel

Intelligence Services in the Information Age
Michael Herman

Espionage and the Roots of the Cold War
The conspiratorial heritage
David McKnight

Swedish Signal Intelligence 1900–1945
C.G. McKay and Bengt Beckman

The Norwegian Intelligence Service 1945–1970
Olav Riste

Secret Intelligence in the Twentieth Century
Edited by Heike Bungert, Jan G. Heitmann and Michael Wala

The CIA, the British Left and the Cold War
Calling the tune?
Hugh Wilford

Britain, America and Anti-Communist Propaganda 1945–53
The Information Research Department
Andrew Defty

Britain, America and Anti-Communist Propaganda 1945–53

The Information Research Department

Andrew Defty

 Routledge
Taylor & Francis Group

LONDON AND NEW YORK

First published 2004
by Routledge
2 Park Square, Milton Park, Abingdon, Oxfordshire OX14 4RN

Simultaneously published in the USA and Canada
by Routledge
270 Madison Ave, New York NY 10016

Routledge is an imprint of the Taylor & Francis Group

Transferred to Digital Printing 2005

© 2004 Andrew Defty

Typeset in Times New Roman by
Newgen Imaging Systems (P) Ltd, Chennai, India

British Library Cataloguing in Publication Data
A catalogue record for this book is available from the British Library

Library of Congress Cataloging in Publication Data
A catalog record for this book has been requested

ISBN 0-7146-8361-2

Printed and bound by Antony Rowe Ltd, Eastbourne

In loving memory of
Michael Hodgson

Contents

List of plates   xi
Foreword   xiii
Acknowledgements   xv
List of abbreviations   xvii

Introduction: historians, the media and British
Cold War propaganda   1

1   The origins of Britain's anti-communist
    propaganda policy, 1945–47   26

2   Launching the new propaganda policy, 1948   63

3   Building a concerted counter-offensive: cooperation
    with other powers, 1948–50   102

4   'Close and continuous liaison': British and American
    cooperation, 1950–51   138

5   A global propaganda offensive: Churchill and
    the revival of political warfare   182

6   A new strategy of political warfare   222

    Conclusion   246

    Bibliography   256
    Index   277

Plates

1 Ralph Murray, head of the IRD from 1948 to 1951   130
2 John Peck, head of the IRD from 1951 to 1954   131
3 An IRD basic paper with the removable cover-slip
   still attached   132
4 A cartoon in the IRD serial, *Inside Soviet China*   133
5 Strip-cartoon serialization of Orwell's *Animal Farm*   133
6 Edward W. Barrett, US Assistant Secretary of State for
   Public Affairs, 1950–52   134
7 C.D. Jackson, Eisenhower's Special Assistant for
   psychological warfare   134
8 Gordon Gray taking the oath of office as Director of
   the Psychological Strategy Board in 1951   135
9 President Truman dedicating the US Coast
   Guard cutter *Courier*   135
10 Truman and Churchill, in the Oval Office in January 1952   136
11 Balloons being released to transport Radio Free Europe
   leaflets into Czechoslovakia in the early 1950s   136
12 Foreign journalists on a tour of British defence
   institutions   137
13 The NATO Caravan of Peace in Portugal in 1954   137

The author would like to thank the following for permission to reproduce photographs: 1 and 2, the Foreign and Commonwealth Office; 3, 4, 5 and 12, the Public Record Office; 6, the Harry S. Truman Library; 7, the Dwight D. Eisenhower Library; 8, 9 and 10, the United States National Archives; 11, Radio Free Europe; 13, the North Atlantic Treaty Organisation.

Foreword

For people living through the so-called 'global war on terrorism', a war without any seeming end, this well-timed book serves to remind us of an earlier conflict in which Britain also aligned itself to the United States in order to combat an enemy that was hell-bent on undermining the Western way of life. A new phrase was invented to describe that earlier conflict, the Cold War, which might appear to be inherently contradictory since it never quite heated up to become a conventional war in which bullets or bombs resulted in the death of Soviet or Anglo-American soldiers. Instead, the Cold War was fought with words. It was a war of ideas between two competing political ideologies and indeed ways of life and, as such, it was a war largely fought out on two fronts: intelligence and propaganda.

As we in the UK have seen with Hutton Enquiry, the line between these two activities is much thinner than is often thought. Propaganda is about saying publicly something in a certain way in order to benefit the source, whereas intelligence is a largely secret activity that is designed to outwit or pre-empt the enemy, but the fact remains that both are dependant on each other. This is especially true in a world characterised by ever-improving communications technologies. At the start of this information age, when television was added to the arsenal of weapons required to wage what is now called 'information warfare', the media were in the front line of the Cold War. Andrew Defty's book carefully documents the strategies, the risks and the techniques adopted in the deployment of propaganda by democratic regimes that perceived themselves to be involved in a war of national survival against the Soviet Union. Although historians have known about the Information Research Department for some time as the principal – but highly secret – organisation for the British contribution to the Western propaganda campaign, we have never been treated to such a thorough treatment that recognises the fusion between intelligence and propaganda.

The Cold War lasted for just over forty years. If the war on terrorism lasts anything like as long – and even if it doesn't – this book will provide a template for how future historians should approach the present struggle for global hearts and minds.

Philip M. Taylor
University of Leeds
February 2004

Acknowledgements

Throughout the research for this book, the archival research has been informed and enhanced by the recollections of a number of individuals involved with the Information Research Department (IRD) who kindly offered to tell me about their experiences of the Department. I am particularly grateful to Adam Watson and John Cloake, who offered detailed recollections and were kind enough to comment on earlier drafts from this book. I would also like to thank Brian Crozier, Aubrey Essex, Hilary King, Lord Christopher Mayhew, Lord Owen, Eric Runacres, John Snodgrass, Mary Tucker, Sir Peter Wilkinson. Several other former members of the IRD provided information but preferred not to be named. Their remarks were no less insightful for that and I am grateful for their help.

This book began life as a PhD thesis at the University of Salford. I owe a great deal of thanks to my supervisor Sheila Kerr, who was an inspiration long before I began this research, and has been supportive and encouraging and given generously of her time long after her responsibility for my supervision should have ended. I also owe a particular debt of gratitude to Richard Aldrich, who pointed me down some useful avenues in the course of my research and has been instrumental in turning my thesis into this book. Many others have provided useful information, advice and encouragement. I would particularly like to thank the following people: Nick Cull, John Garrard, E.D.R. Harrison, Skipper Jones, John Keiger, Paul Maddrell, Davina Miller, Gary Rawnsley, Tony Shaw, Vera Tolz, Ralph White and John W. Young.

Research such as this would be impossible without a great deal of institutional support and I am grateful to the European Studies Research Institute of the University of Salford which provided considerable financial support. I am also grateful for a research grant provided by the Harry S. Truman Library Institute. Such institutions are, of course, comprised of individuals and I am indebted to the staff of many archives and libraries notably: the Public Record Office, the US National Archives, the Harry S. Truman and Dwight D. Eisenhower Presidential Libraries, the Lauinger Library at Georgetown University, the Liddell Hart Centre for Military Archives, McMaster University Library, the NATO Media Library, the National Museum of Labour History, the Palace Green Library at Durham University, and the University libraries of Salford and Manchester. I would like to express particular thanks to Margaret Bryan of the Foreign and Commonwealth Office Library and Records Department, who patiently dealt with my numerous questions about the nature and progress of the declassification of the IRD papers. Permission to quote from private papers was granted by the Trustees of the Liddell Hart Centre for Military Archives, King's College, London. Part of Chapter 4 has already appeared in the journal *Intelligence and National Security* and I acknowledge its repetition here.

Above all I would like to thank my family and friends who have supported me throughout this project. I am grateful for many things: for looking after the children while I wrote, for lifts to London, for accommodation and sustenance on my many archival visits, for encouragement when it was going well and for not asking when it wasn't. I owe a particular debt of gratitude to my mother who has given me so much. I would like to apologise to my own children, Matthew and Isobel, who thankfully care not a jot for Cold War propaganda, but because of it, have had to endure a grumpy father, and been forced to watch far too much television, while I surrounded myself with books and papers. Most of all I would like to thank my wife, Shona, who has been unwavering in her support and encouragement. However, if she will forgive me, I would like to dedicate this book, not to Shona, as I originally intended, but to her father, Michael Hodgson, who died as this book went to press. Michael and I shared a passion for history, and it is a source of great regret that I was not able to complete this book sooner. He was a great help, an inspiration and I will miss him greatly.

Abbreviations

ACUE	American Committee for a United Europe
AFRS	American Forces Radio Service
BBC	British Broadcasting Corporation
BIS	British Information Service
CAB	Cabinet (UK)
CCF	Congress for Cultural Freedom
CFA	Committee for a Free Asia
CIA	Central Intelligence Agency (USA)
CIPC	Colonial Information Policy Committee (UK)
COI	Central Office of Information (UK)
Cominform	Communist Information Bureau
COS	Chiefs of Staff (UK)
CRD	Cultural Relations Department (UK)
CRO	Commonwealth Relations Office (UK)
DBPO	*Documents on British Policy Overseas*
DWS	Diplomatic Wireless Service
ECA	Economic Cooperation Administration (US)
EEC	European Economic Community
FAOH	Foreign Affairs Oral History Program
FBI	Federal Bureau of Investigation (US)
FBIS	Foreign Broadcast Information Service (US)
FCO	Foreign and Commonwealth Office (UK)
FO	Foreign Office (UK)
FOIA	Freedom of Information Act (US)
FRUS	*Foreign Relations of the United States*
GCHQ	Government Communications Headquarters (UK)
IBD	International Broadcasting Division of State Department (US)
IIA	International Information Administration (US)
ILO	Information Liaison Officer (UK and US)
IOD	International Organizations Division of CIA (US)
IPD	Information Policy Department (UK)
IPWG	Information Policy Working Group (NATO)
IRD	Information Research Department (UK)
JIC	Joint Intelligence Committee (UK)
JIPC	Joint Information Policy Committee (UK)
KMT	Koumintang, Chinese Nationalist party

LCS	London Controlling Section (UK)
LHCMA	Liddell Hart Centre for Military Archives
LIO	Labor Information Officer (US)
LSE	London School of Economics
MDAP	Mutual Defence Assistance Pact
MI5	Security Service (UK)
MI6	Secret Intelligence Service, *see* SIS (UK)
MOD	Ministry of Defence (UK)
MSA	Mutual Security Administration (US)
NARA	National Archives and Record Administration (US)
NATIS	North Atlantic Treaty Information Service
NATO	North Atlantic Treaty Organisation
NCFE	National Committee for a Free Europe
NIIS	NATO International Information Service
NMLH	National Museum of Labour History
NSC	National Security Council (US)
NUS	National Union of Students (UK)
OCB	Operations Coordinating Board (US)
OIC	Office of International Information and Cultural Affairs (US)
OPC	Office of Policy Coordination (US)
OSS	Office of Strategic Services (US)
OWI	Office of War Information (US)
PAO	Public Affairs Officer (US)
PCIIA	President's Committee on International Information Activities
PPS	Policy Planning Staff (US)
PR	IRD departmental designation in Foreign Office papers (UK)
PRO	Public Record Office (UK)
PSB	Psychological Strategy Board (US)
PUSC	Permanent Under Secretary's Committee (UK)
PUSD	Permanent Under Secretary's Department (UK)
PWE	Political Warfare Executive (UK)
RFE	Radio Free Europe
RG	Record Group
RIAS	Radio in the American Sector
RIO	Regional Information Office (UK)
RL	Radio Liberty
SEAC	South East Asia Command
SIS	Secret Intelligence Service, *see* MI6 (UK)
SOE	Special Operations Executive (UK)
SSU	Strategic Services Unit (US)
TUC	Trades Union Congress (UK)
USIA	United States Information Agency
USIS	United States Information Service
VOA	Voice of America
WAY	World Assembly of Youth
WFDY	World Federation of Democratic Youth
WFTU	World Federation of Trade Unions
WYO	World Youth Organization

Introduction

Historians, the media and British Cold War propaganda

Writing in 1989, Britain's leading historian of Government propaganda, Philip M. Taylor, described the Cold War as 'the apogee of the twentieth-century struggle for hearts and minds...by its very nature a global propaganda conflict, the alternative to real war.'[1] In the absence of military conflict, propaganda was one of the principal means by which protagonists on both sides of the Iron Curtain sought to project their power, and undermine their enemies. Propaganda was also a vital tool for the creation of domestic support for policies of military expansion which were costly, and with the development of atomic weapons, not without considerable risk to the population. Yet, as Taylor later observed, the role of propaganda as an instrument of national and foreign policy is often neglected in the mainstream historiography of the Cold War.[2] This is particularly true in the case of the Western allies. In an important essay, W. Scott Lucas claims that the use of ideology as a driving force behind US Cold War strategy has been ignored, largely because ideology was always associated with the expansionist policies of the communist powers. Lucas suggests that, 'if an eager student devoured the work of American historians on the Cold War' he would have to be remarkably perceptive to obtain from them any examination of a US ideological campaign.[3] Any student hoping to feast on the role of propaganda in British Cold War history, will find their diet similarly unsatisfying.

It is a central contention of this book that from early in the Cold War Britain developed a propaganda apparatus designed to fight the Cold War on an ideological front, and that in the period from 1945 to 1953 the role of propaganda grew from being an adjunct to foreign policy to become an integral part of British Cold War strategy. Britain was the first country to formulate a coordinated response to communist propaganda. In January 1948, the Government launched a new propaganda policy designed to 'oppose the inroads of Communism, by taking the offensive against it.'[4] It also established a new Foreign Office department, the Information Research Department (IRD), to coordinate Britain's Cold War propaganda. The development of this anti-communist propaganda policy, and the organization and methods of the IRD, are the main focus for this study. It will also reveal that from the earliest stages in the development of Britain's response to communist propaganda, the degree to which such activities could be coordinated with the US Government was a primary consideration. Although Britain's new propaganda policy stated explicitly that it was up to Britain 'as Europeans and as a Social Democratic Government' and 'not the Americans' to give a lead to the forces of anti-communism,[5] it will be shown that cooperation, and eventually coordination of propaganda activities, with the United States became a defining feature of Britain's anti-communist propaganda policy. This was particularly the case following the launch of the US 'Campaign of Truth' in 1950. Faced with a formidable and highly organized communist propaganda machine, officials in both Britain and the USA came to realize the value of a unified response. As both nations developed their own policies for offensive anti-communist propaganda, cooperation became an increasingly important element, as Britain and the USA sought to 'shoot at the same target from different angles.'[6]

The absence of any detailed examination of the role of propaganda in British Cold War history can be at least partly explained by the fact that, as with the British intelligence and security services, successive British governments were at pains to conceal the fact that they maintained a Cold War propaganda apparatus, or even had a policy for responding to communist propaganda. Although the IRD grew to become one of the largest departments in the Foreign Office, its activities were cloaked in secrecy. According to the Foreign Office Order Book for 1951, 'the name of this department is intended as a disguise for the true nature of its work, which must remain strictly confidential.'[7] The IRD did not feature in the published versions of any of the major enquiries into Britain's post-war information activities,[8] and official statements as to its function, were to say the least ambiguous. Although the IRD was listed in the annual *Diplomatic List*, and even featured in Lord Strang's account of the Foreign Office, the description of its functions was brief and ambiguous: 'Responsibility for the compilation of information reports for Her Majesty's Missions abroad.'[9]

The IRD's dissolution in 1977 did see a significant expansion on this statement with the admission that copies of these reports 'were also sent to a number of interested people in the United Kingdom, including journalists and broadcasters.'[10]

However, the refusal of successive Governments to release the bulk of IRD papers to the Public Record Office (PRO) served to discourage many serious historians from embarking on a study of this aspect of British Cold War history. This veil of secrecy was finally lifted when the '1993 White Paper on Open Government' initiated a systematic review of previously retained papers, under the so-called 'Waldegrave Initiative'.[11] In the wake of the Waldegrave Initiative, historians, with the support of interested individuals such as Lord Mayhew, pressed for the early release of the IRD archive.[12] In February 1994, the Foreign Secretary, Douglas Hurd, agreed that these 'interesting papers' should be reviewed for release, and the first batch of IRD records were transferred to the PRO in August 1995.[13] This archival windfall has provided the principal source for this book.

The first accounts of the IRD were written by investigative journalists shortly after the Department was dissolved in 1977. Given that the IRD's work was directed largely at the media, it is perhaps not surprising that the Department has been the object of indignant press fascination. Under lurid headlines such as, 'Death of the department that never was' and 'How the FO waged secret propaganda war in Britain', these early accounts described how the resources and propaganda techniques developed in the Second World War were redirected to fight the Cold War.[14] The main criticism in most of these first accounts was that the IRD's propaganda was directed primarily at a domestic audience. In the most hostile examination, David Leigh claimed that, rather than countering Soviet propaganda, the IRD became 'an instrument of news management' that 'poisoned the wells of journalism,' and deceived, 'people who read books and newspapers (and sometimes even those who actually wrote for them) about what is going on in the world.' Uncooperative journalists, Leigh claimed, were blacklisted and the BBC was 'dragooned into functioning as an arm of government' and '*required* to accept batches of undercover IRD material.'[15] The central argument in most of these accounts is that, by only presenting negative information about the Soviet Union, the Government deliberately suppressed a balanced analysis of Soviet actions. This, argued Richard Fletcher, was, 'a serious subversion of the democratic process,' and may even have prolonged the Cold War.[16]

Another characteristic of the first accounts of the IRD, which was to re-emerge when the IRD papers were released, was the identification of prominent figures or 'celebrities' who cooperated in the Government's propaganda campaign. In an article in 1978, a left-wing magazine, *The Leveller*, named 31 journalists whom they claimed received IRD material, including media stalwarts such as Peter Snow, John Tusa and Peregrine Worsthorne.[17] Investigative journalist, Paul Lashmar, later suggested that the reputation of prominent academics such as Robert Conquest were built upon work derived from material provided by the IRD.[18] Similarly, Duncan Campbell and Andy Thomas, drawing on a document found at the PRO, attempted to show 'how Whitehall schemed to inveigle Michael Foot, Bertrand Russell and a host of prominent intellectuals into the official propaganda machine.' Campbell and Thomas conceded that the Foreign Office rejected this particular proposal, but concluded that 'the nastiest and most embarrassing material...never makes it to the Public Record Office.'[19]

Herein lies the justification for much of this early sensational writing on IRD. The intelligence historian, Richard J. Aldrich, has observed, that it is axiomatic that the lengthy closure of government files has provided 'an invitation to entrepreneurial writers to speculate in an over-imaginative way on the nature of the "dirty secrets" that such archives supposedly contain.'[20] The IRD has been no exception. Early reports claimed that all IRD files had been destroyed to save the government's embarrassment, whilst others suggested that the retention of the IRD files was illegal.[21] The overall result was that the IRD was implicated in a whole range of devious plots, from undermining the Wilson government to human rights abuses in Northern Ireland.[22] As late as 1995 when IRD papers were finally being reviewed for release, one journalist speculated that the: 'IRD still sounds like the place where the most political skeletons are buried.'[23]

When the release of IRD papers began in 1995 there was a fresh burst of media interest in the Department's activities. Although the reports which followed the declassification of the IRD papers were generally less hostile than earlier accounts,[24] they reflected the same preoccupations. Once again the media concentrated on the high profile 'celebrities' named in the documents, including Denis Healey, Bertrand Russell and Stephen Spender.[25] Particular attention focused on the revelation that, in 1949, George Orwell provided the IRD with a list of alleged crypto-communists and fellow-travellers, 'who should not be trusted as propagandists.'[26] Orwell's anti-communism is of course well known, as it was at the time, and Orwell's biographers had long recorded that the writer kept a notebook of 'suspect' individuals.[27] Nevertheless, the fact that Orwell passed this information on to a secret propaganda department was seen by many as a betrayal of the Left.[28] The revelation has spawned a cottage industry in studies of Orwell and the secret state, sustained by the publication, in 1998, of Peter Davison's monumental edition of Orwell's complete works, which included his annotated list of crypto-communists and fellow-travellers.[29] The list Orwell handed to the IRD was not declassified until 2003.[30] Yet, whilst Orwell's supposed role as a 'state informer' has been exhaustively examined, few have recognized the far more significant contribution he made to fighting communism by allowing his work to be used by various agencies involved in Cold War propaganda. More thoughtful studies by Phillip Deery, Tony Shaw and Peter Davison have sought to focus greater attention on the importance of Orwell's work as an instrument of anti-communist propaganda, rather than the actions of Orwell himself.[31]

Concerns about the IRD's domestic operations were also repeated following the first releases of IRD papers. The documents, it was claimed, proved that the BBC was 'conscripted' into the Foreign Office campaign and provided further evidence of an establishment conspiracy to manipulate the Labour Government.[32] *The Times* columnist, Simon Jenkins, described the Foreign Office as 'obsessed' with deceiving the Labour Party, and in *The Guardian* Stephen Dorril claimed that Attlee's Government was 'hoodwinked' into creating a black propaganda unit by hardliners in the Foreign Office and the Ministry of Defence who were 'fascinated by the clandestine.'[33] Many of these stories were recycled in the first popular history of the IRD which followed shortly after the first release of IRD papers. Remarkably, *Britain's Secret Propaganda War, 1948–1977*, by the investigative journalists Paul Lashmar and James Oliver, made only scant use of the newly released material. Instead Lashmar and Oliver drew heavily on the emerging scholarship on British Cold War propaganda, to trace IRD involvement in Korea, Malaya and Suez and, with the aid of interview material, provided some new information on the IRD's role in the 'confrontation' in Indonesia in the 1960s, in Northern Ireland, and most remarkably the campaign for British entry to the European Economic Community (EEC) in the 1970s.[34]

A prevailing trend in these recent accounts of the IRD, most prominent in the work of Lashmar and Oliver, has been to repeat the criticisms of the IRD expressed by journalists in the 1970s and 1980s. Those journalists writing shortly after the IRD's dissolution were influenced by the revisionist interpretation of the Cold War, popular at the time. This interpretation rested on the assumption that the people of Western democracies were tricked by cynical leaders into supporting an aggressive policy of economic imperialism through the propagation of a myth that monolithic communism threatened their national survival.[35] The collapse of the Soviet bloc saw this interpretation tested by new evidence from Soviet archives and memoirs which suggested that the scale of Soviet domestic suppression and communist subversion abroad was such that Western leaders, and indeed propaganda, may even have underestimated the Soviet threat.[36] However, in recent years historians investigating the scale of, principally US, covert activities in the Cold War have revived the revisionist interpretation. These commentators, predominantly working on what has become known as 'the cultural Cold War', have revealed covert attempts by the US Government to influence opinion in the West on a scale not previously appreciated. Their identification of a wide-scale campaign to manufacture an anti-communist consensus at home and abroad, on a scale comparable with Soviet subversion, has naturally led to suggestions of moral equivalence.[37]

The most influential example of this new revisionist school is Francis Stonor Saunders's study of the CIA and the cultural Cold War, *Who Paid the Piper?* Through prodigious archival research and interviews with those involved, Saunders reveals an extensive state-private network of covert funding for cultural, intellectual and artistic movements in Europe which went some way beyond the well-documented CIA funding for the Congress for Cultural Freedom. Saunders identifies many of the key individuals involved this network, such as Arthur Koestler, Malcolm Muggeridge and Nicholas Nabokov, and asks difficult questions of those who took CIA dollars, while claiming intellectual independence. Saunders disputes the claim that the CIA's financial investment came with no strings attached, and that the CIA 'was merely interested in extending the possibilities for free and democratic cultural expression.' She forcefully argues that cultural activities were manipulated to meet the ends of US Cold War strategy and that support for certain individuals and groups went hand-in-hand with the suppression of dissenting views.[38]

Saunders's book is certainly an important work. It was fêted by those on the liberal Left, such as Edward Said, while some of those involved in the activities Saunders covers, such as Peter Coleman and Peregrine Worsthorne, were roundly critical.[39] Saunders lively style and her unrelenting emphasis on a network of personal associations connecting the intellectual and political arenas, undermines or supports her thesis depending on your position. However, the most effective criticisms have been made by those scholars working on the cultural Cold War, who have questioned Saunders' tendency to attribute every development in the cultural and intellectual arena to the guiding hand of CIA paymasters. In common with much popular writing on propaganda, Saunders tends to exaggerate the influence of the propagandist while presenting the target audience as passive recipients. Her most measured critic, Hugh Wilford, has argued that the response of British intellectuals to the CIA's cultural Cold War effort was, 'more complex and varied than allegations of hoodwinking would have one believe.' There were, Wilford argues, elements of 'resistance, cooperation and appropriation' in their response which in varying degrees mitigated against the imposition of American values and direction.[40]

Although Saunders deals only tangentially with the work of the IRD, she similarly overstates the impact of British propaganda. Saunders claims that the principal problem facing the British Government in the post-war years was to dismantle 'the untruths it had systematically constructed' in the war years 'that communism was politically decent.'[41] In fact, British propaganda in the Second World War was carefully designed to counter the tendency of the British public to 'forget the dangers of communism in their enthusiasm over the resistance of Russia.'[42] If the British public was inclined to take a different view it is testament not to the skill of British propagandists but the achievements of the Red Army on the Eastern Front. The IRD could not hope to manufacture a consensus regarding the Soviet threat in the post-war years without the change in public perceptions brought about by events such as the communist subversion of democracy in Czechoslovakia in 1948. Indeed, the IRD did not so much seek to construct a new image of the Soviet menace as build upon the powerful residual anti-communism of many of those on the British Left. Moreover, Saunders' case for US dominance in the field of anti-communist propaganda underestimates the pioneering anti-communist propaganda activities of British Government agencies, including the IRD, and the extent to which the IRD was able to use its close cooperation with the US as a means of exerting a restraining influence on US activities.

The popular history of the IRD has benefited considerably from the emergence of a body of scholarship on British Cold War propaganda. The IRD's origins and *modus operandi* were examined in detail in an article by Lyn Smith published in the London School of Economics (LSE) journal *Millennium* in 1980.[43] Smith sought to fill in some of the gaps in the earlier press reports and show in particular that, as well as influencing opinion at home, propaganda was also used as 'part of the government's mechanism for conducting relations with other states.' Smith's article was based largely upon a series of documents covering the period 1947–49, provided confidentially by Christopher Mayhew.[44] As Parliamentary Under-Secretary in the Foreign Office in the late 1940s, Mayhew had been instrumental in formulating Britain's anti-communist propaganda policy. Given the origins of the article, it is not surprising that Smith placed considerable emphasis on Mayhew's role in launching the new propaganda policy. Nevertheless, Smith also uncovered a great deal of information about the IRD's operations and contacts throughout its existence. The Department, she revealed, produced two categories of material. The first consisted of secret and confidential studies designed for high-level consumption by heads of state. The second was less highly classified and suitable for dissemination by British missions to local contacts to be used on an unattributable basis. In the production of this material the IRD drew on secret service sources as well as information gathered openly by diplomats in British missions. It consisted of carefully selected factual material dealing with deficiencies of the Soviet system and the advantages of Western social democracy:

> All of this was energetically reproduced and distributed to a great variety of recipients. These included: British Ministers, MPs and trade unionists, the International Department of the Labour Party and UN delegates, British media and opinion formers including the BBC World Service, selected journalists and writers. It was also directed at the media all over the non-communist world, information officers in British Embassies of the Third World and communist countries, and the Foreign Offices of Western European countries.[45]

Smith, however, found no evidence to suggest that any of these recipients were deceived about the origins of the material they received, and those who passed on the material unattributably did so willingly, confident of its veracity. Mayhew pointed out that IRD material was not forced on MPs, rather 'if some anti-Stalinist MP wanted information or briefing on some subject, then we were only too happy to send him the facts.' Smith also spoke to many journalists who received IRD material. They were, she wrote, aware that the material 'was produced by the FO backroom boys' and selected the facts required for their particular needs. Most significantly, Smith's interviews with representatives of the BBC Overseas Services refuted the idea that the BBC was in any way deceived or forced into using IRD material. Sir Hugh Greene, Head of the BBC Eastern European Services in 1949 and 1950, did not find the IRD intrusive in any way. It was, he told Smith, 'just another source of factual information... The BBC always had complete editorial authority – the freedom to take or leave IRD material, and that's what we did.'

Similarly, Smith has reviewed a great many of the books which IRD covertly sponsored by authors as diverse as Susan Strange, Robert Conquest, Bertrand Russell and Leonard Schapiro, yet she found, 'no evidence that writers' views were trimmed to particular political lines...rather it was the case that if their independent opinions fitted in with IRD requirements then their output would be used.' Nevertheless, in conclusion, Smith conceded that the IRD's influence may not have been entirely positive. It was certainly a major hidden influence on opinion at home and abroad, and, she speculated, the process of selecting material on communism may have resulted in a distorted picture of the Soviet bloc.[46]

Smith's path-breaking article set out the organization and methods of British Cold War propaganda. Since then historians have sought to integrate these activities into a broader historical context. Scholars have generally approached the study of IRD from two distinct fields of historical enquiry: intelligence studies and communications history. Those historians from what D.C. Watt has termed the 'British school of intelligence studies' have generally adopted a wide definition of the term 'intelligence' which encompasses a whole range of covert activity including the collection and interpretation of information, special operations, covert propaganda and internal security. These historians have, according to D.C. Watt, 'come to consider positive clandestine action to influence the policy and opinion of other states an important part of the whole intelligence/covert action range.'[47] A small group of historians, led by Philip M. Taylor have sought to integrate the IRD into wider studies of British propaganda in the twentieth century, and in particular the use of propaganda in a series of conflicts in the post-war years – most notably, Malaya, Korea and Suez.[48] Recent attempts by these two separate but not unrelated groups of historians to integrate the activities of the intelligence services and the media into scholarship on international relations has led directly to the development of a body of scholarly literature on British anti-communist propaganda. This has created a curious paradox whereby IRD is given equal weight in studies of the most open aspect of diplomacy – government publicity, and in studies of its most secret aspect – intelligence.[49]

Historians of intelligence and the Cold War have sought to place the IRD within the context of an expanding post-war intelligence community in which many of the clandestine techniques developed during the Second World War were resurrected to deal with the new threat from communism. In 1987, the intelligence historian, Wesley K. Wark, wrote that the IRD was 'a true child of the high-tension atmosphere of international politics into which it was born.' In the early years of the Cold War, faced with a concerted Soviet offensive, of which propaganda was just one part, Foreign Secretary, Ernest Bevin, who was initially sceptical of the value of anti-communist propaganda, authorized a response designed to mirror the Soviets' own offensive campaign. The nature of Britain's response, Wark claimed, was defined by the experience of two World Wars which had served to 'foster an enthusiasm for unorthodox methods of political warfare.'[50]

Raymond Smith has shown that this enthusiasm was most prevalent among senior officials in the Foreign Office who from 1946 began to advocate a defensive/ offensive response to Soviet propaganda modelled on wartime methods of propaganda and subversion. Smith argued that, despite Bevin's reservations, officials proved adept at developing British Soviet policy along their own lines. In an interpretation which highlights Bevin's administrative weakness, Smith concluded that, through proposals for more targeted anti-communist propaganda activities, most notably in Iran, officials 'chipped away' at Bevin's resistance and moved the Foreign Secretary towards a more offensive strategy which culminated in the creation of the IRD in January 1948.[51]

The suggestion that senior officials were responsible for British policy towards the Soviet Union has led revisionist historians, such as Peter Weiler, to argue that the IRD was part of a concerted campaign to manufacture consensus in the Labour movement in Britain. In a critical assessment of *British Labour and the Cold War*, Weiler argued that the first years of the post-war Labour Government saw the rejection of the communist and non-communist Left in the Labour Party and the trade unions, and the incorporation of the Labour movement into the hegemonic values and ideology of the state. Foreign Office propaganda, Weiler suggested, was central to this process. British labour's growing hostility towards the Soviet Union, Weiler argued, may have owed as much to the manipulation of opinion by élites in the Foreign Office as to Soviet actions.[52]

Although Weiler provided important evidence of the Foreign Office's domestic anti-communist activities, several historians have contested his assertion that the domestic consensus regarding Soviet intentions was manufactured by the Foreign Office. Anthony Carew has argued that in promoting anti-communism in the Trades Union Congress (TUC), the Government was effectively pushing against an open door. Moreover, Carew has shown that the Government's involvement with the TUC was not motivated by domestic concerns, but by the desire to counter communism in the international trade union movement.[53] Similarly, in *The Secret State*, a study of British internal security in the twentieth century, Richard Thurlow argued that Weiler overstated his case by suggesting that labourism was hijacked by establishment élites. Thurlow noted that far from being led by the nose, democratic socialists had long recognized the horrors of Stalinism. When these socialists formed the Government in 1945, Thurlow wrote, they established a 'symbiotic and dialectical relationship' with the Establishment in which both recognized the need to guard against the communist threat. The creation of the IRD, Thurlow argued, was the result of a convergence between the policies of the Labour Government and the interests of the Whitehall Administration, 'rather than the effects of anti-communist propaganda or a semi-conspiratorial incorporation of the Labour movement bureaucracy into the structure of the Capitalist State.'[54]

The convergence of Labour policies and Foreign Office thinking has been examined in the most detailed study of the origins of Britain's anti-communist propaganda by W. Scott Lucas and C.J. Morris, which appeared in Aldrich's edited volume, *British Intelligence, Strategy and the Cold War, 1945–51*, in 1992.[55] Aldrich opened the volume with an essay on the post-war reorganisation of the British intelligence community, which placed the IRD within the context of a Whitehall Administration struggling to cope with a Cold War conducted 'by all means short of war.'[56] Lucas and Morris set the Foreign Office proposals for a response against the background of Bevin's need to accommodate the left-wing of the Labour Party. The new propaganda policy, they argued, emerged when the Foreign Office plan was wedded to a new tenet of British foreign policy, the positive projection of a British-led 'Third Force' linked to the Empire and Commonwealth and independent of the USA and the Soviet Union. They suggested, however, that the 'Third Force', may have been merely, 'a device to win ministerial support' for the Foreign Office strategy. Within a year, they claimed, the 'positive' element had disappeared from Britain's propaganda, and the offensive element was modified and expanded. Lucas and Morris claimed that the IRD shifted quickly from 'Third Force propaganda' to 'political warfare' which went beyond what was originally described as a 'defensive/offensive' to include support for subversive operations being carried out by the intelligence services and, eventually, operations in support of British interests outside the communist bloc. They argue that because the Government failed to establish effective control, the IRD became 'a service department, "on call" to support the latest projects of other departments and agencies.' As a result, they concluded, the IRD evolved from anti-communist to 'anti-anti-British.'[57]

Many facets of the IRD's operations, at home and abroad, behind the Iron Curtain, and in the colonies, have been drawn together in Richard J. Aldrich's vast history of British and American Cold War secret intelligence, *The Hidden Hand*.[58] In one of the first works to take advantage of the declassified IRD papers, Aldrich focuses on the operational aspect of the Government's anti-communist propaganda policy in an effort to shed some light on how the Cold War was fought:

> Cold War fighting, and a growing conviction that the Cold War could be won through special operations or covert action, was critical in determining the character of this struggle. By the early 1950s, operations to influence the world by unseen methods – the hidden hand – became ubiquitous and seemed to transform even everyday aspects of society into an extension of this battleground.[59]

In Britain, Aldrich argues, clandestine operations to counter communist influence began as early as 1945. By the time the IRD was created in 1948, 'it was playing catch-up with obscure sections of Whitehall that were ahead in authorising counter-measures against the Soviets.'[60] Not least amongst these was the Cultural Relations Department of the Foreign Office, which since late 1945 had mounted an orchestrated campaign to counter communist influence in international youth organizations.[61] Responsibility for such activities was soon passed to the IRD. Aldrich is careful, however, not to describe a simple continuum between wartime and Cold War clandestine operations. The IRD, he asserts, was different from the diverse bodies dealing with wartime propaganda in that it was entirely under Foreign Office control.[62] Moreover, Aldrich paints a vivid picture of Bevin successfully resisting sustained pressure from the Chiefs of Staff for more aggressive propaganda and special operations aimed at the liberation of Eastern Europe.[63]

The detailed research of historians such as Wark, Lucas and Morris, and Aldrich has shed considerable light on the Cold War origins of Britain's anti-communist propaganda policy. A second group of historians have placed the policy in a much broader context. These historians, led by Philip M. Taylor, have explained the origins of Britain's anti-communist propaganda policy as part of an historical trend towards the acceptance by governments that propaganda, 'a major requisite of modern warfare,' is 'no less essential to the maintenance of peace, power and prestige.'[64] This, Taylor claimed, was no less true for British governments than it was for the totalitarian regimes of Nazi Germany and Soviet Russia. Taylor has shown that, despite a traditional antipathy towards propaganda, by the 1950s British governments accepted that machinery for the effective employment of propaganda had become an essential weapon in the national arsenal, 'part of the normal apparatus of diplomacy of a Great Power.' This view was not only based on the experiences of two World Wars but also the ravages of the inter-war years. In the 1920s and 1930s successive governments gradually and reluctantly came to recognize the importance of projecting Britain abroad, firstly as an aid to trade, and later as a response to anti-British totalitarian propaganda. This experience, Taylor argued was soon adapted to the harsh realities of the post-war world.[65]

Taylor has also identified several distinctive features of British overseas propaganda. These were established at the time of the British Government's first foray into propaganda activities during the First World War, and were confirmed by experience of British propagandists in future conflicts. The most important was that effective propaganda was based upon the truth. In marked contrast to totalitarian governments' advocacy of the 'Big Lie', British governments have found the selective presentation of the facts a more effective, and more palatable, employment of propaganda. Despite this, British governments have also been keen to hide their propaganda activities. British governments, it was claimed, did not engage in 'propaganda,' they told the truth. Consequently, agencies responsible for directing propaganda overseas have usually operated in secret. The Foreign Office, in particular, has favoured an indirect approach to the dissemination of propaganda. The reason for this, was outlined by Sir Robert Cecil in 1916: 'official propaganda known to be such was "almost useless".'[66] Unlike the totalitarian governments, the British government eschewed direct appeals to mass opinion and targeted their propaganda at élite opinion formers. As Taylor has also shown, for the Foreign Office in particular, mass public opinion was almost incomprehensible and only to be influenced indirectly. 'Foreign Office-inspired propaganda was directed towards the opinion-makers, such as journalists, publicists and politicians, rather than to the mass of foreign peoples.' The principle being that it was better to influence those who can influence others than to attempt a direct appeal to the mass of the population.[67] These principles were to influence Foreign Office thinking in the production of propaganda during the Cold War, and were the source of some friction when the Labour Government proposed a new propaganda policy based upon an appeal to the masses.

Taylor's work has inspired a series of detailed case studies of British propaganda. Studies of propaganda during the Korean War, the Suez crisis and colonial insurgencies in Malaya, Kenya and Cyprus have served to illustrate British governments' growing appreciation of the importance of propaganda and the media.[68] These studies have also illustrated that during the Cold War the communist threat came to dominate all of Britain's overseas propaganda. In 1995, Susan Carruthers revealed that the IRD was closely involved in Britain's response to colonial insurgency. As a result, Carruthers observed, whether or not communism was a principal factor in the unrest, 'the IRD's very *raison d'être* meant it was almost bound to exaggerate the communist threat.'[69] Although the IRD's involvement supported the claims of Lucas and Morris that the IRD moved from anti-communist to anti-anti-British propaganda, Carruthers suggests a more subtle thesis. In its engagement in colonial campaigns, she concluded, the IRD's principal concern remained anti-communism. 'If it was anti-anti-British, it was so precisely because it was anti-communist.'[70]

Tony Shaw and Gary Rawnsley reached similar conclusions in their respective examinations of propaganda during the Suez crisis. Both have also suggested that the IRD was far more at home in dealing with Cold War crises such as the Hungarian uprising and the war in Korea.[71] In contrast to the crude attempts to shoehorn the communist threat into the presentation of colonial unrest, the campaign in Korea, Shaw concluded, 'bore out the value to the British Government of a propaganda department whose priority was anti-communism':

> The IRD's ability to devise and disseminate material demonising the monolithic Soviet bloc in various forms to suit different audiences showed subtlety and imagination. (It also contrasted with the communists' overly crude and ultimately counter-productive tendencies.) The non-attributable (or 'grey') nature of its output added to the public's impression that politicians were reflecting opinion rather than seeking to lead it... The department's true research skills in tracking and countering communist propaganda helped the UN to keep a step ahead of its rivals in general throughout the conflict.[72]

The literature suggests there were two influences on the generation of Britain's anti-communist propaganda policy. The first was the threat from Soviet propaganda and subversion and the need to formulate a response using means 'short of war.' In order to do so the British Government, it is claimed, fell back on the lessons of the recent past and resurrected a series of covert wartime agencies. Others have sought to place these developments within the context of a world in which the advent of a mass media, and the development of conflicts which increasingly affected the whole of the population, led governments to embrace propaganda as a tool of diplomacy. British propaganda in the Cold War, it is argued, did not merely represent a resurrection of wartime agencies, but was the application of principles developed in the Foreign Office since the First World War. The most accurate assessment, of course, lies in a synthesis of these views.

There is little consensus as to how Britain's anti-communist propaganda policy developed after 1948. Although the work of Carruthers, Rawnsley and Shaw has addressed British propaganda in a series of conflicts in the 1950s and 1960s, there has been little examination of the role of propaganda in building a concerted counter-offensive to the Soviets in the early Cold War. In particular, the 'Third Force' aspect of Britain's propaganda policy has been inadequately explored. It is generally assumed that the positive aspect of the new propaganda policy was never implemented, and the IRD in particular has been criticized for neglecting this aspect. It is also unclear as to what was the principal target for British anti-communist propaganda. Revisionists have stressed the domestic element. Others, such as Lucas and Morris, suggest that British propaganda quickly developed an offensive element directed at subversion in Eastern Europe. Lucas later suggested, that by the mid 1950s the IRD was turning its attention to lesser opponents in the Middle East and Africa, leaving anti-communist work primarily to the USA.[73]

In the literature there is, in particular, a certain myopia with regard to the relationship between British and US anti-communist propaganda. Most of the work from Lyn Smith onwards has highlighted some degree of cooperation between British and US propagandists. Those who have employed US sources, such as Smith, Fletcher and Wark have indicated that US information staff in the field were kept informed of the IRD's activities. Moreover, it has been shown that at a series of meetings in London in 1950, British and US officials exchanged details of their respective propaganda programmes and agreed to 'close and continuous liaison' on all aspects of anti-communist propaganda.[74] However, this relationship has not been examined in detail. In general, it is argued that although Britain led the field by providing a coordinated response to communist propaganda as early as 1948, Britain's modest propaganda activities were soon swamped by the superior resources of the USA.[75] The release of the IRD papers has done little to change this perception. In 1995, Scott Lucas wrote that by the 1950s the IRD was a pale shadow of the CIA propaganda machine, 'it would be the US, with its own propaganda means and ends, that would define the image of the Free World.'[76] Similarly, in 1998, Hugh Wilford reviewed the first two batches of IRD papers to be released. Wilford detected in the files 'a growing tendency towards Anglo-American cooperation in the publicity crusade against communism, both between headquarters and between representatives in the field.' Yet, with only a small amount of material to review, Wilford fell back on the easy assumption made in much of the secondary literature that the British campaign was soon eclipsed, 'as leadership of the anti-communist crusade passed to the Americans.' The Foreign Office's most powerful motive for cooperating, Wilford suggested, was to take advantage of the 'superb resources' of the USA.[77] It is remarkable, and perhaps a little surprising that Britain's contribution to Anglo-American anti-communist propaganda has been so denigrated, when studies of other aspects of Anglo-American cooperation, most notably intelligence, have found ample evidence of the value of Britain's contribution of expertise and experience in a field dominated by US resources.[78]

The declassification of material under the Waldegrave Initiative has clearly opened the field for serious historical enquiry into British propaganda during the Cold War. Although historians have already begun to mine this rich seam, the body of literature on British Cold War propaganda can not compare with the vast literature on the use of propaganda in the two World Wars. Much of the emerging literature on British propaganda during the Cold War years has tended to reflect this interest in the role of propaganda in wartime with detailed studies of propaganda in Korea, Malaya and the Suez. It is also evident that some fields of propaganda activity, notably broadcasting, have attracted considerable attention,[79] whilst others, such as the press and publishing, have received little attention.[80] Only a few historians, most notably Aldrich, have used the declassification of material under the Waldegrave Initiative to return to the development of British policy towards the Soviet Union in the early Cold War years, and examine the role of propaganda in peacetime.[81]

This study has benefited from access to a large volume of material released under the Waldegrave Initiative.[82] Most significantly, since 1995, almost all the policy files of the Foreign Office Information Research Department from the period under scrutiny have been transferred to the PRO. The content of this extensive archive has shed considerable new light on British anti-communist propaganda policy, and provides the main source for this study.[83] The Waldegrave Initiative has also seen the release of a large number of files relating to anti-communist propaganda in the records of other Foreign Office and government departments, and the return of previously retained material to collections of private papers of British public servants.[84]

There is a methodological bonus in researching the work of organizations responsible for propaganda, even a secret department such as the IRD. That is, that such organizations depend upon the widespread dissemination of their product. Even when their methods are secret, their output is not. Thus, propaganda material generated by the IRD was distributed widely across Whitehall, and beyond. Even before the recent release of IRD files, enough material relating to British Cold War propaganda had slipped past the 'weeders' in the records of other government departments to allow a number of authoritative accounts of the IRD's work. This has been augmented by the release of further material under the Waldegrave Initiative. In researching this book, documents pertaining to the IRD's activities have been found in the records of government departments as diverse as the Central Office of Information, the Colonial Office and the Ministry of Labour, and a host of other Foreign Office regional and information departments, and embassy files.

The nature of the IRD's work was such that evidence has also survived in collections outside the PRO. Although the IRD's methods were clandestine, unlike the intelligence and security services its product was designed for widespread distribution outside of Whitehall. The International Department of the Labour Party under the direction of Denis Healey was an early and avid consumer of IRD material. A large number of IRD briefing papers and some correspondence may be found in the Labour Party archives.[85] The BBC also received IRD reports and recommendations, and those working on Western broadcasting during the Cold War have found much evidence of the IRD's work in the BBC archives.[86] A review of the IRD files at the PRO reveals a host of other organizations in receipt of IRD material, including the Church of England, the TUC, the National Council for Social Services, the National Union of Students and the Congress for Cultural Freedom. Some historians have already begun to sift the archives of these organizations for examples of Foreign Office propaganda.[87] Many prominent individuals, journalists and academics worked with the IRD and some of this material survives in collections of private papers.[88] The IRD also distributed material to a large number of foreign governments. While this study has drawn on a wealth of material from the US archives, the Australian historian, Phillip Deery, has found extensive evidence of the IRD's activities in the National Archives of Australia.[89] Further examples of IRD's output must reside in the archives of the foreign ministries of a large number of nations across Europe and Asia.[90]

The wealth of material now available does not, however, provide a complete picture of British efforts to counter communist propaganda. The IRD's archive is itself far from complete. Significant numbers of files remain classified and may well remain closed for some considerable time. British clandestine activities in peacetime remain a more sensitive subject than similar operations during war. Most of the files of the wartime Political Warfare Executive were declassified under the 30-year rule, whilst records of its peacetime equivalent, the IRD, have only recently been released. Even following the Waldegrave Initiative, the release of a great volume of files relating to intelligence and special operations in the Second World War has not been matched by the release of files from the early post-war years. It is apparent that files from the post-1945 period are subject to a much more careful review, and their release has therefore been somewhat slower and more erratic.[91] The files of the IRD have certainly been carefully weeded. Some files have been retained in their entirety. In more cases, sensitive material has been removed from files or the policy of blanking out sensitive sections has been employed. Some extant material relates to the IRD's relations with the Secret Intelligence Service (SIS), although numerous reports from MI5 can be found in the IRD files.[92] Information on the coordination of clandestine activities with other powers, such as the USA, is perhaps the most sensitive. Particularly when it relates to covert activities in other friendly countries – such as British and US efforts to counter communism in France and Italy.

In addition to the continued classification of material, perhaps a more serious problem facing historians researching British Cold War propaganda is the destruction of records. The intelligence historian Richard Aldrich has warned historians against growing fat on the processed diet of records selected for preservation in national archives while 'the bulk of contemporary history heads to the incinerators unseen and largely uncontested.'[93] Of course, not all official documents are selected for permanent preservation, nor should they be. Nevertheless, it is clear that policies for the preservation of material of historical interest have not been applied consistently across Whitehall, and particular concern has been expressed about the preservation policies of covert agencies. No lesser body than the Lord Chancellor's Advisory Council on Public Records has expressed concern about security and intelligence agencies applying their own criteria for the selection of material.[94] The Foreign Office, along with the Cabinet Office, preserves the largest proportion of papers, more than 80 per cent of the political papers are judged to be of historical interest, of which over 95 per cent are released.[95] Nevertheless, there is a substantial gap in the documentary record of British Cold War propaganda. Although the policy files of the IRD have been preserved, much of the Department's output, the propaganda itself, has not. In 1982, the Lord Chancellor's Department stated that apart from a handful of papers on general themes: 'The items distributed by IRD to other FO departments and journalists were in the main ephemeral and not considered to be of sufficient historical importance to be selected for permanent preservation.'[96]

Although this statement caused several commentators at the time to fear that the whole of the IRD archive had been pulped,[97] it referred only to the IRD's output. (An, admittedly vast, number of briefing papers, on a whole range of issues, produced by the IRD on a weekly or monthly basis throughout its 30-year existence.) Some of the IRD's output may be found in the Department's policy files, and selected examples survive in files of other Government departments.[98] However, only two whole series of the IRD's briefing papers were selected for permanent preservation, as examples of the IRD's product.[99] This is only a tiny fraction of the IRD's output and the series chosen only represent the IRD's early concern with countering communism in Europe and the Far East. It is remarkable that other series of briefing papers produced to deal with particular situations, such as the Suez crisis, or particular issues, such as the communist attitude to religion, were not considered worthy of preservation.[100]

Faced with British official secrecy, early studies of the IRD suggested that much information regarding British anti-communist propaganda could be gleaned from US sources.[101] In the USA, as in Britain, the end of the Cold War has prompted a new policy of openness regarding the declassification of government documents. In April 1995, President Clinton issued Executive Order 12958 requiring government agencies to release, with few exceptions, material retained for over 25 years. Although the sheer scale of classified material due for review, coupled with a certain reticence on the part of the CIA, has led to some disquiet regarding the application of this policy, recent studies of US covert activity in the early Cold War have made extensive use of recently declassified material from the National Archives of the USA.[102] Moreover, as Aldrich has observed, US records policy is such that the United States Archives are often represented as some kind of 'Wonderland' where classified British documents may be found in abundance.[103] This is, of course, only partly true. Agreements between the State Department and the British Government detailing the categories of material that London requests be withdrawn from US files, coupled with the CIA's 'third agency rule' has meant that the release of documents relating to cooperation with allies in covert activities is rare.[104] Nevertheless, the scale of Anglo-American cooperation in anti-communist activities in the early Cold War, covert and overt, in every corner of the globe, was such that much material has slipped through the net of official secrecy. More particularly, it is clear that while documents pertaining to liaison between British and US intelligence agencies have been carefully screened, the work of information staff has attracted less attention. A whole network of cooperation between the IRD and information staff in US embassies, and in particular the information liaison arrangements between the British Embassy in Washington and a whole range of US agencies may be traced in the records of the US State Department.

When the documentary record is incomplete supplementary information is often found in the recollections of those involved in clandestine activities. This study has benefited from the memoirs, correspondence and interviews with those involved in British anti-communist propaganda. Memoirs provide a predictably patchy insight into British anti-communist propaganda. In the memoirs of some of the most senior officials involved in British overseas information activities, Sir Robert Marrett, Ivone Kirkpatrick and Paul Gore-Booth, the IRD is notable by its absence.[105] As their accounts were all written before the IRD's dissolution, and Marett's book in particular is otherwise so comprehensive, the omission can only be explained by considerations of official secrecy. Although the publicity surrounding the release of the IRD papers prompted a number of former officials to speak out in support of the department's work, some remain reluctant to refer to their work for fear of breaching official secrecy.[106]

The utility of memoirs is also reduced by the nature of service in the Foreign Office. In many cases a tenure in the IRD was only a small part of a long Foreign Office career. For example, Cecil Parrott, who joined the IRD in its first and formative year, referred in his memoirs only to, 'a preliminary run of a year in one of the Information Departments of the Foreign Office,' after which he was transferred to the United Nations Political Department.[107] Even those who recall their work in more detail often provide little substantive information about propaganda policy or operations. As one of the largest departments in the Foreign Office, the IRD employed a great many people. However, it seems much of the IRD's work was rather mundane, comprising mainly of detailed research, foreign press reading and the production of briefing papers. The dissemination of this information in the field, was often no more interesting. Dame Stella Rimington, the former Director-General of MI5 worked in the IRD's Delhi office in the late 1960s:

> Nobody ever told me what was going on there. I was merely told to carry out the rather basic task of stuffing envelopes with all sorts of printed material, which was sent out from London, and posting them off to a whole series of

addresses. It was very important, I was told, to get the right stuff in the right envelopes – not everyone got everything – and the whole operation, and in particular the names and addresses were very secret... Whether any of it had any effect I was not in a position to judge, though I did notice from time to time articles in the newspapers which seemed to have drawn on the stuff I had put in the envelopes.[108]

Of course, Rimington adds, she now knows that the IRD was responsible for influencing public opinion by planting stories hostile to Britain's enemies and favouring the British position.

It is often the recipients of this material who have provided the most detailed accounts of the IRD's methods. Journalists such as Brian Crozier, Richard Beeston, Peregrine Worsthorne and Roland Challis, who received confidential briefings from the Foreign Office or were employed as temporary contract staff by the IRD, have less to fear from the guardians of official secrecy and have been more candid in accounts of their dealings with the Foreign Office.[109] Similarly, politicians have traditionally had less regard for official secrecy than officials worried about their pension, even former heads of the Security Service. Thus, the most detailed, and some of the earliest, accounts of Britain's anti-communist propaganda policy came from those who, as Government Ministers, were responsible for its formulation. Christopher Mayhew, who was instrumental in creating the IRD, revealed the existence of the British Government's anti-communist propaganda policy as early as 1969.[110] He has since produced two detailed accounts of his role in British anti-communist propaganda policy.[111] Denis Healey, who as Secretary of the Labour Party's International Department in the late 1940s was a frequent recipient of IRD material, and David Owen, who as Foreign Secretary presided over the department's demise, have also provided information on the IRD's methods.[112]

Beyond the published recollections of individuals involved in Cold War propaganda, interviews provide a useful additional source. Interviews can, of course, provide vital colour to any narrative, and may provide deeper insight into the documentary record. However, they are particularly valuable when researching activities conducted on the fringes of the covert world such as British Cold War propaganda. While the broad outlines of British propaganda policy may be effectively traced in the archives, the IRD's *modus operandi* is less clear. The IRD's propaganda material was distributed largely by personal contacts between IRD officials and a whole range of opinion formers at home and abroad, journalists, intellectuals, MPs and trade union officials. The kind of informal arrangement whereby such individuals were persuaded to take IRD material, or even write for the Department, is rarely reflected in the documentary record. The personal reflections of those involved are also particularly useful when trying to establish the dynamics of Anglo-American relations. While there were certainly formal arrangements for British and US liaison in the field of anti-communist propaganda, a great deal of consultation and cooperation was conducted on an informal level, over drinks at the Embassy, whisky in the White House, or dinner at the home of some senior figure. In one notable example, following Eisenhower's election, the British Information Liaison Officer in Washington, Adam Watson, had monthly meetings at the White House with Eisenhower's psychological warfare chief, C.D. Jackson. These were informal meetings which ranged widely across the problems of the Cold War, no minutes were taken, and save for brief references in Jackson's daily log, the only surviving record lies in the memory of Adam Watson. While old age, natural reserve and uncertainties over the limits of official secrecy prevent many from sharing their recollections, those who do, such as Watson, are extremely valuable witnesses to history.[113]

There is now almost an embarrassment of riches for anyone wishing to research the work of this once secret department, and this study can only make a modest contribution to this field. More detailed and varied studies will certainly follow as the archive of the IRD is mined more deeply. This book does not aim to provide a comprehensive assessment of British propaganda from 1945 to 1953. The Labour Governments of 1945–51 presided over perhaps the greatest expansion of the British Government's propaganda apparatus until the election of the Labour Government in 1997. Propaganda was used widely by the Labour Governments: to explain their policies at home and abroad; to reassure Britain's allies, most notably the USA, about Labour's socialist policies; to promote trade; to counter colonial insurgency; to promote good relations with the newly independent colonies; and to undermine Britain's enemies. This study will focus on just one, very important, aspect of this, the use of propaganda to counter communism. It will show how the Cold War became the defining characteristic of British propaganda policy at home and abroad, and how propaganda was elevated from being an adjunct to policy to become Britain's principal weapon for fighting the Cold War. Under Churchill, it will be shown, an ever expansive role was defined for this weapon as the means with which to bring an end to the Cold War.

This study will be limited to an examination of anti-communist propaganda *policy*. It will show how that policy expanded to become an integral part of Britain's strategy for dealing with the Soviet threat, but it does not seek to present a detailed account of the implementation of that policy. Although the organization and methods of the IRD will be assessed, details of specific propaganda campaigns or operations will be included only insofar as they illustrate the overall direction of Britain's anti-communist propaganda policy. In the period under consideration the IRD launched two major propaganda campaigns: to publicise the use of forced labour in the Soviet Union, and to counter the Soviet peace campaign. In addition, the Department was involved in psychological warfare campaigns in the Malayan emergency and the Korean War. Each one of these campaigns could be the subject of a more detailed examination, and others have already begun this work.[114] These campaigns will only be considered here within the context of Britain's overall strategy for combating communist propaganda.

This study will also concentrate on one specific aspect of Britain's anti-communist propaganda policy: cooperation with the USA. This is not, however, a comparative study of British and US anti-communist propaganda. It does not aim to provide a detailed assessment of America's response to communist propaganda, this has been extensively covered elsewhere.[115] It is a study of British anti-communist propaganda policy, and the extent to which that policy was coordinated with Britain's principal Cold War ally, the USA. The study is comparative only in that British cooperation with the USA, will be viewed in the context of British cooperation with other powers in the field of anti-communist propaganda. It will reveal a wide and complex network of cooperation and consultation in the organization and dissemination of anti-communist propaganda between Britain and other powers, most notably in the Commonwealth, and within the North Atlantic Treaty Organisation (NATO). This will serve to illustrate two fundamental points. Firstly, that cooperation with like-minded governments was an important part of Britain's anti-communist propaganda policy. Secondly, that the degree of cooperation with the USA went some way beyond that with any other power. As such, it serves not only to enhance our understanding of British policy towards the Soviet Union, but also British policy towards her other allies and the USA in particular.

Finally, it is not the intention of this study to examine the effectiveness of British propaganda in the Cold War. It is notoriously difficult to assess the impact of propaganda, particularly if it is directed at a foreign audience. One may identify propaganda policies, and assess the output of propaganda agencies, but it very difficult to gauge how the propaganda is received. This is as much a problem for the propagandist as it is for the historian. A review of the IRD's operations in 1951 observed that it was becoming, 'increasingly difficult to assess precisely the results directly due to Information Research Department.'[116] Some assessment can be made through records kept by the IRD, of all known uses of its material, although these are far from complete. Even where such records are available, as they are for some of the IRD's major campaigns, accounting column inches devoted to a particular propaganda line in the press, provides no indication of how many people read a particular article or whether they were receptive to the information it contained. What is clear is that the resources devoted to the anti-communist propaganda policy were considerable and suggest that successive British governments were convinced of the vital importance of such work and presumably its impact.

Notes

1 P.M. Taylor, 'The Projection of Britain, 1945–51', in J.W. Young and M. Dockrill (eds), *British Foreign Policy 1945–1956* (London: Macmillan, 1989), p. 10.
2 Taylor, 'Through a Glass Darkly? The Psychological Climate and Psychological Warfare of the Cold War', in G.D. Rawnsley (ed.), *Cold-War Propaganda in the 1950s* (London: Macmillan, 1999), p. 225. See also Taylor, 'Back to the Future? Integrating the Press and Media into the History of International Relations', *Historical Journal of Film, Radio and Television*, 14, 3 (1994), pp. 321–9.
3 W. Scott Lucas, 'Beyond Diplomacy: Propaganda and the History of the Cold War', in Rawnsley, *Cold-War Propaganda in the 1950s*, pp. 11–30. Lucas sought to correct this deficiency in, *Freedom's War: The American Crusade against the Soviet Union* (New York: New York University Press, 1999).
4 'Future Foreign Publicity Policy,' CP(48)8, 4 January 1948, CAB 129/23, PRO.
5 *Ibid.*
6 Foreign Office circular to British Missions, 12 May 1948, PR 229/1/G, FO 1110/6, PRO.
7 Reference on the Information Research Department for the Foreign Office Order Book, 22 March 1951, FO 1110/383, PRO.
8 Cmnd.9138, *Summary of the Report of the Independent Committee of Enquiry into the Overseas Information Service: The Drogheda Report* (London: HMSO, April 1954); Cmnd.225, *White Paper on Overseas Information* (London: HMSO, 1957); Cmnd.2276, *Report of Committee on Overseas Representation, 1962–63* (London: HMSO, 1964); Cmnd.4107, *Report of the Review Commission on Overseas Representation 1968/69: The Duncan Report* (London: HMSO, July 1969); *Fourth Report from the Expenditure Committee (Defence and External Affairs Sub-Committee): Central Policy Review Staff Review of Overseas Representation*, Session 1977–78, Parliamentary paper, 286–1, p. lxxix.

9 The IRD was listed in the Diplomatic List each year, from 1949 until its dissolution in 1977; the description of its activities remained the same throughout that time: *The Foreign Office List and Diplomatic and Consular Yearbook* (London: Harrison & Sons Ltd, 1950–64); *Diplomatic Service List* (London: HMSO, 1965–77). Lord Strang was similarly reticent in *The Foreign Office* (London: George Allen & Unwin, 1955), p. 211, 'Appendix II: Departmental Allocation of Work, October 1954.' The IRD's role is described as: 'Research and provision of material on special subjects.'

10 *Parliamentary Debates: Commons*, vol. 943, p. 182, 1 February 1978, Written Answer.

11 Cmnd.2290, *White Paper on Open Government* (London: HMSO, July 1993).

12 Lord Mayhew, *Parliamentary Debates: Lords*, 25 October, 1993; Institute of Contemporary British History Conference, 'The Waldegrave Initiative on PRO Releases: One Year On', 24 November 1993; B. Cathcart, 'Eden's Lessons of Suez Revealed, 37 Years On', *The Independent*, 28 November 1993; R.J. Aldrich, 'Open More Archives', Letter to *The Daily Telegraph*, 9 February 1994.

13 See the Foreign Secretary's announcement of the pending release of the first batch of IRD papers in *Parliamentary Debates: Commons*, 22 February 1994; see also the PRO website for subsequent releases: http://www.pro.gov.uk/releases

14 D. Leigh, 'Death of the Department That Never Was', *The Guardian*, 27 January 1978, p. 13; R. Fletcher, G. Brock and P. Kelly, 'How the FO Waged Secret Propaganda War in Britain', *The Observer*, 29 January 1978, p. 2; D. Leigh, 'UK Propaganda Machine Worked On In Peacetime', *The Observer*, 20 December 1981, p. 3; R. Fletcher, 'How the Secret Service Shaped the News', *The Guardian*, 18 December 1981, p. 13. See also books by investigative journalists, J. Bloch and P. Fitzgerald, *British Intelligence and Covert Action* (London: Junction, 1983), and D. Leigh, *The Frontiers of Secrecy: Closed Government in Britain* (London: Junction 1980).

15 Leigh, *Frontiers of Secrecy*, pp. 218–24.

16 This point is most consistently argued in, R. Fletcher, 'British Propaganda since World War II: A Case Study', *Media, Culture and Society*, 4 (1982), pp. 97–109. Fletcher, an investigative journalist, wrote some of the first press reports regarding the IRD and expanded upon them in this journal article.

17 'The Ministry of Truth', *The Leveller*, 13 (March 1978), pp. 11–13.

18 P. Lashmar, 'Covert in Glory', *New Statesman and Society* (3 March 1995), pp. 14–15. Conquest worked in the IRD in the late 1940s and early 1950s; see R. Conquest, 'In Celia's office, Orwell and the Cold War', *Times Literary Supplement*, 21 August 1998, pp. 4–5.

19 D. Campbell and A. Thomas, 'The FO and the Eggheads', *New Statesman*, 27 February 1981, pp. 13–14.

20 R.J. Aldrich, 'Never-Never Land and Wonderland? British and American Policy on Intelligence Archives', *Contemporary Record*, 8, 1 (Summer 1994), p. 136.

21 D. Leigh, 'The 30-Year-Old Secrets which Cannot Be Told', *The Observer*, 3 January 1982; *ibid.* 'Secret Cold War Files Are Scrapped by Foreign Office', *The Observer*, 28 February 1982; Lashmar, 'Covert in Glory.'

22 S. Dorril and R. Ramsay, *Smear!: Wilson and the Secret State* (London: Grafton, 1992), pp. 110, 130–1, 216, 298, 322; D. Leigh, *The Wilson Plot: The Intelligence Services and the Discrediting of a Prime Minister* (London: Heinemann, 1988), pp. 7–9, 70; P. Foot, *Who Framed Colin Wallace?* (London: Macmillan, 1989).

23 R. Ramsay, 'Views from Vauxhall Cross', *New Statesman and Society*, 7 April 1995, pp. 52–3. After the first tranche of papers were released, speculation continued as to what secrets remained hidden: see P. Anderson, 'Best Is Yet To Come From Propaganda Unit's Archives' *New Statesman and Society*, 25 August 1995, p. 7.

24 W.S. Lucas, 'The British Ministry of Propaganda', *The Independent on Sunday*, 26 February 1995; *ibid.* 'Ministry of Truth Comes Out of the Closet', *The Sunday Times*, 13 August 1995; N. Bethell, 'How Labour Kept Stalin At Bay', *The Times*, 18 August 1995.

25 'Celebrity Team Used In Secret Anti-Soviet Campaign', *The Times*, 17 August 1995; 'Poet Used As Secret Weapon', *The Independent*, 17 August 1995; 'Healey Served As

Covert Linchpin In War Of Words', *The Times*, 18 August 1995; 'Healey Was Conduit For Anti-Soviet Propaganda', *The Independent*, 18 August 1995.

26 'Orwell Was Recruited To Fight Soviet Propaganda', *The Times*, 11 July 1996; 'George Orwell's Cold War', *The Times*, 12 July 1996; 'Orwell Offered Writers' Blacklist To Anti-Soviet Propaganda Unit', *The Guardian*, 11 July 1996; 'Orwell Is Revealed In Role Of State Informer', *The Daily Telegraph*, 12 July 1996.

27 B. Crick, *George Orwell: A Life* (London: Penguin, 1980), p. 556; M. Shelden, *Orwell: The Authorized Biography* (London: Heinemann, 1991), pp. 467–9.

28 'Orwell's Little List Leaves Left Gasping For More', *Independent on Sunday*, 14 July 1996; 'Orwell Is Revealed In The Role Of State Informer', *The Daily Telegraph*, 12 July 1996; 'Orwell's Debutante Friend Tells Of Role In Writer's "Betrayal" List', *The Daily Telegraph*, 13 July 1996; P. Worsthorne, 'Why the Right Are Wrong About Orwell', *The Spectator*, 27 July 1996. Orwell was defended by his biographers and various others, mainly in the right-wing press: see B. Crick, Letter to the Editor, *The Guardian*, 12 July 1996; D. May, 'George Orwell's Cold War', *The Times*, 12 July 1996; M. Peake, 'Fears That Made Orwell Sneak On His Friends', *The Guardian*, 13 July 1996; A. Roberts, '*Animal Farm*'s Rich Crop of Humbug', *The Sunday Times*, 14 July 1996; A. Neil, 'Patriot Orwell Left In Cold', *The Daily Mail*, 15 July 1996; N. Podhorertz, 'Revenge of the Smelly Little Orthodoxies', *National Review*, 27 January 1997.

29 P. Davison (ed.), *The Complete Works of George Orwell*, vol. 20 (London: Secker & Warburg, 1998), p. 3,732. M. Shelden and P. Johnstone, 'Socialist Icon Who Became Big Brother', *The Daily Telegraph*, 22 June 1998; 'Revealed: George Orwell's Big Brother Dossier', *The Daily Telegraph*, 27 June 1998; G. Wheatcroft, 'Big Brother with a High Moral Sense', *The Independent*, 28 June 1998; T. Naftali, 'George Orwell's List', *The New York Times*, 29 July 1998; C. Hitchens, '1984 and All That', *The Nation*, 24 August 1998.

30 The list may be found in FO 1110/189, PRO. After so much interest, with the notable exception of a series of articles in *The Guardian*, the release of Orwell's list passed almost unnoticed in the press. 'Blair's Babe', *The Guardian*, 21 June 2003; T. Garton Ash, 'Love Death and Treachery', *The Guardian Review*, 21 June 2003; 'Orwell Hitlist Member Says Illness Clouded Author's Mind', *The Guardian*, 24 June 2003; T. Garton Ash, 'Under the Blanket', *The Guardian*, 10 July 2003.

31 P. Deery, 'Confronting the Cominform: George Orwell and the Cold War Offensive of the Information Research Department, 1948–50', *Labour History*, 73 (November 1997) pp. 219–225; T. Shaw, *British Cinema and the Cold War: The State, Propaganda and Consensus* (London: I.B. Tauris, 2001), pp. 91–114; P. Davison (ed.), *Orwell and Politics* (London: Penguin, 2001), pp. 501–9.

32 'BBC Was Conscripted into MI6's Anti-Communist Crusade', *The Guardian*, 18 August 1995; 'BBC Chiefs Bowed To Pressure From Our Man In Moscow', *The Independent*, 18 August 1995; 'Propaganda Unit Run Secretly "to foil Labour left" '; *The Times*, 18 August 1995; 'Healey Served As Covert Linchpin In War Of Words', *The Times*, 18 August 1995; 'Labour's Role In Secret Anti-Communist Plan Revealed', *The Guardian*, 18 August 1995.

33 S. Jenkins, 'Spies Bungling For Britain', *The Times*, 19 August 1995; S. Dorril, 'The Puppet Masters', *The Guardian*, 18 August 1995.

34 P. Lashmar and J. Oliver, *Britain's Secret Propaganda War, 1948–1977*, (Stroud: Sutton, 1998). Some of Lashmar and Oliver's revelations found contemporary resonance in a Eurosceptic British press: see G. Neale, 'Revealed: How MI6 Men Funded Drive To Join Europe'; *The Sunday Telegraph*, 27 April 1997; P. Lashmar and J. Oliver, 'How MI6 Pushed Britain To Join Europe', *The Sunday Telegraph*, 27 April 1997; P. Lashmar, 'Triumph of the Euro-spooks', *The Guardian*, 1 January 1999. In general, Lashmar and Oliver's account found a receptive audience in the media: see the following reviews, 'The Arthur Daleys of Diplomacy', *The Independent*, 18 February 1999; '1948 and 1984', *Times Literary Supplement*, 12 March 1999. For more cautious reviews, see H. Wilford in *Intelligence and National Security*, 14, 2 (1999), p. 211; T. Shaw, 'The Politics of Cold War Culture', *Journal of Cold War Studies*, 3, 3 (2001), pp. 59–76.

35 J.L. Gaddis, 'The Emerging Post-Revisionist Synthesis on the Origins of the Cold War', *Diplomatic History*, 7 (Summer 1983), pp. 171–90.
36 C. Andrew and V. Mitrokhin, *The Mitrokhin Archive: The KGB in Europe and the West* (London: Allen Lane, 1999); A. Weinstein and A. Vassiliev, *The Haunted Wood: Soviet Espionage in America – The Stalin Era* (New York: Random House, 1999); A. Applebaum, *Gulag: A History of the Soviet Camps* (London: Allen Lane, 2003); M. Amis, *Koba the Dread: Laughter and the Twenty Million* (London: Jonathan Cape, 2002); J.L. Gaddis, 'Out of the Woodwork', *Times Literary Supplement* (30 April 1999); N. Stone, 'McCarthy Was Right', *The Spectator*, 14 May 1994; S.S. Rosenfeld, 'Soviet Archives are Showing That Western Hardliners Had It Right', *International Herald Tribune*, 23 January 1995; R. Conquest, 'Small Terror, Few Dead', *Times Literary Supplement*, 31 May 1996. When his US publisher suggested a new edition of *The Great Terror* with a new title, Conquest reportedly replied, 'Well, perhaps "I Told You So, You Fucking Fools". How's that?', K. Amis, *Memoirs* (London: Hutchinson, 1991) p. 146.
37 On new revisionism, see R.J. Aldrich, ' "Grow Your Own" Cold War Intelligence and History Supermarkets', *Intelligence and National Security*, 17, 1 (2002), pp. 135–52; B. Cumings, 'Revising Post-Revisionism Revisited', in M. Hogan (ed.), *America in the World: The Historiography of American Foreign Relations Since 1941* (Cambridge: Cambridge University Press, 1995), pp. 127–39.
38 F.S. Saunders, *Who Paid the Piper? The CIA and the Cultural Cold War* (London: Granta, 1999).
39 E. Said, 'Hey, Mister, You Want Dirty Book?', *London Review of Books*, 30 September 1999; M. Bradbury, 'How the CIA Promoted the Post-Modern', *The Times*, 1 July 1999; P. Worsthorne, 'How Western Culture was Saved by the CIA', *Literary Review*, July 1999; P. Coleman, 'Supporting the Indispensable', *The New Criterion*, 18, 1 (September 1999); P. Coleman, Book review, *Intelligence and National Security*, 17, 3 (2002), pp. 192–3; D.C. Watt, 'The Proper Study of Propaganda', *Intelligence and National Security*, 15, 4 (2000), 143–63.
40 H. Wilford, 'Literati Dine Out On the Cultural Cold War', *The Times Higher Education Supplement*, 4 July 2003; H. Wilford, *Calling the Tune? The CIA, the British Left and the Cold War* (London: Frank Cass, 2003); see *also* T. Shaw, 'The Politics of Cold War Culture.' *Journal of Cold War Studies*, 3, 3 (2001), pp. 59–76.
41 Saunders, *Who Paid the Piper?*, pp. 58–9.
42 Policy Committee minutes, 4 September 1941, INF 1/676, PRO; see also P.M.H. Bell, *John Bull and the Bear: British Public Opinion, Foreign Policy, and the Soviet Union 1941–1945* (London: Edward Arnold, 1990).
43 L. Smith, 'Covert British Propaganda: The Information Research Department, 1947–77', *Millennium: Journal of International Studies*, 9, 1 (1980), pp. 67–83.
44 In the article, Smith referred to these documents as 'a collection of British official documents which have come into my possession from a confidential source.' In her introduction to Mayhew's final volume of memoirs, which she edited, Smith revealed that Mayhew had been the source of these documents: see C. Mayhew, *A War of Words: A Cold War Witness* (London: I.B. Tauris, 1998), p. ix.
45 Smith, 'Covert British Propaganda', pp. 69–70.
46 *Ibid.* pp. 72–82.
47 D.C. Watt, 'Intelligence Studies: The Emergence of a British School', *Intelligence and National Security*, 3, 2 (1988), pp. 338–41; R.J. Aldrich (ed.), *British Intelligence, Strategy and the Cold War, 1945–51* (London: Routledge, 1992), pp. 1–10; D.C. Watt, book review, *Intelligence and National Security*, 12, 4 (1997), p. 224.
48 Taylor, 'Back to the Future?'; Taylor, 'The Projection of Britain Abroad, 1945–51'; Taylor, *British Propaganda in the Twentieth Century: Selling Democracy* (Edinburgh: Edinburgh University Press, 1999); S.L. Carruthers, *Winning Hearts and Minds: British Governments, the Media and Colonial Counter-Insurgency, 1944–1960* (Leicester: Leicester University Press, 1995); T. Shaw, 'The Information Research Department of the British Foreign Office and the Korean War, 1950–53', *Journal of Contemporary History*, 34, 2 (1999), pp. 263–81; G.D. Rawnsley, *Radio Diplomacy and Propaganda: The BBC*

and VOA in International Politics, 1956–64 (Basingstoke: Macmillan, 1996); Shaw, *Eden, Suez and the Mass Media: Propaganda and Persuasion During the Suez Crisis* (London: I.B. Tauris, 1996).

49 See, for example, Taylor, 'The Projection of Britain Abroad, 1945–51'; R.J. Aldrich, 'Secret Intelligence for a Post-War World: Reshaping the British Intelligence Community, 1944–51', in Aldrich, *British Intelligence, Strategy, and the Cold War*, pp. 15–49.

50 W.K. Wark, 'Coming In From the Cold: British Propaganda and Red Army Defectors, 1945–1952', *International History Review*, 9, 1 (February 1987), pp. 48–73.

51 R. Smith, 'A Climate Of Opinion: British Officials and the Development of British Soviet Policy, 1945–7', *International Affairs*, 64, 4 (Autumn 1988), pp. 635–47.

52 P. Weiler, *British Labour and the Cold War* (Stanford, CA: Stanford University Press, 1988), pp. 189–229. For a similar, although less convincing, examination of the IRD's domestic role, see B. Porter, *Plots and Paranoia: A History of Political Espionage in Britain 1790–1988* (London: Unwin Hyman, 1989), pp. 192–3.

53 A. Carew, 'The Schism Within the World Federation of Trade Unions: Government and Trade Union Diplomacy', *International Review of Social History*, 29, 3 (1984), pp. 297–335; A. Carew, *Labour under the Marshall Plan: The Politics of Productivity and the Marketing of Management Science* (Manchester: Manchester University Press, 1987), pp. 75–7.

54 R. Thurlow, *The Secret State: British Internal Security in the Twentieth Century* (Oxford: Blackwell, 1994), pp. 268–311.

55 W.S. Lucas and C.J. Morris, 'A Very British Crusade: The Information Research Department and the Beginning of the Cold War', in Aldrich, *British Intelligence, Strategy and the Cold War*, pp. 85–110.

56 Aldrich, 'Secret Intelligence For A Post-War World', pp. 16–20.

57 Lucas and Morris, 'A Very British Crusade.'

58 R.J. Aldrich, *The Hidden Hand: Britain, America and Cold War Secret Intelligence* (London: John Murray, 2001); see, in particular, chs 5 and 20.

59 *Ibid.*, p. 5.

60 *Ibid.*, p. 134.

61 The work of the CIA's remarkable International Organisations Division (IOD) in this field from 1951 has been well documented, but Aldrich is almost unique in highlighting the pioneering work of the British. Aldrich, *The Hidden Hand*, pp. 122–41. See also J. Kotek, *Students and the Cold War* (London: Macmillan, 1996). On the CIA's IOD, see C. Meyer, *Facing Reality: From World Federalism to the CIA* (New York: Harper Row, 1980).

62 Aldrich, *The Hidden Hand*, p. 131.

63 *Ibid.*, pp. 142–59.

64 Taylor, 'The Projection of Britain Abroad, 1945–51', pp. 9–10.

65 *Ibid.* See also A. Adamthwaite, 'Britain and the World, 1945–9: The View from the Foreign Office', *International Affairs*, 61, 2 (1985), p. 223.

66 Taylor, *British Propaganda in the Twentieth Century*, p. 18.

67 *Ibid.*, pp. 5–29.

68 Shaw, 'The IRD and the Korean War'; Rawnsley, 'Radio Diplomacy and Propaganda'; Shaw, *Eden, Suez and the Mass Media*; Carruthers, *Winning Hearts and Minds*; S.L. Carruthers, ' "A Red Under Every Bed?": Anti-Communist Propaganda and Britain's Response To Colonial Insurgency', *Contemporary Record*, 9, 2 (Autumn 1995), pp. 294–318.

69 Carruthers, ' "A Red Under Every Bed?" ', p. 311.

70 *Ibid.*, p. 312.

71 Rawnsley, *Radio Diplomacy and Propaganda*; G.D. Rawnsley, 'Cold War Radio in Crisis: The BBC Overseas Services, the Suez Crisis and the 1956 Hungarian uprising', *Historical Journal of Film, Radio and Television*, 16, 2 (1996), pp. 197–219; Shaw, 'The IRD and the Korean War.'

72 Shaw, 'The IRD and the Korean War', pp. 279–80.

73 S. Lucas, 'The Dirty Tricks That Were Made in England', *The Independent on Sunday*, 20 August 1995.
74 Wark, 'Coming in From the Cold', pp. 52–3; T. Barnes, 'The Secret Cold War: The CIA and American Foreign Policy in Europe, 1946–1956, Part II', *The Historical Journal*, 25, 3 (1982), pp. 649–70; R.J. Aldrich (ed.), *Espionage, Security and Intelligence in Britain, 1945–1970* (Manchester: Manchester University Press, 1988), pp. 185–7.
75 Wark, 'Coming In From The Cold', p. 53; Wilford, 'The Information Research Department: Britain's Secret Cold War Weapon Revealed', *Review of International Studies*, 24 (1998), pp. 366–9; T. Barnes, 'Democratic Deception: American Covert Operations in Post-War Europe', in D.A. Charters and M.A.J. Tugwell (eds), *Deception Operations: Studies in the East–West Context* (London: Brassey's, 1990), pp. 297–321.
76 Lucas, 'The Dirty Tricks That Were Made In England.'
77 Wilford, 'The Information Research Department.'
78 J. Bamford, *The Puzzle Palace* (London: Penguin, 1983); J. Richelson and D. Ball, *The Ties That Bind: Intelligence Cooperation between the UKUSA Countries* (London: Allen & Unwin, 1985); J. Ranelagh, 'Through the Looking Glass: A Comparison of United States and United Kingdom Intelligence Cultures', in H. Peake and S. Halperin (eds), *In the Name of Intelligence: Essays in Honour of Louis Pforzheimer* (Washington, DC: NIBC, 1994).
79 See, for example, Rawnsley, *Radio Diplomacy and Propaganda; ibid.*, 'Cold War Radio in Crisis'; M. Nelson, *War of the Black Heavens: The Battles of Western Broadcasting in the Cold War* (London: Brassey's, 1997).
80 T. Shaw, 'The British Popular Press and the Early Cold War', *History*, 83, 269 (1998), pp. 66–85; J.A. Oliver, 'Britain and the Covert War of Words: The Information Research Department and Sponsored Publishing', MA Thesis, University of Kent at Canterbury, 1995.
81 Aldrich, *The Hidden Hand.*
82 On the Waldegrave Initiative, see R.J. Aldrich, 'The Waldegrave Initiative and Secret Service Archives: New Materials and New Policies', *Intelligence and National Security*, 10, 1 (1995), pp. 192–7; R.J. Aldrich, 'Did Waldegrave Work? The Impact of Open Government Upon British History', *Twentieth Century British History*, 9, 1 (1998), pp. 111–26.
83 For a review of the early papers, see FCO Historians, *IRD: Origins and Establishment of the Foreign Office Information Research Department, 1946–48*, History Note no. 9 (London: FCO/LRD, 1995); Wilford, 'The Information Research Department.'
84 A. Defty, 'Organising Security and Intelligence in the Far East: Further Fruits of the Waldegrave Initiative', *Study Group on Intelligence Newsletter*, 16 (Winter 1997/98), pp. 2–5. The Foreign Office is particularly helpful in providing consolidated lists of newly released material. FCO Library and Records Department, *List of Papers Released from the Previously Retained FCO Archive*, 4th edn (London: FCO/LRD, 1997; reprinted 1998); *FCO Released Papers*, (FCO/LRD, 2000), available at: http://www.fco.gov.uk. For up-to-date information regarding releases, see the PRO website: http://www.pro.gov.uk
85 See, in particular, Box – Anti-Communist Propaganda, International Department Papers, Labour Party Archives, NMLH. See also A. Flinn, 'National Museum of Labour History Archive and Study Centre', *Contemporary Record*, 7, 2 (1993), pp. 465–72.
86 See, in particular, Nelson, *War of the Black Heavens.*
87 D. Kirby, 'Divinely Sanctioned: The Anglo-American Cold War Alliance and the Defence of Western Civilization and Christianity, 1945–48', *Journal of Contemporary History*, 35, 3 (2000), pp. 385–412; *ibid., Church, State and Propaganda: The Archbishop of York and International Relations: A Political Study of Cyril Forster Garbett, 1942–1955* (Hull: Hull University Press, 1999); Kotek, *Students and the Cold War*; H. Wilford, '"Unwitting Assets?": British Intellectuals and the Congress for Cultural Freedom', *Twentieth Century British History*, 11, 1 (2000), pp. 42–60.
88 Box 2, File – Foreign Office, 1948, Morgan Phillips papers, NMLH; Correspondence with Foreign Office and John Peck, Bertrand Russell papers, MacMaster University; Davison (ed.), *Orwell and Politics*, pp. 501–9.

89 P. Deery, 'Covert Propaganda and the Cold War: Britain and Australia, 1948–1955', *The Round Table*, 361 (2001), pp. 607–21.

90 IRD material can certainly be found in the archives of the French Ministry of Foreign Affairs. Correspondence between Massigli, ambassador in London, and Bidault, Foreign Minister, enclosing copies of the following IRD periodicals: 'The Interpreter', 'Tendances de la Propagande Communiste', and 'Developments in International Organizations.' Massigli to Bidault, 21 April 1953; Massigli to Bidault, 22 June 1953; Massigli to Bidault, 16 November 1953, Ministry of Foreign Affairs, Paris. Series: Europe, 1944–60. Sub-series: URSS – Box 158. I am grateful to Professor John W. Young for this information.

91 Aldrich, 'Did Waldegrave Work?'

92 See, for example, Bagot, Box no. 500 [MI5] to J. Peck, which contains paper on 'Second World Peace Congress, Sheffield/Warsaw 1950', January 1951, PR 5/28, FO 1110/370; M.J.E. Bagot, Box no. 500 [MI5], to G.N. Jackson, IRD, 15 October 1951, which contains paper, 'Commonwealth, British Colonial and United Kingdom representation at the III World Festival of Youth and Students – Berlin, August 1951', PR 48/306, FO 1110/406, PRO.

93 Aldrich, *Hidden Hand*, pp. 6–7; *ibid.*, 'Grow Your Own.'

94 Lord Chancellor's Advisory Council on Public Records, *Review of Security Service Selection Criteria* (London: Public Record Office, 1998).

95 R. Bone, 'Recent Changes in FCO Records Policy', in FCO Historical Branch (ed.), *Changes in British and Russian Records Policy*, Occasional Paper no. 7 (London: FCO, November 1993); FCO Historical Branch, *FCO Records: Policy, Practice and Posterity*, 1782–1993, History Notes no. 4 (London: FCO, November 1993).

96 Quoted in, 'Secret Cold War Files Are Scrapped by Foreign Office', The Observer, 25 February 1982, p. 4.

97 *Ibid.*

98 For example, copies of the first 21 issues of the 'IRD Digest' from 1948 and 1949 may be found in the files: FO 371/71713, FO 371/71714, PRO.

99 IRD basic papers, which ran from 1948 may be found in class FO 975; *The Interpreter*, a periodical from the 1950s may be found in class FO 1059, PRO.

100 Examples of these serials may be found elsewhere. The files of the International Department of the Labour Party contain, the first 17 issues of *Middle East Opinion*, dated from August 1956 to January 1958, and issues number 28–39 of *Communist Propaganda and Developments in the Middle East*, dated from December 1956 to January 1958, Box – Middle East Opinion, LPID, NMLH. The IRD's 'Religious Digest' was launched in 1951, file, FO 1110/382, PRO.

101 Wark, 'Coming in from the Cold', pp. 51–3; Fletcher, 'British Propaganda since World War II,' pp. 99–102.

102 S. Lucas, *Freedom's War*; Wilford, *Calling the Tune*.

103 Aldrich, 'Never-Never Land and Wonderland?'

104 *Ibid.*; Z. Karabell and T. Naftali, 'History Declassified: The Perils and Promise of CIA Documents', *Diplomatic History*, 18, 4 (1994), pp. 615–34.

105 R. Marett, *Through the Back Door: An Inside View of Britain's Overseas Information Services* (London: Pergamon, 1968); I. Kirkpatrick, *The Inner Circle* (London: Macmillan, 1959); P. Gore-Booth, *With Great Truth and Respect* (London: Constable, 1974).

106 R. Conquest, 'In Celia's Office: Orwell and the Cold War', *Times Literary Supplement*, 21 August 1998; R. Conquest, *Reflections on a Ravaged Century* (London: John Murray, 1999), pp. 160–3; Aubrey Essex, Letter to the Editor, *The Times*, 7 December 1998; Former IRD officials, correspondence with author, September 1996 and January 1997.

107 C. Parrott, *The Serpent and the Nightingale* (London: Faber & Faber, 1977), p. 47.

108 S. Rimington, *Open Secret: The Autobiography of the Former Director-General of MI5* (London: Hutchinson, 2001), pp. 74–5. Of course, being a woman, Rimington's work was almost certainly at the clerical/secretarial end of the IRD's work. Fay Weldon, who joined the IRD in 1952, paints a similar picture in 'My Career As A Spy', *The Sunday Times*, 6 December 1998; *ibid., Auto Da Fay* (London: Flamingo, 2002), pp. 240–4.

109 B. Crozier, *Free Agent: The Unseen War 1941–1991* (London: Harper Collins, 1993); R. Beeston, *Looking for Trouble: Life and Times of a Foreign Correspondent* (London: Brassey's, 1997); R. Challis, *Shadow of a Revolution: Indonesia and the Generals* (Stroud: Sutton, 2001), pp. 94–103; P. Worsthorne, *Tricks of Memory: An Autobiography* (London: Weidenfeld & Nicolson, 1993). The BBC's John Simpson also provides an amusing account of an interview he had to join IRD in 1966. Simpson apparently declined the post when told that he would merely be required to write reports about other countries and would not get to carry a gun, *Strange Places, Questionable People* (London: Macmillan, 1998), pp. 13–14.

110 C. Mayhew, *Party Games* (London: Hutchinson, 1969), pp. 85–6.

111 C. Mayhew, *Time to Explain* (London: Hutchinson, 1987); *ibid., War of Words: A Cold War Witness* (London: I.B.Tauris, 1998).

112 D. Owen, *Time to Declare* (London: Michael Joseph, 1991); D. Healey, *The Time of My Life* (London: Michael Joseph, 1989). Tony Benn also records the IRD's demise in his diaries, *Conflicts of Interest: Diaries, 1977–1980* (London: Hutchinson, 1990).

113 It is clear that many individuals are reluctant to speak about their work for fear of breaching their statutory obligations under the Official Secrets Act. In an effort to resolve such difficulties, the Institute of Contemporary British History in cooperation with the Cabinet Office has produced a useful, *Guidelines For Former Officials at Scholarly Interviews and Witness Seminars*: http://www.ihr.sas.ac.uk/icbh

114 P. Deery, 'The Dove Flies East: Whitehall, Warsaw and the 1950 World Peace Congress', *Australian Journal of Politics and History*, 48, 4 (2002), pp. 449–68; Carruthers, *Winning Hearts and Minds*; Shaw, 'The IRD and the Korean War.'

115 See, for example, Lucas, *Freedom's War*; W.L. Hixson, *Parting the Curtain: Propaganda, Culture and the Cold War, 1945–1961* (London: Macmillan, 1997).

116 Anti-communist propaganda operations, 27 July 1951, PR 126/5, FO 1110/460, PRO.

1 The origins of Britain's anti-communist propaganda policy, 1945–47

In January 1948, Britain launched a new propaganda policy designed to 'oppose the inroads of communism by taking the offensive against it.' Britain's 'future foreign publicity policy' was outlined in a paper presented to the Cabinet at its first meeting of 1948. It stated that since the end of the War, Soviet propaganda, had carried on 'a vicious attack against the British Commonwealth and against Western democracy.' The time had come to 'pass over to the offensive and not leave the initiative to the enemy, but make them defend themselves.' It also claimed that it was up to Britain, as a European social democratic government, and not the Americans to take the lead in uniting the forces of anti-communism.[1]

Although the USA had also begun to respond to communist propaganda, in January 1948 Britain led the way by developing a policy and an organizational machinery to provide a coordinated global response to hostile communist propaganda. This chapter will examine the formulation of this new propaganda policy. It will identify the factors which, between the end of the War and the drafting of the Cabinet paper at the end of 1947, influenced Britain's decision to go over to the offensive. It will also argue that from the earliest stages Britain's response to communist propaganda was paralleled by, and even complemented, the propaganda policy and machinery of the USA.

The first year of peace saw the dissolution of wartime propaganda agencies and the development of new policies for national projection and the creation of new government propaganda agencies to implement these policies. At the same time British and US policy-makers gradually developed complementary perceptions of the Soviet threat, which by the end of 1947 led to the development of a more offensive concept for the use of propaganda. Although the Soviet Union posed a considerable military threat the principal fear was communist subversion of democracy through the use of techniques short of war such as propaganda. Britain's initial response to communist propaganda was a propaganda policy based on the positive projection of Britain's national achievements. As this policy proved increasingly inadequate as a counter to hostile foreign propaganda Britain and the USA developed complementary propaganda policies designed to supplement passive national projection with various defensive and offensive measures. In the case of Britain a series of *ad-hoc* offensive measures led eventually to the adoption of a coordinated global response to communist propaganda by January 1948.

British and American propaganda 1945–46

The British and US Governments emerged from the Second World War convinced of the value of a permanent peacetime propaganda machinery. During the War all the major powers had employed propaganda on an unprecedented scale both at home and abroad. Britain and the USA had developed a complex bureaucratic machinery for the dissemination of government propaganda and the coordination of allied psychological warfare. Before the end of the War, an official committee set up to consider the machinery of government in post-war Britain noted the potential for peacetime employment of propaganda for 'securing publicity and goodwill for Britain abroad and the Government's policies at home.'[2] At the end of the War, British and US leaders expressed their conviction that propaganda was an important tool of policy. In December 1945, the British Prime Minister, Clement Attlee, expressed himself satisfied that the information services 'have an important and permanent part in the machinery of government under modern conditions.' He described the services as 'essential' to keep the public informed about government policy and to ensure that, 'a true and adequate picture of British policy, British institutions and the British way of life should be presented overseas.'[3] In the USA earlier the same year, President Harry S. Truman had observed that, 'the nature of present day foreign relations makes it essential for the United States to maintain information activities abroad as an integral part of our conduct of foreign affairs.'[4] However, initially Truman and Attlee did not envisage peacetime propaganda as a defence against hostile foreign powers. They reverted to concepts of government propaganda which owed more to ideas of national projection and advertising developed in the inter-war years than the lessons of the Second World War. Propaganda was not to be employed in dishonourable and deceitful pursuits as exemplified by the totalitarian dictatorships. In the immediate aftermath of the War, Britain and the USA developed government propaganda as a positive aid to diplomacy. By explaining their position more clearly to foreign powers, they hoped to promote international understanding and more particularly, to improve the prospects for international trade.

Before a peacetime propaganda machinery could be established, both governments had to overcome a widespread antipathy towards the use of propaganda. Although the use of propaganda could be excused as expedient in wartime, many British and US politicians and officials held deep-seated reservations about the employment of government propaganda in peacetime. The maintenance of government agencies for the manipulation of opinion was viewed by many as the preserve of totalitarian dictatorships, and many wartime propaganda agencies were hastily dismantled.[5] In Britain there was a general feeling that government departments generated by wartime necessity should be dissolved. Those agencies responsible for covert propaganda – the Political Warfare Executive and the Special Operations Executive – were dismantled early in 1946. Attlee noted brusquely that 'he had no wish to preside over a British Comintern.'[6] The Ministry of Information was also abolished, and overall responsibility for overseas propaganda was shifted to the Foreign Office, where enthusiasm for such activity was by no means universal. As late as 1952 one senior Foreign Office official wrote sardonically to Sir Robert Fraser, Director of the Central Office of Information, that 'no normal diplomatist, I suspect, can be a real enthusiast about publicity and propaganda.'[7]

In the USA popular support for the dissolution of wartime agencies was if anything more pronounced. Congress and the public had a distaste for the application of wartime methods to the problems of peace and any wartime agency which was not clearly demonstrable as necessary to the Government's peacetime policy was rapidly dismantled. The Office of War Information was dissolved in 1945, and responsibility for overseas propaganda was foisted on an unwelcoming State Department. A handful of officials argued the case for peacetime propaganda but the State Department information programme suffered drastic cuts between 1946 and 1948.[8] The USA's covert propaganda apparatus fared little better. Sensational press articles predicting the creation of a 'super-Gestapo agency' stifled early plans for a post-war intelligence agency.[9] The Office of Strategic Services (OSS) was praised for its wartime achievements and promptly abolished.[10] Although elements of OSS were transferred to other departments there was little apparent concern to preserve its propaganda apparatus. State Department officials considered that maintaining such a capability would be 'contrary to the fundamental premises of our own governmental system and would be honouring the totalitarians by imitating them.'[11]

Britain was the first to overcome such reservations. Faced with a worsening economy and a declining position as a world and imperial power, the Labour Government placed considerable faith in the projection of British power and achievements through propaganda. The social and economic policies of the Labour Government marked a radical departure from Conservative precedents, and Labour was aware of the need to explain its policies to a wide domestic and foreign audience. At home, propaganda was employed on an unprecedented scale to explain the benefits of Labour's economic policies to managers, workers and the public at large.[12] Competition in the world markets and Britain's increasing dependence on the USA's economy made it essential that Britain's case should not be allowed to go unexplained overseas. In the USA in particular, British propaganda was widely employed to explain to sceptical Congressmen that British socialism was not a step on the road to communism.[13]

Beyond the explanation of Labour's socialist policy, this new commitment to national projection served other less tractable ends. The post-war expansion of Britain's overseas propaganda also reflected an awareness of diminished power and the need to convince the world that traditional prestige and skills could compensate for economic and military decline.[14] As the historian Philip M. Taylor has observed:

Propaganda may indeed fail *ultimately* to disguise weakness or the realities of decline but it can provide an illusion of strength and confidence that does serve to aid foreign policy objectives in effective short term ways.[15]

In pursuing these ends, British post-war foreign propaganda reflected a concept of positive national projection developed in the inter-war years. This concept was most famously developed by Sir Stephen Tallents who coined the phrase 'The Projection of England' in a pamphlet published in 1932. Tallents argued that because Britain no longer enjoyed that position of supremacy which had generated its own prestige and had enabled her to remain aloof for long periods in the past, she must forego her traditional insularity and make Britain more widely known and understood in the world. By 'projecting' a balanced interpretation of British civilization and personality, the Government would thereby ensure that its views and policies were clearly understood and appreciated abroad.[16]

In the post-war years, Britain's straitened financial situation invested this theme with new value. One of the first directives sent to British information officers by the Foreign Office Information Policy Department (IPD) was entitled 'The Projection of Britain'. The paper was designed to explain British policy and aid 'the spread of British ideas and British standards' abroad. The principal themes were to be industrial welfare and the new social legislation of the Labour Government.[17] Initially at least, the overriding objective of the 'Projection of Britain' was to foster the nation's economic well-being. When Bevin wrote to information officers announcing the continuation of information activities he suggested that one of the most important objectives for the post-war years would be the 'promotion of British exports, and the explanation of British trading policy.'[18] Bevin also believed that propaganda could be used overseas as a suitable tool for the projection of British social democracy. The Labour Party's election manifesto had stated that Britain 'must play the part of brave and constructive leaders in international affairs,' promoting worldwide prosperity through their own example of high production and a steady improvement in living standards.[19] 'The Projection of Britain' was likewise designed to depict Britain as a leading exponent of social democracy and the leading power in the development of progressive welfare legislation.[20] This was overseas propaganda at its most positive. The Government was clearly proud of its achievements and Bevin in particular was 'anxious that our light should not remain under a bushel.'[21]

Projecting British achievements had traditionally been the job of the BBC and the British Council. In the post-war years, implementing this national projection on an unprecedented scale was facilitated by the retention of significant elements of Britain's wartime information apparatus. The ease and speed with which post-war propaganda was instituted and expanded suggests that the dissolution of wartime information agencies was largely superficial. The Ministry of Information's functions were divided between various government departments that, in many cases, expanded their information activities accordingly. In 1945 the Foreign Office had only two departments responsible for overseas propaganda, by 1947 it had nine.[22] Although the Ministry of Information was abolished, under a new system government information activities were coordinated by a high level committee under the chairmanship of the Lord President of the Council, Herbert Morrison. The retention of a Minister of Information was considered 'politically dangerous,' but Morrison effectively became minister responsible for the information services.[23] In a candid discussion with US officials in 1945 Britain's last Minister of Information, Edward S. Williams, noted that the disappearance of the formal Ministry would not result in the termination of 'most of the present functions of the Ministry.'[24] Britain's covert propaganda agencies also continued to operate after their official dissolution. Problems related to the occupation in Europe, the Mediterranean and Asia ensured that the Political Warfare Executive (PWE) continued to function,[25] and that institutional ties between British and US propagandists continued. The vast Psychological Warfare Division (PWD) which had operated in all theatres became a much reduced Allied Information Service, operating in the former Axis states. Its principal function was political re-education concentrating on 'public information, "consolidation" propaganda, counter-propaganda and much political intelligence.'[26]

Not surprisingly, whilst the Labour Government was keen to advertise its achievements, it was less eager to reveal the manner in which these achievements were publicized. In response to several enquiries from information officers regarding what to tell foreign governments about the reorganization of British information services, the IPD produced a directive outlining the need for discretion. Requests for information about British organizations were not to be discouraged, but the IPD noted, 'it is important not to give the impression that it is the intention of His Majesty's Government to build up a powerful publicity machine abroad.' It was suggested that requests for information should be used as an opportunity to publicize Britain by describing the output of these services rather than the organization. It was they claimed, 'more useful to tell other clients what we can provide than how we do it.'[27]

The one notable exception to this rule on discretion was the USA. In 1945 the Foreign Office and the State Department exchanged detailed information regarding their plans for peacetime propaganda. These informal discussions were carried out by officials on both sides of the Atlantic. In the USA, representatives of the British Information Services met with State Department officials.[28] In London, Embassy staff discussed developments directly with the Minister of Information.[29] These meetings were not confined to areas of mutual interest but covered the whole range of British information apparatus. The extent to which these relations differed from those with other powers is indicated by the fact that although British information officers had been instructed to be particularly careful not to reveal the scale of information activity to representatives of foreign powers, in 1946, the Foreign Office and the State Department exchanged lengthy and precise details regarding the budgets and personnel involved in overseas propaganda.[30]

These discussions revealed that US plans for peacetime propaganda were considerably less ambitious than Britain's. The State Department described its information activities as, 'facilitative and supplemental.' The State Department merely sought to keep channels of information open so that interested parties might learn about American life, if they wished. The British thought this approach 'too limited and negative,' preferring 'an active programme of presenting British life, virtues and policy to the world through all available media.'[31] Although America's first post-war propaganda did seek to present a balanced interpretation of the USA's national attributes, there was no active programme of explanation or persuasion. It was believed that the facts of American life were exemplary and sufficient to influence world opinion without the employment of any techniques of persuasion. In a secret history of American psychological operations written in 1951, Dr Edward P. Lilly described the American position in 1945 as follows:

> If the world were given straight facts about American objectives and desires, men would necessarily recognise the cooperative position of the United States... The unadulterated facts speak for themselves and are more acceptable to the common man than government opinion influencing efforts. America had no selfish post-war policies, and therefore we needed only channels to insure that all peoples knew the American policy.[32]

Like the British, the US government was concerned that this programme of national projection should not be seen as propaganda. In a speech in January 1946,

William B. Benton, the Assistant Secretary of State for Public Affairs, called for a dignified 'information' programme, as distinguished from 'propaganda' with its unfavourable connotations. He made it clear that he intended to present a 'full and fair picture' of the USA. 'The State Department does not intend to engage in so-called propaganda,' he announced.[33] Benton's statement was perhaps closer to the truth than he intended. Despite his efforts, the USA's information programme virtually disappeared in the immediate post-war years. State Department officials were largely disinterested or hostile to the propaganda activities that they had inherited. Congressional hostility was even more pronounced and appropriations for overseas information were reduced by more than half between 1946 and 1948.[34] The US Government's most well-established information agency, the Voice of America (VOA), almost collapsed under the combined assault of Congressional budget cuts, and the hostility of private news agencies no longer prepared to service a government propaganda agency.[35]

Despite such pressures, with the support of Truman and the efforts of individuals such as Benton, elements of America's wartime information apparatus were retained to support peacetime policy. Following the liquidation of the Office of War Information, ten new divisions were established in the State Department under a new Office of International Information and Cultural Affairs (OIC).[36] Further continuity was provided in the War Department, who viewed the employment of propaganda somewhat more favourably than their colleagues in the State Department. The American Forces Radio Service (AFRS), directed at GIs in the occupied territories, fulfilled an important propaganda function. Its activities were supplemented by stations such as Radio in the American Sector (RIAS) and Radio Red-White-Red which targeted the home audience in occupied Germany and Austria.[37] More significantly, the War Department provided a hospitable environment in which America's offensive propaganda developed. On the same day President Truman signed the Executive Order abolishing the OSS, he also wrote to Secretary of State Byrnes asking him to formulate plans for a comprehensive and coordinated intelligence programme.[38] In the ensuing reorganization, the operational assets of OSS, including its covert propaganda capability, were absorbed in the War Department's new Strategic Services Unit (SSU). Whereas the State Department rejected covert propaganda as incompatible with a peacetime information programme, the SSU were keen to retain the propaganda assets of OSS.[39] Moreover, in the debate over the development of a peacetime intelligence agency, Truman's directive that the agency should perform 'such other functions and duties' related to national security, was generally interpreted to encompass a wide range of activities, including propaganda.[40]

In the first year of peace the British and US Governments displayed an ambivalent attitude to the continued operation of government information services. Public statements by leaders and officials suggested that propaganda was now an established feature of government activity. However, the public dissolution of wartime information agencies gave the impression that such activity was largely curtailed. In these reorganizations the British information services fared somewhat better than their US counterparts. Although the British governments were keen to disguise the scale of their propaganda activities, there was no suggestion that such activity should not continue, merely that it should be more discreet. Indeed, it seems apparent that after the initial demobilization, the Foreign Office, in particular, quickly stepped up its propaganda activity. In the USA, in contrast, there was a strong feeling that government propaganda should be stopped altogether. Appropriations were dramatically reduced and a handful of advocates were forced to fight for the survival of an overseas propaganda programme within the State Department. There was, however, one important area of continuity. Elements of the USA's covert propaganda apparatus were retained in the War Department and it was from within the burgeoning intelligence community that a new plan for offensive propaganda would emerge. However, initially at least, the propaganda policies of both nations remained focused on the positive presentation of national achievements. US confidence led many to believe that positive policies spoke for themselves, that other nations would naturally be interested in US democracy and all that was required was a facilitative programme to distribute factual information where it was wanted. In contrast, Britain's declining status as a world power, coupled with a growing dependence on international trade, led her to place considerable faith in the ability of propaganda to disguise national weakness and elicit international economic support. Although both nations retained elements of their wartime propaganda apparatus neither yet had a policy for responding to hostile foreign propaganda.

British and American perceptions of the Soviet threat

As the war drew to a close policy-makers in Britain and the USA were unsure of Soviet intentions, and were forced to make assumptions about Soviet aims and objectives based on Soviet behaviour and ambivalent statements by the Soviet leadership. The Soviets had been courageous and formidable allies. The Red Army drove the Nazis out of the USSR, across Eastern Europe and back into Germany. The USSR was the dominant power of the Eurasian land mass and occupied much of continental Europe. The communists in Europe had also gained considerable political strength. Communist Party membership had soared during the War, particularly in Eastern Europe but also in France, Italy and Finland where the communist vote comprised 20 per cent of the electorate in 1945. Meanwhile, Germany, Japan and Italy were defeated, France was humiliated, and Britain was weakened.[41] In the view of Western policy-makers, the Soviets were quick to capitalize on their advantages. Early in 1945, under Soviet pressure, communist-controlled governments were formed in Romania, Bulgaria and Poland. In March 1945, the Soviet Union denounced the Turco–Soviet non-aggression pact and began to put pressure on Turkey over control of the Dardanelles, a threatening stance compounded by the ongoing communist insurrection in Greece. In Iran, the Soviets sought to strengthen their position by promoting aspirations for autonomy of non-Iranian groups in the Soviet occupied north. In February 1946, in his first major post-war address, Stalin dismissed any prospect of coexistence between capitalist and communist powers. He described the War as an inevitable crisis of the 'last stage of capitalism,' in which 'our victory means, in the first place, our Soviet system has won.' He called for a fundamental redistribution of raw materials and markets among countries according to their economic weight, something which he stated could not be achieved under present capitalist conditions.[42] According to the former Soviet foreign minister, Maxim Litvinov, 'there has been a return in Russia to the outmoded concept of security in terms of territory – the more you've got the safer you are.'[43]

From 1945 until mid-1946, British and US policy-makers developed an, often complementary, perception of the Soviet threat. As the War drew to a close, British and US military planners viewed Soviet military potential with alarm. In the aftermath of the War, the postponement of elections in Eastern Europe, the presence of Soviet troops in Iran, and Soviet pressure on Greece and Turkey served to further undermine faith in Soviet goodwill. Concerns regarding Soviet intentions in Eastern Europe and the Middle East were supported by numerous reports from British and US missions which highlighted the growth in hostile Soviet propaganda. Such reports provided the basis for a perception of the Soviet threat based upon political and not military fears. British and US policy-makers and officials did not believe that the Soviet Union was ready to embark upon an imminent war. They did, however, fear the spread of Soviet influence through communist subversion. Western observers were concerned that the Soviet Union retained the potential to influence events beyond its borders through a well-organized network of communist parties and agents. Once they had established control in Eastern Europe, it was feared that the Soviets would attempt to weaken and subvert Western democracies by a series of clandestine and overt methods short of military confrontation. Soviet actions in the immediate aftermath of the War did little to dispel these fears.

During the War, British and US leaders had divergent views regarding the prospects for continued three-power cooperation after the defeat of Nazi Germany. Churchill regarded cooperation with the Soviet Union merely as an alliance of convenience. Relations between Britain and the Soviet Union had been characterized by ideological and geopolitical hostility since 1917 and Churchill was under no illusion that hostile relations would resume after the war. On his way to the Teheran conference in 1943 Churchill told Macmillan, 'Germany is finished... Russia is the real problem now.'[44] In contrast Roosevelt was determined to maintain cooperation with the Soviet Union as the key to world peace. Elusive as Roosevelt's views are, there is little evidence to suggest that he shared Churchill's view of the Soviet threat. It is apparent that in Roosevelt's vision Russia and the USA would manage world affairs through the United Nations.[45]

It is tempting to ascribe the shifts in British and US policy towards the Soviet Union in 1945 to the changes of administration brought about by the death of Roosevelt and the British general election. However, Soviet actions called into question whether Roosevelt's concept of a post-war order could ever be realized. Truman assumed office promising to continue Roosevelt's policies. Like Roosevelt he was concerned to avoid the appearance of Anglo-American collaboration against the Soviet Union. Throughout 1945, with Secretary of State James Byrnes, Truman sought accommodation with the Soviet Union. Faced with Soviet manoeuvres in Eastern Europe and the intransigent negotiating position of Soviet delegates at the peace conferences, by early 1946 Truman resolved to follow a tougher policy towards the Soviet Union. According to Melvyn Leffler, Truman regarded Soviet actions in Eastern Europe as 'opportunistic, arbitrary and outrageous.'[46] He characterized Soviet behaviour as a continuation of tsarist Russia's expansionist past. Moreover, recent lessons indicated that if totalitarian nations were allowed to gather strength they could threaten the USA. At the end of 1945, on reading a report on the conduct of elections in Eastern Europe, Truman famously expressed himself, 'tired of babying the Soviets.' He wanted the Rumanian and Bulgarian Governments radically changed, Soviet actions in Iran condemned and Soviet designs on Turkey checked. By the beginning of 1946, Truman resolved that, 'unless Russia is faced with an iron fist and strong language another war is in the making.'[47] Shortly afterwards, Truman shared a platform with Churchill in Fulton, Missouri, as the former Prime Minister gave his famous 'Iron Curtain speech'.

In Britain, however, the new Labour Government had fought the general election campaign on the assertion that a socialist government would naturally enjoy closer relations with the Soviet Government than their Conservative predecessors. There was considerable sympathy for the Soviet position among Labour Party activists, and much pro-Soviet sentiment was expressed by the 1945 intake of MPs in their first months in Parliament. In marked contrast to the party rank and file, those in the Labour leadership with firsthand experience of dealing with the Soviets were inclined to be less conciliatory.[48] During the election campaign, Attlee had accompanied Churchill to the Potsdam conference. When he returned to Potsdam as Prime Minister, faced with Stalin's geniality, Attlee was under no illusions about the Soviet's attitude, 'I knew from experience that the Communists had always fought us more vigorously than the Tories because they thought we offered a viable alternative to Communism.'[49] On returning from the San Francisco conference in June 1945, Attlee pronounced the Russians to be 'perfectly bloody to deal with; they tell us nothing yet are setting up puppet governments all over Europe and as far west as they can.'[50] Attlee's choice of Bevin as Foreign Secretary was, according to his press secretary and biographer, Francis Williams, predicated on the fact that, 'Soviet Russia would become tough, aggressive and uncooperative' and Bevin was the most suited, 'by temperament and experience to meet such a situation.'[51] Bevin's anti-communist credentials were undoubted. Although he was committed to a new internationalist, and if possible socialist, world order, he was not prepared to make concessions to the Soviets to achieve it.[52] At Potsdam, Bevin claimed that, Churchill had gone 'too far in throwing baubles to the Soviets.'[53] Unlike Churchill, Bevin would not acquiesce in Soviet attempts to extend their sphere of influence in Eastern and South-eastern Europe. By the spring of 1946, following the first frustrating Council of Foreign Ministers meeting, and Stalin's February speech, Bevin told Attlee that the Russians 'have decided upon an aggressive policy based upon militant Communism and Russian chauvinism and seem determined to stick at nothing, short of war, to obtain their objectives.'[54]

Western leaders' perceptions of the Soviet threat were not, of course, based simply on their experiences of dealing with the Soviets at the peace conferences. Towards the end of the War, military and intelligence agencies in Britain and the USA turned their attention to the potential threat from the Soviet Union's vast military capability. In Britain, the Post Hostilities Planning Staff (PHPS) began preparing studies early in 1944 based on the assumption that the Soviet Union was the next potential enemy.[55] In the USA, the Joint Chiefs of Staff stressed the importance of deterring Soviet aggrandizement in Europe and Asia.[56] By the autumn of 1945, military planners on both sides of the Atlantic were worried that Soviet control of much of Eastern Europe would aid the Soviet Union's economic recovery, enhance its warmaking capacity and deny resources to Western Europe.

British and US intelligence agencies produced their first post-war assessments of Soviet intentions early in 1946. In the light of US possession of the atomic bomb, these assessments stressed that the immediate threat was not Soviet military strength but communist subversion. The principal fear was that following the establishment of Soviet control in Eastern Europe the Soviets would attempt to weaken and subvert Western democracies by a combination of clandestine and overt methods short of military intervention. In March 1946, the British Joint Intelligence Committee (JIC) concluded that although the Soviet Union would avoid any course of action likely to provoke a war, she would respond 'using all weapons, short of war' to any attempt to undermine her position in the satellite states. In addition to securing her frontiers the Soviet Union would adopt a 'policy of opportunism to extend her influence wherever possible without provoking a major war.' According to the JIC, at most risk were those areas where they were least likely 'to come up against firm combined resistance from the United States and Great Britain,' such as the Mediterranean, Turkey and Iran. The JIC identified several methods by which the Soviets would seek to extend their influence: communist parties abroad would play a central role, both in consolidating power in the Soviet orbit and weakening non-communist states; the Soviets would also make use of their position in the United Nations, and various other international organizations such as the World Federation of Trade Unions (WFTU) and the World Youth Organisation (WYO); finally, propaganda would be used to the full, in particular to stir up trouble among colonial peoples.[57]

The first estimate of Soviet intentions and capabilities produced by the American Central Intelligence Group's Office of Research and Evaluation (ORE), also concluded that the Soviet Union would seek to avoid military conflict. Like the JIC, it acknowledged that the Soviet Union would insist upon dominating Eastern Europe. Elsewhere Stalin would pursue an 'opportunistic and grasping' policy. The main targets for Soviet attention would be Greece, Turkey and Iran. The Soviets would also seek to be the predominant influence in the whole of Germany and Austria, and enjoy an influence at least equal to the USA in Japan, China and Korea. In line with the British, this US assessment also stressed that the Soviets believed the success of their policies were dependent upon ensuring that Britain and the USA did not combine as part of a powerful Western bloc. The report identified subversion as the principal method the Soviets would employ to undermine the unity and strength of foreign states. Through local communist parties and propaganda the Soviets would seek to: foment domestic discord, discredit the leadership, promote domestic agitation conducive to a reduction of their target's military and economic strength and to the adoption of foreign policies favourable to Soviet purposes, and incite colonial unrest.[58]

These intelligence assessments were supported by reports throughout 1946 from British and US representatives abroad at the sharp end of Soviet propaganda attacks. These reports suggested a developing propaganda campaign directed at Britain and the USA, and an increase in Soviet propaganda in vulnerable areas. From early in 1946 British and US missions began to report a new and increasingly hostile communist propaganda campaign. According to the US Ambassador in Moscow, the Soviet propaganda campaign combined 'violent attacks on "British imperialism"' with 'grotesque and slightly sinister' depictions of the American way of life.[59] The British Embassy reported that a delegation of Labour MPs to Moscow had been shocked by the 'extent and virulence' of Soviet anti-British propaganda.[60] Reports also suggested that communist propagandists were active in at least some of those areas identified as at most risk from Soviet subversion. A US weekly intelligence summary from August 1946 observed that Soviet propaganda was increasingly aimed at splitting the 'Anglo-America bloc' by playing up Anglo-American differences in the Middle East, and highlighting the competition for markets in India and the Far East.[61] In July 1946, a Parliamentary Delegation to Iran was dismayed by the level of anti-British propaganda by the communist Tudeh Party. On their return they recommended that 'a strong British propaganda drive should be launched' in Iran.[62] British information officers implored the Foreign Office to allow them to respond on a broader scale,[63] and the American Ambassador in Moscow called for a 'vigorous and intelligent American information program.'[64]

Perhaps the most influential assessments of Soviet policy came from British and US representatives in Moscow. From their position near the centre of Soviet power, and often at the forefront of communist propaganda attacks, they dramatically illustrated the dangers of communist subversion. Most famously, in February 1946, George Kennan, chargé d'affaires at the American Embassy in Moscow, sought to define Soviet policy in his 'long telegram' to the State Department. Kennan concluded that Soviet policy was guided by the belief that 'with US there can be no permanent *modus vivendi*.' Stalin believed that 'peaceful coexistence' was impossible, and that the world revolved around socialist and capitalist 'centres' engaged in a constant battle for command of the world economy. Although Soviet foreign policy was not adventuristic the Soviets would seek to expand the limits of Soviet power 'wherever it was considered timely and promising.' This policy, Kennan wrote, would be pursued at an official and a 'subterranean' level, in which the actions of Soviet officials would be supported by a series of measures undertaken 'by agencies for which Soviet Government does not admit responsibility.' According to Kennan the Soviet Union had at its disposal:

> ...an elaborate and far flung apparatus for exertion of its influence in other countries, an apparatus of amazing flexibility and versatility, managed by people whose experience and skill in underground methods are presumably without parallel in history.[65]

Kennan's views were echoed in a series of telegrams from the British chargé d'affaires, Frank Roberts.[66] Roberts concurred with Kennan that the Soviet Union would seek to avoid a major war, but he too found little cause for optimism in this analysis. Instead, Roberts warned that 'increasing attention was devoted to the renewed Marxist-Leninist ideological campaign.' He also emphasized the particular anti-British tone of this campaign. Kennan had noted that of all their perceived enemies the Soviets would wage a relentless battle against the so-called 'false friends of the people', namely moderate socialist or social democratic leaders. Roberts' experience confirmed Kennan's observation. He wrote that, in the new ideological offensive, Britain, 'as the home of capitalism, imperialism and now of social democracy, is a main target.' Moreover, he expanded, such propaganda was not confined to the Soviet Union. All across Europe 'communist propaganda is constantly directed against us.'[67]

Kennan's and Roberts' reports illustrate the degree of convergence between British and US official perceptions of the Soviet threat. They also indicate a marked degree of agreement in their proposed response to Soviet actions. Both suggested a response based on the projection of an image of a healthy and vigorous society to rival the appeal of Soviet communism. The 'self-confidence, discipline, morale and community spirit of our own people', was, according to Kennan, 'a victory...worth a thousand diplomatic notes and joint communiqués.' Only through presenting 'a more positive and constructive picture of the sort of world we would like to see' could the USA hope to guide the rest of the world away from communism. Similarly, Roberts stressed that Britain 'should act as champions of a dynamic faith and way of life with an appeal to the world at least as great as that of the Communist system.' Kennan and Roberts also recognized that an appeal to international opinion would only succeed if coupled with a campaign to disillusion domestic public opinion about Soviet intentions. Both emphasized the need for a campaign to 'educate' the British and US public about the realities of Soviet communism. In conclusion, Kennan and Roberts believed that countering the Soviet threat would involve the coordination of political and military strategy, domestic and foreign policy in a manner comparable with wartime strategy.[68]

Kennan and Roberts were both influential in defining the Soviet threat. Kennan's telegram was widely circulated within the US Government. The Secretary of the Navy, James Forrestal, thought it so inspired he had it despatched to 'hundreds if not thousands' of senior officers in the armed services. Kennan's 'long telegram' has been widely credited with defining the US policy of 'containment' of the Soviet threat for the next 40 years. Kennan returned to Washington shortly afterwards from where he continued to provide detailed assessments of the Soviet threat as head of the new Policy Planning Staff tasked with 'formulating and developing...long-term programs for the achievement of US foreign policy objectives.'[69] Although the impact of Roberts' analysis was less sensational it also struck a resonant chord in the Foreign Office, and was widely read in Government. The Head of the Northern Department, Christopher Warner, described his despatches as 'magnificent' and Bevin instructed that the whole of Roberts' analysis be circulated to the Cabinet.[70]

Roberts' analysis supported a growing consensus within the Foreign Office regarding the hostile nature of Soviet intentions and the need to adopt a more vigorous response. In 1946 senior officials in the Foreign Office began to reassess Soviet intentions. Prompted by the JIC and Roberts' reports from Moscow, they reached rather gloomy conclusions about the limits of Stalin's intentions and advocated a new 'defensive/offensive' strategy to respond to the Soviet threat.[71] The forum in which this response was developed was the Foreign Office Russia Committee. Roberts had recommended the creation of a new body within the Foreign Office to provide analysis of Soviet policy and formulate Britain's global response. The Russia Committee was established in April 1946 and is evidence of the growing awareness of the Soviet threat and the need to provide a coordinated response. The Russia Committee was designed to provide a weekly review of 'all aspects of Soviet policy and propaganda', and consider what response was required, with particular reference to the 'probable degree of support to be looked for from the United States of America, and to a lesser degree from France and others.'[72]

At its first meeting, the committee considered a paper drawn up by Christopher Warner which outlined, 'The Soviet Campaign Against This Country and Our Response To It'. Warner echoed Frank Roberts' telegrams by stressing that the Soviets had returned to a 'pure doctrine of Marx-Lenin-Stalinism' which was naturally antagonistic to British social democracy. In pursuing this doctrinal policy the

Soviets would, according to Warner, 'play an aggressive political role, while making an intensive drive to increase its own military and industrial strength.' Warner's analysis reveals the degree to which recent experience influenced Foreign Office perceptions of the Soviet threat. Highlighting the proselytising nature of communism, Warner noted that, 'we should be very unwise not to take the Russians at their word, just as we should have been wise to take *Mein Kampf* at its face value.' Warner stressed that as Hitler had occupied half of Europe by means short of war there should be no mistake about Soviet intentions.[73] Aggressive Soviet actions were evident around the world: in Eastern Europe, Germany, Iran, Manchuria and Korea, and in the United Nations. British interests worldwide were threatened, in particular by aggressive Soviet propaganda. 'The Soviet Government,' he wrote, 'are carrying on an intensive campaign to weaken, deprecate and harry this country in every possible way.' Wherever they have the opportunity the Soviets would, according to Warner, seek to 'stir up trouble for His Majesty's Government or to weaken their influence.' The threats to Britain were manifold: the establishment of communist governments in countries where hostile influence threatened Britain's national interest; the weakening of friendly elements in such countries; the creation of troubled conditions in the colonies; disruption of recovery outside the Soviet orbit; attempts to divide Britain from their allies; and attempts to discredit Britain as weak and reactionary. Faced with such threats, Warner argued, 'concessions and appeasement' would merely serve to weaken Britain's position while the Soviets built up their industrial and economic strength. Britain, he concluded, must launch a vigorous defence. Taking his lead from the JIC, Warner asserted that if the Soviets were to employ means short of war, such methods should also be Britain's defence:

> The Soviet Government makes coordinated use of military, economic, propaganda and political weapons and also of the communist 'religion'. It is submitted, therefore, that we must at once organise and coordinate our defences against all these and that we should not stop short of a defensive-offensive.[74]

Warner's paper was endorsed by Bevin and Attlee.[75] The general acceptance of the Foreign Office's reassessment of Soviet policy, and, in the USA, the embracing of Kennan's analysis, indicates that on both sides of the Atlantic policy-makers' views of the Soviet threat had crystallized by early 1946. However, public perceptions of the Soviet threat did not necessarily correspond with those of politicians and officials, and this remained an obstacle to a more robust response to the Soviet threat. In September 1946, US intelligence observed that Soviet propaganda which had sought to 'keep alive in the US and UK any active opposition to any firm policy towards the USSR' had met with considerable success. It concluded that many moderate and liberal groups 'have been so divided over the issue of policy toward the USSR that their potentialities for opposing Soviet tactics have been at least neutralised.'[76] If the British and US Governments were going to pursue a tougher policy with the Soviet Union they would also need to address public opinion at home.

The Soviet attempt to promote a more generous policy towards themselves in Britain and the US was largely pushing against an open door. In Britain there remained among the general public a widespread feeling of gratitude for the Soviet contribution to the war effort. Throughout the War, the British public had displayed a marked admiration for the achievements of the Red Army, and by extension, the Soviet regime. As early as 1941, Churchill remarked on the 'tendency of the British public to forget the dangers of communism in their enthusiasm over the resistance of Russia.'[77] By March 1945, the Foreign Office suggested that it was necessary to encourage franker criticism in Britain of Soviet policy and to stop the 'gush of propaganda' eulogizing the Russian war effort and their system of government.[78] When, in September 1945, a Gallup public opinion poll asked the British public if their feelings towards Russia were more or less friendly than a year ago, 16 per cent said they felt more friendly, 54 per cent felt the same, and 19 per cent less friendly. When asked the same question about the USA, only 9 per cent felt more friendly, and 35 per cent less friendly.[79] When questioned again about attitudes towards the Soviet Union in September 1946, 41 per cent now pronounced themselves less friendly, but 41 per cent recorded no change in attitude and 8 per cent still expressed increased friendliness.[80] Moreover, when asked the reasons for the disappearance of allied cooperation, general mistrust and 'each country out for itself' came significantly higher than Russian imperialism and unwillingness to cooperate.[81] Remarkably, when Gallup compiled a list of people most admired by the British public in November 1946, Stalin came seventh, one place above the King and Queen![82]

Remarkably, in the USA, where throughout the War Roosevelt had openly pursued a more accommodating policy towards the Soviet Union, the public was less pro-Soviet than in Britain. Polls carried out by the American Institute of Public Opinion indicate a consistent level of distrust of Soviet policies throughout the War and into peacetime.[83] Nevertheless, they also indicate that public concern about the nation's security was not entirely due to anti-Soviet sentiment. When pollsters asked the public in February 1946 which countries they distrusted, although the Soviet Union led the list with 52 per cent, Britain came in a close second with 41 per cent.[84] Moreover, suspicion of Soviet intentions did not transform into support for a new policy towards the Soviet Union. Following Churchill's 'Iron Curtain speech' at Fulton the British Ambassador, Halifax, concluded that although the majority of 'articulate comment' paid homage to the speaker, it disagreed, 'either with his diagnosis or his cure, or both.' Halifax noted:

> Profound as the uneasiness is about Soviet policies, there is still a reluctance to face the full implications of the facts and a timidity about the consequences of language as forthright as Mr Churchill's.[85]

Halifax's conclusions are supported by opinion polls which indicate that the majority of those polled who knew of Churchill's speech disapproved of his suggestions.[86] This reluctance to respond to Soviet policies reflected a wider feeling in both the USA and Britain, that foreign policy issues were not a major concern as the world recovered from the war. In October 1945, only seven per cent of Americans polled rated world peace as the number one problem facing the country. Jobs and labour unrest were, perhaps predictably, their foremost concerns.[87] In Britain, foreign policy was not included in pollsters' questions regarding the most pressing problems facing the country until 1947. When it was, in July 1947, only 5 per cent considered foreign policy to be the most important problem, far below the food situation at 27 per cent and housing at 13 per cent.[88]

By mid-1946, British and US leaders and officials had reached similar views of the Soviet threat. In responding to this threat, policy-makers faced several problems. Firstly, diplomats and information officers in certain strategic areas – principally Iran, Eastern Europe and the Soviet Union – urgently sought permission to answer specific communist propaganda charges in their respective countries. In addition to the immediate problem of this ongoing communist propaganda campaign, observers feared the potential of communist subversion on a much wider scale. Those such as Kennan and Roberts, who took in the whole vista of Soviet behaviour, recognized that the communist propaganda apparatus was widespread and highly organized. Their analyses suggested that a piecemeal response to individual Soviet attacks would not do. They recommended the global presentation of Western values as a coherent doctrine to rival that of communism. Such an approach would necessitate a propaganda campaign comparable in scale and organization to that of the Soviet Union. Finally, British and US policy-makers faced the problem of mobilizing domestic opinion. British and US representatives abroad who witnessed hostile communist propaganda first hand were quick to advocate a vigorous response; however, the mass of the population of Britain and the USA was not subject to such exposure. For some people at least, the Soviet Union was a valiant ally which had suffered incredible losses and was, not surprisingly, concerned for its future security. A far larger majority cared little for foreign policy issues. They had survived a dreadful war and were more concerned with the immediate problems of domestic regeneration. If policy-makers were to develop a coherent and effective response to Soviet propaganda they would need to employ government propaganda both at home and abroad at a level unprecedented in peacetime.

The development of anti-communist propaganda 1946–1947

Britain took the initiative in responding to communist propaganda. It was, however, an initiative taken with reluctance and followed with caution. Faced with warnings from the JIC, and calls from his most senior diplomats to allow them to react to communist propaganda, Bevin continued to place great faith in 'The Projection of Britain'. His response to anti-British communist propaganda was to propose an ever more forceful presentation of British achievements. In January 1946, Bevin told the Cabinet, 'The best means of preventing the countries of South-eastern Europe from being absorbed into an exclusive Soviet sphere of influence was to provide a steady stream of information about British life and culture.'[89] By emphasizing Britain's industrial welfare, Bevin hoped to 'expose the myth current in many quarters that Soviet Russia is the only country in which attention is given to the welfare of workers.'[90] Although many of those posted abroad considered this response to be somewhat inadequate, the Foreign Office replied to their requests for permission to answer Soviet charges with Bevin's edict that 'no active steps should be taken in the way of counter-attack.'[91] At a joint Central Office of Information and Foreign Office Conference on overseas information, Ivone Kirkpatrick stressed that it was the Foreign Secretary's wish that:

> ... the steady political and publicity attack being made by Russia should not be met by anti-communist propaganda. The policy was that publicity should project the British social system, aspects of industrial welfare etc. being in fact educative.[92]

There is evidence to suggest that this educative approach was paying off. Reports from British missions in Eastern Europe emphasized the 'pathetic and encouraging' appetite of the general populace for British cultural material.[93] Similarly, in Italy (an area considered to be a principal target for communist propaganda), the British Labour Attaché wrote that, 'it would be more profitable to adopt a positive line of pro-British propaganda than the negative line of answering other people's propaganda.'[94] In June 1947, Kirkpatrick informed a production conference on overseas propaganda, that the Foreign Secretary 'considered the tide of communism in Europe had receded, largely owing to the way in which the Russians had conducted affairs, and the way in which they [the British] had presented themselves to the world.'[95]

Bevin's confidence in 'The Projection of Britain' was not, however, shared by all his colleagues in the Foreign Office. From early in 1946, officials in the Foreign Office urged Bevin to adopt a more vigorous response to communist propaganda. Often couched in language reminiscent of the Second World War, this response went beyond the educative approach favoured by Bevin and included elements of offence as well as defence. It was a response which Bevin resisted through 1946 and 1947, yet one which ultimately prevailed. Faced with offensive communist propaganda, officials suggested that British overseas propaganda should concentrate less on projecting national achievements and focus greater attention on countering communist charges. As Ivone Kirkpatrick told the Central Office of Information in July 1946, 'the stage of winning admirers and friends for Great Britain had now passed...the time had come to persuade each country to take action.'[96]

In his paper on the Soviet campaign against Britain, Christopher Warner had begun to outline a new line for responding to offensive communist propaganda. Far from winning friends through the projection of national achievements, Warner stressed that British propaganda should be directed against communism, which should be exposed as totalitarianism. British propaganda should attack and expose the myths the Soviet Government was using to justify its policy, such as: the supposed encirclement of Russia by capitalist powers; the myth that Germany was to be built up against Russia; that Russia gave disinterested support to subject races in contrast to colonial enslavement by capitalist powers; the fallacious distinction between the idea of a 'Western bloc' and the reality of the Russian Eastern bloc; the Russian misinterpretations of 'democracy,' 'cordon sanitaire' and 'collaboration'; and the Soviet habit of calling all non-communists 'reactionaries' and 'anti-democratic'. In addition to this new line in British propaganda, Warner suggested that Britain should offer 'all moral and material support as was possible without endangering their lives' to progressive forces in any country fighting against communism.[97]

Prompted by Warner's paper, Kirkpatrick drafted a detailed proposal for British counter-propaganda. Kirkpatrick was a veteran of wartime propaganda and his proposal contained much to recommend it to Bevin. He outlined several premises for an effective propaganda campaign, including: the cooperation of Government Ministers; the support of the BBC and the domestic media; and the closest coordination of domestic and foreign propaganda. He also cautioned against expectations of dramatic results. The essence of the campaign was to be education and would therefore proceed 'at a steady drip rather than a sudden gush.' However, Kirkpatrick somewhat undermined the impact of his paper by linking his proposals for counter-propaganda with a more hazardous plan for subversion. By drawing on his wartime experience Kirkpatrick crossed a line between advocating actions short of war and the kind of direct intervention which could provoke one. In a much quoted passage, he concluded:

> We have a good analogy in our very successful campaign during the war directed towards stimulating resistance movements in Europe. The V sign was blazoned all over the world, but at the same time we acted. We parachuted men, money and arms into occupied territory... Propaganda on the largest possible scale was coordinated with our policy.[98]

Despite support from senior officials, Kirkpatrick's dramatic plan never received any degree of Ministerial approval. Bevin strongly opposed the scheme and minuted tersely underneath, 'The more I study this the less I like it. I am quite sure that the putting over of positive results of British attitudes will be a better corrective.'[99] Far from sponsoring subversion, Bevin recommended greater publicity for the new Insurance Bill and National Health Bill.[100] Although Kirkpatrick's paper was discussed on several future occasions, on each occasion it was decided that anti-communist propaganda and subversion should be treated separately.[101] In contrast, Warner's paper had been distributed to selected Cabinet Ministers, and received the approval of both Bevin and Attlee.[102] It seems likely that Warner's appeal to unite the forces of social democracy was somewhat more palatable to Bevin than Kirkpatrick's reversion to wartime tactics.

Although Bevin resisted the adoption of a defensive-offensive policy on a global scale, he did authorise such a campaign in several key areas, most notably Iran.[103] The Middle East was essential to Britain's emerging Cold War strategy. Foreign Office concerns about communist propaganda in the area coincided with military plans to use the Middle East as a base from which to attack the Soviet Union in the event of war. The UK was out of range of many important strategic targets, and the Chiefs of Staff considered bases in the Middle East vital to bring the industrial and oil-producing areas of Southern Russia within long-range air attack.[104] In 1945, the JIC had identified the Middle East as an area in which Britain was particularly vulnerable to hostile Soviet propaganda. In June 1946, it reported that the aim of Soviet policy was to 'weaken the British position in that area.'[105] The Foreign Office had already decided to 'go all out for the defence of our interests in the areas which the Chiefs of Staff eventually declared to be of vital importance.'[106] Thus, when the British mission in Teheran began to express concern at the influence of the communist Tudeh Party, the Foreign Office urged Bevin to make an exception to his rule and sanction a general counter-offensive in Iran.[107]

In October 1946, Kirkpatrick drafted a directive for propaganda in the Middle East and, with reservations, Bevin approved it. Kirkpatrick proposed a two pronged counter-offensive designed to present Britain as the nation to which Middle East countries should look for guidance, whilst dealing factually with the Russian campaign of misrepresentations. Bevin's only concern was that the campaign should be predominantly positive and not make the mistake of rousing 'communist enthusiasm by excessive attacks on communism.' As Bevin wished, Kirkpatrick's directive was designed to project positive themes and avoid futile controversy. Britain's progressive social policy was emphasized as was Britain's willingness to extend this commitment overseas in the form of technical and humanitarian assistance. It was, Kirkpatrick claimed, important to 'ram home' to the peoples of the Middle East Britain's interest in the 'independence, security and prosperity' of the region, whilst also publicizing British attempts to influence governments in the area to introduce social reforms and raise standards of living. The anti-communist aspect of the campaign sought to answer Soviet misrepresentations, depict the true state of affairs in Russia, and stress the failure of Russian diplomacy. Aware of Soviet experience in propaganda, Kirkpatrick noted that communist charges should be answered with discretion. It was important to avoid being drawn into debates on subjects chosen by the Soviets and always appear to be on the defensive. The positive work of 'building the new Britain' was to be at the forefront of British propaganda.[108]

These themes were projected on the widest possible scale. In addition to the British Government's information apparatus, the BBC, British companies in the Middle East, and the TUC were all mobilized. Sir Ian Jacob, Controller of the BBC's European Services, had approached the Foreign Office earlier in 1946 to suggest that Britain was being too indulgent in its attitude to Soviet propaganda and that broadcasts might carry more anti-communist material. Jacob was promptly invited to attend meetings of the Russia committee as the only non-Foreign Office member.[109] When the campaign in Iran began in October 1946, Kirkpatrick recommended that Sir William Haley, the Director-General of the BBC, be asked to place the Middle East services under Jacob's control.[110] Although Jacob insisted that the BBC's impartiality should be preserved, he urged the Russia Committee to provide more background information on the USSR, methods of the Soviet Government and British policy in the Middle East.[111] British oil companies were also asked to publicize their efforts to raise the standard of living in Iran.[112] In an effort to ensure their assistance, it was suggested that officials stress the danger of communist disruption of the labour force and that British oil companies, 'can only hope to hold their positions if they order their affairs according to the best *Western* standards.' One company which did much to promote Britain's positive approach to labour welfare was the Anglo-Iranian Oil Company (AIOC). In return for its cooperation Bevin asked the Minister of Supply, the President of the Board of Trade and the Minister of Labour to deal 'rapidly and favourably' with all requests from the AIOC for facilities for their development programme.[113] Kirkpatrick recommended a similar approach to the Imperial Bank in Iran. The TUC was also asked to provide literature on 'a considerable scale.'[114] Finally, in the tradition of successful wartime propaganda, overt propaganda was supported by a certain degree of covert activity. The SIS was brought in to enquire into certain aspects of Persian opinion and carry out any investigation the ambassador might request. Colonel Wheeler, the newly appointed information officer in Teheran, also suggested that Persian agents from India might be introduced for the oral dissemination of 'black' propaganda.[115]

The propaganda campaign in Iran was only the first tentative step towards a global response to communist propaganda. It was nevertheless a significant step. It was the first example of the more active offensive-defensive strategy for responding to Soviet propaganda, involving the coordination of overt and covert propaganda and the close support of the BBC and private organizations. Bevin, however, baulked at requests to expand the campaign to cover the whole of the Middle East.[116] When Sargent suggested that Kirkpatrick's original proposals be reconsidered in the light of the new campaign, Bevin stood firm, 'I am not going to commit myself to the whole of Kirkpatrick's scheme in order to tackle Persia.'[117] The Foreign Office was nonetheless reluctant to allow Bevin's doubts to impede the general progress of the anti-communist campaign. As Raymond Smith has observed, there was a substantial measure of confidence that Bevin's objections could be 'chipped away' as long as the momentum was maintained. Bevin's approval of the campaign in Iran alongside his general approval of Warner's paper proved to be 'the hammer and chisel' by which this was to be done.[118] Officials followed a dual strategy whereby preparations were made so that a more vigorous campaign might be instituted the moment ministerial approval was forthcoming. At the same time, they sought approval for a propaganda counter-offensive in various specific cases, in Germany, France and Italy, and at home in Britain.

In preparation for the expected change in policy, Warner's memorandum was circulated to heads of Foreign Office departments and 30 diplomatic posts.[119] The Russia Committee suggested that British representatives abroad 'should be furnished with the necessary background for any action which *might* be required,' and it should be made clear that 'a departure from the normal practice of non-interference in the internal affairs of other countries *will* be involved.'[120] It was also agreed that, Britain's publicity machine should be maintained 'at full efficiency, in order that it might be able to *meet the possibility* of Ministers approving an all-out anti-communist campaign.'[121] In July 1946, the Russia Committee established a publicity subcommittee to provide more detailed consideration of propaganda measures.[122]

Throughout 1946 the Russia Committee also considered action in response to specific requests from British missions in Italy, France and Finland. In these cases, ministerial approval was apparently not sought although the measures discussed clearly went beyond Bevin's instructions. In Italy, the British Ambassador noted that efforts to prevent the country embracing communism were woefully inadequate. Anti-British propaganda was widespread and the ambassador recommended the creation of an organization like the Political Warfare Executive to carry out offensive propaganda.[123] In response, the Russia Committee recommended that propaganda should compare the low cost of British occupation to Soviet calls for reparations, and suggested that further publicity be given to misdeeds in countries under Soviet occupation. They also considered what opportunities might arise for 'influencing elections in favour of our friends.'[124] Concern that communists might take power through the ballot box was also evident in France. The question of influencing French elections was first discussed in March 1946, and by the end of April it was noted that Kirkpatrick and the French Department were 'doing all that was possible to combat Communist propaganda in the French elections.'[125] When discussing such intervention the question of ministerial approval was rarely mentioned although the Committee was apparently aware of the limitations imposed by Bevin. Its willingness to bypass Bevin's authority was clearly illustrated when the British representative in Finland asked for permission to expose communist myths through a programme of oral propaganda. The Russia Committee noted that such measures went 'somewhat beyond what we are already authorised to do.' Nonetheless they approved the suggestions, and agreed to furnish the Embassy with all possible support, 'provided they are carried out discreetly.'[126]

Ministerial approval was secured in September 1946 for additional anti-communist measures in Germany, and more generally to publicize Soviet breaches of the

Potsdam Agreement.[127] In Germany, British propaganda activities had continued since 1945 under the guise of 're-education,' in what Kirkpatrick later termed the 'battle for the German mind.'[128] The new campaign stepped up these activities and drew attention to Soviet misrepresentations of British policy. Authority was given for 'a campaign of enlightenment' regarding Soviet failure to carry out the Potsdam Agreement.[129] Publicity was given to the production of war material in the Soviet zones of Germany and Austria. Kirkpatrick also arranged for Soviet troop numbers in South-eastern Europe to be publicized by the BBC.[130] In Germany, as in Iran, the Foreign Office sought to avoid 'a slanging match where we are on the defensive and engaged in breathlessly countering Soviet charges.' Officials noted perceptively that, 'the latest Soviet lie will always have greater news value than the latest British denial.' The main task was to explain British policy fully and, where possible, implicitly debunk Soviet propaganda about it. In addition, there was to be a certain amount of factual reporting of conditions in the Soviet zone, with particular emphasis on the Soviet desire for reparations.[131]

The adoption of a more combative response to communist propaganda in Germany is indicative of a general shift in Bevin's attitude at the end of 1946. Prompted by the creation of communist governments in Bulgaria, Romania and Poland in late 1946, Bevin moved towards a tougher line in responding to communist propaganda. In September 1946, Oliver Harvey informed the Russia Committee that they now had 'general authority...to defend ourselves against Russian propaganda attacks.'[132] In January 1947, the propaganda campaign already under way in Germany was extended to cover the whole of Eastern Europe. Bevin told a meeting of British ambassadors from Eastern Europe that following the elections they were 'finally faced with totalitarian, Moscow-controlled governments' in Bulgaria, Romania and Poland, as well as Yugoslavia and Albania. Consequently, the campaign to secure 'free and unfettered elections' in Eastern Europe would come to an end. Instead, British diplomats were authorized to do everything possible to promote the Western way of life and to counteract misrepresentations and anti-British propaganda spread by the communists. The objective was 'to hold the position against the spread of communism in order that Western concepts of social democracy may, if possible, in the course of time be adopted in as many Eastern European countries as possible.' It was also felt that if Britain were to relax the pressure on the Soviets in Eastern Europe, 'we should have to expect increased pressure from the Russians in Western Europe and the Middle East.'[133] In July 1947, Britain's response to communist propaganda attacks in the Middle East were also stepped up when Kirkpatrick's directive for propaganda in Iran was extended to cover the whole of the Middle East.[134]

Britain's initiation of measures to counter communist propaganda coincided with a gradual stiffening of US resolve in its dealings with the Soviet Union, and a widening perspective in regard to the USA's global responsibilities. In early 1946, Warner had recommended that the USA be approached to see if they would take part in a general world-wide anti-communist campaign.[135] However, Foreign Office officials were by no means confident about the degree of support they could expect from the USA. In 1946, there was considerable concern that the USA was not taking a 'realistic' view of the Soviet threat. It was also evident that the US Government was keen to avoid any indication that Britain and the USA were uniting against their former ally.[136] Consequently, the Foreign Office advocated a gradual policy of eliciting

US support in certain key areas, whilst avoiding a general policy of cooperation. The policy was summarized by Christopher Warner:

> ... American dislike of 'ganging up' with us being still so strong, we should probably be well advised to make no general approach to the State Department regarding an anti-communist campaign, but to consult them in each specific case, while seeking as at present to encourage the cooperation of the British and American representatives in the various countries, so that they may whenever possible, send their governments similar appreciations and recommendations.[137]

By 1947 the mood in the USA was changing. Almost half the members of Congress travelled abroad in 1946 and 1947 and their exposure to the privations of post-war Europe and organized communist propaganda, led to the passage of significant legislation in 1947.[138] Truman's annunciation of his doctrine in March paved the way for the massive programme of aid for Europe proposed by Secretary of State, George C. Marshall, three months later. In addition, the National Security Act – which created a permanent intelligence apparatus – was presented to Congress in February; and the Smith–Mundt Bill – which established America's first permanent peacetime propaganda programme – was introduced in May. In both cases, Congressional debate centred on the need to respond to external threats.[139] In July, George Kennan's 'long telegram' was transformed into an anonymous article in the journal *Foreign Affairs*, following which the Russia Committee expressed their satisfaction that US officials and the American public were now under no illusions regarding Soviet intentions.[140] The previous month, Sir Maurice Peterson, British Ambassador in Moscow, informed the Foreign Office that his US counterpart, Walter Bedell Smith, had stated that a 'policy of toughness was now the order of the day.' Smith believed that the Soviets had returned to the tactics of the Comintern and the only method of combating them was 'to return blow for blow and to embark on open political warfare against communism.'[141]

The first step away from the State Department's factual information programme towards the revival of offensive propaganda was taken late in 1946 by a subcommittee of the State-War-Navy Coordinating Committee. The Committee noted the Soviet Union's intensive anti-American propaganda campaign and recommended the establishment of a permanent subcommittee on psychological warfare to develop policies, plans and studies for its use 'in time of war or threat of war.'[142] The development of plans for overt and covert propaganda were taken up by the National Security Council (NSC) in November 1947. The NSC drafted two reports: NSC 4, on the coordination of overt 'foreign information measures'; and NSC 4-A, on covert 'psychological operations'. The former highlighted the USSR's 'intensive propaganda campaign' aimed at damaging the prestige of the USA and undermining the non-communist elements in all countries. It proposed the strengthening and coordination of all 'foreign information measures' under the direction of the State Department. In the annex NSC 4-A the CIA was given authority to conduct 'covert psychological operations' to counteract Soviet and Soviet-inspired activities.[143] On 1 December 1947, almost 18 months after Warner's paper had been circulated to British embassies, the State Department issued a new directive on US information policy. It proposed that in addition to the 'factual, truthful, and forceful presentation of US foreign policy and American ways of living... we should take the offensive in dealing with Soviet policies and anti-American propaganda, as well as those of local communist parties.'[144]

Although the USA's new policy did not immediately result in close cooperation with British attempts to counter communism in Europe, it did result in a certain degree of indirect support for British objectives. Long-established intelligence cooperation yielded information for British propaganda regarding Soviet breaches of the Potsdam Agreement.[145] The assignment of foreign broadcast monitoring to the CIA led to a new agreement with the BBC facilitating greater exchange of monitoring reports. The CIA also considered the establishment of new radio stations in US zones of occupation through the transfer of equipment under British control.[146] In several cases the USA's adoption of a dynamic policy of containing Soviet communism closely resembled the response pursued by the British Foreign Office since 1946. If this policy was not coordinated with those British activities already in progress it certainly supported similar objectives. In Germany, where Britain had begun to answer communist charges in October 1946, General Lucius Clay, Commander of the American occupation forces, announced in October 1947 that the US military government was to launch a campaign against communism in the US zone.[147] In November, US representatives in Austria informed the State Department that they had begun to publicize communist involvement in strikes, demonstrations and various illegal activities.[148] British propaganda in occupied Europe was also supported by the work of the combined Allied Information Service (AIS) which conducted 'concentrated and continuous counter-propaganda to communism.'[149] As early as October 1946 US officials in Germany had urged an increased budget for AIS operations noting that the British side was 'strengthening its personnel and increasing its contributions of money and equipment.'[150]

Like their British counterparts, US officials were also concerned at the prospect of communist electoral victories in France and Italy. The Marshall Plan was widely recognized as a bold attempt to undermine the standing of communists in Western Europe. In October 1947, Averell Harriman, the senior Marshall Plan representative in Europe, called for a psychological offensive to counter communist propaganda in France and Italy.[151] The following month, George Kennan's Policy Planning Staff concluded that the Soviet Union was 'very likely' to order the communist parties in France and Italy to 'resort to virtual civil war' as soon as US occupation forces left Italy.[152] In response, the CIA, under the direction of NSC 4-A, provided funds that helped defeat the communists in the French elections of 1947, and subsidized non-communist elements in French trade unions. They also began a programme of aid for anti-communist forces in Italy in preparation for the elections of 1948.[153]

The Foreign Office was clearly pleased at the increasing alignment of British and US thinking on the Soviet threat. Bevin, however, maintained his resistance to a global campaign against communist propaganda. In July 1947, the Russia Committee decided it would not be politic to request an extension of the propaganda line in the Middle East to the rest of the world. Warner informed the Committee that – until after the Council of Foreign Ministers meeting in November – the Foreign Secretary would not sanction any policy based on open despair of reaching agreement with the Russians.[154]

Although the Russia Committee understood Bevin's position and were satisfied with the developments in responding to communist propaganda abroad, officials were growing increasingly concerned about the state of domestic opinion. The Foreign Office found itself in the position of promoting a foreign propaganda campaign which was increasingly inconsistent with domestic policy. It is axiomatic that effective foreign propaganda must be supported by a corresponding domestic campaign yet, by 1947, British foreign and domestic propaganda were clearly operating on different levels. As Frank Roberts noted in March 1947, despite the progress in persuading the Foreign Secretary to advocate anti-communist measures abroad, the British public remained unenlightened:

> It is surely ridiculous to be enlightening the Arabs and the Persians and other peoples about the true nature of the Soviet State and of Soviet propaganda while leaving our own people in complete abysmal ignorance.[155]

Substantial elements of the British public, and more particularly the left wing of Bevin's own party, still believed that Britain could maintain friendly relations with the Soviet Union. In late 1946, Christopher Warner noted that the BBC Home Service and most of the daily papers were 'studiously uncritical' of the Soviet Union and communist regimes in Eastern Europe. In general it was felt that not enough publicity was given to Soviet anti-British propaganda, and the activities of Soviet-sponsored communist parties in Eastern Europe. In particular, Warner had confidential information that at the *Daily Telegraph* there was a general instruction not to print news critical of the Soviet Union unless it was authoritatively sponsored or emanated from government sources. The same was thought to be true of the Beaverbrook press.[156] There was also a growing concern about the Soviet penetration of various international organizations, which professed to represent international opinion, but were in fact organs of Soviet propaganda. There was, the Russia Committee warned, 'no limit to the extent to which this Soviet technique might spread in getting hold of, for example women's and youth organisations or in forming any sort of international organisation to be used as a sounding board for their anti-British propaganda.' The Russia Committee was particularly concerned about the increasing number of British groups attending such international conferences. Private British organizations, they warned, were often ill-equipped or unwilling to resist communist subversion.[157]

The Labour Party was also a major cause for concern. In May 1946, the Russia Committee expressed alarm that some Ministers, 'took the line that it would be wrong to consider Russia to be hostile to this country'[158]; and as late as August 1947 Warner reminded them that 'in view of the risk of a split in the Labour Party' they could expect no overall directives or public statements on Soviet policy.[159] Left-wing criticism of Bevin's foreign policy had been mounting throughout 1946. In the autumn, *New Statesman* published a series of articles on British foreign policy arguing that Britain should reassert its independence from the USA. In November, over 100 Labour MPs abstained in a vote on a Commons amendment criticizing the Government's foreign policy. At the beginning of 1947, a small group of Labour MPs began to meet and formed an organized campaign for a return to socialism in Labour's foreign and domestic policy. Although this *Keep Left* group pressed for a more amenable policy to the Soviet Union, its foreign policy recommendations were also profoundly anti-American.[160] In 1946, Warner had highlighted the restrictions on Anglo-American cooperation due to America's wish to avoid the appearance of 'ganging up' with Britain. In February 1947, in a remarkable reversal of transatlantic concerns, US intelligence reported that due to domestic pressures the British Government had in recent months 'displayed a nominally independent attitude in foreign relations in contrast to its previous close collaboration with the US.' Although this was not to be interpreted as a trend towards closer collaboration with the USSR, it was noted that it would curtail joint Anglo-American actions with regard to the Soviet Union.[161]

In an effort to disillusion the public about Soviet intentions the Russia Committee proposed a number of measures to influence domestic opinion. It was felt that the Prime Minister and the Foreign Secretary could exert a great deal of personal influence in matters of domestic publicity. In March 1946, Bevin had asked the editor of *The Times* to put a stop to 'the jellyfish attitude of *The Times* on all important matters of foreign affairs', particularly E.H. Carr's pro-Soviet articles.[162] In September, Warner suggested that the Foreign Secretary or the Prime Minister might 'have a word' with some of the editors and proprietors of the daily press to let them know that more publicity for Soviet actions would be helpful to the Government. The Foreign Office also increased its own 'off-the-record' briefings with the press. With regard to the BBC, Warner apparently felt they could apply a little more direct pressure. It was suggested that the Director General should be asked to 'modify' the policy of the Home Service with regard to the Soviet Union. More particularly, it was proposed that the Home Service put on a weekly talk summarizing the attitude of the Soviet media on the chief international topics of the week.[163] Other *ad-hoc* projects included the distribution of the report of the Canadian Royal Commission into Soviet espionage, and a proposal to purchase the English rights to the autobiography of Soviet defector Victor Kravchenko, *I Choose Freedom*.[164]

An ambitious programme to counter communist control of international organizations was launched in 1946. Although these activities involved a range of departments, including the Home Office, MI5 and Special Branch, the lead agency was the Cultural Relations Department (CRD) of the Foreign Office. The CRD had been actively seeking to combat communist domination of international youth organizations since as early as 1945. With the assistance of the intelligence and security services, the CRD closely monitored communist penetration of British youth groups, most notably the National Union of Students (NUS). In 1946, the Department began to organize a series of counter-measures designed to loosen the communist hold on British youth and student groups. The CRD covertly established links with several individuals in non-communist British youth groups to brief them on communist tactics. The CRD also sought to place obstacles in the way of representatives of the NUS wishing to attend communist-dominated youth and student conferences abroad. The Department also organized a rival International Youth Conference to be held in London in August 1948. Officials approached youth organizations privately and indirectly to persuade them to leave the communist-controlled World Federation of Democratic Youth and join the CRD-sponsored rival. The conference was considered a great success and laid the foundations for an alternative non-communist youth organization, the World Assembly of Youth.[165]

A similarly discreet and intensive campaign was launched to influence opinion within the Labour Party. It was a campaign in which the Foreign Office could rely on a considerable degree of support from within the Party itself. Several Labour

MPs cooperated with the Foreign Office to ensure that information about Soviet intentions was distributed to the parliamentary Labour Party. It was decided in 1946 that the Foreign Office weekly review of the Soviet press, and monthly review of omissions and peculiarities in the Soviet press, would be made available to the House of Commons library through Parliamentary Secretary Kenneth Younger.[166] It was also suggested that the Labour Party's series of 'Speakers Notes' would be 'an excellent system for the dissemination of useful information on foreign affairs.' Under-Secretary Christopher Mayhew acted as a channel between the Foreign Office and the Labour Party, through the Party's International Secretary, Denis Healey. Mayhew provided Healey with information on foreign affairs, in return Healey provided information on the state of party and public opinion.[167] More significantly, in 1947, Assistant Under-Secretary Gladwyn Jebb drew up a paper outlining Foreign Office views on British foreign policy. Bevin suggested that Jebb's arguments against the *Keep Left* approach might be embodied in a Labour Party pamphlet. He suggested that Jebb should get together with Denis Healey making sure to keep cooperation 'very dark.'[168] At the 1947 Labour Party conference Healey's pamphlet *Cards on the Table* was distributed to all delegates. The pamphlet was a defence of Labour's foreign policy, designed to persuade Labour supporters of the Soviet Union's 'sustained and violent offensive' against Britain. It also emphasized the importance of British social democracy as an ideological alternative to Russian communism and American capitalism. Although it described an exclusive line-up with the USA as 'dangerous and undesirable', it argued that given Britain's straitened financial situation, the importance of international trade, and the needs of national security, it was unrealistic to believe Britain could pursue a completely independent foreign policy.[169] Dalton endorsed the pamphlet, and Bevin, pleased to have his case put by someone else in the party, reiterated its conclusions in his conference speech.[170]

However, it was not through the efforts of the Russia Committee or individuals such as Healey that British public opinion finally aligned with official perceptions of the Soviet threat. In September 1947, the Soviet Union with eight other European communist parties, including the French and Italian parties, established the Communist Information Bureau (Cominform). With the founding of the Cominform, the Soviet Union officially reverted to the orthodox Bolshevik line that those who were not avowed communists were avowed enemies. It was the final rejection of any prospect of cooperation with the non-communist left in Europe. With this action the Soviets themselves did more to undermine left-wing sympathies in Europe than any of the measures implemented by the British and US Governments. The CIA predicted that the immediate effect would be to reduce the voting strength of the communist parties in Europe and, were it not for the threat of economic crisis, substantially strengthen the position of the moderate non-communist parties in Western Europe.[171] In Britain the Russia Committee, with some relief, noted that the news had 'at last drawn the United Kingdom public's attention to the Russian campaign against this country, which hitherto had gone largely unnoticed.'[172] Bevin informed the Cabinet in November that if no progress were made at the Moscow Conference of Foreign Ministers, he would have to 'ask the Cabinet to consider a fresh approach to the main problems of our foreign policy.'[173]

Bevin's frustration with the Soviets had been building throughout 1947. In May, negotiations for a new Anglo-Soviet treaty collapsed, in July the Soviets withdrew from the Marshall Plan discussions, and at successive Council of Foreign Ministers meetings Bevin strove against Soviet intransigence in the hope of some degree of accommodation. Even following the creation of the Cominform in September, Bevin pressed on in the hope of agreement at the December Council of Foreign Ministers in London. In his frustration following the collapse of these discussions, Bevin finally agreed to consider a global response to communist propaganda. The catalyst for Bevin's acceptance of a new propaganda policy did not come from the Russia Committee but from the Parliamentary Under-Secretary, Christopher Mayhew. Mayhew was part of the British delegation to the UN, and like Bevin, was becoming increasingly disillusioned with the activities of his Soviet counterparts. In late 1947 Mayhew wrote home from the UN:

> My general view is that we should try to discourage the Slavs from using the UN for blackguarding us and the Americans by occasionally pulling a skeleton out of *their* cupboard for a change. True, we fight at a disadvantage, since, unlike the Bolsheviks, we are likely to be cross-examined about our propaganda when we get home; but nobody except an undiluted Christian can listen to Mr Vishinsky for long without answering back once in a while.[174]

In December, while returning to England on the *Queen Elizabeth*, Mayhew drafted a proposal for answering communist propaganda with a campaign of 'Third Force Propaganda'. Bevin read the paper and asked Mayhew to prepare a Cabinet paper outlining his recommendations.[175]

The timing of Mayhew's paper was obviously crucial. It arrived at an opportune moment when Bevin, frustrated by Soviet intransigence, was grasping for new ideas. There is another reason why Mayhew's paper may have held more appeal than previous proposals from the Russia Committee. Mayhew's idea for an effective counter to Soviet propaganda reflected Bevin's own developing interest in a British-led 'Western Union'. Historians have shown that Bevin had a genuine interest in close links with the Continent which, alongside the African colonies and the Middle East, could form a 'third force' in world affairs.[176] At the 1947 Party conference, Bevin effectively stole the thunder of the Left with his own plans for a Western Union. Although the Western Union concept eventually proved untenable, the period from December 1947 to January 1948 marked the peak of enthusiasm for the idea.[177] This was also the period in which Britain's new propaganda policy was prepared and launched. Mayhew entitled his paper 'Third Force Propaganda'. In it he linked the need to answer Soviet propaganda with the hope that Britain could take a leading role in international affairs. He suggested opposing the inroads of communism with a 'Third Force' comprising, 'all democratic elements which are anti-communist and, at the same time, genuinely progressive and reformist, believing in freedom, planning and social justice.' Communism was to be exposed by comparison with 'the broad principles of Social Democracy which in fact has its basis in the value of civil liberty and human rights.' To this Mayhew added there should be a 'positive appeal to Democratic and Christian principles... We must put forward a positive rival ideology.'[178]

It has been suggested that the 'Third Force' concept may have been merely a 'device to win ministerial support.'[179] This does not appear to have been the case. Mayhew did suggest employing a device to make the new propaganda policy more palatable to the Labour Party, but that device was anti-capitalism. In a memo accompanying his paper, Mayhew suggested to Bevin that the new propaganda policy should 'balance anti-communist with anti-capitalist arguments so as to reassure the Parliamentary Labour Party.'[180] Mayhew included in his paper a recommendation that they attack in equal measure the 'principles and practices of communism' and 'the inefficiency, social injustice and moral weakness of unrestrained capitalism.'[181] However, anti-capitalism and the 'Third Force' concept were two different propositions. Anti-capitalism was a negative concept tagged onto Mayhew's paper in an unabashed attempt to sell it to the Labour Party. In contrast, the idea of Britain leading a 'Third Force' was integral to the paper as a whole. It involved the positive projection of social democracy and reflected Bevin's own interest in a British-led 'Western Union'. It had its roots in the 1945 General Election manifesto which presented Britain as a 'brave and constructive leader in world affairs,' and built upon existing ideas about post-war propaganda as embodied in 'The Projection of Britain'.

Mayhew discussed his paper with senior officials, including Kirkpatrick and Warner, on 30 December 1947. There was clearly a consensus regarding the need to launch a counter-offensive against communist propaganda.[182] Although Mayhew was not a member of the Russia Committee and later claimed to have been unaware of the earlier papers by Warner and Kirkpatrick,[183] his paper encapsulated many of the proposals for countering communist propaganda developed by the Russia Committee since 1946. The idea of projecting a positive rival ideology was a common theme in Foreign Office thinking since at least as far back as Roberts' telegrams from Moscow in March 1946. Similarly, the idea of Britain providing a lead to all the democratic forces opposing communism in Europe had been a prominent theme in Warner's memorandum on the Soviet campaign against this country. More generally, the combination of positive national projection with a vigorous response to Soviet propaganda was the framework for propaganda campaigns already in progress in the Middle East, Germany and Eastern Europe. The Foreign Office officials were not, however, entirely happy with the anti-capitalist and 'Third Force' aspects of Mayhew's paper. It was felt that the paper might give the impression that the British Government advocated 'unfavourable reflections on the American way of life.'[184] It was also thought that the term 'Third Force' was inappropriate for the forces of anti-communism to which Britain hoped to give a lead. The term had too many other meanings, including a very specific connotation in French politics, and could not be 'taken over by us and given a different connotation.'[185] Despite these reservations it was decided to link Mayhew's proposal for 'Third Force' propaganda with Bevin's scheme for a spiritual union of the West which was also being drafted as a Cabinet paper. It was suggested that the principal common element in the two ideas was that Britain should provide leadership to other nations with a similar point of view and that 'by emphasising this we could avoid the political difficulties connected with the advocacy of unfavourable reflections on the American way of life.'[186] The idea of anti-capitalist propaganda also had a political value which outweighed obvious practical concerns. Moreover, the Cabinet paper would make clear that in practice this policy should not result in attacks on the USA. With these qualifications Mayhew's paper was drafted by Warner into a Cabinet paper on Britain's 'Future Foreign Publicity Policy,' to be placed before the Cabinet at its first meeting of 1948.[187]

Conclusion

The new propaganda policy presented to the Cabinet in January 1948 was a combination of views advocated by the Russia Committee since early in 1946, and the response of Bevin's Parliamentary colleague, Christopher Mayhew, to a series of more immediate problems. Although the Russia Committee had been advocating an offensive against communist propaganda for some time, Mayhew's timely paper was clearly influential. Mayhew offered Bevin an important compromise in the crucial months at the end of 1947 when Bevin finally accepted the need for a fundamental shift in Britain's policy towards the Soviet Union. Following the formation of the Cominform few in the Labour Party would argue with Mayhew's proposal for a propaganda counter-offensive. However, although the 'Keep Lefters' in the Party and the Cabinet were shaken by the formation of the Cominform they were not stirred from their commitment to a policy of independence from the USA. Mayhew's emphasis on Britain leading a 'Third Force' propaganda campaign, reflected the hopes of the Labour Party and more importantly the Foreign Secretary that a change in Britain's policy towards the Soviet Union need not necessarily lead to a partnership with the dominant USA.

If Mayhew's paper was the catalyst for a new propaganda policy, the composition of that policy had been tried and tested by the Russia Committee in a series of experiments since 1946. By the time Bevin agreed to propose a coordinated global response to communist propaganda, British diplomats were already making a concerted effort to answer communist charges in several areas – most notably, Iran, Germany, Austria, France, Italy and Eastern Europe. The BBC Middle East services were pursuing a general policy of highlighting communist shortcomings, and in October 1947, Jacob concluded that the time had come for the BBC Russian and Eastern European services to make a more forceful presentation of British policy. The Cultural Relations Department of the Foreign Office had developed tactics for countering communist control of international organizations which laid the foundations for the work of the IRD. The Foreign Office and the Labour Party were also working closely to influence domestic political opinion. The activities of the Russia Committee meant that the new propaganda policy presented to Cabinet in January 1948 did not mark a major departure from existing policy. It is evident, however, that there was a certain degree of tension between Mayhew's and the Russia Committee's conceptions of an anti-communist campaign. Despite the avoidance of Anglo-American cooperation in Mayhew's recommendations, in practice by the end of 1947 Britain and the USA had developed remarkably similar responses to the threat from communist propaganda. Although institutionalized cooperation was limited, Britain and the USA were responding to communist propaganda in a similar manner, in the same geographic areas. In the years that followed the propaganda machinery and policies of both nations expanded considerably and the *ad-hoc* measures of the pre-1948 period became institutionalized as a global, coordinated and often unified campaign.

Notes

1 Future Foreign Publicity Policy, C.P.(48)8, 4 January 1948, CAB 129/23, PRO.
2 T. Wieldy, 'From the MOI to the COI – Publicity and Propaganda in Britain, 1945–1951: The National Health and Insurance campaigns of 1948', *The Historical Journal of Film,*

Radio and Television, 6, 1 (1986), p. 4. See also P.M. Taylor, *British Propaganda in the Twentieth Century: Selling Democracy* (Edinburgh: Edinburgh University Press, 1999), pp. 229–33.

3 *Parliamentary Debates: Commons*, 5th series, vol. 417, 17 December 1945; quoted in M. Ogilvy-Webb, *The Government Explains: A Study of the Information Services* (London; Allen & Unwin, 1965), p. 67.

4 Quoted in, J.W. Henderson, *The United States Information Agency* (New York: Praeger, 1969), p. 35.

5 On British antipathy towards peacetime use of propaganda, see M. Grant, 'Towards a Central Office of Information: Continuity and Change in British Government Information Policy, 1939–51', *Journal of Contemporary History* 34, 1 (1999), pp. 49–67; On similar US concerns, see The Development of American Psychological Operations, 1945–1951, By Edward P. Lilly, 19 December 1951, pp. 16–17, Box no. 22; SMOF: PSB Files; Truman Papers, Truman Library; Henderson, *The United States Information Agency*, p. 37.

6 Quoted in M.R.D. Foot, *SOE: An Outline History of the Special Operations Executive 1940–46* (London: Mandarin, 1990), p. 355.

7 D.W. Lascelles, to Sir Robert Fraser, 10 December 1952, XHO1/4953, FO 366/3041, PRO. Lascelles comments, which included an attack on the Foreign Office's anti-communist propaganda, are a remarkable insight into one enduring official view of government propaganda. Interestingly, Lascelles was in the process of drafting Lord Strang's book, *The Foreign Office* (London: George Allen & Unwin, 1955), which he appears to have been largely responsible for writing. Lascelles involvement may explain the unsatisfactory treatment of the information services in the book. See also Sir Robert Fraser's somewhat irritated reply to Lascelles, 1 January 1953, XMOI/5363, FO 366/3042, PRO.

8 Many of those involved testify to State Department hostility towards the information programme. See E.W. Barrett, *Truth is Our Weapon* (New York: Funk & Wagnalls Company, 1953), pp. 52–3; E.W. Barrett, J.M. Begg and J. Noel Macy, Oral History Interviews, Truman Library.

9 Press reports in the *Chicago Tribune*, the *Washington Times, the Herald*, and the *New York Daily News*, 9 February 1945; quoted in T.F. Troy, 'Truman on CIA', *Studies in Intelligence*. Box 7 Fall 1975-Spring 1981, RG 263, NARA. See also W. Trohan, 'US Sets Up "Gestapo"; 1,500 Secret Agents', *Chicago Tribune*, 15 June 1947; Box 56; Papers of George M. Elsey, Truman Library.

10 Executive Order 9621, Termination of the Office of Strategic Services and Disposition of Its Functions, 20 September 1945, *Foreign Relations of the United States (FRUS), 1945–1950, Emergence of the Intelligence Establishment* (Washington, DC: US Government Printing Office, 1996), pp. 44–6.

11 Memorandum from the Secretary of State's Special Assistant for Research and Intelligence (McCormack) to the Assistant Secretary of State for Public and Cultural Relations (Benton), 23 October 1945, in *FRUS, 1945–1950, Emergence of the Intelligence Establishment*, p. 197.

12 S.W. Crofts, 'The Attlee Government's Economic Information Propaganda', *Journal of Contemporary History*, 21 (1986), pp. 453–91.

13 C. Anstey, 'The Projection of British Socialism: Foreign Office Publicity and American Opinion, 1945–50', *Journal of Contemporary History*, 19 (1984), pp. 417–51; See also P.M. Taylor, 'The Projection of Britain Abroad, 1945–51', in J.W. Young and M. Dockrill (eds), *British Foreign Policy 1945–1956* (London: Macmillan, 1989), pp. 9–30.

14 A. Adamthwaite, 'Britain and the World, 1945–9: The View from the Foreign Office', *International Affairs*, 61, 2 (1985), p. 231; Taylor, 'The Projection of Britain Abroad, 1945–51', pp. 10–11.

15 Taylor, 'The Projection of Britain Abroad, 1945–51', p. 9.

16 S. Tallents, *The Projection of England* (London: Faber & Faber, 1932). See P.M. Taylor, 'Cultural Diplomacy and the British Council: 1934–1939', *British Journal of International Studies*, 4 (1978), pp. 244–65; P.M. Taylor, *The Projection of Britain: British Overseas Publicity and Propaganda, 1919–1939* (Cambridge: Cambridge University Press, 1981).

17 'The Projection of Britain', 12 September 1946, P731/1/907, FO 930/496, PRO; Information Newsletter no. 4, 17 October 1946, P1083/1/907, FO 930/498, PRO.
18 Circular no. 7 'Information and Publicity Work in Foreign Countries', E. Bevin, 15 January 1947, P1083/1/907, FO 930/498, PRO.
19 *Let Us Face the Future: A Declaration of Labour Party Policy for the Consideration of the Nation* (London: The Labour Party, 1945), p. 11, Labour Party Archives, NMLH.
20 'The Projection of Britain', 12 September 1946, P731/1/907, FO 930/496, PRO; Information Newsletter no. 4, 17 October 1946, P1083/1/907, FO 930/498, PRO.
21 Central Office of Information, Overseas Production Conference (OP46)1, 30 April 1946, GN1/5 Part A, INF 12/61, PRO.
22 The Department's were: American Information; Cultural Relations; Eastern Europe Information; Far Eastern Information; Information Policy; Latin American Information; Middle East Information; News; and Western Europe Information. Only the Cultural Relations and News Departments existed in 1945.
23 Conclusions of Cabinet Meeting on the Government Publicity Services, 6 December 1945, INF 1/958, PRO; Wieldy, 'From the MOI to the COI', 5.
24 Memorandum of Conversation between Rt. Hon. Edward S. Williams and T.C. Achilles, 'Future Informational Activities of the British Government', 19 December 1945; 841.20200/12-1945, RG 59, NARA.
25 K. Young (ed.), *The Diaries of Sir Robert Bruce Lockhart*, vol. 2, *1939–1965* (London: Macmillan, 1980), p. 492.
26 Office Memo, Wilson to Benton, 'Subject for Discussion with General Eisenhower', 4 October 1946, 811.42700/12-3146, RG 59, NARA. On the PWD during the War, see D. Lerner, *Psychological Warfare against Nazi Germany: The Sykewar Campaign, D-Day to VE-Day* (London: MIT Press, 1971).
27 Information Newsletter no. 5, 'Enquiries from Foreign Governments About the Reorganisation of British Overseas Information Services', November 1946, P991/1/907, FO 930/498, PRO.
28 Memorandum of Conversation between Thomas Baird, Nevile Gardiner, British Information Services, and Mr Macy, Miss Wright, Mr Edwards and Mr Begg, INI, 14 February 1945, 841.20200/2-1445, RG 59, NARA.
29 Memorandum of Conversation between Rt. Hon. Edward S. Williams and T.C. Achilles, 'Future Informational Activities of the British Government', 19 December 1945, 841.20200/12-1945, RG 59, NARA.
30 W. Benton, Assistant Secretary of State, to I. Kirkpatrick, 2 August 1946; I. Kirkpatrick to W. Benton, 7 November 1946, P998/963/907, FO 930/521, PRO.
31 Memorandum of Conversation between Rt. Hon. Edward S. Williams and T.C. Achilles, 'Future Informational Activities of the British Government', 19 December 1945, 841.20200/12-1945, RG 59, NARA.
32 The Development of American Psychological Operations, 1945–1951, by Edward P. Lilly, 19 December 1951, pp. 21–2; SMOF: PSB Files, Box 22, Truman Papers, Truman Library.
33 Henderson, *The United States Information Agency*, pp. 37–8.
34 The Development of American Psychological Operations, 1945–1951, By Edward P. Lilly, pp. 22–5; SMOF: PSB Files; Box 22, Truman Papers, Truman Library. See also Barrett, *Truth is Our Weapon*, pp. 52–6.
35 R.W. Pirsein, *The Voice of America: An History of the International Broadcasting Activities of the United States Government, 1940–1962* (New York: Arno Press, 1979), pp. 111–27.
36 *Ibid.*, pp. 114–16; N.O.Wood, 'Strategic Psychological Warfare of the Truman Administration: A Study of National Psychological Warfare Aims, Objectives and Effectiveness', PhD Dissertation, University of Oklahoma, 1982, pp. 17–30.
37 On AFRS, see The Development of American Psychological Operations, 1945–1951, by Edward P. Lilly, pp. 27–8; SMOF: PSB Files, Box 22, Truman Papers, Truman Library. On RIAS and Red-White-Red, see D.R. Browne, 'RIAS Berlin: A Case Study of a Cold War Broadcast Operation', *Journal of Broadcasting*, 10 (1966), pp. 119–35; Hans Cohrssen, Oral History Interview, Foreign Affairs Oral History Program (FAOH), Georgetown University.

38 Letter from President Truman to Secretary of State Byrnes, 20 September 1945, *FRUS: Emergence of the Intelligence Establishment*, no. 15, pp. 46–7.

39 Memorandum from the Director of the Strategic Services Unit (Magruder), to the Assistant Secretary of War (McCloy), 25 October 1945, *FRUS: Emergence of the Intelligence Establishment*, no. 97, pp. 243–5.

40 Letter from President Truman to Secretary of State Byrnes, 20 September 1945, and Presidential Directive on Coordination of Foreign Intelligence Activities, 22 January 1946, *FRUS: Emergence of the Intelligence Establishment*, nos 15 and 71, pp. 46–7, 178–9. On interpretation, see, for example, Paper prepared for the Secretary of State's Staff Committee, SC-172 Development of a National Intelligence Program, 15 November, 1945, in *ibid.*, no. 46, pp. 111–16. See also A.B. Darling, *The Central Intelligence Agency: An Instrument of Government to 1950* (University Park, PA: Penn State Press, 1990), pp. 67–74; T. Braden, 'The Birth of the CIA', *American Heritage*, 28 (1977), pp. 4–13.

41 M.P. Leffler, *A Preponderance of Power: National Security and the Truman Administration, and the Cold War* (Stanford, CA: Stanford University Press, 1992), p. 3.

42 H. Thomas, *Armed Truce: The Beginnings of the Cold War 1945–46* (London: Sceptre, 1986), pp. 32–44.

43 J.L. Gaddis, *We Now Know: Rethinking Cold War History* (Oxford: Oxford University Press, 1997), p. 23.

44 R. Ovendale, 'Britain, the USA and the European Cold War, 1945–8', *History*, 67 (1982), p. 217.

45 R. Ovendale, *Anglo-American Relations in the Twentieth Century* (London: Macmillan, 1998), pp. 50–4. It is interesting to note that, for all his efforts, Roosevelt's overtures were viewed by the Soviet leadership with the same suspicion as Britain's intentions; see Gaddis, *We Now Know*, pp. 20–3.

46 Leffler, *A Preponderance of Power*, p. 49.

47 *Ibid.*, p. 49.

48 For a detailed examination of the differing party/leadership perceptions of the Soviet Union, see B. Jones, *The Russia Complex: The British Labour Party and the Soviet Union* (Manchester: Manchester University Press, 1977).

49 F. Williams, *A Prime Minister Remembers* (London: Heinemann, 1961), p. 71.

50 Jones, *The Russia Complex*, p. 109. On the Soviet tactics at the peace conferences, see 'Characteristics of the Russians as Negotiators', Report by the Joint Intelligence Sub-Committee on Relations with the Russians, JIC(45)299(0)(Final), 18 October 1945. *Documents on British Policy Overseas (DBPO)*, series 1, vol. 6, no. 41, *Eastern Europe August 1945–April 1946* (London: HMSO, 1991), pp. 151–6.

51 Williams, *A Prime Minister Remembers*, p. 5.

52 Jones, *The Russia Complex*, p. 112; A. Bullock, *Ernest Bevin: Foreign Secretary, 1945–1951* (Oxford: Oxford University Press, 1985), pp. 105–7.

53 P. Weiler, 'British Labour and the Cold War: The Foreign Policy of the Labour Governments, 1945–51', *Journal of British Studies*, 26 (1987), p. 64.

54 *Ibid.*

55 On PHPS, see J. Lewis, *Changing Direction: British Military Planning for Post-War Strategic Defence, 1942–47* (London: Sherwood, 1988), pp. 98–177; V. Rothwell, *Britain and the Cold War, 1941–1947* (London: Jonathan Cape, 1982), pp. 114–23.

56 M.P. Leffler, 'The American Conception of National Security and the Beginnings of the Cold War, 1945–48', *American Historical Review*, 89 (1984), p. 357; *ibid., A Preponderance of Power*.

57 Report by Joint Intelligence Sub-Committee on Russia's strategic interests and intentions, JIC(46)1(0) Final (Revise), 1 March 1946. *DBPO*, series 1, vol. 6, Doc.78, pp. 297–301.

58 ORE-1, Soviet Foreign and Military Policy, 23 July 1946: M. Warner (ed.), *CIA Cold War Records: The CIA Under Harry Truman* (Washington, DC: Central Intelligence Agency, 1994), pp. 65–76.

59 The ambassador to the Soviet Union (Smith) to the Secretary of State, July 23 1946; the ambassador to the Soviet Union (Harriman) to the Secretary of State, January 20 1946; in *FRUS, 1946*, vol. 6, *Eastern Europe; Soviet Union* pp. 676–7, 769.

60 'Publicity in this Country about Russia and Communism', draft Memo by C.F.A. Warner, September 1946, N12400/140/G38, FO 371/56789, PRO.
61 Central Intelligence Group, Weekly Summary, 2 August 1946, W.J. Kuhns (ed.), *Assessing the Soviet Threat: The Early Cold War Years* (Washington, DC: Center for Study of Intelligence, 1997), pp. 67–9.
62 'Parliamentary Visit to South Iranian oilfields, 28 May–10 July 1946', Minutes by Mr Pyman, 26 July, *DBPO*, series 1, vol. 7, *The United Nations: Iran, Cold War and World Organisation, 1946–1947* (London: HMSO, 1995), Calender ii to no. 63, pp. 178–9.
63 Home and Overseas Production Conference, 15 October 1946; Overseas Production Conference, 22 October 1946; COI Overseas Production Conference, FO Information Officers Conference, 14–18 October 1946, GN 1/5 Part A, INF 12/61, PRO.
64 The ambassador to the Soviet Union (Harriman) to the Secretary of State, 20 January 1946, in *FRUS, 1946*, vol. 6, p. 677.
65 Charge in the Soviet Union (Kennan) to the Secretary of State, 22 February 1946, in *FRUS, 1946*, vol. 6, pp. 696–709.
66 Roberts, Moscow to Bevin, 14, 17 and 18 March 1946, in *DBPO*, series 1, vol. 6, no. 80, pp. 305–12, no. 82 pp. 315–26, no. 83 pp. 326–31. On the importance of Roberts' telegrams, see J. Zametica, 'Three Letters to Bevin', in J. Zametica (ed.), *British Officials and British Foreign Policy* (London: Pinter, 1990), pp. 39–97; S. Greenwood, 'Frank Roberts and the "Other" Long Telegram', *Journal of Contemporary History*, 25, 1 (1990), pp. 103–22.
67 Roberts to Bevin, 14 March 1946, in *DBPO*, series 1, vol. 6, no. 80, pp. 305–12.
68 Kennan's policy recommendations are in part 5 of the 'long telegram'–'Practical deductions from standpoint of US policy': Charge in the Soviet Union (Kennan) to the Secretary of State, 22 February 1946, *FRUS, 1946*, vol. 6, pp. 706–9; Roberts' recommendations are in the final of his three telegrams: Roberts to Bevin, 18 March 1946, *DBPO*, series 1, vol. 6, no. 83, pp. 326–31.
69 J.L. Gaddis, *Strategies of Containment: A Critical Appraisal of Post-War American National Security Policy* (Oxford: Oxford University Press, 1982), p. 26.
70 Greenwood, 'Frank Roberts and the "Other" Long Telegram', p. 117.
71 R. Smith, 'A Climate of Opinion: British Officials and the Development of British Soviet Policy, 1945–7', *International Affairs*, 64, 4 (1988), pp. 631–47.
72 Russia Committee terms of reference, 18 April 1946, N5170/5169/G38, FO 371/56885, PRO. See R. Merrick, 'The Russia Committee of the British Foreign Office and the Cold War, 1946–47', *Journal of Contemporary History*, 20 (1985), pp. 453–68. Many additional Russia Committee papers have been declassified since the publication of Merrick's excellent analysis, see Foreign and Commonwealth Office, *List of Papers Released from the Previously Retained FCO Archive*, 4th edn (London: FCO/LRD, July 1997, repr. 1998).
73 For a more detailed assessment of the impact of Hitler on Western perceptions of the Soviet threat, see B. Heuser, 'Stalin as Hitler's Successor: Western Interpretations of the Soviet Threat', in B. Heuser and R. O'Neil (eds), *Securing Peace in Europe, 1945–62* (London: Macmillan, 1991), pp. 17–40.
74 'The Soviet Campaign Against This Country and Our Response To It', C.F.A. Warner, 2 April 1946, N6344/605/G38, FO 371/56832, PRO.
75 Russia Committee meeting, 28 May 1946, N7079/5169/G38, FO 371/56885, PRO. Cabinet distribution in: R. Howe to O. Sargent, 17 May 1946, N6733/140/G38, FO 371/56784, PRO.
76 Central Intelligence Group, Weekly Summary 20 September 1946, Kuhns (ed.), *Assessing the Soviet Threat*, pp. 83–4.
77 Policy Committee Minutes, 4 September, 1941, INF 1/676, PRO.
78 Ovendale, 'Britain, the USA and the European Cold War', p. 228.
79 G.H. Gallup, *The Gallup International Public Opinion Polls: Great Britain 1937–1975*, vol. 1, *1937–1964* (New York: Random House, 1976), September 1945, p. 120.
80 Gallup, *ibid.*, September 1946, p. 139.

81 Gallup, *ibid.*, August 1946, p. 137.
82 Gallup, *ibid.*, November 1946, p. 143. Listed above Stalin were: Churchill, Montgomery, Attlee, Bernard Shaw (!), Bevin and Smuts.
83 The Quarter's Polls, *Public Opinion Quarterly,* 9, 2 (Summer 1945), p. 254; *ibid., Public Opinion Quarterly*, 10, 1 (Spring 1946), p. 115.
84 B.F. Smith, *The War's Long Shadow: The Second World War and its Aftermath – China, Russia, Britain and America* (London: Andre Deutsch, 1986), pp. 152–3.
85 The Earl of Halifax (Washington) to Mr Bevin, 10 March 1946, in *DBPO*, series 1, vol. 4, *Britain and America: Atomic Energy, Bases and Food, 12 December 1945 – 31 July 1946* (London: HMSO, 1987), no. 49, pp. 153–4.
86 The Quarter' Polls, *Public Opinion Quarterly*, 10, 2 (Summer 1946), p. 204.
87 Leffler, *A Preponderance of Power*, p. 39.
88 Gallup, *The International Polls: Great Britain*, January 1947, pp. 148–9.
89 W.S. Lucas and C.J. Morris, 'A Very British Crusade: the Information Research Department and the beginning of the Cold War', in R.J. Aldrich (ed.), *British Intelligence, Strategy and the Cold War, 1945–51* (London: Routledge, 1992), p. 88.
90 COI, Overseas Production Conference, 30 April 1946, GN1/5 Part A, INF 12/61, PRO.
91 COI, Home and Overseas Production Conference, 15 October 1946, GN1/5 Part A, INF 12/61, PRO.
92 COI Overseas Production Conference, Foreign Office Information Officers Conference, 14–18 October 1946, Note by Secretariat, HP(46)29, OP(46)28, GN1/5 Part A, INF 12/61, PRO.
93 Minutes of meeting held on 14 January 1947 on British publicity and cultural work in Eastern Europe, report of W.E. Houston Boswell (Bulgaria), P198/198/950, FO 953/4E, PRO. Cavendish-Bentinck had earlier reported from Warsaw regarding the 'pathetic yearnings' for British cultural material, 'Reestablishment of Cultural Links with Poland', 25 August–2 October 1945, *DBPO*, series 1, vol. 6, Calenders to no. 8, p. 30.
94 Memorandum by Mr Braine, enclosure in letter from Sir L. Charles (Rome) to Sir O. Sargent, 27 August 1946, N11472/140/G38, FO 371/56788, PRO.
95 COI, Overseas Production Conference – Minutes, 25 June 1947, OP(47) 8th Mtg, GN1/5 Part B, INF 12/62, PRO.
96 Central Office of Information Overseas Production Conference, 9 July 1946, OP(46) 9th Mtg, GN1/5 Part A, INF 12/61, PRO.
97 'The Soviet Campaign Against This Country and Our Response To It', C.F.A. Warner, 2 April 1946, N6344/605/G38, FO 371/56832, PRO.
98 Minute by I. Kirkpatrick, 22 May 1946, P449/1/907, FO 930/488, PRO.
99 Bevin Minute, undated, P449/1/907, FO 930/488, PRO.
100 Russia Committee Meeting, 4 June 1946, N7515/5169/G38, FO 371/56885, PRO.
101 Russia Committee Meeting, 31 July 1947, N9345/271/G38, FO 371/66371, PRO; note of meeting held in Mr Mayhew's room to discuss 'Third Force Propaganda', 30 December 1947, N134/31/G38, FO 371/71648, PRO.
102 Russia Committee meeting, 28 May 1946, N7079/5169/G38, FO 371/56885, PRO. See Cabinet distribution in, R. Howe to O. Sargent, 17 May 1946, N6733/140/G38, FO 371/56784, PRO.
103 Draft Memo by Warner, undated (*circa* September 1946), N12400/140/G38, FO 371/56789, PRO.
104 Report by the Chiefs of Staff Committee on the Strategic Position of the British Commonwealth, COS(46)119(0), 18 April 1946, *DBPO*, series 1, vol. 6, no. 90, pp. 356–9; see also Smith, 'A Climate of Opinion', pp. 643–6.
105 Report by the Joint Intelligence Sub-Committee on Relations with the Russians, JIC(45)299(0)(Final), 18 October 1945, *DBPO*, series 1, vol. 6, no. 41, pp. 151–6; Report by Joint Intelligence Sub-Committee on Russia's Strategic Interest and Intentions in the Middle East, JIC(46)38(0)Final(Revise), 6 June 1946, *DBPO*, series 1, vol. 7, no. 58, pp. 161–4.
106 Minutes of meeting to brief Sir M. Peterson, 18 March 1946, N5572/605/G38, FO 371/56832, PRO.

107 Teheran to Foreign Office, no. 749, 26 May 1946, P449/1/907, FO 930/488, PRO.
108 Russia in the Middle East, Publicity Directive, 17 October 1946, GN1/5 Part A, INF 12/61, PRO; COI Overseas Production Conference, OP(46)23, 24 October 1946, GN1/5 Part A, INF12/61, PRO.
109 Russia Committee meeting, 17 September 1946, N12335/5169/G38, FO 371/56886, PRO.
110 COI, Overseas Production Conference, Report by Kirkpatrick on Publicity in the Middle East, OP(46)23, GN1/5 Part A. INF 12/61, PRO.
111 Russia Committee meeting, 17 Oct. 1946, N13583/5169/38G; Russia Committee meeting, 24 Oct. 1946, N13979/5169/38G, FO 371/56886, PRO.
112 Russia Committee meeting, 23 April 1946, N5407/5169/38G, FO 371/56885, PRO.
113 Minute from Howe to Bevin, 13 July 1946, *DBPO*, series 1, vol. 7, no. 63, pp. 175–8.
114 Russia in the Middle East, Publicity Directive, 17 October 1946, GN1/5 Part A, INF 12/61, PRO; COI Overseas Production Conference, OP(46)23, 24 October 1946, GN1/5 Part A, INF12/61, PRO.
115 Lucas and Morris, 'A Very British Crusade', p. 91; Smith, 'A Climate of Opinion', pp. 642–3.
116 Undated Minute, *circa* September 1946, N11812/140/38G, FO 371/56788, PRO.
117 Bevin Minute, 29 May 1946, P449/1/907, FO 930/488, PRO.
118 Smith, 'A Climate of Opinion', p. 641.
119 *Ibid.*; Circular, Committee on Policy towards Russia, O. Sargent, 13 May 1946, N6274/5169/38G, FO 371/56885, PRO.
120 Russia Committee meeting, 7 May 1946, N6092/5169/G, FO 371/56885, PRO.
121 Russia Committee meeting, 6 August 1946, N10437/5169/38G, FO 371/56886, PRO.
122 Lucas and Morris, 'A Very British Crusade', p. 90.
123 Sir L. Charles, British Embassy Rome to O. Sargent, 27 August 1946, N11472/140/38G, FO 371/56788, PRO.
124 Russia Committee meeting, 9 July 1946, N9162/5169/38G, FO 371/56885; Russia Committee meeting, 21 November 1946, N15456/5169/38G, FO 371/56887, PRO.
125 Minutes of meeting to brief Sir M. Peterson, 18 March 1946, N5572/605/38G, FO 371/56832; Russia Committee meeting, 30 April 1946, N5940/5169/38G, FO 371/56885, PRO.
126 Russia Committee meeting, November 1946, N15457/5169/38G, FO 371/56887, PRO.
127 Draft Memo by Warner, undated, *circa* September 1946, N12400/140/38G, FO 371/56789, PRO.
128 Quoted in: K. Jurgensen, 'The Concept and Practice of "Re-Education" in Germany 1945–50', in N. Pronay and K. Wilson (eds), *The Political Re-Education of Germany and her Allies After World War II* (London: Croom Helm, 1985), p. 87.
129 Draft Memo by Warner, undated, *circa* September 1946, N12400/140/38G, FO 371/56789, PRO.
130 A.E. Lambert to R.O. Wilberforce, Control Office for Germany and Austria, 11 September 1946, N11471/140/38G, FO 371/56788; Russia Committee meeting, 7 May 1946, N6092/5169/38G, FO 371/56885, PRO.
131 Foreign Office Minute, Anti-Soviet propaganda in Germany, 15 July 1947, C9768/1554/18, FO 371/64499, PRO.
132 Circular to members of the Russia Committee, O. Harvey, 25 September 1946, N12332/140/38G, FO 371/56788, PRO.
133 Policy in Eastern Europe, January 1947, P198/198/950, FO 953/4E, PRO.
134 Foreign Office to Cairo, 23 January 1948, PR1/1/913, FO 1110/1, PRO.
135 'The Soviet Campaign Against This Country and Our Response To It', C.F.A. Warner, 2 April 1946, N6344/605/G38, FO 371/56832, PRO.
136 P.G. Boyle, 'The British Foreign Office View of Soviet American Relations, 1945–46', *Diplomatic History*, 3 (1979), pp. 307–20; P.G. Boyle, 'The British Foreign Office and American Foreign Policy, 1947–48', *Journal of American Studies*, 16, 3 (1982), pp. 373–89.
137 'The Soviet Campaign Against This Country and Our Response To It', C.F.A. Warner, 2 April 1946, N6344/605/G38, FO 371/56832, PRO.

138 Barrett, *Truth is Our Weapon*, p. 61; R. Makins, Oral History Interview, Truman Library.

139 On the National Security debate, see Darling, *The Central Intelligence Agency*, pp. 166–92; On the Smith-Mundt debate, see S.J. Parry-Giles, 'Rhetorical Experimentation and the Cold War, 1947–1953: The Development of an Internationalist Approach to Propaganda', *Quarterly Journal of Speech*, 80 (1994), pp. 448–53.

140 Russia Committee meeting, 4 December 1947, N14304/271/38G, FO 371/66375, PRO.

141 Sir M. Peterson to Foreign Office, no. 1375, 20 June 1947, N7458/271/38, FO 371/66370, PRO.

142 The Development of American Psychological Operations, 1945–1951 by Edward P. Lilly, pp. 34–7; SMOF: PSB Files, Truman Papers, Truman Library. See also Darling, *The Central Intelligence Agency*, pp. 250–6.

143 NSC 4, Coordination of Foreign Information Measures, 9 December 1947; NSC4-A, Psychological Operations, 9 December 1947, *FRUS, 1945–1950, Emergence of the Intelligence Establishment*, pp. 639–45.

144 US Information Policy with Regard to Anti-American Propaganda, 1 December 1947, enclosure with letter from J. Balfour, British Embassy Washington to Warner, 25 February 1948, PR41/41/G, FO 1110/24, PRO.

145 Although this information was derived from intelligence exchanged with the US, Kirkpatrick suggested that it might be wise to avoid giving the Americans the impression 'that we are using for publicity purposes information which has been given to us confidentially.' Russia Committee meeting, 7 May 1946, N6092/5169/38G, FO 371/56885, PRO.

146 T. Barnes, 'The Secret Cold War: The CIA and American Foreign Policy in Europe, 1946–1956. Part I', *The Historical Journal*, 24, 2 (1981), p. 401; Minutes of the Fourth Meeting of the Intelligence Advisory Board, 9 May 1946, Minutes of the Fifth Meeting of the Intelligence Advisory Board, 10 June 1946, *FRUS, 1945–1950, Emergence of the Intelligence Establishment*, pp. 352–3, pp. 370–1.

147 *Keesing's Contemporary Archives*, vol. 6, *1946–1948* (London: Keesing's Publication's Limited), p. 8,954.

148 American Legation, Vienna to State Department, 26 November 1947, in P. Kesaris (ed.), *Documents of the National Security Council, 6th Supplement* (Bethesda, MD: University Publications of America, 1993), microfilm at Liddell Hart Centre for Military Archives, King's College, London.

149 W.J. Sullivan, British/US Zone Trieste, Desp. no. 17, 31 March 1948, PR176/1/913G, FO 1110/5, PRO.

150 Office Memo, Wilson to Benton, 'Subject for Discussion with General Eisenhower', 4 October 1946; 811.42700/12-3146, RG 59, NARA.

151 Memorandum from the Executive Secretary of the NSC (Souers) to Secretary of Defense Forrestal, 24 October 1947, *FRUS, 1945–1950, Emergence of the Intelligence Establishment*, pp. 627–8.

152 PPS/13 Resume of World Situation, 6 November 1947, in A.K. Nelson, *The State Department Policy Planning Staff Papers, 1947* (London: Garland Publishing Inc., 1983), pp. 129–36.

153 Although these operations expanded considerably in 1948, it seems apparent that they began in late 1947. See The Development of American Psychological Operations, 1945–1951, by Edward P. Lilly, pp. 38–41; SMOF: PSB Files, Box no. 22, Truman Papers; Truman Library; W. Colby and P. Forbath, *Honourable Men: My Life in the CIA* (London: Hutchinson, 1978), pp. 109–10; Barnes, 'The Secret Cold War', pp. 411–13.

154 Russia Committee meeting, 31 July 1947, N9345/271/38, Russia Committee meeting, 14 August 1947, N9549/271/38, FO 371/66371, PRO.

155 F. Roberts (Moscow) to CFA Warner, 15 March 1947, N3303/271/38G, FO 371/66366, PRO.

156 Publicity in this Country about Russia and Communism, draft Memo by CFA Warner, undated, *circa* September 1946, N12400/140/38G, FO 371/56789, PRO.

157 Russia Committee Meeting, 23 April 1946, N5407/5169/G38; Circular to Heads of Political and Functional Departments, Communist Activities in International Federations and Congresses, 25 May 1946, N6274/5169/G38, FO 371/56885, PRO.

158 R. Howe to Sir O. Sargent, 17 May 1946, N6733/140/G38, FO 371/56784, PRO.
159 Russia Committee Meeting, 14 August 1947, N9549/271/G38, FO 371/66371, PRO.
160 The literature on domestic opinion and the influence of *Keep Left* is extensive; see, in particular, K. Harris, *Attlee* (London: Weidenfeld & Nicolson, 1982), pp. 292–308; A. Carew, *Labour Under the Marshall Plan: The Politics of Productivity and the Marketing of Management Science* (Manchester: Manchester University Press, 1987), pp. 230–40; B. Jones, *The Russia Complex*, pp. 121–43; W. Knight, 'Labourite Britain: America's "Sure Friend"? The Anglo-Soviet Treaty Issue, 1947', *Diplomatic History*, 7 (1983), pp. 267–82.
161 Memorandum for the President from Hoyt S. Vandenberg, Director of Central Intelligence, 26 February 1947, PSF: Intelligence File, Box no. 250, Truman Papers, Truman Library.
162 Anstey, 'The Projection of British Socialism', p. 434.
163 Publicity in this Country about Russia and Communism, draft Memo by CFA Warner, undated, *circa* September 1946, N12400/140/38G, FO 371/56789, PRO; Anstey, 'The Projection of British Socialism', p. 434.
164 Russia Committee meeting, 28 August 1946, N11284/5169/38G, FO 371/56886, PRO.
165 R.J. Aldrich, *The Hidden Hand: Britain, America and Cold War Secret Intelligence* (London: John Murray, 2001), pp. 122–8; J. Kotek, *Students and the Cold War* (London: Macmillan, 1996), pp. 168–73.
166 Russia Committee, Publicity Sub-Committee Meeting, 29 July 1946, N9930/5169/G38, FO 371/56886, PRO.
167 Minutes of meeting on Foreign Office relations with the Labour Party and relations with the TUC, 5 November 1947, UNE33/33/96, FO 371/67613, PRO. See also Russia Committee meeting, 7 November 1946, N14607/5169/G38, FO 371/56886, PRO.
168 Anstey, 'The Projection of British Socialism', p. 435.
169 *Cards on the Table: An interpretation of Labour's Foreign Policy* (London: The Labour Party 1947). Denis Healey was not credited as the author at the time. Much discussion at the conference surrounded the question of its authorship, and whether it had been approved by the Foreign Office, ' "Cards on the Table" at the Margate Conference', nd, Labour Party International Department Papers, Denis Healey Articles, 1947–1948, NMLH.
170 *The Labour Party Report of the 46th Annual Conference, May 26–May 30 1947* (London: Transport House), NMLH; ' "Cards on the Table" at the Margate Conference', nd; D. Healey, *The Time of My Life* (London: Penguin, 1990), pp. 105–6; A. Bullock, *Ernest Bevin: Foreign Secretary 1945–1951* (Oxford: Oxford University Press, 1985), pp. 397–8.
171 Implications of the new Communist Information Bureau, 13 October 1947, SMOF: NSC Files, 1947–53, Box no. 2 – CIA Special Evaluations – ORE, Truman Papers, Truman Library.
172 Russia Committee meeting, 9 October 1947, N12137/271/38G, FO 371/66372, PRO.
173 C.M.90(47), 25 November 1947, Cab 128/10, PRO; quoted in Lucas and Morris, 'A Very British Crusade', p. 94.
174 C. Mayhew, *Party Games* (London: Hutchinson, 1969), p. 85.
175 Lord Mayhew, interview with author, May 1996; C. Mayhew, *Time to Explain: An Autobiography* (London: Hutchinson, 1987), pp. 105–8.
176 J. Kent and J.W. Young, 'The "Western Union" Concept and British Defence Policy, 1947–8', in Aldrich (ed.), *British Intelligence, Strategy and the Cold War, 1945–51* (London: Routledge, 1992), pp. 166–92; S. Greenwood, 'Ernest Bevin, France and Western Union', *European History Quarterly*, 14 (1984), pp. 319–38; J. Kent, 'Bevin's Imperialism and the Idea of Euro-Africa', in M. Dockrill and J.W. Young (eds), *British Foreign Policy, 1945–56* (London: Macmillan, 1989) pp. 47–76.
177 Kent and Young, 'The "Western Union" concept', p. 170.
178 'Third Force Propaganda', 6 December 1947, P138/138/950G, FO 953/128, PRO.
179 Lucas and Morris, 'A Very British Crusade', p. 93.
180 Mayhew to Bevin, 6 December 1947, P138/138/950G, FO 953/128, PRO.
181 'Third Force Propaganda', P138/138/950G, FO 953/128, PRO.

182 Meeting to discuss 'Third Force Propaganda', 30 December 1947, N134/31/38G, FO 371/71648, PRO. See also Mayhew's account of this meeting: C. Mayhew, *A War of Words: A Cold War Witness* (London: I.B. Tauris, 1998), pp. 19–20.
183 Lord Mayhew, interview with author, May 1996.
184 Meeting to discuss 'Third Force Propaganda', 30 December 1947, N134/31/38G, FO 371/71648, PRO.
185 Warner to Bevin, 1 January 1948, P138/138/950G, FO 953/128, PRO.
186 Meeting to discuss 'Third Force Propaganda', 30 December 1947, N134/31/38G, FO 371/71648, PRO.
187 Warner to Bevin, Draft Cabinet Paper 'Future of Foreign Publicity Policy', 1 January 1948, P138/138/950G, FO 953/128, PRO.

2 Launching the new propaganda policy, 1948

In March 1946, Ivone Kirkpatrick, the Foreign Office Under-Secretary responsible for information activities, claimed that counter-propaganda would be easy to arrange if the Government decided to attack communism.[1] Kirkpatrick's claim was finally put to the test almost two years later, when the Foreign Secretary conceded the need for a coordinated global response to communist propaganda and launched Britain's new propaganda policy. In the early months of 1948, Britain moved from an *ad-hoc*, piecemeal response to hostile Soviet propaganda to a coordinated and wide-ranging propaganda policy in which the positive 'Projection of Britain' was combined with offensive propaganda designed to oppose the inroads of communism and 'give a moral lead to the forces of anti-communism in Europe and Asia.'[2] The new propaganda policy, which Kirkpatrick had played no small part in formulating, was placed before the Cabinet at its first meeting of 1948. In the months that followed, the short Cabinet paper on 'Future Foreign Publicity Policy' was developed into a detailed propaganda policy in consultation between Bevin, the Cabinet, the Chiefs of Staff, the Foreign Office Russia Committee and a new Ministerial Committee on anti-communist propaganda. Britain's existing propaganda apparatus was redirected to follow the new policy, and arrangements were made to provide new instruments with which to coordinate and implement the new propaganda policy. The change in direction in Britain's propaganda policy was conducted with some urgency against the backdrop of increasing evidence of hostile Soviet intentions in Europe, most notably in the communist-backed coup in Czechoslovakia.

By comparison with the *ad-hoc* response to Soviet propaganda since the end of the War, the new propaganda policy adopted in January 1948 was designed to be highly organized, coordinated and global in scale. It was in several respects a return to the policy and methods of a wartime propaganda counter-offensive. Certainly, the new propaganda policy and the proposed methods for its implementation derived a great deal from Foreign Office experience of overseas propaganda in the two World Wars. A defining characteristic of the new policy was that Britain's response to communist propaganda should be based on the truth. In the projection of British principles, and the description of life behind the Iron Curtain, it was felt that exaggeration was counter-productive and largely unnecessary. Similarly, and perhaps somewhat contradictorily, the defining feature of the newly formed IRD's output was that its source should not be revealed, and the very existence of the new propaganda campaign should remain secret. It was felt that information emanating from unofficial, but otherwise authoritative sources, would have greater impact than an official response to communist propaganda and that the methods for countering communist propaganda should therefore be indirect. These ideas – that the most effective propaganda was based on the truth and that propaganda recognized as emanating from an official source was 'almost useless' – had been guiding principles of the Foreign Office approach to propaganda since the First World War.[3]

However, the new propaganda policy did not mark a return to offensive wartime methods and the IRD was not a resurrected Political Warfare Executive.[4] Bevin firmly resisted calls from Cabinet colleagues and the Chiefs of Staff for a return to wartime methods of political warfare. The phrase 'political warfare' was not to be used even in the closest government circles to describe the new propaganda policy. Moreover, in the administrative arrangements for control of overseas propaganda the wartime models of an executive agency or even an interdepartmental planning staff were eschewed in favour of assigning responsibility for the implementation and coordination of the new propaganda policy to a dedicated Foreign Office department with ultimate responsibility for all overseas propaganda in the hands of the Foreign Secretary alone. Furthermore, the new propaganda policy was not directed at occupied Europe. It was not an offensive strategy designed to undermine communist rule in the Soviet Union and Eastern Europe. Its primary purpose was the consolidation of democracy in those free countries threatened by communism, principally in Western Europe and the Middle East. This was markedly different from the psychological warfare directed at enemy forces and occupied peoples during wartime, and clearly had implications for the methods employed and the tone of the propaganda.

The new propaganda policy also had several distinct features which owed more to the Labour Government's perception of the Cold War, than the Foreign Office's approach to propaganda in previous conflicts. Most notably the new propaganda policy was to be directed at 'the broad masses of workers and peasants' a quite different audience from the educated elite usually targeted by Foreign Office information staff. Bevin's strategy for a Western Union defence was also central to the new line in British propaganda. Consequently, rather than promoting strictly British values the new propaganda policy was based on the 'vital ideas of British Social Democracy and Western civilisation.'[5] This lent a distinctly progressive internationalist hue to the traditional concept of the 'Projection of Britain'.

The 'Future Foreign Publicity Policy'

The Cabinet discussed the new propaganda policy on 8 January 1948. At this meeting Bevin placed a raft of papers before the Cabinet. Alongside the memorandum on 'Future Foreign Publicity Policy', there were memoranda on 'The First Aim of British Foreign Policy', 'Policy in Germany', 'Review of Soviet Policy' and 'Extinction of Human Rights in Eastern Europe'.[6] The broad sweep of these papers effectively set out the Soviet position and Britain's long-term response to that threat. In 'The First Aim of British Foreign Policy', Bevin warned that 'from behind secure entrenchments,' the Russians were 'exerting a constantly increasing pressure which threatens the whole fabric of the West.' In response, Bevin proposed a 'Western Union' backed by the Americans and the Dominions and comprising Scandinavia, the Low Countries, France, Portugal, Italy and Greece and, as soon as circumstances permitted, Spain and Germany. But Bevin was not proposing a simple defensive pact, it was not enough to reinforce 'the physical barriers which reinforce our Western civilisation':

> We must also organise and consolidate the ethical and spiritual forces inherent in this Western civilisation of which we are the chief protagonists. This in my view can only be done by creating some form of union in Western Europe, whether of formal or informal character, backed by the Americans and the Dominions.[7]

The means for mobilizing this spiritual union were set out in the paper on 'Future Foreign Publicity Policy.' It stated that Soviet propaganda had been carrying out a 'vicious attack against the British Commonwealth and against Western democracy.' It was up to Britain 'as Europeans and as a Social Democratic Government,' to take the lead in responding to that threat:

> We should adopt a new line in our foreign publicity designed to oppose the inroads of Communism, by taking the offensive against it, basing ourselves on the standpoint of the position and vital ideas of British Social Democracy and Western civilisation, and to give a lead to our friends abroad and help them in the anti-communist struggle.[8]

The new publicity policy was to be implemented by a small section in the Foreign Office which would collect and disseminate information on communist policy and tactics. In addition to the existing government information services, experience had shown that the fullest cooperation of the BBC would be 'desirable'. The paper suggested other channels which reflected the Labour Party's own anti-communist efforts. Anti-communist material would be made available to Ministers for use in their public speeches, and information was to be sent to Labour Party and trades union officials and through them to trade unionists abroad. Foreign trade unionists and non-Communists from abroad were to be given the opportunity of studying British life and institutions. London, it was hoped, would become 'the Mecca for Social Democrats in Europe.'[9]

The paper set out in some detail the guiding principles for the new publicity policy. These combined an offensive element designed to 'attack and expose Communism,' and a positive presentation of 'something far better.' Britain, the paper stated, 'must provide a positive rival ideology' based on Democratic and Christian principles. Despite the reservations of the Foreign Office the anti-capitalist aspect of Mayhew's original paper remained. In contrast to 'totalitarian Communism and *laissez-faire* capitalism' it stated Britain should offer 'the vital and progressive ideas of British Social Democracy and Western Civilisation.' The new propaganda policy should 'advertise our principles as offering the best and most efficient way of life.' The principles and practices of communism were to be denigrated by comparison, as was the 'inefficiency, social injustice and moral weakness of unrestrained capitalism.' The main target for Britain's propaganda was to be the broad masses of workers and peasants in Europe and the Middle East, and the main arguments used were designed to appeal to this group. Thus, considerable emphasis was to be placed on the standard of living of 'ordinary people' in the Soviet bloc and the comparative benefits of life in the West. The aim of the new propaganda policy was to expose the Soviet 'workers' paradise' as 'a gigantic hoax.' Britain's new propaganda should also stress the civil liberties issue and the many analogies between Nazi and communist systems. The foreign policy of communist states was also to be targeted. Soviet foreign policy was to be portrayed as the 'stalking horse of Russian imperialism' and the satellites represented as 'Russia's new colonial empire.' Finally, it stated, the time had come to answer Soviet misrepresentations about Britain. British representatives abroad who had for so long urged the adoption of a more offensive line in Britain's response to Soviet propaganda were now to be provided with the 'ammunition' to reply.[10]

The Cabinet was generally supportive of the proposed moves to consolidate the forces of Western Europe. There was also qualified support for the new line in British propaganda. The Secretary of State for the Colonies, it was noted, had already sought to promote democratic principles in the colonies through the press, films, broadcasting, promotion of trade union movements and guidance to students from the colonies studying in the UK. With regard to publicity in Europe the possibility of establishing a Western European broadcasting station was mentioned. However, concerns were expressed about the anti-Soviet aspect of the new propaganda policy. It was feared that too much emphasis on the anti-Soviet aspect might alienate the socialist forces in Western Europe and those Eastern European countries which, 'though dominated politically by communists, still had a Western outlook.' Bevin replied that it would be impossible for him to give an effective lead without being critical of Soviet policy. But, he stressed, it was his intention 'mainly to concentrate on the positive and constructive side of his proposals.' With these reservations and assurances the Cabinet approved the new propaganda policy.[11]

In fact, the new propaganda policy had in effect already been launched by the Prime Minister, Clement Attlee, in a party political broadcast on 3 January, several days before the new line was discussed by the Cabinet. Attlee had seen drafts of the papers which were to be presented to the Cabinet on 8 January and had invited Christopher Mayhew to Chequers during the Christmas recess to discuss his paper on 'Third Force' propaganda.[12] Attlee's subsequent speech paraphrased large sections of the Cabinet papers on foreign policy and future publicity policy. It had two main themes: the deterioration in the international situation brought about by the Soviet Union; and the leading role Britain should play as a 'Third Force' in the world between communist totalitarianism and US capitalism. In recognition of his hosts, Attlee began by highlighting the freedom of political debate in the West epitomized by the BBC which provided a platform 'for free and unfettered controversy' unrestricted by the Government or private interests. He compared this to the situation in Russia and the satellites where, 'the voice of criticism is silenced' and 'only one view is allowed.' Attlee went on to attack the pretence by which the Soviet Union would limit freedom and suppress opposition whilst masquerading 'as upholders of democracy.' Far from being a workers' paradise, he characterized the Soviet Union as a place of growing inequality where the lack of political freedom had a direct impact on standards of living:

> Where there is no political freedom, privilege and injustice creep back. In Communist Russia 'privilege of the few' is a growing phenomenon, and the gap between the highest and lowest incomes is constantly widening.[13]

Attlee went on to explain how Soviet communism was endangering world peace with a 'new kind of imperialism – ideological, economic and strategic' which threatened the welfare and way of life of the other nations of Europe. At the other end of the scale from Soviet suppression, Attlee set the USA with its commitment to individual liberty and human rights. But Attlee also criticized US capitalism which was, he said, characterized by extreme inequality of wealth. It was, he claimed, up to Britain – situated geographically, economically and politically between these 'two great continental states' – to 'work out a system of a new and challenging kind, which combines individual freedom with a planned economy, democracy and social justice.'[14]

Attlee's speech was widely covered in the press where the new tone did not go unnoticed. Most newspapers gave particular prominence to the harsh anti-communist aspect of the speech and, in general, welcomed it.[15] Those in the Foreign Office who had been responsible for devising the new propaganda policy also welcomed Attlee's robust speech. Mayhew wrote in his diary at the time that the speech was 'ruder to the USA than even I think wise' but later praised the criticism of the Soviet Union which although 'mild by later standards' was, 'a useful send-off to our propaganda campaign.'[16] In the Russia Committee, Sir Ian Jacob, Controller of the BBC's European Services, stressed that if the new policy was to be successful the Prime Minister's broadcast should be followed by other ministerial speeches on which the BBC could base their publicity.[17]

The anti-communist message was reinforced by the Deputy Prime Minister, Herbert Morrison, in a speech to Labour Party members on 11 January. Morrison began by expressing his sorrow at the rift in Anglo-Soviet relations since 1945. He blamed this rift on increasingly hostile Soviet propaganda. Although the Government had sought active cooperation with the Soviet Union they had been frustrated by 'untruthful and malicious attacks...by the reckless propaganda machines of the Russian communists.' In the face of such attacks, Morrison said, Britain could no longer be expected to lie down. Moreover, he said, Britain could not be happy when 'country after country in Eastern and South-eastern Europe find themselves subject to undemocratic and unrepresentative Communist Governments.' Morrison responded, like Attlee, with an attack on the imperialist Soviet foreign policy. He did not pull his punches, the Communist Parties of the world he said, were merely, 'the servile automatic outposts of the Soviet Foreign Office.' The communist takeovers in Eastern Europe were characterized by suppression of other parties, curtailment of press freedom, 'wholesale witch-hunting', and unjudicial execution of non-communist leaders. Morrison contrasted Soviet imperialism with British colonialism. Whereas Soviet action in Eastern Europe was exploitative, the aim of British colonialism, he claimed, was 'development' based on 'the cooperation and goodwill of the colonial peoples themselves.' Soviet actions in Eastern Europe were more akin to the totalitarian rule of Nazi Germany. Like Attlee, Morrison expressed indignation that Soviet actions in Eastern Europe were cloaked in the language of freedom, democracy and anti-fascism when it was increasingly clear that the communists were displaying all the characteristics of the extreme Right. 'I have never admitted that the Communists are on the Left' he stated baldly, 'they are on the Right.' Finally, he concluded, by pursuing these provocative policies the communists 'are not only running the risk of war at some time, but...are impeding the economic progress of mankind[.]'[18]

The speeches by Attlee and Morrison clearly served to launch the new propaganda policy, but the most effective annunciation of the new line in British foreign policy was provided by the Foreign Secretary himself in his formidable contribution to the foreign affairs debate in the Commons, 22 January. In this speech, Bevin unveiled his ideas for a Western Union defence against Soviet aggression. As Attlee and Morrison had done earlier that month, Bevin began with a bitter attack on Soviet attitudes which had led to the breakdown in East–West relations since 1945. He related his own attempts to work with the Soviets at successive Council of Foreign Ministers meetings and revealed how weary he was of the consistently hostile attitude of Soviet delegations. Britain had, he claimed, always tried to cooperate with the peoples of Eastern Europe but 'the activities of the Cominform, like those of its predecessor the Comintern, afford the greatest hindrance to mutual confidence and understanding.' He described the 'ruthless' progression of communism in Eastern Europe, and like Morrison compared the communists' creation of 'police states' in Europe with those of Hitler and Mussolini. In response, Bevin called for a moral rearmament of the West. Although Bevin was more careful than Attlee not to advocate a breach with the USA, the time had come, he said, for the nations of Western Europe to think of themselves as a unit. To draw more closely together and mobilise 'such a moral and material force as will create confidence and energy in the West and inspire respect elsewhere.' He continued:

> How much these countries have in common. Our sacrifices in the war, our hatred of injustice and oppression, our Parliamentary democracy, our striving for economic rights and our conception and love of liberty are common among us all. Our British approach, of which my rt. hon. friend the Prime Minister spoke recently, is based on principles which also appeal deeply to the overwhelming mass of the peoples of Western Europe. I believe the time is ripe for a consolidation of Western Europe.[19]

Bevin's speech was broadly welcomed – just as Attlee's speech had been – and the general reaction indicated the emergence of a broad consensus among the Government, the Opposition, officials and the press regarding Soviet intentions and the need for a robust response.[20] It won the support of the Conservative Opposition. Eden replied that Western Union should be pursued with 'the greatest possible vigour,'[21] and one Conservative MP recorded the relief on the Opposition benches that Bevin 'did not intend to allow the Bolshies to run Europe if we could help it.'[22] On his own side of the House, Bevin won the support of most of the Left Wing who embraced the idea of Britain, independent of the USA, leading a predominantly socialist Europe. The press, who had largely missed the 'Third Force' aspect in Attlee's speech, were enthusiastic about Bevin's idea. *The Times*, for example, noted that although much of Bevin's vision remained to be worked out they welcomed his call for 'an association of friendly nations' in Europe and the colonies, 'wide enough to win strength and independence together,' and acclaimed this as 'a challenge and a call to action.'[23]

This speech by Bevin, following those of Attlee and Morrison, marked a clear and very public shift in Britain's policy towards the Soviet Union. It was a public statement that the Government, and Bevin in particular, had finally moved to a position, long held in the Foreign Office, that any kind of compromise with Moscow was doomed to failure. Relations had irrevocably broken down and the time had come for Britain to respond to Soviet hostility. Although the central feature of Bevin's speech was a rallying cry for a European 'Third Force', the language and tone adopted by Bevin, Attlee and Morrison in these three speeches to describe the breakdown of East–West relations and Soviet action in Eastern Europe also served to launch Britain's new propaganda policy. None of the speakers referred explicitly to a British propaganda campaign, indeed one feature of the speeches was an indignant condemnation of hostile Soviet propaganda since 1945. 'Propaganda', Bevin told the Commons 'is not a contribution to the settlement of international problems.'[24] Yet these speeches, especially when taken together, were themselves part of the new intensive and coordinated anti-communist propaganda campaign. They clearly followed the guiding principles set out in the Cabinet paper on 'Future Foreign Publicity Policy', and laid out the themes to be pursued in Britain's anti-communist propaganda. Each Minister explained their more strident tone by reference to the increasingly hostile tone of Soviet propaganda. This was followed in each case with a forthright attempt to 'expose the myths of the Soviet paradise,' in many cases in comparison with the benefits of Western social democracy. Thus, Soviet moves in Eastern Europe were branded the 'new imperialism' and compared unfavourably, by Morrison, with paternal British colonialism. Each compared the economic and political freedoms of the West with the suppression of civil liberties in Soviet-occupied territory, and followed the line that Soviet communism was a form of totalitarianism analogous to Nazi Germany. Moreover, Soviet actions – like those of Nazi Germany – were clearly represented as a threat to world peace. Finally, both Attlee and Bevin advertised an alternative to Soviet communism which in the evocative yet vague language of the 'Third Force' projected a positive aim to balance the offensive/defensive tone of the anti-communist aspect of the new propaganda policy. That these themes were drawn out in major foreign policy statements by three of the most senior Government Ministers is indicative of the importance of this new line in British propaganda, and of at least some degree of Cabinet consensus regarding the anti-Soviet aspect of the new propaganda policy.

Following this prominent launch, the Cabinet paper on 'Future Foreign Publicity Policy' was passed to the Russia Committee for consideration of how the new propaganda policy was to be implemented on a broader front. Christopher Warner, who in January 1948 took over from Kirkpatrick as Assistant Under-Secretary responsible for information activities, told the Committee that Britain's new propaganda would draw out two main themes: that the West provided higher standards of living than the Soviet system; and that a communist regime involved the suppression of political liberties. The positive side of the new propaganda policy was less clear but would be based on the policy outlined in the paper 'The First Aim of British Foreign Policy', and unveiled by the Foreign Secretary in his Commons speech. It would seek to create 'some form of union in Western Europe...backed by the Americans and the Dominions.' Propaganda material would be prepared for use abroad and designed to appeal not only to intellectuals but also the workers and peasants. At home, material would be available to Ministers and the Labour Party, visits would be encouraged from foreign trade unionists, and courses would be developed for representatives of foreign anti-communist parties.[25]

The discussion in the Russia Committee was significantly different from the Cabinet's consideration of the new policy. Whereas the Cabinet minutes reveal concern regarding the strength of the anti-communist aspect of the new policy, several members of the Russia Committee raised concerns about the policy of attacking 'unrestrained capitalism', an issue apparently not discussed by the Cabinet.[26] In particular, they stressed the risk of attacking the USA and other democratic parties of the Right. Warner drew attention to the qualification in the Cabinet paper which said that they should not attack or appear to attack any member of the Commonwealth or the USA, and Ivone Kirkpatrick replied somewhat obliquely that the phrase was 'of general application and expressed the view that no difficulties would arise over the practical interpretation of it in preparing publicity material.'[27] It was suggested that rather than attacking the Right as such, taking the lead from Attlee's speech the line should be that communism was a form of totalitarianism. Rather than attacking capitalism and communism in equal measure, the policy would be to attack totalitarianism on the Right and Left. This was not quite the same interpretation of the paper as that of the Cabinet. Indeed, far from attacking US capitalism the Committee discussed whether Britain should coordinate anti-communist propaganda with the USA and other friendly countries. At this stage, though, any suggestion of Anglo-American cooperation was treated with caution. Warner stated that the right general policy would be to exchange information on propaganda with the USA whenever appropriate, but that Britain should not have a general agreement to consult with them or to take the same line.[28]

The Committee discussed the implementation of the new policy in different regions. Sir Ian Jacob, Head of the BBC European Services, enquired whether the propaganda would go so far as to encourage opponents of Communism in Europe. Kirkpatrick replied that whilst this was an aim in Western Europe, as regards the satellites, the intention was 'to attack the suppression of freedom' but not to incite opponents of the existing regimes. It was suggested that a special directive would be required for Eastern Europe. The Committee also identified problems in implementing the new policy in the Middle East, given that the new policy was to be directed at 'the mass of workers and peasants.' Although publicity channels existed among such groups in Europe, British propaganda in the Middle East had traditionally been directed at the educated élite. Given these problems, it is evident that initially at least the focus for the new policy would be Western Europe. In Germany, where Britain's propaganda was already taking a more aggressive line, the new policy could take immediate effect. Moreover, it was suggested, this should be done with some urgency given recent evidence of planned communist disturbances in the Ruhr.[29] Similarly, Gladwyn Jebb and Robin Hankey drew attention to reports of plans for communist direct action in France and Italy in March. Jebb concluded the discussion by suggesting that Warner 'should make his plans on the assumption that some major Communist offensive might take place in the early spring and that all possible publicity ammunition would be required in repelling it.'[30]

In fact, it was events in Eastern Europe which injected a sense of urgency into the new propaganda policy. The Soviet-backed coup in Czechoslovakia in February 1948 galvanized anti-communist sentiment in Britain, within the Labour Party in particular, and led to calls for Britain to adopt a more offensive propaganda policy. In the Foreign Office, according to Gladwyn Jebb, the effect of the coup in Prague was, 'electrical.' 'If the Russians could do this to one European democracy nearly three years after the end of the war, what was to prevent them doing it to other European countries, and notably in Western Europe?'[31] The impact on opinion in the Labour Party was even more marked. Bill Jones, historian of Labour's relations with the Soviet Union, describes the Party's response to the coup as the culmination of a process of reinterpretation of Soviet foreign policy towards a new 'almost hostile, image of the Soviet Union.'[32] *Tribune* reported events under the unequivocal headline 'Murder in Prague', whilst, in the *Daily Herald*, Michael Foot lamented the most 'tragic week since the end of the war.' On 3 March, the Labour Party's National Executive Committee issued a fierce condemnation of Soviet actions stating that Czechoslovakia had 'fallen victim to aggression from without aided by treachery from within.'[33] Two days later, Bevin submitted a memorandum to the Cabinet on 'The Threat to Western Civilisation'. In it he outlined the fast-growing threat of Soviet expansion and the steps Britain should take to frustrate them. It was now clear, Bevin stated, that Soviet policy aimed for nothing less than world domination:

> The immensity of the aim should not betray us into believing in its impracticability. Indeed, unless positive and vigorous steps were shortly taken by those other states in a position to take them, it may well be that within the next few months – or even weeks – the Soviet Union would gain political and strategic advantages which would set the great communist machine in action, leading either to the establishment of a world dictatorship or more probably to the collapse of organised society over immense stretches of the globe.[34]

The Cabinet's response to Bevin's stark warning reveals a marked shift in opinion since Bevin placed his previous review of Soviet policy before them in January. The Cabinet continued to support Bevin's plans for Western Union defence, but also recommended a significant expansion of Britain's anti-communist propaganda. In contrast to their cautious acceptance of the new propaganda policy two months earlier, in which they stressed that 'too much emphasis should not be placed on its anti-Soviet aspect,'[35] the Cabinet now accepted that 'the weapon of propaganda must be used to the full.'[36] It was even suggested that 'some organisation on the lines of the wartime Political Warfare Executive' could be established. The discussion that followed ranged across the kind of measures which could be used in a new campaign of political warfare. There were certain directions it was suggested, in which the Labour Party, not the Government, might be the most effective instrument for conducting propaganda, particularly among the social democratic parties in Western Europe. It was also suggested that the Christian Churches might be allied to the defence of Western civilization. The International Council of Christian Churches might be persuaded to work with the Government, and it was noted, there had been growing sympathy with social democracy in the Catholic Church. The campaign could also extend to economic warfare in which more generous terms or 'more aggressive methods' could be adopted in trade with Eastern European states. It was also recommended that a special effort should be made to concentrate propaganda on the Eastern European countries which were nearest to Western Europe. The aim of this proposed campaign of political warfare was 'to provide the people of Europe with the leadership in Western Europe which governments have so far failed to provide, but its scope should be worldwide.'[37]

This call for a return to political warfare was echoed elsewhere in Whitehall. In March, the Chiefs of Staff expressed disquiet at what they perceived to be the defensive nature of Bevin's recent proposals for responding to the Soviet threat. They were surprised that the new policy was designed to defend Britain rather than taking the offensive against Soviet propaganda, and they disapproved of the allocation of anti-communist propaganda to a 'small section' in the Foreign Office. The 'Cold War' they claimed could not be waged as an adjunct of diplomacy. The Chiefs of Staff advocated a propaganda policy more closely integrated with defence and coordinated by a resurrected Political Warfare Executive. The Defence Minister told Bevin that the Chiefs of Staff felt they had an important stake in this matter. They wanted an integrated Cold War strategy combining political warfare, economic warfare and special operations. Through this policy they hoped to take the offensive against Soviet internal organization or to disrupt the military or industrial connections between the Soviet Union and the satellites.[38]

Bevin, however, was reluctant to sanction such an offensive strategy and restrained calls for a return to political warfare of the kind employed during the War. Bevin responded to events in Prague by consolidating his plans for a Western Union defence of Europe. The most immediate result was the signature, on 17 March 1948, of a mutual defence pact between Britain, France and the Benelux countries. At the same time, instead of planning subversion in Eastern Europe, more detailed plans were formulated to counter the spread of communism in the free world. The Chiefs of Staff were asked to formulate defence plans to support Bevin's Western Union policy.[39] In response to the Cabinet's new found enthusiasm for propaganda, a Ministerial Committee on anti-communist propaganda was convened to consider the general application of the new propaganda policy.[40]

However, before the first meeting of the Ministerial Committee, the question of political warfare was decided at an informal meeting between the Foreign Secretary, the Prime Minister, the Chancellor of the Exchequer and the Minister of Defence. Bevin was concerned that discussions that were likely to cover covert activities by the intelligence services should not be disclosed to Ministers generally, and that future discussions of political warfare were to be confined to this small informal group. At this meeting it was decided that the phrase 'political warfare' was not to be used in any description of Britain's publicity policy, and that there was no reason to recreate a body like the wartime Political Warfare Executive.[41] The reasons for this policy of restraint were set out in a memorandum by the Cabinet Secretary, Norman Brook. The comparison with wartime political warfare, Brook wrote, was inappropriate, impracticable and indeed 'dangerous.' Although conditions behind the Iron Curtain were comparable with wartime conditions in enemy-occupied Europe, Britain was not responding to those conditions with the same wide range of activities both overt and covert as had been employed during the War. Indeed, consideration had not been given as to what methods of 'black' propaganda might be employed under the new policy. Moreover, it was far from clear that the application of wartime methods of political warfare would be practicable in combating the westward spread of Soviet influence in peacetime. Thus, Britain was not at that time employing methods of political warfare, nor was it clear whether such methods would be desirable in the future. There were also no practical reasons for reconstituting a Political Warfare Executive to direct such activities. The PWE had been necessary because ministerial responsibility for such activities had been divided between the Foreign Secretary and the Ministers of Information and Economic Warfare. In 1948, all overseas information activities, including 'black' propaganda, were the sole responsibility of the Foreign Secretary, and Bevin was not about to relinquish this control.[42] Although Bevin conceded that some machinery was necessary to enable the Chiefs of Staff to make their contribution, Bevin would continue to exercise sole ministerial responsibility for overseas propaganda policy, and, in particular, to decide the extent to which 'black' propaganda methods were to be applied in particular countries.[43]

Bevin began the first meeting of the Cabinet Committee on anti-communist propaganda by reiterating the reasons for his refusal to countenance a return to political warfare. In spite of the views of at least some of the Cabinet and the Chiefs of Staff, Bevin stated clearly 'it is my considered view that we should not incite the peoples of the Iron Curtain countries to subversive activities.' Although he did not object in principle to the use of 'black' propaganda, for 'severely practical reasons' he felt it was of limited use in present circumstances. Drawing on the comparison with political warfare in the Second World War, Bevin pointed out that 'we discouraged resistance movements from activity until our arms were at hand.' It was useless to stir up resistance to existing regimes unless there was a practical prospect of their being overthrown and in present circumstance Bevin stated 'we should be doing ourselves and our friends in those countries [behind the Iron Curtain] a great disservice if our publicity now urged them to active resistance.' Propaganda in countries behind the Iron Curtain was to be limited to official statements carried by the BBC, and open promotion of 'the virtues and achievements of Western methods, and that to a limited extent.'[44] There were also financial limitations on the implementation of political warfare. The amount of money available for all kinds of propaganda was limited and in peacetime conditions Bevin felt that open propaganda paid a better dividend than subversive activities. In peacetime, Bevin concluded, overt propaganda was more important than covert propaganda, and usually much cheaper.[45]

Bevin then presented the Committee with an expanded version of the January Cabinet paper on future foreign publicity which outlined the work that was underway in the Foreign Office to implement the new policy. Focusing on overt media, Bevin outlined three main channels for the dissemination of material under the new propaganda policy. Firstly, the reproduction in the foreign press of ministerial speeches, official and semi-official statements by Government spokesmen, and articles from the press in this country. In order for this to be effective it was important for all official, and especially ministerial statements to be 'framed with the new publicity policy in mind.' In an effort to ensure consistency within the Labour Party Bevin said officials were constantly studying Party publicity on foreign affairs with the assistance of the Party's General Secretary, Morgan Phillips, and International Secretary, Denis Healey. Arrangements were also in hand for liaison between the Foreign Office and the Chiefs of Staff to ensure that Service statements were framed with consideration for their effect abroad. The second major channel for disseminating propaganda abroad was the BBC and the official London Press Service. Bevin stated that the BBC's Sir Ian Jacob was fully apprised of the new policy and programmes were generally planned in line with the Government's publicity policy. However, Bevin rejected suggestions that the Government's relationship with the

BBC should be altered to allow official direction on the content of overseas broadcasts. 'It would raise very serious issues here and might well diminish the influence and reputation in foreign countries of the BBC's broadcasts.' The third main channel for disseminating propaganda abroad was through the staff of Britain's embassies, legations and consulates. In addition to the work of specialist information staff, it was, Bevin said, up to all the diplomatic staff working abroad to help with publicity work, 'each in their own sphere and with their own contacts.'[46] As with official statements at home, the new policy was to be applied broadly and consistently.

With regard to the themes to be pursued, Bevin reiterated the importance of combining offensive anti-communist material with a positive projection of both British values and the Western Union. He concluded with an important statement of his priorities for the new propaganda policy:

> This is only the beginnings of what is to be done, but I think it is on the right lines. I would only add that while anti-Communist publicity is important, I attach greater importance to publicising positive achievements in the field of Western Union, economic recovery and social improvement. Moreover, I am certain that we must be careful not to increase the fear of war and of the Russian and Communist strength.[47]

Although Bevin's proposals were somewhat removed from the dramatic suggestions for a return to political warfare discussed by the Cabinet, Bevin's plan was no less ambitious in its scope. Rather than seeking a return to wartime propaganda methods, Bevin grasped the fact that opportunities for essentially overt propaganda in peacetime were much greater. Certainly, outside the Iron Curtain countries, Britain gained 'by being able to use in peacetime all the various types of overt publicity which could not be used in occupied countries during the war.' What was far more important than the development of covert channels of influence was a propaganda campaign that was closely coordinated, intensive and, above all, consistent. The defining feature of Bevin's proposals was that the new propaganda policy depended on consistent application from the highest level to the most mundane, from Minister's speeches, to personal contacts between British officials and representatives of foreign governments, the media and the public.

Organising the new propaganda policy

The Cabinet paper on future foreign publicity policy recommended that the only new machinery necessary to implement the new propaganda policy would be a 'small section in the Foreign Office to collect information concerning Communist policy, tactics and propaganda and to provide material for our anti-Communist publicity through our Missions and Information Services abroad.'[48] Christopher Warner, as Assistant Under-Secretary concerned with information activities, was briefed to establish the new machinery. Warner informed the Russia Committee that for administrative purposes the new propaganda policy would be organized around three key functions:

1   An *offensive* branch, which would attack and expose communist methods and policy and contrast them with 'Western' democratic and British methods and policy.

2   A *defensive* branch, which would be concerned with replying to Soviet and communist attacks and hostile propaganda.
3   A *positive* branch, which would deal with the 'build-up' of the Western Union conception.[49]

From the outset it was decided to separate the positive aspect of the new policy from the defensive and offensive aspects. Consideration of positive publicity was assigned to a new working party in the Foreign Office.[50] This working party on the 'spiritual aspects of Western Union' was chaired by Warner and comprised senior Foreign Office officials, including Gladwyn Jebb, P.M. Crosthwaite, head of the Western Department, Paul Gore-Booth, incoming head of the European Recovery Department, heads of Foreign Office information departments and the renowned Director-General of the wartime PWE, Sir Robert Bruce Lockhart. The working party was briefed for the not inconsiderable feat of putting meat onto the bones of the Western Union concept which Bevin had outlined in the Commons. Its terms of reference were to 'examine the common factors to the Western Union countries, other than the political, strategic and economic which can contribute to building up the Western Union conception.' It was to recommend measures to build up the Western Union through publicity and cultural agreements, to consider which countries should be included in the Western Union for the purpose of such work, and to consider which could be brought into consultation over information work, and how.[51]

The more substantial, and specifically anti-communist, offensive and defensive aspects of the new policy were to be handled by the new Foreign Office information department. A circular telegram to missions outlining the new propaganda policy set out the terms of reference for the new department:

> ...to collate information concerning Communist policy, activities and propaganda, to prepare the material of our long-term anti-Communist publicity for dissemination through His Majesty's Missions and the Information Services abroad, to prepare quick replies to Communist propaganda attacks and to brief Government spokesmen at home and at conferences abroad on the Communist propaganda lines and replies thereto.[52]

After some discussion, the new department was given the innocuous title Information Research Department (IRD). According to the Foreign Office Order Book, 'the name of this department is intended as a disguise for the true nature of its work, which must remain strictly confidential.'[53] There were several reasons for this secrecy. Initially the primary concern was that the Soviet Union should not be alerted and launch a propaganda counter-offensive before the new propaganda policy was properly organized. Warner cautioned the Russia Committee that if Britain launched an anti-communist propaganda offensive before being fully equipped they ran the risk of provoking a 'violent reaction on the part of the Russians and unless we could reply to such a reaction fully and effectively, we should be left at a disadvantage.'[54] Thus, it was decided that, initially, the existence of the new policy would be kept secret.

It has been suggested that the Soviets knew about the new propaganda policy from the start through Guy Burgess, the Soviet agent in the Foreign Office. Christopher

Mayhew has recalled how he appointed Burgess to a position in the IRD early in 1948. He showed, Mayhew recalled, 'a dazzling insight into communist methods of subversion and propaganda, and I readily took him on.' Burgess lasted only a few months before he was sacked by Mayhew for being 'dirty, drunk and idle.'[55] Nevertheless, it has been suggested that in this time Burgess made a tour of British missions to brief officials about the IRD, and was able to 'pass on a full account of IRD's operations to Moscow.'[56]

Nothing has been found in the IRD files about Burgess or his position in the Department, and other early recruits have no recollection of reading any of Burgess's work.[57] Nevertheless, it is apparent that at this time Burgess was passing a large number of government documents to his Soviet controllers.[58] Moreover, a report in a Polish newspaper in April 1948, suggested that the new propaganda policy had been compromised, most probably by Burgess. This article, repeated in the *Soviet Monitor* in Britain, referred to recent instructions to British missions regarding an intensified anti-communist campaign, 'including propaganda and the dissemination of false rumours.'[59] It may also be significant that, in September 1951, shortly after the defection of Burgess and Maclean to Moscow, a meeting of British information officers from Western Europe was informed that, 'the communists themselves were aware of what we were doing.'[60]

However, given that Burgess was only in the IRD for 'a few months' at the beginning of 1948,[61] it is unlikely that he could have passed on a vast amount of information regarding the IRD's operations. It seems highly unlikely that Burgess was entrusted with touring British missions to inform them of the IRD's work. All British missions were informed of the new policy in a circular telegram in January 1948.[62] In the extensive replies there is no reference to a personal visit from anyone from the new department. Although it seems likely that Burgess passed on a copy of this circular, more specific directives regarding propaganda in different regions were not drafted until the summer of 1948 when Burgess had almost certainly left the IRD. Similarly, he would have been unable to give the Soviets advance warning of the IRD's first set-piece campaign regarding Soviet forced labour, launched in the United Nations in October 1948.[63] It is also unlikely that the Soviets were surprised that the British Government had decided to launch an offensive against communist propaganda, and one might question what they could do about it. The Soviet counter-offensive that the Foreign Office feared certainly did not materialise. By December 1949, it was decided that it was no longer necessary to conceal the fact that Britain was conducting anti-communist propaganda abroad through official channels.[64]

Nevertheless, the unofficial channels used by the IRD remained concealed. The existence of the IRD, and its methods were to remain secret. The IRD's output was effectively 'grey' propaganda, that is propaganda emanating from an unidentifiable source. Those who received propaganda material from IRD, such as information staff, Ministers, journalists and the BBC, were aware of its origin but were expected to pass this material on without revealing its source. 'Non-attributability' according to Foreign Office historians was a 'central and distinguishing feature of IRD material.'[65] This had several important advantages: it allowed the widest possible circulation for the IRD's output, whilst protecting the existence of an officially inspired anti-communist propaganda campaign. It was believed that anti-communist propaganda would have greater impact on the recipient if it were not seen to emanate from official sources.[66] Secrecy also allowed the IRD to enlist prominent individuals to the anti-communist cause who might otherwise be reluctant to lend their name to material with an official imprimatur. As the IRD head wrote in May 1948:

> It would embarrass a number of persons who are prepared to lend us valuable support if they were open to the charge of receiving anti-communist briefs from some sinister body in the Foreign Office, engaged in the fabrication of propaganda directed against the Soviet Union.[67]

Initially the IRD had a fairly modest establishment. The original staff requirements were for ten members including four clerical staff. The department's organization was similarly modest and reflected its collating role. Initially it comprised only three sections: an Intelligence Section, an Editorial Section and a Reference Section. The Intelligence Section was responsible for acquiring material from across Whitehall including other departments' papers, reports from missions and colonial posts, as well as press and broadcast monitoring. The Editorial Section prepared the output material. The Reference Section provided a comprehensive library where all material was carefully indexed and stored, 'ready to be pulled out a moment's notice when required.'[68] From this modest base, the Department soon expanded with the establishment of additional sections for geographical areas, the United Nations, NATO, economic affairs, international organizations, and war planning.[69]

From the beginning the general profile of the staff was somewhat different to the standard Foreign Office recruitment. Recruits were drawn from the existing information departments, but also from individuals with experience in publicity outside the Foreign Office, including wartime propagandists and journalists. Among early recruits there was a tendency to appoint those with experience of unconventional warfare. The head of department, Ralph Murray, had spent the War in the PWE. His Assistant, Milo Talbot, was a veteran of the Ministry of Economic Warfare. Another early recruit, Peter Wilkinson, attributed his appointment to his wartime service in the SOE, which meant he had 'closer connections with the intelligence community than most members of the foreign service.'[70] Murray was a popular head of department, with considerable experience in publicity work. Aside from his wartime service in the PWE, Murray had worked in the BBC and in 1945 he had headed the public relations branch of the new Control Commission for Austria. In 1946, he was sent to South-east Asia to head the British information services in the region.[71] For expertise on communism the Department looked to those with experience of the Soviet Union. Early recruits to the Intelligence Section included Jack Brimmell and Hugh Lunghi, both recently returned from the Russian Secretariat in the Moscow Embassy. In 1949, Talbot was replaced as Murray's assistant by Adam Watson, who had just completed a four-year appointment at the Moscow Embassy.[72] Others had firsthand experience of the communist takeover of Eastern Europe. Cecil Parrott came to the Department from the Information Office in the British Embassy in Prague, where he had witnessed the communist coup of 1948, and Robert Conquest had watched the communist takeover of Bulgaria from his position as press officer in the British Embassy in Sofia.[73]

The Department also relied increasingly on 'contract' staff: émigrés from Eastern Europe and freelance journalists. Leslie Sheridan, another SOE veteran, was

Murray's first 'import from the world of professional publicity,' when he was appointed to head the Editorial Section in 1949. Sheridan was, according to Murray, 'extremely good value,' and more appointments followed.[74] In the late 1940s, H.H. Tucker, the chief foreign sub-editor for *The Daily Telegraph*, worked for the IRD on a freelance basis providing 'a professional touch to some of the briefs and background papers.' Tucker joined the Foreign Office in 1951 and eventually rose to the post of assistant to the head of IRD.[75] These appointments of contract staff were considered one of the great strengths of the IRD, but also gave the department a rather unconventional complexion. For one early recruit, the IRD provided a somewhat unexpected, and not entirely happy, introduction to Foreign Office life:

> I came with a First in History from Cambridge and was surprised and bemused to be lodged in such a way-out department. It lived in a rabbit warren in Carlton House Terrace... There were a lot of temporaries, a good many of them from the journalistic world. The atmosphere was hard working and somewhat frenzied!...not what I had expected from the FO and within eight months or so I was happily transferred to one of the traditional departments.[76]

The Department was housed in the elegant Carlton House Terrace, in what had once been the German Embassy. The conditions, however, were hardly ideal. The IRD occupied the servants' quarters on the top floors of Numbers 17 and 18. The tiny lift is well remembered by former officers as 'The Meat Safe'.[77] One of the houses still had Crockford's Gambling Club occupying the lower floors. The other was occupied by the Information Policy Department and Foreign Office regional information departments. Despite their proximity, one early recruit recalls, 'we had regular, but not very close, contacts.'[78] Nevertheless, the Department's location did have a certain cachet. Aubrey Essex who joined the IRD in 1960 recalls that, 'as an address one could dine out on the strength of it.' On important State occasions, such as the Trooping of the Colour and visits of foreign statesmen, 'we could turn out on the terrace overlooking The Mall and Horse Guards for a grandstand view, and rub shoulders with the rich and famous of Crockfords Club.'[79] The novelist, Fay Weldon, who spent a brief spell in the IRD in the early 1950s, recalls watching the Queen's coronation procession from Carlton House Terrace, although her abiding memory is of the 'splendid bathrooms.'[80]

The starting budget reflected the Department's modest establishment. The IRD was established with £7,500 generated by economies in the other information departments. In addition, the Treasury agreed a lump sum of £150,000 as a starting budget. Despite these modest beginnings it is clear that ambitious plans were already anticipated. In approaching the Treasury for funding, Harold Caccia suggested that, in addition to the costs of establishment, the Treasury might wish to consider the possibility of additional operational expenditure. This extra expense, 'probably substantial, but at present incalculable,' Caccia said, would be necessary to expand IRD's activities at home and abroad, including increased BBC broadcasts, possibly involving extra wavelengths.[81] Others suggested that the expenditure might rise to between one quarter million to a million pounds.[82] It may be that Caccia deliberately pitched his proposal high in order to ensure that at least the minimum requirement was forthcoming. However, Warner was disturbed that suggestions for expansion were being made before the Department had actually begun work. He reassured the Treasury that they were, 'going quite cautiously about the new policy' and any further plans would be 'examined ruthlessly from the point of view of the most rigid economy.'[83]

From the outset it was intended that funding for the new department should be discreet. In putting its proposals to the Treasury, the Foreign Office noted that it was 'undesirable that undue public attention should be drawn to this new activity.' They were particularly anxious that the lump sum should not be listed as an additional item in the published estimates for information expenditure. As a result, the Foreign Office devised a plan whereby the additional £150,000 was disguised under other items of publicity in the estimates. Thus, an extra £30,000 was added to the proposed estimate for publicity in the press; £80,000 to films, and photography; £20,000 to broadcasting; and £20,000 to miscellaneous expenses.[84] This was the only occasion on which such a method was used. When Murray proposed further expenses of £100,000, in September 1948, it was agreed that funding for the IRD would now be provided under the secret vote,[85] where it remained until 1973. Secret funding served a number of purposes: it hid the IRD from unwanted public attention; it also allowed the Department freedom to recruit staff unrestricted by the limitations of civil service pay and conditions. This became particularly important as the department's began to recruit more journalists and émigrés from outside the normal ranks of civil service appointments. Such specialists were not paid according to civil service rates, and 'in some cases the recipients led double lives, and could not let it be known that they received a salary from IRD.'[86]

The IRD's modest establishment reflected the intention that the Department would play a supplemental role in implementing the new propaganda policy (the Department arrived rather late in the post-war development of Britain's propaganda apparatus and it seems apparent that initially its role was to *supplement* the work of Britain's already substantial information apparatus). As IRD's terms of reference indicated, although the Department was to coordinate the anti-communist aspect of the new propaganda policy, it was only to play a supporting role in the collection and dissemination of anti-communist material. The paper on 'Future Foreign Publicity Policy' had suggested the creation of a 'small Section in the Foreign Office' which would 'collate' information on communism, and disseminate this material through the 'usual channels.'[87] The IRD was to provide a central collection point for material on communist activities and this material would be disseminated through the Government's existing information apparatus.

The new department collated information on communist policy and practices from across Whitehall. Foreign Office departments were asked to forward to IRD all papers on Soviet and communist policy, organization, tactics and propaganda in the Soviet Union, Europe and the Middle and Far East. Items on the conditions in territories under communist rule were particularly valuable, especially regarding material which, if exposed, would be likely to diminish communism's hold over its adherents or its appeal to neutrals.[88] It was felt that the detailed papers of the Foreign Office Research Department (FORD) and the press reading facilities of the Russian Secretariat at the Moscow Embassy would be particularly valuable. Detailed intelligence requirements were submitted to the intelligence authorities at home and those in exceptional positions in the field, such as the Intelligence Division in Hereford and the Intelligence Organization in Vienna.[89] Most importantly, British representatives abroad were asked to provide 'any material' likely to be of value for anti-communist propaganda. They were to forward any material which, if widely known, would 'expose, damage and help defeat the Communists and... encourage anti-communists by illustrating the frauds, deficiencies and drawbacks of communism and the superiority of the policies and way of life of those who share our beliefs.' Missions in Eastern Europe in particular were expected to provide 'much useful material for anti-Communist publicity.'[90]

The IRD's intelligence requirements were broad and somewhat unusual but clearly reflected the themes which were to be pursued in the new propaganda policy. Not surprisingly, the rather general request for any material likely to damage the communists met with a muted response from British missions. Although they were quick to recommend the kind of material they could use locally, information officers were less helpful in providing the IRD with material on which it could base its propaganda. It is apparent that British representatives abroad had little understanding of the kind of material which could be used in the new propaganda policy. For example, the British Embassy in Prague felt unable to help because it believed that any information it could provide would not be 'sufficiently dramatic or instructive' to be of use in other countries. Others simply ignored the request.[91] Consequently, in March 1948, the IRD issued more specific intelligence requirements, asking missions to provide details of the hierarchy, personalities, finance, propaganda, strategy and tactics of communist organizations in their territories.[92] Missions behind the Iron Curtain were informed that, although their despatches provided a great deal of political information, the IRD was also interested in the details of everyday life under communist rule. To assist this, the IRD provided a generic list of individuals – the worker, the peasant, the public servant, the professional, the trader, the student and the parent – about whom they required information.[93] By the end of 1949 the Department had established long and detailed requirements for intelligence from communist-dominated countries, under the headings: labour conditions, social conditions, political conditions, cultural conditions and religious conditions. These included requests for specific information on such topics as: wages, housing conditions, medical standards, the cost of commodities, organization of secret police and individuals involved, and support or suppression of local customs and laws.[94] This emphasis on the details of everyday life under communist rule became the staple of the IRD's intelligence requirements. It was clearly novel to British information staff abroad and was, according to Murray, an 'eye-opener' for the intelligence authorities at home.[95]

Within the IRD, this material was drafted into briefing papers designed to provide information staff abroad with anti-communist background material for use in discussions with local contacts or for unofficial local distribution. These 'basic papers' comprised the bulk of the IRD's output. In their subject matter the papers followed the guiding principles set out in the new propaganda policy. In keeping with the new policy's aim to disillusion the people of Europe and the Middle East about Russia's pretence to be a 'worker's paradise' the first papers focused heavily on life under communist rule. The first basic paper was entitled 'The Real Conditions in Soviet Russia' and was followed by other papers, including: 'Conditions in the New Soviet Colonies'; 'Labour and Trade Unions in the Soviet Union'; 'Peasant Collectivization in Areas Under Soviet control'; and 'Daily Life in a Communist State'.[96] These papers provided basic information on everyday life behind the Iron Curtain, the kind of public interest details which might be taken up by the popular press. 'The Real Conditions in Soviet Russia', for example, described the common man's living conditions in the Soviet Union: the low wages; the high cost of basic foodstuffs; the prohibitively expensive consumer goods; the overcrowded housing; the poor working conditions; and an education system which was 'far behind Western standards.'[97] Other basic papers focused on the threat to world peace from communist foreign policy. The first paper to be considered mature enough for printing was the 'Essence of Soviet Foreign Policy'. This was followed by papers on the 'Communist Conquest of the Baltic States' and 'The facts of Soviet Expansionism'.[98] Finally, some papers offered more sophisticated analyses of the 'principles and practices of communism.' These included a lengthy paper on 'The Foundations of Stalinism' by the Northern Department's Soviet expert, Thomas Brimelow. Brimelow's paper was based on Stalin's statements as head of the Communist Party. It was followed by a companion piece entitled 'The Practice of Stalinism', by W. Barker of the Russian Secretariat in the Moscow Embassy.[99] These detailed papers were clearly designed for consumption within the Government or distribution to foreign politicians and opinion-formers. Both papers were given widespread distribution within Whitehall. Initially up to 700 copies of Brimelow's paper were printed, 55 of which went to the Foreign Office News Department compared with 130 copies for the JIC.[100]

In July 1948, in response to requests from some missions for shorter, more pointed material, the basic papers were supplemented by a weekly 'Digest' of news stories regarding Soviet and international communism. The Digest was divided into two sections. The first part consisted of a detailed treatment of one topical event. The second part comprised recent information on communist activities under a number of broad headings including: labour affairs, agrarian affairs, the Islamic world, human rights and international movements.[101] The Digest was intended to provide quotable material on events that were not necessarily common knowledge. The information was presented in a form easily used by information officers who were expected to pass selected items to their contacts rather than hand over whole issues of the Digest. In order to make the material more useful to editors, where possible, stories were attributed to a named source.[102] The IRD also made use of the Foreign Office system of guidance telegrams, or Intels, which were designed to provide embassies with quick answers to incorrect information about British policy. Murray, however, found the Foreign Office telegraphic system somewhat unsuited to the exigencies of effective rebuttal. 'They take too long to draft and clear, they go Saving and arrive too late,' he complained.[103]

Although the tone of the IRD's output was certainly anti-communist, the papers they produced were not intended to present an inaccurate picture of Soviet communism. The Foreign Office stuck to the long-held view that the most effective propaganda was straight news and facts. Indeed, some of the basic papers, such as those by Brimelow and Barker, were thoughtful and well-balanced assessments of Soviet policy. Moreover, for propaganda purposes, conditions in Soviet-controlled territory were such that it was felt that exaggeration was not necessary. In order to 'expose the myths of the Soviet paradise' it was felt sufficient merely to present the harsh realities of life under Soviet rule. The impact of the basic papers on life behind the

Iron Curtain was predicated on the fact that conditions behind the Iron Curtain were poor and that such information was not widely available in the West. Although the Foreign Office Minister, Hector McNeill, felt the papers were a little overstated for a British audience,[104] Christopher Warner thought the first papers were perhaps 'too dully written' and in need of 'pepping up':

> But when I say pepping up I do not mean exaggerating the facts; for the papers are strictly factual and it would be very difficult and, I am sure, a mistake for us to water down the facts. Our whole object is to enlighten those who have no idea how unpleasant the conditions in Communist-controlled countries are.[105]

The only deception involved the dissemination of this material. The material in the digests was meant for unofficial distribution and was designed to be used unattributably. The basic papers and digests were printed 'white' with no indication of authorship, sometimes undated, and, most importantly, no indication of their origin in the British Foreign Office. Distribution outside of official circles was to be on a strictly unattributable basis. A detachable cover sheet attached to each basic paper outlined how the material was to be used:

> The attached material is for the use of His Majesty's Missions and Information Officers in particular.
> The information contained in this paper is, as far as it is possible to ascertain, factual and objective. The paper may, therefore, be used freely as a reference paper, but neither copies of it nor the material contained in it should be distributed officially without the sanction of the Head of Mission. It and/or the material in the paper, however, may be distributed unofficially in whatever quarters seem useful so long as it can be assured that there will be no public attribution of material or of the paper to an official British source.
> This note must be detached from any copy of the material before it passes beyond official use.[106]

Although the preparation of 'grey' anti-communist propaganda was the IRD's principal role, the new propaganda policy required a change in the policy of other agencies with responsibility for Britain's overseas information activity. The policy of Britain's overt propaganda agency, the Central Office of Information, was changed to reflect the new anti-communist line, and arrangements were made to more closely coordinate covert propaganda with the new propaganda policy. In addition to the preparation of anti-communist propaganda, the IRD sat at the centre of the machinery for coordinating the new propaganda policy across Whitehall. Through a network of liaison committees and informal contacts, the Department collated information on communism, generated anti-communist propaganda for dissemination abroad, and oversaw the implementation of the anti-communist propaganda policy by Britain's other propaganda agencies. On the one hand, this was a matter of budgetary restraint. For example, rather than establish its own production facilities, the IRD was instructed to employ the technical expertise of Britain's existing information apparatus, most notably the Central Office of Information. On the other hand, as Bevin had directed, it located overall control of the new propaganda policy firmly within the Foreign Office.

Assigning anti-communist propaganda to a dedicated Foreign Office department was meant to ensure effective control and the coordinated implementation of the new propaganda policy. It also gave the IRD influence over Britain's instruments of overseas propaganda out of proportion to the Department's own size and resources.

Information activities in Britain's colonial possessions were the responsibility of the Commonwealth Relations Office and the Colonial Office, but concerns about communist attacks on the Western colonial exploitation, coupled with the rise of communist movements in some British colonies, meant that the new propaganda policy being developed in the Foreign Office was also applicable in the colonies.[107] In July 1948, the Cabinet Committee on anti-communist propaganda established the Colonial Information Policy Committee (CIPC) to coordinate the propaganda activities of the Foreign Office, the Commonwealth Relations Office and the Colonial Office. The CIPC was chaired by Christopher Mayhew and comprised Parliamentary Under-Secretaries and officials from the three Departments along with Robert Fraser, Director General of the Central Office of Information, and Jacob, from the BBC.[108] The CIPC terms of reference were 'to coordinate the collection and presentation of publicity material regarding British colonial policy and administration.'[109] Although initially the three Departments were to remain wholly independent in the conduct of this propaganda, the dominant role of the Foreign Office in directing anti-communist propaganda was soon evident. In November 1948, the CIPC terms of reference were expanded 'to stimulate and concert the dissemination of publicity designed to counter Communist propaganda in countries overseas, especially in the self-governing and Colonial countries of the Commonwealth and neighbouring territories.'[110] Moreover, although the Colonial and Commonwealth Relations offices prepared publicity material projecting the British way of life and the benefits of colonial administration, material for combating communist propaganda in the colonies was usually supplied by the Foreign Office.[111]

Machinery was also established for liaison on anti-communist propaganda between the Foreign Office and the Chiefs of Staff. The ostensible purpose of this liaison was to ensure the supply of military intelligence that could be of use for propaganda purposes. Informal committees were established in each of the Service Departments, comprising the Director of Plans, the Director of Intelligence and the Public Relations Officer. These informal committees would collate information from the Services at home, and British military attachés abroad, and pass any relevant information through the Secretary of the Chiefs of Staff Committee to the head of the IRD. The aims of this liaison were threefold: to ensure that military intelligence about the strength and weakness of the enemy was made available to the Foreign Office; to ensure that intelligence about Britain's military strength and that of Britain's allies was available to the Foreign Office; and to ensure that routine announcements made by the Service Departments were framed in line with the new propaganda policy.[112] In the light of their frustration at the slow pace of Britain's planning for political warfare, it is apparent that the Chiefs of Staff hoped this channel of communication would also afford them some influence over the direction of Britain's cold war propaganda:

Once this channel of communication is established we contemplate that information and advice would flow through it in both directions. It would enable the Chiefs of Staff and the Service Departments to make their contribution towards the conduct of anti-Communist propaganda. It would also enable the Foreign Office to keep the Services informed of the propaganda measures which they were taking.[113]

Significantly, on the Services' recommendation, this liaison organization had been modelled on that which served the needs of the wartime PWE, and 'would form a working nucleus which could be rapidly expanded in case of need.'[114] Faced with such pressure from the Service Departments, the Foreign Office asserted its authority over the application of the new propaganda policy. It was later agreed that although the Service Committees would not be debarred from making practical suggestions for activities in the field, 'it rested with the Foreign Office whether any such suggestions were acted on or not in the light of political considerations.'[115]

Whilst the IRD handled the distribution of unattributable briefing material it also oversaw the application of the new policy by Britain's overt propaganda agency the Central Office of Information (COI). The COI was not a policy department and only rarely originated propaganda campaigns in its own right. Since its establishment in 1946, the COI's function was to supply government departments with technical publicity advice and provide a number of common distributive services. Although the COI maintained no staff overseas it provided British embassies abroad with books, pamphlets, posters, and photographs. It also ran the London Press Service (LPS). This telegraphic service provided British missions with a daily bulletin on diplomatic, industrial, social and economic affairs. It was not a current news service but was designed to provide commentary on the assumption that the 'hard news' had already reached foreign posts through the news agencies and the BBC. It was a free, attributable service unrestricted by secrecy and copyright and was designed for diplomats, information officers and the local press to use in whatever manner they saw fit.[116]

Since 1946, the COI's overseas services had been geared towards the 'Projection of Britain'. Following the approval of the new propaganda policy in January 1948, the COI was provided with a new directive in which they were required to 'take every suitable opportunity that offers for drawing the comparison between the merits of our own methods in Britain, the Commonwealth and the Empire, and the vices and dangers of Communist methods'. Although it was encouraged to exercise 'tact and discretion', the COI's output was to be 'forthright and effective in our comparison, and on occasion in our denunciation of Communist methods.'[117] In February 1948, the IRD head, Ralph Murray, outlined a detailed plan for the employment of COI services. He suggested that the LPS should increase its emphasis on labour affairs in Europe, and might even carry a regular commentary on Soviet affairs which would enable them to include a great deal of IRD material. In order to facilitate the new policy Murray suggested that LPS should establish direct and daily contact with IRD. He proposed that the directive for COI photoprint editors should be altered to include subjects to emphasize the contrast between conditions in the West and behind the Iron Curtain. In particular, they might be asked to prepare feature sets illustrating 'What Liberty Means', with pictures of 'guardians of civil liberties in the democracies' and contrasting illustrations of the secret police in communist-dominated areas.[118]

Murray was particularly keen to use COI contacts to develop a series of signed feature articles from well-known commentators. It was felt that signed articles had a much greater impact than official statements, particularly on foreign audiences, and they were frequently requested by Information Officers.[119] Murray proposed that articles should be commissioned from writers, 'out of the ordinary run' of COI contributors;[120] and, like the IRD basic papers, these articles were to focus on comparative standards of living between the Western democracies and the Soviet 'paradise', and to stress civil liberties. Although 'tactically' Murray said, they should probably be angled to fit in as part of the 'Projection of Britain', 'each article should be equipped with a powerful sting in its tail.'[121] The IRD could provide the writers with material to help in their research but 'for reasons of discretion' it was suggested that COI should commission the papers.[122] In October 1948, the IRD presented the COI with a detailed list of topics for feature articles, these included: communist penetration of the Middle East; Soviet secret police action; a comparison of Soviet and Nazi aggression in action; Soviet disregard for human rights; and a series of signed articles on 'Impressions of the USSR' and 'The Russian Economic Grip on the Iron Curtain Countries'.[123]

The COI was not entirely happy with its involvement in the new propaganda policy. Robert Fraser, Director General of the COI, thought it unwise for the COI to produce anti-communist material as part of its general service for the Foreign Office. It was not, he believed, in the interests of the COI to 'get mixed up with secret or semi-secret work.'[124] When reviewing IRD's progress in August 1948, Murray described efforts to mobilize the COI as 'quite fruitless.' He bemoaned 'interminable negotiations' over the improved LPS output, the production of a bulletin on Labour affairs and anti-communist feature output, and 'equally fruitless' negotiations over films, photographs, strip cartoons and books.[125] Nevertheless, cooperation between the Foreign Office and the COI did bear some fruit. The COI secured a number of impressive commissions for feature articles, including a series on conditions in the Soviet Union from Edward Crankshaw, articles on Soviet and fascist methods and on Soviet sabotage of atomic energy written by Malcolm Muggeridge, and articles on Soviet penetration of the Middle East written by Elizabeth Monroe.[126] The IRD and the COI also established close and effective cooperation in the development of anti-communist themes in the LPS services. The LPS maintained a daily contact with the IRD. By March 1949, the IRD was pleased that suggestions for the emphasis of LPS bulletins met with absolute cooperation, and the use of IRD themes was 'very satisfactory in quantity...and far from bad in quality.' The only regrets arose from the natural limitations of the LPS service – material needed to reach LPS by 10 am, it did not carry news, and it could not carry signed articles.[127]

Arrangements were also made to coordinate IRD's anti-communist propaganda with the activities of Britain's covert propaganda agencies. Although Bevin had given his Cabinet colleagues the impression that any covert propaganda was impracticable in the present circumstances, at least one Minister was informed confidentially, early in 1948, that '"black" activities were in fact going on to a limited extent.'[128] Responsibility for 'black' propaganda was, however, somewhat disjointed. Covert propaganda was divided between MI6, which handled 'black' propaganda, and a body in the Ministry of Defence responsible for deception planning, the London Controlling Section (LCS). (The LCS, which was established during the War to prepare strategic deception plans, had been preserved within the Ministry of Defence as a reservoir of specialist skills and knowledge.[129])

An examination of the organization of 'black' propaganda and deception in early 1948, concluded there was very little coordination between the agencies responsible. The Cabinet Secretary, Norman Brook, wrote that he could not 'see any clear dividing line between "black" propaganda and deception.' 'Deception', he observed, 'is only one aspect of "black propaganda".' Yet the activities were divided between two departments which did not appear to have any arrangements for cooperation.[130] Moreover, it is apparent that the SIS was ill prepared for 'black' propaganda activities. In January 1948, Air Chief Marshall Sir John Slessor had expressed dismay at the SIS's inadequate plans for covert propaganda.[131] Norman Brook also found that the SIS was not properly equipped to handle 'black' propaganda. 'Functionally,' he wrote, 'it is an intelligence-collecting organization' which handled propaganda due to circumstances, in that it had inherited the remnants of the SOE and so controlled the channels through which 'black' propaganda was disseminated. However, in a remarkable admission, Brook commented, 'I don't believe that "C" himself knows anything about propaganda; and I have not been able to get any assurances that he has on his staff anyone who does.'[132]

The organization of the new propaganda policy attempted to provide improved coordination of 'black' propaganda, by making arrangements to allow the Foreign Office an overview of such activities. Coordination with the SIS was established through Sir Stewart Menzies, Director General of the SIS, who maintained contact with Christopher Warner in the Foreign Office, and with the Director of Plans in the Service Departments.[133] A separate informal contact was established between Warner and a representative of the LCS.[134] Through this machinery the IRD was able to coordinate 'black' activities with the rest of the Government's overseas propaganda activities. It also went some way towards providing closer coordination of the two agencies responsible for covert propaganda. As there was little apparent appetite for closer coordination from the secret agencies themselves, this effectively left the Foreign Office as the only agency with an overall view of Britain's 'black' propaganda activities, and, more importantly, the coordination of these activities with the new propaganda policy. As Brook observed, the liaison machinery left the problem of coordination in the hands of the Foreign Office on the basis that, 'the Foreign Office are responsible for policy on both sides and must be left to see that the executive agencies of propaganda, "black" and "white" carry out that single policy.'[135]

Clearly the organization of the new propaganda policy placed the new Foreign Office department in an influential position. In addition to the job of collating and disseminating anti-communist material the IRD oversaw all of Britain's anti-communist propaganda activities overseas. This central coordinating role for the Foreign Office may have been exactly what Bevin intended. There was to be no return to the wartime organization for political warfare with an executive agency outside the Foreign Office responsible for the preparation and application of offensive and defensive propaganda. In the Cold War the Foreign Office was to retain overall control and it established the primary agency for the preparation of Britain's anti-communist propaganda, and the central coordinating authority for the application of the new propaganda policy across Whitehall, in the IRD.

Moreover, in the months following its creation, the IRD's role expanded rapidly. It soon became clear that the original intention that the IRD would merely act as a central collection point for anti-communist material for distribution through existing channels was unworkable. By August 1948, although the IRD had grown to

16 personnel, Murray found it impossible to increase 'this slow laboured trickle of output' without an enlarged establishment. He needed competent editorial staff, reference section assistants and specialist readers of the Russian and Iron Curtain press 'for our purposes.'[136] The IRD also struggled to secure the cooperation of some other government departments which viewed its activities with a certain distaste. As Aubrey Essex recalls, the IRD 'had many critics both within government and within the Foreign Office. The idea of a department whose principal commodity was propaganda – albeit anti-Communist propaganda – was anathema to such people.'[137]

The reluctance of some government departments to become involved in the new propaganda policy, coupled with the specialist nature of the IRD's anti-communist campaign, led the IRD to develop its own capabilities. The COI's reluctance to produce material without an official imprimatur led the IRD to develop its own production facilities, and commission its own anti-communist feature articles.[138] Although the Department continued to commission material through intermediaries, in 1949 the IRD secured the services of a number of prominent individuals who were willing to work directly with the IRD in the production of signed feature articles; these included Richard Crossman, MP, Will Lawther, President of the National Union of Mineworkers, J.A. Hough of the British Cooperative Union, and the journalist and former communist, Norman Ewer.[139] In 1949, the Department also appointed new staff with prominent contacts in intellectual circles, most notably Celia Kirwan, the sister-in-law of Arthur Koestler and a friend of George Orwell. Similarly, Adam Watson, who joined the IRD in mid-1949, was 'friendly with many of the leading figures of the "literary Left"', including Bertrand Russell and Orwell's wife, Sonia. Sonia was, according to Watson, 'well aware, more so than Orwell himself, about the value of publicity.' She had worked for the intellectuals' magazine *New Writing* and with Cyril Connolly on *Horizon*, and was a 'very useful contact' for Watson in his efforts to find left-of-centre intellectuals to write for the IRD.[140]

The Department also developed its own substantial research and intelligence sections. Members of the Foreign Office Research Department (FORD), whose role mostly closely resembled that of the IRD, resisted a proposed merger with the IRD on the grounds that, 'they are not and do not wish to be propagandists.'[141] IRD officials also had reservations about the suitability of such departments for propaganda work. Although the FORD's detailed papers were admired in Whitehall it was felt that a 'short readable document' was more effective for propaganda purposes.[142] Murray noted that 'pure FORD research minds are not necessarily what I need', and Warner observed that 'persons selected for research in FORD are averse to and totally unsuited for anything in the nature of propaganda.'[143] Similarly, in 1949, when Foreign Office inspectors recommended the creation of a separate Russian and satellite intelligence department to service the needs of all Foreign Office departments, the IRD resisted the dilution of their intelligence cadre.[144] Warner argued it was impracticable for the same people to do intelligence work for different purposes, namely political, economic and propagandist. Without an intimate knowledge of Soviet propaganda, and also of the particular themes and campaigns on which the IRD were working, it would be impossible for the intelligence analyst to pick up useful items.[145] By mid-1949, the IRD had expanded to 52 personnel and the intelligence section alone numbered 21.[146] Although the IRD continued to use the facilities of the Government's existing research and propaganda agencies, the development of its own capabilities meant the 'small section' created in 1948 to coordinate Britain's anti-communist propaganda continued to expand almost throughout its existence.[147]

Implementing the new propaganda policy: dissemination – methods and media

Once the machinery for coordinating the new propaganda policy had been established, the IRD set about organizing channels through which anti-communist propaganda could be disseminated. The Cabinet paper on 'Future Foreign Publicity Policy' stated that the new department would 'provide material for our anti-communist publicity through our Missions and Information Services abroad.' It also suggested that anti-communist material should be made available to Ministers, and to Labour Party and Trade Union officials on an informal basis.[148] In a circular telegram to British missions outlining the new policy, diplomats were instructed that preparations would take some time and they should not therefore, 'initiate any general change to the new policy in local publicity pending further instructions.' They were merely required to make 'observations and suggestions' regarding the methods and media to be adopted, the character of material required and the probable effect of the new policy on the work of their information staff.[149]

British missions were at the forefront of communist propaganda attacks and the IRD was heavily dependent on British representatives abroad to provide information on communist propaganda for use in Britain's response, and also to implement the new propaganda line. In the early months of 1948, in the phoney-propaganda war before the IRD began its work, the themes to be pursued in the new propaganda policy, and the channels through which that propaganda was to be disseminated, were delimited in a series of telegrams between the IRD and British missions abroad. A circular to all British missions, on 23 January, outlined the broad framework of the policy defined by the Cabinet paper on 'Future Foreign Publicity Policy'. It listed five broad themes. The new policy should: advertise British principles as the best way of life compared with communism and unrestrained capitalism; stress the civil liberties issue, pointing to the many analogies between fascist and communist systems; highlight the destructiveness of communist foreign policy; answer Soviet misrepresentations about Britain; and in all this to take care to emphasize the weaknesses and deficiencies of communism, not its strength.[150]

Missions were told that the target audience for the new policy was to be the 'broad masses of workers and peasants.' The principal target area was to be Western Europe, where it was stated that the new policy was designed to give a lead and lend support to democratic elements resisting the inroads of communism. It was stated that the new policy would also require 'special application' in the Middle East and certain Far Eastern countries such as India, Pakistan, Burma, Ceylon, Malaya, Indonesia and Indo-China. An additional circular was sent to Middle East missions which were informed that they should for the time being continue to implement the anti-communist measures set out in the directive of October 1946, 'Russia in the Middle East'.[151] British embassies in Eastern Europe and in Russia were also given specific instructions. It was accepted that these missions would not be able to carry out anti-communist measures locally, but it was hoped the positive side of the new policy could be implemented. Such anti-communist activity as was possible was to be limited to repeating suitable material from ministerial and official statements covered by the BBC. They were to avoid 'any incitement to subversive activity.' These missions were, however, vitally important in providing material on conditions behind the Iron Curtain for use in Britain's anti-communist propaganda.[152]

The reaction of British missions to the new propaganda policy was somewhat mixed. Although it was broadly welcomed, some aspects of the new policy were questioned and it was obvious that the policy as it stood was not applicable in all regions. Several missions questioned the wisdom of attacking 'unrestrained capitalism.' In the Middle East, it was pointed out, capitalism was generally associated with the ruling class and big foreign oil companies, 'who already have enough trouble on their hands without the aid of our official policy.'[153] Similarly, in some countries – for example, in Latin America – communists were already attacking 'American imperialism' and an attack on capitalism would naturally be assumed to be directed against the USA.[154] The proposed appeal to democratic Christian principles was another feature of the new policy which was not of universal application: in Catholic Latin America, Britain did not appear an appropriate champion of Christian values, and in the Middle East an emphasis on Christian principles was hardly likely to be profitable.[155] The British Middle East Office in Cairo concluded, not without some truth, that the new policy seemed to have been designed with Europe in mind. With regard to countering communist influence further East it was effectively a step back from the 1946 publicity directive 'Russia and the Middle East' which sought to defend Britain *and the USA* against Soviet charges of aggressive imperialism and reply to Soviet misrepresentations 'with all the means at our disposal.'[156]

Missions were asked to comment in particular on the methods and media of dissemination likely to be most fruitful in implementing the new policy in their region. Their replies suggested that five broad channels would be used for the dissemination of Britain's new anti-communist propaganda: the press; broadcast media, principally the BBC; books; visual media, such as film and posters; and personal contacts. The extent to which each of these channels could be employed varied considerably depending on local circumstances. In Eastern Europe information officers were clearly aware of their vulnerable position and stressed the need for discretion. Belgrade and Prague, for example, both cautioned that they could not take the offensive through their existing overt information programmes, such as reading rooms, for fear of giving the authorities an excuse to shut down their information departments.[157] It was widely felt in Eastern Europe that the BBC was the 'safest and most useful method' for the dissemination of information.[158] Nevertheless, there was scope for implementing the new policy more discreetly through the development of personal contacts. According to the Helsinki Embassy, such a policy should aim for 'maximum influence; minimum display.'[159] The embassy in Prague stated boldly that 'active anti-communist propaganda' in Czechoslovakia was by no means impossible, although such activity would need to be indirect. Material could reach the Czech public through personal contacts with anti-communist politicians, non-communist newspaper and magazine editors, and reliable leading Czechs from other walks of life who could disseminate material amongst their own political or professional circles.[160]

90   *Launching the new propaganda policy, 1948*

In Western Europe, where information departments in British embassies operated with greater freedom, a more varied range of media was suggested. The embassy in Madrid, for example, offered a long and diverse list of methods for disseminating anti-communist material including the BBC Spanish Service, embassy bulletins, films, photographs for the press and window displays, posters, lectures and verbal propaganda by means of 'calls'.[161] In some countries in Western Europe a more discreet approach to anti-communist propaganda was still recommended. In France and Italy, on the frontline of the struggle against communism in Western Europe, it was suggested that, although propaganda could openly project British achievements and espouse the virtues of Western democracy, the dissemination of anti-communist propaganda should be more indirect. In Rome, the ambassador, Sir Victor Mallet, said that the embassy and consulates should not be used for the direct dissemination of anti-communist material for two reasons. Firstly, feelings were running so high between the communist and non-communist parties, that the sacking of party publicity offices was a growing pastime and British information offices would do well to stay out of the arena. Secondly, the strength of anti-communist feeling in the majority of Italian newspapers was such that there was little need to disseminate such material officially from the embassy. Instead, Mallet recommended, anti-communist material should be disseminated discreetly through personal contacts with sympathetic sections of the press and non-communist political parties.[162] Similarly, in France, the ambassador said that British officials should avoid any overt anti-communist statements, but should seek to 'personally inspire public men, editors, publishers and writers with material for their own activities in this field.' He even suggested that a confidential arrangement could be made with small press agencies in France to include IRD material in their services.[163]

Outside of Europe, as the Russia Committee had predicted, there were problems with the proposal to direct the new policy at the 'broad masses of workers and peasants.' In the Middle East, the existing propaganda policy targeted the educated élite. In response to the new policy, the British Middle East Office in Cairo argued in favour of maintaining existing policy. Students and graduates, they suggested, would be a more appropriate target than uneducated workers and peasants: 'the semi-educated townee is the most dangerous class in the Middle East... It is they who usually start the trouble.'[164] A detailed programme of anti-communist measures from the embassy in Baghdad identified three groups in the Middle East to whom anti-communist propaganda could be directed. The small professional and English-speaking class had the most to lose from communism and therefore was largely opposed to communism already; propaganda directed at this class would be preaching to the converted. The student class was the most susceptible to the blandishments of communism; however, students' grasp of English was often rudimentary and an approach to them, it was felt, was best made in Arabic. Finally, the remaining masses were largely illiterate and must be approached by 'visual methods, the radio and a whispering campaign.'[165]

Reaching these groups required different methods than those employed in Europe, with a greater emphasis on visual and oral media, and a need for more material in local languages. The educated classes, Baghdad suggested, should be influenced through anti-communist material placed in the local press.[166] The ambassador in Cairo reported that various local newspapers were already following an anti-communist line and would welcome more material.[167] This material, Baghdad suggested, could be provided both locally and through London. It was noted that every overseas newspaper subscribed to some syndicated service in the UK for its feature articles. Editors of services in Britain should be encouraged to increase the production of anti-communist material. It was even suggested that a feature service might be set up in London to feed articles to the Arab world. Local information officers would also ensure that articles were translated and placed in the local press, and that the producing newspaper was distributed to all posts. Thus, articles placed in just one local newspaper would be repeated throughout the region, thereby obscuring their origin and impressing upon the reader the seriousness with which communism was regarded in many countries.[168] This technique, described by the IRD's John Cloake, as 'place, pick-up and play back,' became an important part of the IRD's dissemination procedure. Although, Cloake recalls, it had an unfortunate consequence, as 'we spent quite a lot on "second-rights" in buying back our own material!'[169]

Baghdad also suggested that the semi-educated should be targeted with 'cheap literature that can be placed in the many hole-in-the-wall bookshops.'[170] The idea of producing cheap books for sale or distribution to reading rooms and libraries was suggested by a number of posts. In the Far East the British representative in Burma recommended 'a special campaign of cheap simple literature for popular bookshops or for presentation to schools and associations.' Similarly, the information staff in Batavia called for cheap books by non-official British writers focusing on the Soviet Union and its international behaviour but 'preferably free from polemic.'[171]

Baghdad suggested an ambitious programme of visual propaganda to target the illiterate masses. This included: a poster campaign showing the consequences of forced labour and collectivization; a feature film with a Middle East setting depicting the progressive infiltration of communism into a country; and newsreels. There was concern, however, that newsreels would need to become more hard-hitting. Current newsreels, according to Baghdad, tended to present British achievements 'rather effetely.' 'Such subjects as the Chelsea Arts Ball, bathing beauties and sports are not calculated to inspire confidence in us.'[172] Other posts also stressed the value of visual media for targeting a mass audience. Short films in local languages were recommended in the Far East, and Cairo suggested the return of cinema vans which had been widely used to bring newsreels to isolated areas during the War.[173]

Finally, the most important medium for reaching the illiterate masses was oral propaganda. This ranged from the most powerful medium of broadcasting to small-scale whispering campaigns. As in Europe, the BBC was the most important overt medium for the new policy and could openly carry the government line, in the form of ministerial statements, to the largest audience. There were also a number of local services. Some army stations, like Radio South East Asia Command (SEAC), were directed at British troops abroad but had built up large local audience. Other services broadcast in local languages under British direction, most notably Sharq al-Adna.[174] Covert oral propaganda was also considered. The Foreign Office and the SIS had begun to organize the covert oral dissemination of anti-communist propaganda through agents in Persia early in 1947. A more widespread programme was now advocated. One notable channel was the Brotherhood of Freedom, a secret anti-Nazi society established in Cairo by the British Ministry of Information in the Second World War. Modelled on the Muslim Brotherhood, which stressed religious plurality and a secular democratic political system, the Brotherhood of Freedom had spread across the region and had over 40,000 members by the end of the War. In the post-war years, the Brotherhood had continued to operate, promoting social reform, counteracting false ideas about the advantages of communism and stressing the need for mutual cooperation under the UN.[175] Although the Brotherhood's origins were widely known, it was highly regarded and its experience, local organization and contacts could, it was felt, once again serve the interests of Britain's propaganda policy.[176]

Although the IRD's principal role was the provision of anti-communist material to British information officers abroad, the Department was also given the task of briefing government spokesmen at home 'on Communist propaganda lines and replies thereto.' The new propaganda policy had, of course, been launched in a series of ministerial speeches and Bevin was keen that all official statements were to be 'framed with the new propaganda policy in mind.'[177] In addition to the material prepared within the IRD, information officers abroad were instructed to make use of anti-communist statements reaching them through the normal diplomatic channels or repeated in the media. In particular, they were to draw attention to statements by prominent members of the Government, the Labour Party and the TUC. Christopher Mayhew observed that speeches by government Ministers which were:

> automatically sent all over the world by the news agencies, foreign correspondents and the BBC, can put over in a few hours His Majesty's Government's attitude on an essential theme in a way that explanations by Heads of Missions and the work of our Information Officers in the field can seldom, if ever, achieve.[178]

But, as Mayhew indicated, if official statements were to play an important part in Britain's propaganda abroad, it was important to maintain a consistent line at home. Consequently, IRD material was distributed 'on a strictly personal and confidential basis' to Percy Cudlipp of the Cooperative Movement, Herbert Tracey, publicity Director for the TUC and the Labour Party, and Denis Healey, head of the Labour Party's International Department.[179] Mayhew also suggested that IRD material should be regularly sent to all Cabinet Ministers, and that the Foreign Office should circulate anti-communist speakers' notes or talking points to all Ministers and selected MPs. In a revealing insight into the remaining Cabinet divisions regarding the Soviet threat, the Minister of State, Hector McNeill, rejected Mayhew's suggestion for a general circulation: 'By all means let them have the stuff on a personal basis, but a general circulation would be highly dangerous.' Instead, the IRD drafted a stock of personal letters from Mayhew to selected senior Ministers enclosing a selection of the IRD's output, and urging its use in forthcoming speeches.[180] The first batch went to Attlee, Herbert Morrison and the Minister of Defence, A.V. Alexander. Attlee was, of course, 'glad to lend all the assistance in my power to our overseas anti-Communist propaganda campaign.'[181]

On 27 March 1948, British missions were informed that the IRD had begun work and that information staff abroad were free to begin implementing the new propaganda policy. In response to concerns expressed by several posts regarding the application of the new policy in their regions, they were cautioned that the new policy should be implemented 'with due regard to local political and general conditions' and that they should keep the Foreign Office informed of any activities, proposals and requirements. Those organizing the propaganda policy in the Foreign Office and the IRD remained aware that the Soviet propaganda machine was well established and highly organized, and they were careful not to become involved in a full-scale propaganda war before British defences were established. Shortly before the IRD began work, the IRD head, Ralph Murray, warned that 'we must have an efficient intelligence machine, and an efficient output machine before it is any good taking a leaf out of the Soviet book.'[182] Given the diversity and ambitious nature of some of the suggestions received from British missions abroad, it is apparent that, initially at least, the IRD wished to keep a close rein on the application of the new policy. By exercising such control the IRD was able to ensure consistency in British propaganda, while at the same time discouraging any action likely to provoke an unwanted reaction from the Soviets:

> You will appreciate...that it is most important that in our general presentation of Soviet policy, institutions, doctrine and practices the lines taken by different posts should be consistent. You should therefore be cautious as regards local interpretation of general issues and rely as far as possible on the output of material from here which though meagre to begin with will, it is hoped, be more satisfactory in the near future.[183]

Posts were told that they would shortly be receiving propaganda material in support of the new policy from three sources. They would receive a supply of basic papers from the IRD on various aspects of conditions in the Soviet Union and of events in Iron Curtain countries, designed to meet the requirements expressed in their comments on the new policy. In addition, their attention was drawn to the fact that, due to recent events in Czechoslovakia, attitudes towards communist organizations had crystallised in the Labour Party and the TUC and that there had been clear ministerial statements to this effect. Such information would reach them through the normal official and unofficial channels and should be given due prominence in their information work. Thirdly, they were informed that arrangements were being made with the COI for the LPS and their other services, both written and visual, to take account of the new policy in their official publicity material.[184]

Conclusion

Britain's new propaganda policy was developed and organized in the early months of 1948. In these formative months the guiding principles for Britain's Cold War propaganda policy were established, and the British Government's principal Cold War propaganda instrument, the Foreign Office Information Research Department, was created. The IRD's methods were informed by Foreign Office experience of propaganda in two World Wars. This experience dictated that the most effective propaganda was the truth and that propaganda of any kind was most likely to be believed if it was not seen to emanate from an official source. There were other parallels with propaganda during wartime. Some, although by no means all, of the IRD's early recruits came with experience of working in propaganda during the Second World War. Also, not surprisingly, many of the suggestions from British information staff abroad for channels and methods to be employed in the new propaganda policy were based on wartime experiences. The views of many information staff regarding the central role of the BBC in the new propaganda policy reflected a long-held assumption about the importance of accurate news as the backbone of British propaganda. This view was encapsulated by the founding father of the BBC, Lord Reith, in the aphorism, 'News is the shocktroops of propaganda.'[185] More specific suggestions – such as the employment of cinema vans, covert whispering campaigns and the use of the Brotherhood of Freedom in the Middle East – all owed a great deal to activities of the wartime Ministry of Information and the PWE.

These wartime antecedents, coupled with its rather unconventional methods, set the IRD apart from many in the Foreign Office, who continued to view propaganda with a certain degree of distaste. Although the Department was originally established to collate material from across Whitehall, and to prepare anti-communist material for dissemination through established channels, the Department's specific intelligence requirements, coupled with the reluctance of established government departments to become involved in propaganda work, meant that the IRD was soon forced to develop its own substantial intelligence and distribution facilities. The organizational structure which gave the IRD a central coordinating role for all British anti-communist propaganda, both overt and covert, also placed the Department in a very powerful position in Whitehall's Cold War apparatus. The seeds of the IRD's dramatic growth were planted early. One can see in these early months the roots of the IRD's emergence as a powerful independent force in the development and conduct of British Cold War policy.

However, Bevin resisted calls for a return to wartime methods of political warfare, and dictated that the new department should not be a resurrected PWE. He was careful to ensure that the Cold War propaganda apparatus was not modelled on wartime precedents, but was organized in such a manner that overall control rested with the Foreign Office. The propaganda policy itself was closely linked to Bevin's hopes for a Western Union defence. Propaganda designed to incite unrest behind the Iron Curtain was strictly forbidden. The new propaganda policy was principally designed to disabuse those individuals in the free world labouring under the illusion that the Soviet Union was a 'workers' paradise.' This anti-communist material was to be combined with the positive projection of British values and the benefits of progressive Western social democracy. Certain radical elements of the new propaganda policy created problems for the Foreign Office and were modified somewhat by British information officers in the field. Nevertheless, in the years that followed, the policy's aim – 'to give a lead to our friends abroad and help them in the anti-communist struggle' – would closely follow the development of collective defence, and involve British propagandists increasingly in the moral support of Britain's allies firstly as part of a 'Third Force' based on the Brussels Treaty Organization and later in an Atlantic alliance with the USA.

Notes

1 Minutes of meeting to brief Sir M. Peterson, 18 March 1946, N5572/605/38G, FO 371/56832, PRO.
2 Future Foreign Publicity Policy, CP(48) 8, 4 January 1948, CAB 129/23, PRO.
3 Philip M. Taylor, *British Propaganda in the Twentieth Century: Selling Democracy* (Edinburgh University Press, 1999); see, in particular, ch. 1 – 'Opening Pandora's Box,' pp. 5–29.
4 The view of IRD as a reconstituted Political Warfare Executive is a common misperception in the literature on British Cold War propaganda; see, in particular, Lashmar and Oliver, *Britain's Secret Propaganda War*; Philip M. Taylor, 'The Projection of Britain

Abroad, 1945–51', in J.W. Young and M. Dockrill (eds), *British Foreign Policy 1945–1956* (London: Macmillan, 1989) pp. 9–30; W.K. Wark, 'Coming in from the Cold: British Propaganda and Red Army Defectors 1945–1952', *International History Review*, 9, 1 (1987), pp. 48–72.

5 Future Foreign Publicity Policy, 4 January 1948, CP(48)8, CAB 129/23, PRO.

6 Cabinet conclusions, 8 January 1948, CM2(48), CAB 128/12, PRO.

7 The First Aim of British Foreign Policy, 4 January 1948, CP(48) 6, CAB 129/23, PRO. For detailed examinations of Bevin's Western Union strategy, see Kent and Young, 'The "Western Union" Concept', pp. 166–92; J. Kent and J.W. Young, 'British Policy Overseas: The "Third Force" and the Origins of NATO – In Search of a New Perspective', in B. Heuser and R. O'Neill (eds), *Securing Peace in Europe, 1945–62* (London: Macmillan, 1992), pp. 41–61; G. Warner, 'Britain and Europe in 1948: The View from the Cabinet', in J. Becker and F. Kniping (eds), *Power in Europe? Great Britain, France, Italy and Germany in a Post-War World, 1945–1950* (Berlin: De Gruyter, 1986), pp. 27–44.

8 Future Foreign Publicity Policy, 4 January 1948, CP(48)8, CAB 129/23, PRO.

9 *Ibid.*

10 *Ibid.*

11 Conclusions of Cabinet meeting held on 8 January 1948, CM 2 (48), CAB 128/12, PRO.

12 On the background to Attlee's speech, see C. Mayhew, *A War of Word: A Cold War Witness* (London: I.B. Tauris, 1998), pp. 21–2. See also Kent and Young, 'British Policy Overseas: The "Third Force" and the Origins of NATO', pp. 48–9.

13 Broadcast by the Rt. Hon. C.R. Attlee, MP, 3 January 1948, Box – 'Anti-Communist Propaganda,' International Department Papers, The Labour Party Archives, NMLH.

14 *Ibid.*

15 See, in particular, *The Times*, 5 January 1948. Significantly, although anti-communism was widely covered only *The Economist* gave prominence to the 'Third Force' aspect: 'Freedom and Order,' *The Economist*, 10 January 1948.

16 Mayhew, *A War of Words*, pp. 21–2.

17 Russia Committee meeting, 15 January 1948, N765/765/G38, FO 371/71687, PRO.

18 Speech by Herbert Morrison at meeting of East Midlands Regional Council of the Labour Party, 11 January 1948, Box – Anti-Communist Propaganda', International Department, Labour Party Archives, NMLH.

19 *Parliamentary Debates: Commons*, 5th series, vol. 446, 22 January 1948.

20 Kent and Young, 'British Policy Overseas: "The Third Force" and the Origins of NATO', p. 51. On the subject of government–press consensus, Tony Shaw writes that 'It is difficult to speak of a free-thinking press devising its approach to foreign affairs entirely independently of government by early 1948', in 'The British Popular Press and the Early Cold War', *History*, 83, 269 (1998), pp. 66–85.

21 *Parliamentary Debates: Commons*, 5th series, vol. 446, 22 January 1948, col. 423.

22 S. Ball (ed.), *Parliament and Politics in the Age of Churchill and Attlee: The Headlam Diaries 1935–1951* (Cambridge: Cambridge University Press, 1999), p. 539.

23 Kent and Young, 'British Policy Overseas: The "Third Force" and the Origins of NATO', p. 51.

24 *Parliamentary Debates: Commons*, 5th series, vol. 446, 22 January 1948.

25 Russia Committee meeting, 15 January 1948, N765/765/G38, FO 371/71687, PRO.

26 It should be noted that the Minutes of the Russia Committee meetings are more detailed than Cabinet Minutes, and include, for example, the names of speakers.

27 Russia Committee meeting, 15 January 1948, N765/765/G38, FO 371/71687, PRO.

28 *Ibid.*

29 Rumours of a planned programme of communist subversion and sabotage in the Ruhr began to circulate in January 1948; see S. Ollivant, 'Protocol M', in D.A.Charters and M.A.J. Tugwell (eds), *Deception Operations: Studies in the East West Context* (London: Brassey's, 1990), pp. 275–96.

30 Russia Committee meeting, 15 January 1948, N765/765/G38, FO 371/71687, PRO.

31 *The Memoirs of Lord Gladwyn* (London:Weidenfeld & Nicolson, 1972), p. 213.

32 B. Jones, *The Russia Complex: The British Labour Party and the Soviet Union* (Manchester: Manchester University Press, 1977), pp. 176–9.

33 *Ibid*. E. Barker, *The British between the Superpowers, 1945–50* (London: Macmillan, 1983), pp.105–6.

34 The Threat to Western Civilisation, CP(48)47, 3 March 1948, CAB 129/25, PRO.

35 Conclusions of Cabinet meeting held on 8 January 1948, CM 2 (48), CAB 128/12, PRO.

36 Conclusions of Cabinet meeting held on 5 March 1948, CM19(48), CAB 128/12, PRO.

37 *Ibid*.

38 Barker, *The British Between the Superpowers*, pp. 107–8; For COS staff views, see also R. Murray Minute, 6 May 1948, PR290/137/13G, FO 1110/38, PRO.

39 Kent and Young, 'The "Western Union" Concept and British Defence Policy', p. 178.

40 Lucas and Morris, 'A Very British Crusade: The Information Research Department and the Beginning of the Cold War', in Aldrich, (ed.), *British Intelligence, Strategy and the Cold War,* p. 101.

41 Anti-Communist Propaganda, undated Minute of meeting held on 12 March 1948, CAB 21/2745, PRO.

42 'Political Warfare,' Memo by Norman Brook, 10 March 1948, approved by Attlee, CAB 21/2745, PRO.

43 Anti-Communist Propaganda, undated Minute of meeting held on 12 March 1948, CAB 21/2745.

44 Anti-Communist Publicity: Memo by the Secretary of State for Foreign Affairs, 30 April 1948, GEN231/1, FO 1110/9; see also the Cabinet Secretary's brief for the Prime Minister for the first meeting of the Cabinet Committee on anti-communist propaganda, 'Anti-Communist Propaganda', Memo by Norman Brook, 10 May 1948, CAB 21/2745, PRO.

45 *Ibid*.

46 Anti-Communist Publicity: Memo by the Secretary of State for Foreign Affairs, 30 April 1948, GEN231/1, FO 1110/9, PRO. For minutes and papers of Ministerial Committee on anti-communist propaganda, see CAB 130/37, PRO.

47 Anti-Communist Publicity: Memo by the Secretary of State for Foreign Affairs, 30 April 1948, GEN231/1, FO 1110/9, PRO.

48 Future Foreign Publicity Policy, 4 January 1948, CP(48)8, CAB 129/23, PRO.

49 Russia Committee meeting, 29 January 1948, N1372/765/G38, FO 371/71687, PRO.

50 Minutes of Russia Committee meeting, 29 January 1948, N1372/765/G38, FO 371/71687; Office Circular no. 21, Information Research Department, 25 February 1948, XS03/95H(1/48), FO 366/2759, PRO.

51 Notes of First Meeting of Working Party on 'Spiritual Aspects of Western Union,' 19 February 1948, P2476/1474/950; Warner to Sargent, 13 February 1948, P1474/1474/950, FO 953/144, PRO. For a personal insight into the working party see Lockhart's diary entry for 20 February 1948:

> Lunched today at Savoy after attending a fantastic meeting at the FO on aspects of Western Union other than political and strategical. After an hour and a half's argle-bargle, after which I had to leave, we had just cleared point one on an agenda of twelve subjects.
>
> > K. Young (ed.), *The Diaries of Sir Robert Bruce Lockhart,* vol. 2, *1939–1965* (London: Macmillan, 1980) p. 648

52 Circular telegram no. 6, 23 January 1948, PR1/1/913G, FO 1110/1, PRO.

53 Reference on the Information Research Department for the Foreign Office Order Book, 22 March 1951, FO 1110/383, PRO.

54 Russia Committee meeting, 15 January 1948, N765/765/38G, FO 371/71687, PRO.

55 C. Mayhew, *Time to Explain: An Autobiography* (London: Hutchinson, 1987), pp. 109–10. Burgess's position in the IRD was first revealed in B. Page, D. Leitch and P. Knightley, *Philby: The Spy Who Betrayed a Generation* (London: Andre Deutsch, 1968), p. 203. Their account is very similar to Mayhew's and he may well have been their source for this information.

56 A. Boyle, *The Climate of Treason* (London: Coronet edition, 1980); P. Lashmar, 'Covert in Glory,' *New Statesman and Society* (3 March 1995), pp. 14–15; Lashmar and Oliver, *Britain's Secret Propaganda War*, pp. 37–8.

57 John Cloake, letter to author, October 2002.

58 Y. Modin, *My Five Cambridge Friends* (London: Headline, 1994), pp. 135–65; C. Andrew and O. Gordievsky, *KGB: The Inside Story of Its Foreign Operations from Lenin to Gorbachev* (London: Sceptre, 1991), pp. 398–402.

59 Soviet Monitor, 7 April 1948, AN1614/1195/G45, FO 371/680684, PRO. I am grateful to Dr Sheila Kerr for drawing my attention to this document. See S. Kerr, 'The Secret Hotline to Moscow: Donald Maclean and the Berlin Crisis of 1948', in A. Deighton (ed.), *Britain and the First Cold War* (London: Macmillan, 1990), pp. 71–87.

60 Minutes of Western European Information Officers Conference, 12–14 September 1951, PR121/7, FO 1110/458, PRO.

61 Mayhew, *Time to Explain*, p. 109.

62 Circular no. 6, 23 January 1948, PR1/1/913G, FO 1110/1, PRO.

63 Mayhew, *A War of Words*, pp. 35–7.

64 GEN231/3rd meeting, Confidential annex, 19 December 1949, Anti-Communist Policy and machinery, CAB 130/37, PRO.

65 FCO Historians, *IRD: Origins and Establishment of the Foreign Office Information Research Department 1946–1948*, History Notes no. 9 (London: FCO/LRD, 1995), p. 9.

66 *Ibid.*

67 Murray to Group Captain D.C. Stapleton, MoD, 14 May 1948, PR290/290G, FO 1110/38, PRO.

68 John Cloake, letter to author, October 2002.

69 IRD Office Memo, T.S. Tull, 12 November 1952, PR89/58, FO 1110/516, PRO.

70 Sir Peter Wilkinson, letter to author, November 1996.

71 *Ibid.* John Cloake, letter to author, October 2002.

72 H.A. Caccia to J.I.C. Crombie, Treasury, 15 January 1948; C.F.A. Warner Minute, 9 February 1948, XS03/95H (5/48)G, FO 366/2759; Report on the work of the Information Research Department, 1 August to 31 December 1949, PR110/5, FO 1110/359, PRO.

73 C. Parrott, *The Serpent and the Nightingale* (London: Faber and Faber, 1977); R. Conquest, 'In Celia's Office: Orwell and the Cold War', *Times Literary Supplement*, 21 August 1998. For a useful profile of Conquest, see 'Scourge and Poet', *The Guardian*, 15 February 2003.

74 Report on the work of Information Research Department, 1 August 1949–31 December 1949, PR110/5, FO 1110/359, PRO. Among those proposed but not recruited were Harman Grisewood controller of the BBC Third Programme and the historian Elisabeth Barker: Young (ed.), *The Diaries of Sir Robert Bruce Lockhart*, vol. 2, p. 648.

75 Mary Tucker, wife of H.H. Tucker, letter to author, November 1996. H.H. Tucker died on 30 August 1996.

76 IRD official from 1949 to 1950, letter to author, 4 October 1996.

77 Aubrey Essex, letter to author, January 2003.

78 John Cloake, letter to author, October 2002.

79 Aubrey Essex, letter to author, January 2003.

80 Fay Weldon, *Auto Da Fay* (London: Flamingo, 2002), pp. 240–4.

81 H.A. Caccia to J.I.C. Crombie, Treasury, 15 January 1948, XS03/95H (5/48)G, FO 366/2759, PRO.

82 Walter Stewart Roberts, Minute, undated, XS03/954 (5/48)G, FO 366/2759, PRO.

83 C.F.A. Warner to J. Wardley, Treasury, 10 February 1948, XS03/95H (7/48)G, FO 366/2759, PRO.

84 W.S. Roberts, to D.B. Pitblade, Treasury, 22 January 1948, XS03/95H (5/48)G, FO 366/2759, PRO.

85 'Reorganisation of Information Research Department', Memo by R. Murray, 21 September 1948, XS03/95H (10/48)G, FO 366/2759, PRO.

86 Information Research Department's Finances, 9 January 1950, FO 1110/128, PRO.

87 Future Foreign Publicity Policy, 4 January 1948, C.P.(48)8, CAB 129/23, PRO.

88 Office Circular no. 21 Information Research Department, O. Sargent, 25 February 1948, XS03/95H (1/48), FO 366/2759, PRO.
89 Progress Report: Information Research Department, 1 January–31 July, 1949, FO 1110/277, PRO.
90 FO to HM Representatives, Circular telegram no. 6, 23 January 1948; FO to Helsingfors, no. 11, 23 January 1948, and to Warsaw, Prague, Budapest, Bucharest, Sofia, Belgrade, PR1/1/913G, FO 1110/1, PRO.
91 Prague to FO, no. 11, 7 February 1948, PR2/1/913G, FO 1110/1, PRO.
92 Foreign Office to HM Representatives, Circular Telegram no. 10, 3 March 1948, PR40/1/913G, FO 1110/2, PRO.
93 Foreign Office to Prague, no. 262, 10 March 1948; also to Warsaw, Budapest, Bucharest, Sofia and Belgrade, PR64/57/913G, FO 1110/25, PRO.
94 Intelligence Requirements, IRD, October 1949, PR2840/9/G, FO 1110/187, PRO.
95 Progress Report, Information Research Department, 1 January–31 July 1949, FO 1110/277, PRO.
96 IRD basic papers may be found in class FO 975, PRO. 'The real conditions in Soviet Russia', FO 975/1; 'Conditions in the New Soviet Colonies: The Police States of Eastern Europe', FO 975/2; 'Labour and the Trade Unions in the Soviet Union', FO 975/5; 'Peasant Collectivisation in Areas under Soviet Control', FO 975/9; 'Daily Life in a Communist State', FO 975/17, PRO.
97 'The Real Conditions in Soviet Russia', FO 975/1, PRO.
98 'Essence of Soviet Foreign Policy', FO 975/10; 'Communist Conquest of the Baltic States', FO 975/12; 'The Facts of Soviet Expansionism', FO 975/8, PRO.
99 M. Peterson, Moscow to Bevin, 24 March 1948, Minute by C.R.A. Rae, 6 April 1948, N3820/207/38, FO 371/71670; 'The Practice of Stalinism', FO 975/21; 'The Foundations of Stalinism', FO 975/22, PRO.
100 Partial distribution list in a Minute by C.R.A. Rae, 27 April 1948, N3820/207/38, FO 371/71670, PRO.
101 Lucas and Morris, 'A Very British Crusade', p. 97. The first 19 issues of the Digest can be found in FO 371/71713 and FO 371/71714, PRO.
102 FCO Historians, *IRD: Origins and Establishment*, p. 13.
103 R. Murray, Memo, August 1948, FO 366/3759, PRO. On the Intel system, see 'Purpose of the Intel', Memo by M.G.L. Joy, 11 November 1947, W8450, FO 371/65578, PRO.
104 McNeill Memo, 12 May 1948, PR472/57/913, FO 1110/128, PRO.
105 Warner Minute, 16 June 1948, PR472/57/913, FO 1110/28, PRO.
106 FCO Historians, *IRD: Origins and Establishment*, p. 9, quoted from FO 975/14, PRO. The extract in the FCO History Note does not include the last line regarding detaching the cover sheet. Another version of the cover sheet instructions may be found in: R.J. Aldrich (ed.), *Espionage, Security and Intelligence in Britain, 1945–1970* (Manchester: Manchester University Press, 1998), p. 179.
107 Colonial Office Circular despatch, 'Publicity Policy in Regard to Communism', 2 April 1948, FO 1110/5, PRO.
108 Lucas and Morris, 'A Very British Crusade', p.105; Anti-Communist Propaganda, 2nd Meeting, 22 July 1948, GEN231, CAB 130/37, PRO.
109 Committee on Colonial Information Policy Meeting, 1 October 1948, PR826/23/913G, FO 1110/21, PRO.
110 FCO Historians, *IRD: Origins and Establishment*, p. 14; Mayhew to Secretary of State, 27 November 1948, PR1165/23/913, FO 1110/22, PRO.
111 Colonial Office Circular despatch, 'Publicity Policy in Regard to Communism,' 2 April 1948, FO 1110/5, PRO.
112 Anti-Communist Propaganda: Liaison between Foreign Office and Chiefs of Staff, Memo by the Secretary of the Cabinet, 31 March 1948, GEN231/2, CAB 130/37, PRO.
113 Anti-Communist Propaganda, Memo by the Secretary of the Cabinet, March 1948, PR137/137/913, F1110/38, PRO.
114 *Ibid.*

115 Inter-Service Committee on Propaganda Dissemination, Minutes of meeting held 4 May 1948, PR313/137/913, FO 1110/38, PRO.
116 T. Fife-Clark, *The Central Office of Information*, (London: Allen & Unwin, 1970); Cmnd.7567, *Annual Report of the Central Office of Information for the Year 1947–48* (London: HMSO, November 1948).
117 'Publicity Policy in Regard to Communism in Relation to COI Standard Services', PR173/1/913G, FO 1110/5, PRO.
118 Murray Minute, 19 February 1948, PR139/139/13G, FO 1110/39, PRO.
119 Memo by Murray, August 1948, XSO3/95H, FO 366/2759, PRO.
120 Murray Minute, 2 March 1948, PR139/139/913, FO 1110/39, PRO.
121 Murray Minute, 19 February 1948, PR139/139/G, FO 1110/39, PRO.
122 Murray Minute, 2 March 1948, PR139/139/913, FO 1110/39, PRO.
123 Programme of Anti-Communist Articles, PR797/375/913, FO 1110/60, PRO.
124 R. Fraser to Hadfield, 30 November 1948, PR1226/1/913G, FO 1110/15, PRO.
125 Murray Minute, August 1948, XSO3/95H, FO 366/2759, PRO.
126 Memo from Barnes to Lovell, 20 October 1948, PR922/375/913, FO 1110/60, PRO.
127 Maclaren (IRD) Minute, 23 March 1949, PR846/846/913, FO 1110/123, PRO; G.W. Aldington to M. Lovell (COI), 28 April 1949, P2807/53/950, INF 12/418. (This document, which relates IRD's wish for signed articles on LPS, is retained and therefore unavailable at the PRO. I am grateful to Margaret Bryan of the FCO Records and Historical Services for providing me with a copy.)
128 Anti-Communist Propaganda, Memo for the Prime Minister, by Norman Brook, 17 April 1948, CAB 21/2745, PRO.
129 Aldrich (ed.), *Espionage, Security and Intelligence in Britain*, p. 229.
130 Memo for Sir Edward Bridges, 20 April 1948, CAB 21/2745, PRO.
131 Quoted in Aldrich (ed.), *Espionage, Security and Intelligence in Britain*, pp. 191–2.
132 Memo for Sir Edward Bridges, 20 April 1948, CAB 21/2745, PRO.
133 Anti-Communist Propaganda, Memo by the Secretary of the Cabinet, March 1948, PR137/137/G, FO 1110/38, PRO.
134 Minute by Warner, 5 June 1948, PR358/1/913G, FO 1110/9, PRO.
135 Memo for Sir Edward Bridges, 20 April 1948, CAB 21/2745, PRO.
136 FCO Historians, *IRD: Origins and Establishment*, p. 7; Murray, Minute, August 1948, FO 366/2759, PRO.
137 Aubrey Essex, letter to author, January 2003.
138 FCO Historians, *IRD: Origins and Establishment*, p. 17; Warner to Mr Hadfield, COI, 30 November 1948, PR1226/1/913G, FO 1110/15, PRO.
139 Report on the work of the Information Research Department, 1 August–31 December 1949, PR110/5, FO 1110/359, PRO.
140 Adam Watson, telephone interview with author, August 2003.
141 H.A. Caccia, Minute, 23 September 1948, XS03/95H (10/48)G, FO 366/2759, PRO.
142 Information Section, British Embassy Rangoon to IPD, 23 July 1948; IRD to Information Section, Rangoon, 2 September 1948, PR612/57/913, FO 1110/29, PRO.
143 'Reorganisation of Information Research Department', R. Murray, 21 September 1948; Warner, Minute, 21 September 1948, XS03/95H(10/48), FO 366/2759, PRO. A review of Foreign Office research facilities in 1949 recommended that the two departments should remain separate but stated that it would be beneficial if the intelligence sections of FORD and IRD could share a room or at least be situated in close proximity: Minutes of meeting to discuss use made by departments of FORD, 7 September 1949, XS03/28H(15/49), FO 366/2823, PRO. Remarkably FORD and IRD remained in separate buildings until 1973, when the research sections of the two departments were finally merged. Interview with former IRD official, January 1996.
144 'Reorganisation of Research Department', August 1949, XS03/28H(15/49), FO 366/2823, PRO.
145 Warner, Minute, 2 September 1949, XS03/28H(15/49), FO 366/2823, PRO.
146 Progress Report: Information Research Department 1 January–31 July 1948, Ralph Murray 13 August 1949, FO 1110/277; Intelligence section figures in 'Reorganisation of

Research Department.' FO Memo, undated, *circa* August 1949, XSO3/28H (15/49), FO 366/2823, PRO.

147 Anecdotal evidence suggests indicates that the IRD continued to expand almost unhindered until 1973. At its peak in the 1960s and early 1970s it became the largest department in the Foreign Office with a staff of up to 300, and an annual budget of over £1 million. Interview with former IRD official, January 1996; interview with Brian Crozier, February 1997.

148 'Future Foreign Publicity Policy', 4 January 1948, CP(48)8, CAB 129/23, PRO.

149 Circular telegram no. 6, 23 January 1948, PR1/1/913G, FO 1110/1, PRO.

150 Circular Telegram no. 6, 23 January 1948, PR1/1/913G, FO 1110/1, PRO.

151 FO to Middle East missions, no. 6, Saving, 23 January 1948, PR 1/1/913G, FO 1110/1, PRO. 'Russia in the Middle East,' Publicity Directive, 17 October 1946, GN1/5 Part A, INF 12/61, PRO; see ch. 1.

152 FO to Helsingfors, Warsaw, Prague, Budapest, Bucharest, Sofia, Belgrade, Moscow, 23 January 1948, PR1/1/913G, FO 1110/1, PRO.

153 Jack Troutbeck, British Middle East Office, Cairo to Warner, 19 March 1948, PR136/1/913G, FO 1110/4, PRO.

154 British Embassy, Lima to Foreign Office, 29 March 1948, PR134/1/913G, FO 1110/4, PRO.

155 Despatch from Caracas, 19 March 1948, FO 1110/5, quoted in FCO Historians, IRD: Origins and Establishment, p. 8.

156 'Russia in the Middle East.' Publicity Directive, 17 October 1946, GN1/5 Part A, INF 12/61, PRO.

157 Prague to Foreign Office, .5 February 1948, PR2/1/913, Belgrade to Foreign Office, 17 February 1948, PR16/1/913, FO 1110/1, PRO.

158 Belgrade to Foreign Office, 17 February 1948, PR16/1/913G, FO 1110/1, PRO. See also Sofia to Foreign Office, 16 February 1948, PR3/1/913, Prague to Foreign Office, 5 February 1948, PR2/1/913G, FO 1110/1, PRO.

159 Helsinki to Foreign Office, 9 February 1948, PR4/1/913G, FO 1110/1, PRO.

160 Prague to Foreign Office, 5 February 1948, PR2/1/913G, FO 1110/1, PRO.

161 Madrid to Foreign Office, 11 February 1948, PR9/1/913G, FO 1110/1, PRO.

162 V. Mallet, British Embassy, Rome to Bevin, 24 February 1948, PR24/1/913G, FO 1110/1, PRO.

163 J.E. Cowburn, British Embassy, Paris to Bevin, 9 March 1948, PR60/1/913G, FO 1110/3, PRO.

164 Jack Troutbeck, British Middle East Office, Cairo to Warner, 19 March 1948, PR136/1/913G, FO 1110/4, PRO.

165 'Anti-Communist Measures', H. Mack, British Embassy, Baghdad, to Foreign Office, 17 March 1948, PR138/1/913, FO 1110/4, PRO.

166 *Ibid.*

167 Sir R. Campbell, British Embassy, Cairo to Foreign Office, 9 March 1948, PR58/1/913, FO 1110/3, PRO.

168 'Anti-Communist Measures', H. Mack.

169 John Cloake, letter to author, October 2002.

170 'Anti-Communist Measures', H. Mack.

171 Rangoon, to Foreign Office, 17 March 1948, PR82/1/913, FO 1110/3; Batavia to Foreign Office, 25 March 1948, PR126/1/913G, FO 1110/4, PRO.

172 'Anti-Communist Measures', H. Mack.

173 Batavia to Foreign Office, 25 March 1948, PR126/1/913G, FO 1110/4, PRO; Sir R. Campbell, British Embassy, Cairo to Foreign Office, 9 March 1948, PR58/1/913, FO 1110/3, PRO.

174 'Anti-Communist Measures', H. Mack.

175 The Brotherhood of Freedom was set up by the renowned travel writer Freya Stark, who worked for the Ministry of Information in the Middle East during the Second World War. For a detailed account, see Stark's biography: Jane Fletcher Geniesse, *Freya Stark: Passionate Nomad*, (London: Chatto & Windus, 1999), pp. 261–74, 287–306. For the Brotherhood's post-War role, see Memo by R.W. Fay, 29 April 1947, J2166/164/16, FO 371/63033, PRO.

176 For discussion of utility of Brotherhood of Freedom, see Sir R.Campbell, British Embassy, Cairo to Foreign Office, 9 March 1948, PR58/1/913, FO 1110/3; Warner to Troutbeck, BMEO Cairo, 4 May 1948, and Minutes on file, PR136/1/913, FO 1110/4, PRO.
177 Anti-Communist Publicity: Memo by the Secretary of State for Foreign Affairs, 30 April 1948, GEN231/1, FO 1110/9, PRO.
178 Mayhew Memo for Secretary of State, 9 July 1948, PR445/142/913, FO 1110/41, PRO.
179 P. Weiler, *British Labour and the Cold War* (Stanford, CA: Stanford University Press, 1988), p. 216; Mayhew Memo for Secretary of State, 9 July 1948, PR445/142/913, FO 1110/41, PRO.
180 Mayhew Memo, 24 March 1948, PR142/142/913; Mayhew Memo for Secretary of State, 9 July 1948; Warner Minute, 13 July 1948, PR445/142/913, FO 1110/41, PRO.
181 Attlee to Mayhew, 20 July 1948, PR445/142/913G, FO 1110/41, PRO.
182 Ralph Murray Minute, 18 March 1948, PR 148/1/913G, FO 1110/4, PRO.
183 Circular Telegram no. 13, 27 March 1948, PR 147/1/913G, FO 1110/4, PRO.
184 *Ibid.*
185 Taylor, *British Propaganda in the Twentieth Century*, p. 234.

3 Building a concerted counter-offensive

Cooperation with other powers, 1948–50

> I feel that the major danger is not that we might have our hands tied too much by working in cooperation, but that, by working in isolation, we should fail to make our influence sufficiently felt in building up a concerted counter-offensive. Other countries need our moral encouragement in the feeble efforts most of them put up to defend themselves against communist political warfare.
>
> Christopher Mayhew, May 1949[1]

Cooperation with like-minded people to provide a coordinated response to communist propaganda was a primary objective of Britain's new propaganda policy. Although the policy was conceived as a distinctly British social democratic response to communist propaganda, it was not solely concerned with the defence of Britain and the colonies against communist propaganda and subversion. The threat of communist subversion in Europe and the Middle East, coupled with Bevin's strategy for Western Union defence, meant that, in addition to responding to communist propaganda attacks on Britain, the new propaganda policy also sought to consolidate the forces of anti-communism in the free world. Moreover, as Mayhew suggested, in seeking to build a concerted counter-offensive, British policy-makers had little faith in the ability of the rest of the free world to provide an effective response to communist propaganda. It was, therefore, up to Britain to 'give a moral lead to the forces of anti-communism in Europe and Asia.'[2] In addition to defending Britain against communist propaganda, the Cabinet paper which set out Britain's 'Future Foreign Publicity Policy', stated that Britain should provide an arsenal of anti-communist propaganda for its allies: '[W]e must see to it that our friends in Europe and elsewhere are armed with the facts and the answers to Russian propaganda. If we do not provide this ammunition they will not get it from any other source.'[3]

Once the new Foreign Office Information Research Department was established, its head, Ralph Murray, turned his attention to these wider aspects of the new propaganda policy. In reviewing the progress of the new propaganda policy in August 1948, Murray observed:

> We should be more active in our contacts with the Americans... And surely we should be approaching the Dominion Governments soon, tricky though they may be. And we should surely be exploring the potentialities of cooperation with our co-signatories of the Five-Power Treaty, which presumably must come some day. I cannot tackle these issues as if they are weary side-issues, which they are not.[4]

The liaison envisaged by Murray would involve Britain in cooperation at various levels with the 'forces of anti-communism' abroad. At the most basic level, cooperation was a one-way street in which the Foreign Office provided foreign governments with the product of the IRD's research. In this case, the governments involved were themselves the target of the IRD's propaganda; information was provided in the hope that they might be influenced to adopt a more serious view of the communist threat. Closer cooperation was afforded to those governments such as the Brussels' Powers which largely shared Britain's perception of the Soviet threat. These countries were offered the product of Britain's anti-communist propaganda policy, they were also informed of the existence of the anti-communist propaganda policy, as well as the role and something of the methods of the IRD. At this level, it was hoped that cooperation would involve a reciprocal exchange of propaganda material and possibly the adoption of similar policies and methods by the governments involved. Yet, even at this level, although governments were informed about the IRD's indirect methods, details of the IRD's activities in their countries were not revealed to them – the benefits of cooperation were weighed against the overarching concern that the IRD's existing information activities should not be in any way curtailed or undermined. This concern was also behind Foreign Office reticence towards efforts to establish a multilateral response to communist propaganda through the Brussels Treaty and NATO. On practical grounds, the Foreign Office had no faith in the ability to conduct effective propaganda through an international committee, particularly as Britain was the only European nation with an established information apparatus. It was also felt that Britain's anti-communist propaganda would be blunted if exposed to the consideration and possible veto of her European allies. When an international information service was finally established under NATO, British officials ensured that they were in a position to provide NATO with anti-communist material and exert an influence over NATO propaganda policy. At the same time, the IRD continued its own anti-communist activities within the NATO countries.

In marked contrast to the various degrees of cooperation extended to other powers, the US Government was taken entirely into Britain's confidence regarding the new propaganda policy, the methods adopted, the activities undertaken and the development of cooperation with other Powers. Despite serious concerns in the Foreign Office about the effectiveness of US propaganda, and the state of the US propaganda machine, the level of cooperation between the Foreign Office and the State Department's information apparatus was far above any other bilateral cooperation Britain established in the field of anti-communist propaganda. Cooperation was instituted between London and Washington and the exchange of propaganda material began shortly after the launch of the new propaganda policy. Cooperation was encouraged between the BBC and the VOA and, in contrast to IRD's relationship with other Powers, cooperation was also extended to the field. British and US information officers around the world were given broad discretion to develop cooperative strategies with each other. It was established at an early stage that Britain and the USA would not seek to combine their propaganda output, and the policy of cooperation would be characterized by Britain and the USA aiming to 'shoot at the same target from different angles.'

'Shooting at the same target from different angles': the new propaganda policy and cooperation with the USA

In conception at least, the new propaganda policy appeared to reject cooperation with the USA. The Cabinet paper on 'Future Foreign Publicity Policy' stated that it was up to the British 'as Europeans and as a social democratic government, and not the Americans, to give the lead in spiritual, moral and political sphere' to the forces of democracy in Europe. British social democracy was to be the rallying point for the new policy. The inroads of communism were to be opposed by a 'Third Force' comprising 'all the democratic elements...which are anti-Communist and, at the same time, genuinely progressive and reformist, believing in freedom, planning and social justice.' The paper also stated that in the interest of balance, as well as decrying totalitarian communism, the new policy would attack the 'inefficiency, the social injustice and moral weakness of unrestrained capitalism.' Although it cautioned that in practice this should not involve attacking or appearing to attack the Commonwealth countries or the USA, the principles of British social democracy were to be held up as offering the best and most efficient way of life.' [5]

There were also pragmatic concerns regarding the effectiveness of US propaganda, and the intentions of US propagandists. 'Future Foreign Publicity Policy' criticised US propaganda for emphasizing the strength of international communism, as this tended to 'scare and unbalance the anti-communists while heartening fellow-travellers and encouraging the communists to bluff more extravagantly.'[6] Christopher Warner was more forthright in a letter to Sir John Balfour, the British Ambassador in Washington. 'On the whole,' he wrote, 'the Americans seem to be very ham-handed in their anti-Communist and anti-Soviet publicity.'[7] Warner was particularly worried that the USA might employ propaganda to provoke subversive action in the Soviet satellites, something which was expressly forbidden under Britain's new propaganda policy.[8] Warner also doubted the reliability of the intelligence on which the Americans based their propaganda. It is axiomatic that effective propaganda is dependent on a steady flow of reliable intelligence. Although the USA had access to a large volume of intelligence, Warner felt that an agreement to exchange information was liable to 'open the floodgates' and let through a volume of information 'the reliability of which might sometimes be in doubt, and which would in any event be too great for us to cope with at the present stage.' It was, Warner felt, better to develop Britain's own sources of information.[9] At a meeting of the Russia Committee, Warner suggested that the right general policy 'would be to exchange information on publicity with the Americas wherever appropriate.' But, he stated, 'it would be wrong to have a general agreement to consult them and to take the same line. We must keep our hands free.'[10] At the same time, Warner felt Britain could use its influence to encourage the Americans to be more subtle in their propaganda.[11]

Despite these reservations, the US Government was provided with details of the new propaganda policy at the earliest opportunity. In February 1948, W.P.N. Edwards, head of the British Information Service (BIS) in the USA, discussed Britain's new propaganda policy with Bill Stone, the outgoing head of the State Department information programme. Meanwhile, the incoming head of the State Department's overseas information programme, George Allen, stopped in

London, on his way back to Washington to take up his new post, to discuss British and US propaganda policies. In these discussions it was not, however, intended to reveal the new propaganda policy to the Americans in its entirety. The Foreign Office was unsure about how the US Government might react to the new direction in British foreign policy, in particular Bevin's plans for a British-led Western Union. Significantly, when a copy of the Cabinet paper entitled the 'First Aim of British Foreign Policy' was sent to the Americans in mid-January, the section on the 'Third Force' was omitted.[12] Similarly, when officials in Washington were asked to discuss the new propaganda policy with the State Department, they were warned that, given the proposed attack on capitalism, care was required when outlining the details of the new propaganda policy to US officials. Warner noted that certain expressions and phrases in the 'Future Foreign Publicity Policy', and the subsequent circular telegram, had been included for 'rather special reasons' and would require 'rather special explanation to our United States friends.' It was felt, therefore, that the Americans should not be shown a verbatim copy of the telegram.[13]

However, as a result of confusion between the Washington Embassy and the Foreign Office, the Americans were shown rather more of the details of the new propaganda policy than was originally intended. Early in February, Warner met with information officers from the American Embassy in London, Gallman and Charles. They informed Warner that, in Washington, Edwards had shown Stone a document outlining Britain's new propaganda policy. In return, Gallman and Charles gave Warner a copy of a new US directive detailing their response to communist propaganda. Warner mistakenly believed that Edwards had shown Stone the circular telegram in its entirety. He was somewhat taken aback by this but, believing that the damage had already been done, and feeling somewhat obligated by the Americans' candour, he gave them a copy of the Foreign Office circular telegram detailing the new propaganda policy in full.[14] In fact, Edwards had not shown Stone the whole of this telegram. In a letter, which was not received in London until after Warner had entertained Gallman and Charles, Edwards wrote that he had taken care to omit 'any controversial aspect' from the document given to Stone.[15] By this time it was too late: in the bureaucratic confusion Britain's new propaganda policy had been revealed in full to representatives of the US Government, only one month after it was presented to the British Cabinet.

To Warner's surprise and relief, the Americans were remarkably unconcerned by the anti-capitalist aspect of the new policy. In fact, US officials enthused about Britain's plans and felt that the distinctive approach could compliment their own attempts to counter communist propaganda. George Allen told Warner that there would be 'considerable advantages if [Britain's] shots came from a different angle from the American, so long as they both landed in the same target.'[16] In Washington, Edwards was surprised by a similar lack of concern shown by Stone. It was, Stone felt, only natural that Britain should preach concepts of social democracy, in which the majority of Britons believed, just as the State Department must extol those capitalist virtues which the majority of Americans favoured.[17] The independent approach in Britain's new propaganda policy did not dissuade US officials from proposing cooperation. Stone informed Edwards that he was anxious to develop 'the maximum cooperation between us in working out and implementing the new policy.'[18] In both London and Washington, these first meetings following the launch of the new propaganda policy concluded with suggestions from the US representatives that senior officials from each country's information programme should meet again soon to exchange views with regard to future cooperation. In the meantime, any formal cooperation was eschewed in favour of a general exchange of information between officials in London and Washington and, if appropriate, information officers in the field. The shape of the policy was agreed by Warner and Allen and was to follow the lines of existing cooperation on political matters:

> [T]hat we should exchange information and ideas where desirable without any obligation on either side only to act after consultation had resulted in agreement. This exchange of information would take place, no doubt, both between Foreign Office and State Department and between their representatives in the field.[19]

The Foreign Office sent a circular telegram to British missions informing them of this arrangement. The telegram made clear that cooperation in the field was to be on a strictly *ad-hoc* basis. The guiding principle was encapsulated in the phrase that Britain and the USA should aim to 'shoot at the same target from different angles.' The telegram did make one further suggestion that set an important precedent for Britain's anti-communist propaganda. It gave British information officers discretion in cases where there was a risk of British and US propaganda overlapping to make 'temporary arrangements' to avoid this. It was made clear that this should not result in Britain abandoning any field of activity or geographic area in favour of US propaganda. However, it did establish a precedent for a division of labour in propaganda activities and raise the possibility of conceding certain responsibilities to the USA.[20]

The first example of British and US cooperation in the field was in Italy, where the IRD began its anti-communist campaign. The British and US Governments had been concerned for some time about the prospect of a communist victory in the elections in Italy in April 1948. At the end of February 1948, Warner wrote to the British Embassy in Rome that the first priority for the newly formed IRD was to 'have some influence on the course of events in Italy between now and the elections in April.' The first IRD basic papers, which focused on conditions behind the Iron Curtain, were produced with an eye on the requirements in Italy. Warner instructed the ambassador in Rome, Sir Victor Mallet, to distribute the unattributable papers to 'key men in Rome and the provinces who are carrying on an anti-communist campaign' including 'party organisers, writers in anti-communist papers and anti-communist Parliamentary candidates.'[21] Mallet welcomed the new propaganda policy and agreed to the discreet dissemination of material to sympathetic sections of the press and other personal contacts. The embassy had, he said, already been asked for anti-communist material by the Christian Democrat Party.[22] As the elections approached a small committee chaired by the ambassador was formed in the Rome Embassy to coordinate Britain's anti-communist propaganda.[23]

In early March, the Russia Committee considered what action might be taken in consultation with the Americans to prevent the communists gaining power in Italy.[24] The embassy in Rome was asked for its comments on US policy in Italy and replied that the US Embassy placed its main hope in the publicity associated with the open political support and great economic help the USA was giving to Italy. They were also told in strict confidence that the US embassy had for some time been feeding the Italian anti-communist press with material 'very much on the lines now proposed for our information services.' Given the similarities of the two campaigns, the embassy asked for permission to 'coordinate our arrangements with [the US Embassy] to avoid overlapping, waste of effort and possible risk of contradiction between our respective lines.'[25] The Foreign Office replied that subject to the avoidance of arrangements which might tie Britain's hands, they could exchange information with the US Embassy and make *ad-hoc* arrangements to avoid overlapping and hampering each others' efforts.[26] The cooperation in Italy was reinforced by contacts in Washington where the State Department provided Balfour with a copy of its special guidance for US information officers on the elections in Italy. The Foreign Office reciprocated by providing the State Department with copies of the first seven IRD basic papers which had been produced specifically for use in Italy, and a brief outline of British propaganda activities in Italy.[27]

Although it is difficult to determine exactly what impact British and US propaganda efforts had on the outcome of the Italian elections on the 18 April, the desired Christian Democrat victory was achieved.[28] The propaganda campaign in Italy was an important test for Britain's new propaganda policy. It was the first campaign undertaken by the IRD, and it was organized in great haste before the Department was fully established. It was also a test for cooperation with the USA. Shortly after British information staff began distributing IRD material in Italy, it became apparent that British efforts mirrored a propaganda campaign by the US Government which was already underway. British officials in Rome, London and Washington quickly established an exchange of information with their US counterparts which enabled them to coordinate their propaganda policies and output.

However, it was not Britain, 'as Europeans and a social democratic government,' who gave a lead to the forces of anti-communism in Italy. Although the elections in Italy were effectively a battle between communism and the non-communist Centre-Left, US support, both overt and covert, was more decisive than the IRD's campaign. The propaganda campaign undertaken by the US Government in Italy was an ambitious operation involving considerable overt support backed by the psychological effects of the Marshall Plan, and the first significant covert political operation by the CIA.[29] Moreover, although it is significant that Britain and the USA cooperated so closely in such a formative operation for both powers, it is not clear just how much the two sides revealed to each other about the more covert aspects of their activities in Italy. Certainly the State Department directive on information activities in Italy, given to the Foreign Office, made no mention of the covert support for the Christian Democrats being organized by the CIA.[30] Similarly, when Warner discussed IRD's activities in Italy with the American Information Officer in London, he was careful not to mention that the Christian Democrat Party had asked the British embassy for anti-communist material.[31] This raises the tantalising possibility that Britain and the USA were both providing material support to the Christian Democrats without informing each other. What is clear is that although the propaganda campaign in Italy was by no means a joint effort, Britain played an important role in supplementing US support of the non-communist Left in Italy. This kind of independent pursuit of common objectives was to become characteristic of British and US cooperation in the field.

By mid-1948, senior Foreign Office officials began to consider the question of expanding cooperation with the USA. In August, Ralph Murray noted that, 'we should be more active in our contacts with the Americans.'[32] Aside from the exchange of information in Rome, in most areas liaison in the field had failed to develop. This was due not least to the fact that US missions had not received instructions from the State Department regarding the exchange of propaganda material with the British.[33] Warner was particularly frustrated at the lack of progress. Although Britain had provided the Americans with details of IRD's plans and productions, he complained to the Washington Embassy, 'we are much more in the dark about what they are doing.'[34] Warner proposed to visit Washington in the autumn of 1948 to discuss propaganda activities with the State Department.[35] It is apparent that he had begun to consider a closer degree of cooperation than he had suggested in January 1948. In advance of his visit, Warner wrote to the British Embassy in Washington that 'there should be plenty of room for cooperation in fighting the Cold War – exchange of ideas and of material – and perhaps for some division of labour in the field.' Warner had previously counselled against the joint production of propaganda and especially the use of US intelligence. He now suggested that the agenda for his visit to the USA might include consideration of 'concerting material' and cooperating in the collection of intelligence for use in propaganda.[36]

Warner's visit to Washington, in October 1948, placed British and US cooperation in anti-communist propaganda on a formal footing. However, in several respects, the visit was also something of a disappointment to Warner. It served to illustrate the degree to which Britain's response to communist propaganda was more advanced than that of the USA. The US information programme had suffered drastic budgetary cuts since the end of the War and was only just beginning to recover. In the same period the State Department's information apparatus had undergone four major reorganizations. The most recent of these had taken place since the appointment of the new Assistant Secretary of State, George Allen, in February 1948. Consequently the information apparatus Warner came to view was strained and barely operational. Since the passage of the Smith–Mundt Act early in 1948 the information programme had received increased appropriations. But, Warner discovered, the State Department was only now sending out information officers to many posts and he suspected that the US propaganda machine abroad was only just being established. Warner noted that, although State Department officials were as enthusiastic as ever to cooperate in anti-communist propaganda, they were considerably less active than Britain. The State Department's Office of International Information was not producing anything comparable to the IRD's basic papers and was not providing its officers in the field with the kind of detailed information on Soviet affairs that the IRD regularly sent to British missions. There was little effort to insert articles in the local press or distribute, 'officially or semi-officially', material which attacked or exposed communism. As far as Warner could establish, US activities consisted almost entirely of reproducing anti-communist material published in the USA.[37]

Although the limited output of the Office of International Information meant there was little prospect of a fruitful exchange of material with the IRD, Warner discovered that material comparable to IRD's briefs was being generated by the State Department's Office of Intelligence Research (OIR).[38] In particular, the OIR produced a series of papers entitled 'Soviet Affairs Notes' which in subject matter closely resembled the IRD's series of basic papers. The OIR's 'Soviet Affairs Notes' series had been running for several years and covered similar topics to the IRD briefs. The papers aimed to provide 'reliable information to counteract misrepresentations in regard to Soviet developments and policies.' Although the lack of an organized propaganda campaign meant that the papers almost certainly had not enjoyed the large audience of the IRD's briefs they were distributed under similar conditions. Like the IRD briefs the only indication of origin was on a detachable cover-sheet. This sheet stated in bold letters that: 'In disseminating the material outside of the US Government, the cover sheet must be detached and neither the Department of State nor the US Government may be cited as a source.'[39]

It was agreed that the OIR papers would form the basis for an exchange of propaganda material with Washington. The first batch of 'Soviet Affairs Notes' was despatched to the IRD in October 1948. In return, copies of IRD basic papers and digests were distributed to the Office of International Information and the Division of Eastern European Affairs in the State Department, and to the Policy Planning Staff.[40]

This exchange of basic propaganda material was apparently profitable. The subject matter of IRD and OIR papers was often the same and this exchange provides one example of how cooperation allowed Britain and the USA to develop their propaganda along similar lines and attack the same targets, albeit from different angles. For example, one of the first 'Soviet Affairs Notes' received by the IRD was a paper entitled, 'The Inadequacy of Soviet Economic Statistics'. This paper described how the Soviet Government rarely published economic data and, 'even when published, the information is not only meagre, but much too often ambiguous and incomplete, serving the purpose of equivocation or concealment rather than enlightenment.'[41] Shortly afterwards the IRD produced their own paper entitled 'Soviet Statistics: A Study in Secrecy'. This paper described the 'obscurantist process' by which the Soviet Government, through:

> strict censorship…enforces a statistical blackout which affects a great variety of subjects, ranging from production and consumption to unemployment and cost of living. The result is to render impossible any sound comparisons between the Soviet Union and other countries.[42]

Warner's visit established the first formal agreement for the exchange of anti-communist propaganda material between the British and US Governments. It was agreed that the State Department and the IRD would exchange basic research papers including IRD's basic papers and digests, and the State Department's Soviet Affairs Notes and information directives, and intelligence on conditions behind the Iron Curtain. The locus for this exchange was to be Washington, where a British Embassy official, Denis Allen, would liaise with the Political Division of the State Department. It was also decided that any proposals for joint Anglo-American propaganda would pass through the same channel. In order to prevent confusion and duplication it was decided not to establish a similar liaison through the American Embassy in London.[43]

Warner also discussed the possibility of cooperation in the field of broadcasting, with Charles Thayer, the newly appointed director of the VOA. The State Department had taken control of all VOA broadcasts to foreign countries on 1 October 1948. State Department officials told Warner that they now considered the VOA to be their 'principal weapon in dealing with communism.'[44] There had, however, been concern in London about the strident tone of VOA broadcasts. Warner informed Thayer that there had been criticism from some British posts which regarded VOA broadcasts as 'overdone and antagonising to many listeners,' although the most vigorous anti-communists preferred them to the BBC. There was, Warner concluded, 'probably advantage in employing both types of broadcast – the vigourous American and the balanced British.' Thayer suggested the arrangement of a 'quick "tie-up"' with the BBC on certain occasions so that BBC and VOA broadcasts might support each other. Warner advised that the VOA should approach the BBC directly, although he agreed to raise the matter with Jacob in London. It was also agreed that copies of the State Department's directives to the VOA would be passed to the IRD through Allen in Washington, and Thayer provided a detailed overview of the resources used by the VOA to which the IRD might want access. These included State Department research papers, telegrams from US missions, Russian émigré literature and a card index of quick responses to communist propaganda attacks.[45]

Some officials in London, however, remained reluctant to promote closer ties between the BBC and the VOA. Mrs Ruthven-Murray of the IPD wrote a strongly worded minute advising against the suggestions made in Washington. 'The VOA,' she wrote, 'is not only inaccurate in substance but also tactless and hectoring in tone.' There was, she observed, a large gap between the BBC's policy of 'reflecting the policies and views of HMG', and actually undertaking anti-communist propaganda:

> With all its faults … the BBC continues to maintain a high reputation for telling the truth and in the long run is believed. The VOA may impress those elements who are longing for the day of salvation from the West, but even those elements can never be quite sure that what they have heard is true.[46]

The IRD, however, was in favour of cooperation, at least between the Foreign Office and the VOA. Adam Watson asserted that there was little harm in the Foreign Office exchanging material with the VOA and the State Department. Far from following the same line as the VOA, Watson observed, such an exchange would save time and prevent duplication. As a result, an exchange was allowed to develop on the basis that, 'if they say it, we needn't.'[47]

The success of this cooperation between the Foreign Office and the VOA, was illustrated when Charles Thayer visited London in February 1949. In addition to meetings at the BBC, Thayer met with Warner, Murray and Watson. He informed them that the VOA was one of the largest consumers of their material in Washington. In fact, it appears that the IRD's anti-communist material was more suited to the VOA broadcasts than the BBC. Warner and Murray complained that they were not having much success in pressing their material on the BBC. The BBC's policy of accepting only 'friendly advice' was making for 'strained relations' and delays. Nevertheless, Thayer reassured them, as a result of his meetings with the BBC, he felt the BBC and the VOA was successfully dividing the field. It would, he said, be a mistake, 'if the BBC and ourselves got into a contest for calling the Russians names.'[48]

Perhaps the most important result of Warner's visit was an agreement that there should be 'constant contact and cooperating between our information offices in the field.' That British and US information officers should have the authority 'to show and discuss with their opposite numbers any directives or guidance instructions which they received, and discuss, where appropriate, action upon them.' Warner also ensured that, on this occasion, the State Department and the Foreign Office would both issue circulars to their overseas posts, outlining the policy for cooperation.[49] Both telegrams stressed that nothing should be done that gave the impression that Britain and the USA were pursuing any kind of joint propaganda policy. In the words of the Foreign Office telegram, Britain and America would 'continue to attack the same objectives from different angles.' However, when it came to describing the basis upon which cooperation was to be undertaken the formulation of the telegrams revealed a subtle difference. The Foreign Office suggested that cooperation might take the form of division of research and 'sometimes coordination of attack', but otherwise gave its representatives relative freedom, stating that 'the details of cooperation should be left to each post to work out on its merit.'[50] In contrast, the State Department advocated an 'amicable exchange of views' but stressed that information officers must retain 'complete independence of action and operation.' Moreover, it suggested, the basis for any exchange should be a carefully calculated quid pro quo:

> The Department perceives no objection to the exchange of views with corresponding British officers relative to our general policy inasmuch as it is to the Department's advantage to receive corresponding information concerning British plans and policy.[51]

Only a few US missions reacted to the State Department's cautious tone. The US Ambassador in Iceland, who had been informed of the contents of the Foreign Office telegram, noted that the Foreign Office instructions were 'couched in mandatory terms, which stand out in contrast to the permissive terms of the Department's instructions.' In particular, he was concerned that the Foreign Office did not seem to caution against joint action. In his view the Foreign Office and State Department instructions were 'so much at variance in tone and intention' that he would not sanction any cooperation.[52] Similarly, the US Public Affairs Officer in Bolivia, where the British and US information services had worked closely in the past, interpreted the telegram as urging more restraint in the future. He confidently reassured the State Department that they had recently restricted such cooperation and would in the future make no further arrangements![53]

Nevertheless, most US missions welcomed the State Department's sanction for cooperation. Many were only too pleased that they now had official approval to respond to the approaches made by the British six months earlier. Although the vast majority of posts reported 'close and informal contacts' between their respective information staff, cooperation did of course vary from country to country. The closest cooperation was often in countries where communist propaganda was most hostile. British and US Embassies behind the Iron Curtain reported that their enforced isolation often prompted close and friendly relations, a degree of contact which facilitated cooperation.[54] The form of cooperation also varied greatly. Some posts merely informed each other about their plans for propaganda and reported back to their governments. Several exchanged propaganda material, principally the IRD's *Digest* and the OIR's *Soviet Affairs Notes*. The US representative in Stockholm also provided a useful 'Handbook of Quotations about the Soviet Union'.[55] In embassies with a more advanced propaganda apparatus, equipment was exchanged. In Karachi, United States Information Service (USIS) films were shown by the British Information Service film van.[56] In other cases, the British and US embassies shared translation work. In a few cases there was also a certain degree of operational cooperation. For example, in Korea and Bangkok, US information staff agreed to distribute unattributable British propaganda material along with their own.[57] Similarly, in Manila, the British representative reported wholehearted American cooperation, in which 'we have arranged to "plant" some of their stuff and vice versa.'[58] Nevertheless, even in those posts where cooperation extended this far, British and US information staff were careful to maintain the appearance of independent action. Information officers in the field were perhaps more aware than anyone of the importance of independent propaganda programmes. As the US representative in Warsaw observed, informal cooperation allowed Britain and the USA to 'shoot at the same target from different angles'; conversely the maintenance of separate programmes gave communist propagandists two targets to shoot at rather than one.[59]

'Third Force' propaganda: the Brussels Treaty Organization and the colonies

In early 1948, the developing cooperation between Britain and the USA led a number of British posts to question whether they could reveal the existence of Britain's new propaganda policy to other friendly governments.[60] If there was a defining feature of Bevin's plans for a British-led Western Union, it was his call to 'organise and consolidate the ethical and spiritual forces inherent in this Western civilisation.'[61] Central to this was the extension of the new propaganda policy to involve cooperation with Britain's allies in Europe and the Commonwealth. The Cabinet paper, 'Future Foreign Publicity Policy', stated that Britain would 'give the lead in spiritual, moral and political sphere to all the democratic elements in Western Europe.' Similarly, it warned communism would make headway in the Middle East, India, Burma, Ceylon, Malaya, Indonesia and Indo-China, 'unless a strong spiritual and moral lead…is given against it, and we are in a good position to give such a lead.'[62]

However, the Foreign Office informed missions that, initially at least, there was to be no exchange of information with Britain's other allies, comparable to that with the USA. Although information officers were free to pass IRD material – subject to the usual restrictions on attribution – to politicians and officials in friendly governments, the existence of the IRD and its methods were to be kept secret. In April 1948, the Embassy in Holland was instructed that:

> The facts that a definite decision to carry out a planned anti-communist publicity campaign has been taken, that special machinery for this purpose has been set up, are, as you will appreciate, highly confidential here, and the only foreign government to which we have disclosed this decision and the lines of the campaign is the United States.[63]

The Foreign Office did not begin consideration of European cooperation on anti-communist measures until after the signature of the Brussels Treaty between Britain, France, Belgium, the Netherlands and Luxembourg, on 17 March 1948. The question of coordinating propaganda measures by the Brussels Powers was then considered by the Foreign Office Working Party on the spiritual aspects of the Western Union. In April 1948, Murray presented the Working Party with a proposal for a joint information executive to be established by the Brussels Pact Consultative Council. Murray's proposal was based on article III of the Brussels Treaty which stated that:

> The High Contracting Parties will make every effort in common to lead their peoples towards a better understanding of the principles which form the basis of their common civilisation and to promote cultural exchanges by conventions between themselves or by other means.[64]

Murray proposed that, rather than simply employing this article to promote cultural exchanges, 'we should seek to make active use of the Treaty.' The aim, Murray said, should be 'to get general and practical cooperation in our pro-Western Union and anti-communist propaganda drive without detracting in any way from our own independent efforts.' Through the Brussels Treaty, Murray suggested, the path could be smoothed for Britain's own propaganda efforts, while they could also aim to achieve internationally what could not be done nationally. For example, Murray suggested the establishment of an international newspaper, international feature and photoprint services, and international 'indoctrination courses or courses of instruction and inspiration in the anti-communist fight.' In order to facilitate this effort, Murray suggested the creation of a joint information executive to arrange the exchange of information, make recommendations for possible cooperation, distribute information material and run courses of instruction in anti-communism.[65]

The Working Party was not in favour of Murray's proposal. It was observed that a joint information executive would face difficulties arising from conflicting policies of the Powers in, for example, the Middle East. The meeting was also reminded that Bevin had been against the growth of large information services under the United Nations. There were too many organs of propaganda already and what was needed were fewer and better ones. The proposal ultimately foundered on the fact that, in contrast with the USA, none of Britain's co-signatories to the Brussels Treaty had a substantial propaganda machine of their own. Sir Ivone Kirkpatrick was afraid that joint machinery might interfere with the efficiency of Britain's own propaganda effort whilst offering little in return.[66] It was decided that it would be a mistake to set up a five-Power committee to plan joint propaganda work as Britain was the only country with 'an elaborate Information Services machinery' and a worldwide broadcasting system. Consequently, any proposals for five-Power propaganda would almost certainly result in practice in Britain receiving 'all sorts of requests to use our machine for publicity on behalf of the other countries.' It was decided, therefore, not to inform the Brussels Powers about the British organisation for countering communist propaganda, and not to seek cooperation. The Working Party agreed only that periodic discussions between officials to exchange ideas and consider specific proposals 'might well have advantages.' [67]

The question of cooperation with the European allies was allowed to languish until October 1948, when Bevin himself raised the issue at a meeting with the French Foreign Minister, Robert Schumann, and the US Secretary of State, George Marshall. Bevin thought that the West was at a disadvantage on the propaganda front as 'the Russians spoke with one voice and we tended to show divergent and contradictory views.' The time had come, he said, to discuss the coordination of propaganda in the same way that they discussed the coordination of intelligence and other such matters. He did not propose a formal coordinated programme but 'a general exchange of information and ideas.' In a revealing insight into the shift in Bevin's thinking on the response to Soviet propaganda, he concluded, 'we had after all been very good at psychological warfare during the war.'[68]

Later that month, at the Brussels Pact Consultative Council, Bevin once again called for exchange of ideas on countering communist propaganda and a general pooling of propaganda material. Significantly, at this meeting, Bevin also revealed the existence of the British organization for countering communist propaganda. The Belgian Foreign Minister, Spaak, praised the volume of information on conditions behind the Iron Curtain used by British representatives at the UN. Bevin replied that a small body had been set up in Foreign Office which produced regular reports which might be of use to the other Brussels Powers. It was agreed that although no attempt should be made to coordinate the propaganda of the five Powers, each would make available to the other governments 'information which might be useful in dealing with the problem of the ideological aspect of defence.'[69]

Following the discussions in the Consultative Council, Embassies in the Western Union, capitals were instructed to exchange propaganda material, including IRD papers, with their host governments.[70] Murray also made a tour of the European capitals to explain the IRD's work and discuss arrangements for exchanging propaganda material.[71] This exchange of propaganda material did yield some results. Although the Belgians appeared to view the provision of IRD material as obviating their own need to produce anti-communist propaganda material,[72] the French expressed an interest in developing their own organization on the lines of the IRD.[73] The French Government had also passed one of the IRD's papers to a French writer who had published a series of articles based on it.[74] There was also some success in Holland, where the Dutch Government undertook to disseminate IRD material to the Dutch trade unions.[75] Despite these achievements, the Foreign Office remained concerned about the disproportionate effort Britain was exerting in the propaganda field. The exchange of propaganda material with the Brussels Powers was largely a one-way street; by mid-1949, the IRD had distributed 28 basic papers to the Brussels Powers, and received only 'one or two fairly interesting papers in return' from the French Government.[76]

Cooperation with the Brussels Powers remained on a different level to that with the USA. Firstly, the exchange of propaganda material with the Brussels Powers was only conducted at an inter-governmental level through contacts in the relevant European capitals. Concerns regarding potential conflicts of interest between the Brussels Powers in regions such as the Middle East and South-East Asia meant there was to be no cooperation in the field. The exchange was also limited to propaganda material. There was to be no consultation on propaganda policies or coordination of propaganda activities.[77] In March 1949, Bevin instructed British embassies in South-East Asia that there had been no agreement to do joint propaganda, or even to coordinate the main lines of it. 'We have no confidence in any attempt to conduct publicity by means of an international committee':

> In the case of the Americans, however, cooperation is more intimate and reciprocal, and is extended to the field, whereas in the case of the Brussels Powers it is intended that the exchange of information should in general be confined to the capitals.[78]

There were also concerns about the security implications of cooperation with the Brussels Pact governments, particularly the French. The new propaganda policy had been revealed in full to representatives of the US Government, yet in developing cooperation with the Brussels Powers, as late as October 1948, the IRD was suggesting that, 'a lot could be done by…communicating the results of research without actually notifying to the Government in question that we were engaged in anti-communist activities.'[79] In particular, Murray was concerned that foreign governments should not be aware of the extent of the IRD's existing contacts in their countries, 'apart from any political rumpus that might ensue, we should forfeit a certain amount of press cooperation and confidence which at the moment we enjoy.'[80]

Consequently, when the decision was taken to circulate material to the Brussels Powers governments, the IRD began to develop two categories of material. 'Category A' consisted of 'secret and confidential objective studies of Soviet policies and machinations which are designed for high-level consumption by heads of states, Cabinet members etc.' 'Category B' was less highly classified information suitable for careful dissemination by staff of British missions to suitable contacts who could use it unattributably as factual background material.[81] Whilst 'Category A' material was exchanged with the governments of the Brussels Powers, the IRD continued to disseminate 'Category B' material directly to contacts in the Western Union countries. It was decided not to inform the host governments about these arrangements, to the obvious discomfort of some of the diplomatic staff concerned. The reason was twofold: to protect the confidential nature of IRD's work; and also out of concern that in some countries communist sympathizers in the Government might seek to curb the IRD's activities.[82]

This two-tier approach to cooperation with the Brussels Powers set a precedent for intergovernmental cooperation with the colonies – as with the Brussels Powers anti-communist propaganda work began in the colonial territories some time before the host governments were informed of Britain's anti-communist campaign. British High Commissioners were provided with copies of all IRD material, and instructions on its dissemination to local contacts. As early as February 1948, British information staff in India began to distribute anti-communist material to informal contacts in the local press.[83] In August 1948, the IRD issued a directive regarding counter-propaganda on colonial issues. It sought to counter 'misrepresentations of our colonial policies and the state of affairs in our colonies,' whilst at the same time drawing attention to 'Soviet behaviour in and towards the backward areas of the former Tsarist empire, and towards other areas on which she has laid her hands.' Information staff were instructed to extract information from the directive, and where the opportunity arose, 'endeavour to find publicity for it.'[84]

Cooperation with Commonwealth governments was not considered until November 1948 when the CIPC considered the question of whether the governments of India, Pakistan and Ceylon would be ready to exchange anti-communist propaganda material.[85] The slow start to intergovernmental cooperation with the Commonwealth was not least due to the attitude of the Commonwealth Relations Office (CRO), whose support for the IRD's campaign was less than wholehearted. In October 1948, Foreign Office representatives on the CIPC expressed concern that the CRO were not doing 'everything that might be done...in the field of anti-communist propaganda.' They were particularly concerned that the CRO proposed to leave India, Pakistan and Ceylon out of the distribution of IRD material, presumably because the governments in these territories were not directly threatened by the communists. The Foreign Office were inclined to view the communist threat in the colonies, particularly in India and Pakistan, somewhat more seriously than the CRO. The IRD was not simply concerned with the internal communist threat but the implications of communist propaganda for regional or global security. 'The growth of communism in India and Pakistan,' Ralph Murray observed, 'is intimately related to the growth of it in the foreign territories of S.E. Asia and also in Malaya. We therefore have a strong, if indirect, interest in successful publicity measures being undertaken in India and Pakistan.' By way of example, Murray pointed to 'the dangerous tendency in the Indian provincial press, and to some extent in the metropolitan press as well, to swallow Soviet colonial propaganda, particularly concerning Malaya, hook, line and sinker.'[86]

In December 1948, when the CRO finally agreed to approach Commonwealth governments, cooperation was modelled on the exchange of propaganda material with the Brussels Powers.[87] However, as with the Brussels Powers, the IRD was concerned that cooperation should not jeopardise the security of their activities. In a letter to the Commonwealth Secretary, Patrick Gordon Walker, Christopher Mayhew noted that, 'we shall have to be satisfied that there would not be undue risk of leakage either to the public or to the communists that the British Government were supplying such material.' The governments of some of the Dominions, Mayhew observed would have a number of inexperienced officials working in their departments, 'which I suppose are most probably penetrated by the communists.'[88] Thus the governments of India, Pakistan and Ceylon were offered the IRD's 'Category A' research material on Russia and the orbit, 'much as we do the Brussels Powers,'[89] but were not informed about arrangements for the dissemination of the IRD's 'Category B' material in their countries. The US embassy in London reported:

> Foreign Office and CRO are agreed that dissemination category B material... in India, Pakistan and Ceylon on exactly same lines as used in non-Commonwealth countries without embarrassing GOI [Government of India] or GOP [Government of Pakistan] by asking their permission. IRD has had no 'kick-back' from other countries where category B program working and is prepared assert if question raised that dissemination factual category B material is normal function British missions present world situation. Exceptionally, instructions British High Command Colombo gave him discretion to mention category B material to Ceylon Government.[90]

The objectives of cooperation with the Commonwealth governments were not, however, entirely the same as those with the Brussels Powers. Although the IRD's principal complaint about the exchange of anti-communist material with the Brussels Powers was that they received little in return, in exchanging material with Commonwealth governments it is apparent that the Foreign Office expected little in return. This was because the primary objective of cooperation with governments in the colonies appears to have been to disabuse the governments themselves of any misperceptions about the dangers of communism. In contrast to cooperation with the Brussels Powers, rather than supplying colonial governments with material for use in their own propaganda, the purpose was to educate senior politicians about the communist threat. Mayhew suggested that, even if security from leaks could not be assured, the Dominions governments could be provided with material of 'a safe nature' in the form of studies of certain questions. If the colonial governments did not make use of this material for publicity, he concluded, 'it would serve the purpose of educating them.'[91] Similarly, Sir Archibald Nye, the British High Commissioner in Delhi, warned that although the Indian Government recognized the Soviet threat, Nehru was not inclined to view the threat as a regional one, and continued to think in terms of internal action against communism. Nye discussed with Nehru the possibility of an exchange of information on communism and received 'a friendly response,' although Nehru felt India would be able to offer little in return. Nye recommended that the Foreign Office adopt 'an oblique teaching' approach, making available to the Indian Government the IRD's 'Category A' research material, which made clear communist views and what they had done elsewhere. The Foreign Office were not concerned that the Indians could offer little material in return. The Counsellor of the British Embassy in New Delhi told officials in the US Embassy, 'the proposed exchange would probably be almost exclusively a one-way street.' In relating this information to the State Department, the US Embassy observed that Sir Archibald Nye was 'more interested in the gradual change in Nehru's attitude towards communism than in the substance of information which may be exchanged.'[92]

It is clear then that in developing intergovernmental cooperation with the colonies the Commonwealth governments themselves were as much a target for Britain's anti-communist propaganda as they were potential partners in any anti-communist campaign in their region. In both Western Europe and the Commonwealth, cooperation at the intergovernmental level was clearly designed to alert friendly governments to the communist threat and at best stimulate them into launching their own anti-communist propaganda campaigns. However, it is apparent that cooperation with governments in Europe and the Commonwealth was not the primary means by which the Foreign Office sought to counter communism in those regions. Before any approach was made at an intergovernmental level, the IRD began to influence opinion in Europe and the colonies directly through the cultivation of contacts in the press, trade unions and political parties in those regions, with some success. Consequently, when the IRD began to establish machinery for cooperation with European and Commonwealth governments, it was, at least in part, designed to shield the IRD's direct attempts to influence opinion in those regions from the governments involved.

The contrast with the degree of cooperation enjoyed with US Government could not have been more marked. Whilst the US Government was informed of the new propaganda policy less than one month after the British Cabinet, Britain's plans for 'Third Force' propaganda were not revealed to friendly governments in Europe until October 1948, and to Commonwealth governments until almost a year after the new policy was launched. Moreover, the degree to which the Foreign Office was prepared to cooperate with Britain's allies in Europe and the Commonwealth, fell some way short of the level of cooperation enjoyed by British and US information officers in London and Washington, and in the field.

The principal difference was that Western Europe and the colonies were regions threatened by communism, and as such were primary targets for Britain's anti-communist propaganda. The USA was not. Of course, as the IRD was strictly forbidden from carrying out propaganda activities within the USA itself, there was less need to conceal the IRD's activities from the US Government.[93] However, it is also clear that Britain's attempts to develop intergovernmental cooperation with other Powers merely served to illustrate that the USA was the only state with a propaganda machine and a policy for countering communist propaganda comparable to that of the UK. In so much as any 'Third Force' developed in the field of anti-communist propaganda through 1948 and 1949, it was limited to the dissemination of the product of Britain's new propaganda policy to a growing number of governments in Europe and the colonies.

The decline of Third Force propaganda: anti-communist propaganda and NATO

A series of events, beginning with the Soviet blockade of Berlin in June 1948 and culminating with the signature of the North Atlantic Treaty in April 1949, signalled the demise of Bevin's Western Union concept, and with it the Third Force aspect of Britain's anti-communist propaganda. British difficulties in stimulating anti-communist activities by the co-signatories of the Brussels Pact reflected wider concerns about the viability of the Western Union defence which emerged in British official circles towards the end of 1948. Britain had neither the military might to make a firm commitment to continental defence, or the necessary economic strength to support a Western European bloc. These problems were thrown into relief, from mid-1948, by the Berlin blockade. By the end of the year Bevin's hopes for a Third Force independent of the USA appeared increasingly untenable. In early 1949 the new Permanent Under-Secretaries' Committee, created in the Foreign Office to consider long-term planning, presented its first paper, entitled, 'A Third World Power or Western Consolidation?' It concluded:

> A weak, neutral Western Europe is undesirable and a strong independent Western Europe is impracticable at present and could only come about, if at all, at the cost of the remilitarisation of Germany.
> The best hope of security for Western Europe lies in a consolidation of the West on the lines indicated by the Atlantic Pact.[94]

In the spring of 1949 Britain's commitment to the Atlantic alliance heralded the end of Bevin's plans for a British-led Third Force independent of the USA. The creation of the Atlantic alliance also forced a re-evaluation of Britain's Third Force response to communist propaganda, and the policies for coordinating anti-communist propaganda activities with allies in Europe and the USA.

This was a relief for those officials in the Foreign Office, who had been somewhat sceptical about the 'Third Force' aspect of the new propaganda policy. As early as April 1948, in a British propaganda directive for Germany, Warner had questioned whether 'positive' projection of the 'British way of life' should be replaced by the projection of 'Western...principles and practices.'[95] Following the signature of the North Atlantic Treaty the overall tone of Britain's overseas propaganda was shifted to project 'Western' values. A new directive for British Information Officers indicated that Britain's positive publicity would no longer be based upon 'the vital and progressive ideas of British Social Democracy and Western European civilisation' but a more inclusive 'belief in the virtues, practices and values of Western democracy.' In place of the problematic presentation of British Social Democracy as the best alternative to totalitarian communism *and* unrestrained capitalism, Information Officers were told to stress that, 'the Western democratic way of life has more to offer and is more worthwhile than Soviet communism.'[96]

Embracing the Atlantic alliance did not, however, mean the abandonment of the idea that Britain should give a lead to the forces of anti-communism in Europe. As Britain prepared to sign the Treaty, Christopher Mayhew submitted a proposal to Bevin in which he stressed that Britain should continue to 'take a strong lead in encouraging western democracies in combating communist propaganda in their own countries.' Mayhew suggested that some machinery be established within the alliance to allow members to 'help each other in the task of counter-propaganda' and exchange propaganda material with a view to formulating a unified anti-communist publicity directive:

> We have already achieved some success in this... Discussions have been held with the Brussels Treaty powers and our anti-communist publicity material has now a very wide circulation throughout the world. But there is a definite need to continue giving moral encouragement and material assistance to weaker governments in the anti-communist field, and I hope very much that the signature of the Atlantic Pact will lead to close cooperation between the signatories on this subject.[97]

Following the ratification of the North Atlantic Treaty, Gladwyn Jebb drafted a more detailed proposal for the creation of a NATO subcommittee to promote anti-communist propaganda. In this cautious proposal, Jebb warned that care would be required, to ensure that a NATO subcommittee would not hinder Britain in developing its own anti-communist offensive, and that it would not commit Britain to 'undesirable co-ordination of propaganda policy with the other signatories.' Nevertheless, he felt it would be useful to exchange information and ideas in the field of 'ideological defence.' It would also provide an opportunity for 'stimulating the laggards and imparting the benefit of our experience and techniques and that of the Americans.'[98]

The experience of exchanging information with the Brussels Treaty Powers meant that some in the Foreign Office were cautious about pursuing further arrangements for coordinating anti-communist propaganda with Britain's European allies. Bevin minuted that he was 'not enthusiastic for more machinery.'[99] In considering Jebb's proposal, the Foreign Office mantra was repeated, that 'you cannot actually *do* publicity by means of an international committee.'[100] As with the Brussels Treaty Organization, the principal sticking point was that none of the European partners had a propaganda machinery comparable to Britain's. Only the USA had a similar capability and there was concern that Britain's efforts should not be diluted by the lack of impetus from the other members of NATO. Jebb's proposal received a qualified approval, but the Foreign Office position was clear. The terms of reference of a NATO subcommittee should be limited to the development of positive ideals with which to promote the North Atlantic Treaty and counter communist propaganda attacks. The importance of maintaining Britain's freedom of action was paramount. Finally, it was asserted, Britain and the USA would need to take a leading role in any NATO propaganda organization.[101]

Although the predominant view in the Foreign Office was sceptical of the coordination of anti-communist propaganda with anyone other than the US Government, Mayhew's and Jebb's proposals for a NATO directive on anti-communist propaganda were prescient. Across the Atlantic, US officials had also begun to examine the potential for a Western response to communist propaganda based on the Atlantic alliance. In 1949, the US Government began to reassess their plans for responding to communist propaganda, and the question of liaison with other countries in this field came under scrutiny. In December 1949, the State Department produced a paper on the status of cooperation with Britain in combating communist propaganda which sought to assess firstly, whether cooperation with Britain should be expanded, and secondly whether cooperation should be offered to other selected governments, in particular the French.[102] The State Department felt that cooperation with other powers would become necessary as part of US involvement in international agreements such as the North Atlantic Treaty. In early 1950, a State Department paper entitled 'Capturing Initiative in Psychological Field' stated there was an urgent need for 'a ringing pronouncement setting forth the common objectives of the free world.' In order to achieve this it proposed that the United States should:

> ... promote cooperation with the information services of other governments to the end that, while they speak with many voices, they promote a clearer understanding of their identity of interest in the struggle to preserve freedom and coordinate their efforts to penetrate the Iron Curtain with generally agreed propaganda themes.[103]

Significantly, it was decided that the views of the British Foreign Office were to be obtained before a direct approach was made to any other government.[104] At the Foreign Ministers Conference, in London in 1950, the US delegation suggested to the British that as the USA and the UK had special skills in this field they should 'lend a helping hand' to other nations such as France.[105] The British, chastened by their attempts to stimulate the Brussels Treaty Powers, displayed little enthusiasm for the US suggestion and, prior to the joint meetings, British and American officials agreed that 'Cold War' problems, including anti-communist propaganda, should be discussed bilaterally. According to the British representative, Shuckburgh, 'our own cold warriors will probably not be ready to share their methods and secrets with representatives of the other 11 countries, and any general Atlantic cold war efforts would therefore be much more formal than real.'[106]

Consequently, the question of a NATO propaganda programme was confined to a bilateral meeting between Christopher Warner and Edward Barrett, the newly appointed Assistant Secretary of State for Public Affairs. Warner and Barrett reached an informal agreement on the broad functions to be carried out by the new NATO propaganda machinery. In their discussions it is apparent that the British view prevailed. As a result of the British experience with the Brussels Treaty Organization, and their subsequent opposition to any attempt to organize propaganda through an intergovernmental committee, it was decided the NATO information staff should not issue its own publicity but should coordinate information and stimulate propaganda through the existing information programmes of the individual governments. It was recommended that the information functions should be entrusted to a highly-qualified British or US expert, working directly under the Chairman of the Council of Deputies and the proposed information machinery in many respects reflected the position of the embryonic IRD within the Foreign Office. It would provide a central collection point for information suitable for propaganda purposes and disseminate this information to member governments to use as they saw fit. There would be no joint propaganda directives and there was no suggestion that NATO would become involved in anti-communist propaganda. Information staff would simply make suggestions as to how the information programmes of member countries 'might improve their contribution to the common goal of making the North Atlantic Treaty better understood.'[107]

Despite British misgivings, the US Government did pursue liaison with the information services of other powers, and continued to press for more coordinated propaganda efforts through NATO. In February 1950, prompted by increasingly hostile communist propaganda attacks on NATO and the Mutual Defence Assistance Pact in France, the US Embassy in Paris established a Franco–American consultative committee on NAT-MDAP publicity. This informal committee brought together US officials and representatives of the French Ministries of National Defence and Information. It provided the French with information and made suggestions for propaganda designed to create a sense of confidence in the French public and counteract communist propaganda.[108] However, in attempting to organize a coordinated propaganda campaign through NATO the USA were increasingly frustrated. Following his visit to London in May 1950, Barrett called at Paris, Rome and Florence to discuss information matters with French and Italian Ministers. Although the French were clearly flattered to be consulted, Barrett found that neither they nor the Italians had any arrangements for important foreign or domestic information work. Barrett did not wish to establish any exchange of material with the French or Italians, but he did set up procedures for 'exchange of ideas' to 'offset any feeling that we were playing ball exclusively with the British.'[109] At the Foreign Ministers Conference in Washington, in August 1950, prompted by 'the good psychological reaction to Korea,' the US delegation once again stressed the need for coordinating the propaganda activities of the NATO countries. 'NATO information activities should be initiated serving as a central point for the stimulation of independent national activities. No "Deminform" is intended but general propaganda increase is desirable.'[110] However, the European allies remained reluctant to commit to a more coordinated propaganda programme. To the undoubted exasperation of the US delegation, the French replied that they had no specific ideas to put forth, and the British stressed that 'coordination should not mean combination.'[111] Later, when pressed by the Americans for their views on a NATO propaganda programme, the French Government stressed that each country must tailor their propaganda to national problems, and the implementation of a propaganda programme was a national responsibility – a view echoed by the Italians and the Danes.[112]

When the NATO International Information Service (NIIS) was established in November 1950, its terms of reference attempted to reconcile the European view that propaganda was a national responsibility with the American desire for a more coordinated international propaganda programme. The service was headed by a Canadian, Theodore F.M. Newton, and the information staff were loaned from the member countries. It was in effect an information committee, with no general or operational budget, designed to operate through existing agencies and outlets of the member governments. The terms of reference were broadly along the lines of those proposed by Warner and Barrett, with one notable addition. Alongside the promotion of the positive ideals of the North Atlantic Treaty, NATO information staff would actively seek to counter communist propaganda. Following a recommendation from the French, it was agreed that the NATO governments would each nominate an official to sift information from all sources on the USSR and particularly on living conditions under Soviet rule, and pass it to NIIS for dissemination to member countries.[113]

Despite this apparent change of heart on the part of the French, the creation of the NATO information machinery remained an uneasy compromise between those who advocated a vigorous NATO propaganda programme, and those who believed such activities were best left to the member states. Predictably it failed to win wholehearted approval from the two nations with the greatest interest in the Western propaganda offensive, Britain and the USA. Although the terms of reference had been expanded, the US State Department had hoped for a more vigorous and aggressive NATO information programme. They were unhappy that the NIIS was so small, appointed and paid for by member governments, and forced to work through the information services of member states. Under the present arrangements they observed, the NIIS would not be able to fulfil its potential, 'because of the inadequacies of national information services, their lack of interest in its suggested projects and programs, and in some cases outright opposition.' The State Department envisaged an international information service appointed by and operating through NATO itself. Rather than being subject to the varied propaganda capabilities of the member states, such a service could provide material support as well as stimulating and encouraging the domestic programmes of the member states. The work of the NIIS, in the view of the State Department, should have been more offensive, 'whatever is merely defensive in the work of NIIS should be relegated to a distinctly secondary place.' The fact that the West was not prepared to take the offensive in a military sense, 'need not mean the role of the free world must be a negative or passive one.' However, the State Department concluded pessimistically, concern over the state of the NATO information service came mainly from the Americans, 'the Europeans, by and large, appear to like it the way it is.'[114]

The British, however, were also unhappy at the shape of the NATO information programme, although for quite different reasons. The IRD were surprised and dismayed that counter-propaganda had been added to the terms of reference of the NIIS. The IRD had two concerns. Firstly, they might find it difficult to place their own propaganda material if similar material was emanating from a NATO agency. Secondly, with a NATO agency doing anti-communist propaganda, member governments might ask the IRD to discontinue their activities in Europe. Within the IRD, John Peck observed, 'this does not matter in the least provided that the NATO channel produces results better than or as good as our present efforts,' but he clearly felt it would not.[115] Murray feared that 'all that will result will be additional work for us and others, to no effect.' He believed that the major task of a NATO information office should be positive rather than counter-propaganda. He suggested the addition of a preamble to the NIIS terms of reference stating that NATO 'cannot intervene with anti-communist propaganda in the internal responsibilities of member governments and that such intervention might indeed do more harm than good.'[116]

In December 1950, the IRD tried to head-off NATO plans for counter-propaganda in a hastily convened meeting between Newton, the head of the NIIS, and John Peck of the IRD. Newton informed Peck that the NATO deputies were divided into two groups. One headed by the French, and to a certain extent the Americans, appeared to visualize the NATO information office growing into a sort of counter-Cominform. The other, headed by the UK and Canada, regarded it more as a clearing house for information which would take great care not to interfere with the existing machinery of member governments. Newton had no clear idea about how to reconcile the conflicting opinions, but he reassured Peck that he strongly supported the second view, and was 'determined not to duplicate or obstruct any work which we might be doing.'[117]

This meeting also allowed Peck to impress upon Newton the importance of the IRD's work and the desirability of NIIS working closely with IRD when dealing with counter-propaganda. Given the British experience in this field, Peck recommended that Newton should appoint a Briton, Mr Newton, currently at the BBC, as his assistant responsible for counter-propaganda. Peck gave the NIIS head a full and frank overview of the IRD's methods of operation. He described in detail the multitude of sources from which IRD derived the raw material for counter-propaganda. It was a considerable undertaking to collate and digest this material and Peck suggested it would be a 'costly and needless duplication of effort' for NATO to embark on this. 'A view with which Newton heartily agreed.' Peck also provided Newton with examples of the IRD's output, a copy of the fortnightly 'Trends in Communist Propaganda', and a specimen basic paper, 'The Soviet Peace Campaign'. Newton felt this was precisely the level at which the IRD and the NIIS could best cooperate and he agreed that if IRD could provide him with material in this form 'he would endeavour to get it disseminated as widely as possible in governmental circles in the NATO area.' Peck expressed IRD's concerns about saturating the market, and given the existing wide distribution of this material, the wish to avoid NATO being identified as an IRD channel. In order to counter this it was suggested IRD could rewrite some of the material in a slightly different form, 'since the facts could bear repeated reiteration.'[118]

Peck's meeting with Theodore Newton was something of a coup for the IRD. This early meeting with the new head of the NIIS gave Peck a prime opportunity to offer the IRD's services and to position the IRD as the principal supplier of NATO's anti-communist propaganda. Although Newton informed Peck that 'any government could join in on this, if we happened to be the most prolific nobody could object.'[119] With the provision of specially modified material, the NIIS gave the IRD another outlet for its material at the intergovernmental level. At the same time there was no question of the NIIS replacing the IRD's work. Following the same two-tier approach to cooperation with the Brussels Pact Powers, Peck recommended that the 'IRD should continue their present activities throughout the NAT territories where they are now operating until something happens which makes it necessary or desirable to discontinue our operations.'[120]

In addition to providing a extra channel for IRD material, the IRD also gained influence over the direction of NATO's anti-communist propaganda. The appointment of a British representative as Newton's assistant responsible for counter-propaganda gave the Foreign Office an influential input into NIIS planning. Moreover, the newly appointed head of the NIIS was only too pleased to accept the assistance the IRD offered. Newton asked Peck if the IRD could provide him with a draft directive on counter-propaganda which he could put up to the Council of Deputies 'as his own and that we would not be connected with it in any way.'[121] These contacts helped to place the IRD at the centre of activities to counter communism in Western Europe. Their expertise was such that other European governments began to look Britain for advice in this sphere.[122] The IRD's influence in the NATO information service also allowed them to distribute their own unattributable material, whilst continuing to press NATO to refrain from any overt anti-communist propaganda which might undermine Britain's efforts.[123] However, the question of whether NATO itself should actively seek to provide a unified response to hostile communist propaganda, or whether such counter-propaganda was the preserve of individual nations was the subject of debate within the alliance for some years to come.[124]

Conclusion

The provision of anti-communist propaganda material to like-minded governments was an increasingly important part of the IRD's work. By July 1949, the IRD's Adam Watson observed that it was clear that the IRD would need

> ...to supply more governments with material about the workings of communism as time goes on... We already supply the four Brussels Powers and the seven Commonwealth Powers. We have an embryo system for Iraq, though the Iraqi Government has not had much. We may soon send stuff to all the governments in the Atlantic Treaty. And we are preparing to send stuff to the German Government.[125]

The same degree of cooperation was not, however, extended to all governments. By mid-1949, the IRD had established several distinct levels at which cooperation with foreign governments was instituted. Sharing the product of Britain's anti-communist effort at an inter-governmental level with allied governments under the Brussels Treaty and later the North Atlantic Treaty became an important part of the IRD's work, as did liaison with the Dominion Governments. There were also attempts to persuade other nations to follow Britain's example in responding to communist propaganda. However, although the product of Britain's anti-communist effort was freely shared with allied governments, the degree to which they were taken into Britain's confidence about the existence of a coordinated anti-communist campaign, and the organization of the IRD in particular, varied from country to country. In developing intergovernmental cooperation in the field of anti-communist propaganda, the Foreign Office had two overriding concerns. Firstly, that the existence of Britain's anti-communist propaganda policy should not be revealed, and that the IRD's discreet methods and confidential contacts should not be jeopardized by public disclosure. Secondly, that by revealing their methods to foreign governments, the IRD's activities in that particular country should not be curtailed. Consequently, security concerns weighed heavily on considerations regarding which countries to cooperate with, and the level of cooperation was defined by the degree to which foreign powers were taken into Britain's confidence regarding Britain's anti-communist propaganda policy and methods.

At the same time as cautious approaches were made to friendly governments, the IRD continued to carry out anti-communist activities in those states through unofficial contacts with the 'forces of anti-communism' within them. Arrangements were made for cooperation with individuals, trade unions, political parties, journalists and publishers abroad which in many respects went beyond the degree of cooperation afforded to individual governments. Only the USA was exempt as a target for British anti-communist propaganda.

In spite of Britain's commitment to a policy of 'Third Force propaganda' independent of the USA, and reservations about US propaganda, the USA was the only country to which the new propaganda policy was revealed in its entirety, and with whom Britain actively sought to coordinate propaganda policies. The development of this close and unique level of cooperation contrasted with Britain's slow and cautious approach to cooperation with other Powers in Europe and the colonies. Although Britain's attempt to cooperate with other Powers was part of a genuine attempt to give a lead to the forces of anti-communism in Europe and Asia, these attempts also served to illustrate that the USA was the only other power with a propaganda machinery and policy capable of providing an effective response to communist propaganda.

Notes

1 Mayhew Minute, 8 May 1949, PR795/91/G, FO 1110/270, PRO.
2 Future Foreign Publicity Policy, CP(48)8, 4 January 1948, CAB 129/23, PRO.
3 *Ibid.*
4 Minute by R. Murray, August 1948, XS03/95H, FO 366/2759, PRO.
5 Future Foreign Publicity Policy, CP(48)8, 4 January 1948, CAB 129/23, PRO.
6 *Ibid.*
7 Warner to Balfour, 16 February 1948, P138/138/G, FO 953/128, PRO.
8 Warner Minute, 19 March 1948, PR41/41G, FO 1110/24, PRO.
9 Warner to Balfour, 16 February 1948, P138/138/G, FO 953/128, PRO.
10 Russia Committee, minutes of meeting held on 15 January 1948, N765/765/G38, FO 371/71687, PRO.
11 Warner to Balfour, 16 February 1948, P138/138/G, FO 953/128, PRO.
12 Kent and Young, 'British Policy Overseas: The "Third Force" and the Origins of NATO', p. 48.
13 Warner to Balfour, 16 February 1948, and 28 February 1948, P138/138G, FO 953/128, PRO.
14 Warner to Balfour, 26 February 1948, P138/138/G, FO 953/128, PRO.

15 W.P.N. Edwards to Warner, 19 February 1948 [received 6 March], PR41/41/G, FO 1110/24, PRO.

16 Warner to Balfour, 26 February 1948, P138/138/G, FO 953/128, PRO.

17 W.P.N. Edwards to Warner, 19 February 1948, PR41/41/G, FO 1110/24, PRO. John Lewis Gaddis has identified a certain degree of enthusiasm for the 'Third Force' among State Department officials: J.L. Gaddis, 'The United States and the Question of a Sphere of Influence in Europe 1945–49', in O. Riste (ed.), *Western Security: The Formative Years* (New York: Norwegian University Press, 1985), p. 78; Kent and Young, 'British Policy Overseas', p. 44.

18 W.P.N. Edwards to Warner, 19 February 1948, PR41/41/G, FO 1110/24, PRO.

19 Warner to Balfour, 26 February 1948, P138/138/G, FO 953/128, PRO.

20 Foreign Office circular, 12 May 1948, PR229/1/G, FO 1110/6, PRO.

21 Warner to Mallet, 24 February 1948, PR 1/1/913G, FO 1110/1, PRO. This operation has been covered by H. Wilford, 'The Information Research Department: Britain's Secret Cold War Weapon Revealed', *Review of International Studies*, 24 (1998), pp. 358–9.

22 Mallet to Foreign Office, 24 February 1948, PR24/1/913G, FO 1110/1, PRO.

23 Warner to Balfour, 12 April 1948, PR196/1/913G, FO 1110/5, PRO.

24 Minutes of Russia Committee meeting, 4 March 1948, N2915/765/38, FO 371/71687, PRO.

25 Rome to Foreign Office, 18 March 1948, PR93/1/913G, FO 1110/3, PRO.

26 Foreign Office to Rome, 14 April 1948, PR93/1/G, FO 1110/3, PRO.

27 Balfour to Warner, 31 March 1948, enclosure: Department of State, Office of Information and Educational Exchange, Special Guidance, Elections in Italy, 19 March 1948; Warner to Balfour, 12 April 1948, PR196/1/913G, FO 1110/5, PRO.

28 Clearly other factors had at least as much impact on the election result as the intervention, overt and covert, of other Powers, not least De Gasperi's clever exploitation of fears of communism and even more decisively the Vatican. *See* J.E. Miller, 'Taking Off the Gloves: The United States and the Italian Elections of 1948', *Diplomatic History*, 7 (1983), pp. 35–55; D.W. Ellwood, 'The 1948 Elections in Italy: A Cold War Propaganda Battle', *Historical Journal of Film, Radio and Television*, 13, 1 (1993), pp. 19–33; C.E. Martinez and E.A. Suchman, 'Letters from America and the 1948 Elections in Italy', *Public Opinion Quarterly*, 14, 1 (Spring 1950), pp. 111–25.

29 The literature on the American intervention in the 1948 elections is now voluminous; see, in particular, Miller, 'Taking Off the Gloves'; Ellwood, 'The 1948 Elections in Italy'; T. Barnes, 'The Secret Cold War: The CIA and American Foreign Policy in Europe, 1946–1956 Part I', *The Historical Journal* 24, 2 (1981), pp. 399–415.

30 Department of State, Office of Information and Educational Exchange, Special Guidance, Elections in Italy, 19 March 1948 PR196/1/913G, FO 1110/5, PRO.

31 Warner to Balfour, 18 March 1948, PR99/1/913G, FO 1110/3, PRO.

32 Minute by R. Murray, August 1948, XS03/95H, FO 366/2759, PRO.

33 P.F.D. Tennant, British Embassy, Paris to Foreign Office, 28 May 1948, PR383/1/913, FO 1110/9, PRO. In fact, in spite of the lack of direction from Washington, Paris was one of the few places where US information staff did exchange material with their British counterparts.

34 Warner to Hoyer-Millar, British Embassy, Washington, 22 September 1948, PR801/1/G, FO 1110/14, PRO.

35 Warner to Sir J. Balfour, 24 June 1948, PR497/1/913G, FO 1110/11, PRO.

36 Warner to Hoyer-Millar, British Embassy, Washington, 22 September 1948, PR801/1/G, FO 1110/14, PRO.

37 Memo by C.F.A. Warner, 6 October 1948, PR865/865/913, FO 1110/128, PRO.

38 *Ibid.*

39 'Soviet Affairs Notes,' 1948, PR1178/865/913, FO 1110/129, PRO. For State Department instructions to missions on use of 'Soviet Affairs Notes', see Acheson, State Department to American Consul, British Guiana, 5 May 1949, 800.00B/5–549, RG 59, NARA.

40 D. Allen, British Embassy, Washington to R. Murray, 23 October 1948, PR943/865/913, FO 1110/128, PRO.

41 'Soviet Affairs Notes, no. 18, The Inadequacy of Soviet Economic Statistics', 1 December 1948, PR1178/865/913, FO 1110/129, PRO.
42 'Soviet Statistics: A Study in Secrecy', FO 975/40, PRO.
43 Memo by C.F.A. Warner, 8 November 1948, PR1034/865/913, FO 1110/128, PRO.
44 Memo by C.F.A. Warner, 6 October 1948, PR865/865/913, FO 1110/128, PRO.
45 C.F.A. Warner, record of talk with Charles Thayer, 10 October 1948, PR901/865/913G, FO 1110/128, PRO.
46 B. Ruthven-Murray Minute, 26 October 1948, PR901/865/913G, FO 1110/128, PRO. See also A. Watson Minute, 8 December 1948, PR1259/10/913, FO 1110/16, PRO.
47 Watson Minute, 28 October 1948, PR901/865/913G, FO 1110/128, PRO.
48 Report of European Trip, December 1948–January 1949, by Charles Thayer, IBD, Box no. 11, Papers of Charles W. Thayer, Truman Library.
49 Memo by C.F.A. Warner, 6 October 1948, PR865/865/913, FO 1110/128, PRO.
50 Foreign Office Circular Telegram, 29 November 1948, PR1034/865/G, FO 1110/128, PRO.
51 Foreign Service Serial no. 932, Cooperation with British Information Services, 17 November 1948, 841.20200/11-17-48, RG 59, NARA.
52 American Legation, Reykjavik, to State Department, 13 January 1949, 841.20200/1-1349. The American Consul General in Montreal also interpreted the State Department's circular as prohibitive and criticized the department for their 'extreme caution and hesitancy', American Consulate General to State Department, 8 December 1948, 841.20200/12-848, RG 59, NARA.
53 American Embassy, La Paz, Bolivia to State Department, 30 December 1948, 841.20200/12-3048, RG 59, NARA.
54 *See*, for example, American Embassy, Moscow to State Department, 21 December 1948, 841.20200/12-2148; American Embassy, Prague to State Department, 6 January 1949, 841.20200/1-649; American Embassy, Warsaw to State Department, 31 December 1948, 841.20200/12-3148, RG 59, NARA.
55 British Embassy, Stockholm, to IRD, 15 December 1948, PR1295/865/913, FO 1110/129, PRO. See also American Embassy, Colombo to State Department, 17 July 1949, 841.20200/7-1549, RG 59, NARA.
56 American Embassy, Karachi to State Department, 841.20200/12-1748, RG 59, NARA.
57 American Mission in Korea, Seoul to State Department, 7 January 1949, 841.20200/1-749; American Embassy, Bangkok to State Department, 7 April 1949, 841.20200/4-749, RG 59, NARA. See also Information Office, British Legation, Bucharest to IRD, 15 January 1949, PR205/58/G, FO 1110/245, PRO.
58 British Legation, Manila to IRD, 7 January 1949, PR187/52/G, FO 1110/239, PRO.
59 American Embassy, Warsaw to State Department, 31 December 1948, 841.20200/12-3148, RG 59, NARA.
60 *See*, for example, Sir Philip Nicholls, British Embassy, The Hague, to Foreign Office, 18 March 1948, PR118/1/913G, FO 1110/4, PRO; Oliver Harvey, British Embassy, Paris to Foreign Office, 7 April, 1948, PR312/1/913, FO 1110/9, PRO.
61 The First Aim of British Foreign Policy, 4 January 1948, CP(48)6, CAB 129/23, PRO.
62 Future Foreign Publicity Policy, 4 January 1948, CP(48)8, CAB 129/23, PRO.
63 Warner to Sir Philip Nicholls, British Embassy, The Hague, 20 April 1948, PR118/1/913G, FO 1110/4, PRO.
64 Proposal for an Information Executive to be Established by Brussels Pact Consultative Council, R. Murray 19 March 1948, P2604/1474/950, FO 953/145, PRO.
65 *Ibid.*
66 Third Meeting of Working Party on Spiritual Union, 24 March 1948, P2604/1474/950, FO 953/145, PRO.
67 Coordination of Information Activities of Brussels Pact Powers, Memo by C.F.A. Warner, 3 April 1948, P2604/1474/950, FO 953/145; R. Murray Minute, 15 October 1949, PR860/860/G, FO 1110/126, PRO.
68 Extract from Record of Meeting at the *Quai d'Orsay*, 4 October 1948, SU/48/44, FO 800/502, PRO.

69 Extract of Meeting of the Consultative Council, 25 October 1948, SU/48/47, FO 800/502, PRO. See also C. Mayhew, *A War of Words: A Cold War Witness* (London: I.B. Tauris, 1998), pp. 32–3.
70 Foreign Office to Paris, Brussels, The Hague, 11 November 1948, PR1045/860/913, FO 1110/126, PRO.
71 FCO Historians, *IRD: Origins and Establishment of the Foreign Office Information Research Department 1946–48*, p. 19. For Murray's report of this tour, see 'Exchange of Information Regarding Anti-Communist Publicity with the Brussels Powers', R. Murray, 30 November 1948, PR1162/860/913, FO 1110/126, PRO.
72 Mayhew, *A War of Words*, p. 33.
73 'Exchange of Information Regarding Anti-Communist Publicity with the Brussels Powers', R. Murray, 30 November 1948, PR1162/860/913, FO 1110/126, PRO.
74 Progress Report: Information Research Department, 1 January–31 July 1949, FO 1110/277, PRO.
75 'Exchange of Information Regarding Anti-Communist Publicity with the Brussels Powers', R. Murray, 30 November 1948, PR1162/860/913, FO 1110/126; Progress Report: Information Research Department, 1 January–31 July 1949, FO 1110/277, PRO.
76 Progress Report: Information Research Department, 1 January–31 July 1949, Annexe C List of Papers sent to Brussels Powers, FO 1110/277, PRO.
77 'Exchange of Information Regarding Anti-Communist Publicity with the Brussels Powers', R. Murray, 30 November 1948, PR1162/860/913, FO 1110/126, PRO.
78 Foreign Office Circular, 4 March 1949, PR499/9/G, FO 1110/184, PRO.
79 Minutes of CIPC meeting, 15 October 1948, PR952/23/913G, FO 1110/21, PRO.
80 Murray Minute, 15 October 1948, PR860/860/913, FO 1110/126, PRO.
81 US Embassy London to State Department, 20 May 1949, 841.20200/5-2049, RG 59, NARA. These categories of IRD material were first revealed by L. Smith, 'Covert British Propaganda: The Information Research Department, 1947–1977', *Millennium: Journal of International Studies*, 9, 1 (1980), p. 73. Smith and others have assumed that this was the standard format for all the IRD's output and have not explained that this division grew from decision to distribute material to the Brussels Powers. The origins of the division of material may be found in Foreign Office to Paris, Brussels, The Hague, 11 November 1948, PR1045/860/913, FO 1110/126, PRO.
82 Russia Committee meeting, 28 October 1948, N1182/765/38, FO 371/71687; FO to Paris, 11 November 1948, PR1045/860/G; 'Exchange of Information Regarding Anti-Communist Publicity with the Brussels Powers', R. Murray, 30 November 1948, PR1162/860/913, FO 1110/126; Murray Minute, PR459/20/G, FO 1110/205, PRO.
83 British Information Services distribute critical analysis of communism to press of India and expose Soviet aims in Iran, American Embassy, New Delhi to State Department, 13 February 1948, 841.20245/2-1348, RG 59, NARA.
84 Circular no. 0121, Directive Regarding Counter-Propaganda on Colonial Issues, 17 August 1948, PR580/23/G, FO 1110/20, PRO.
85 Mayhew to P. Gordon-Walker, 22 November 1948, PR1159/23/913G, FO 1110/22, PRO.
86 Minutes of CIPC Meeting, 1 October 1948, R. Murray, PR1265/23/913, FO 1110/22, PRO.
87 J.P. Cloake Minute, 18 December 1948, PR1265/23/913, FO 1110/22, PRO.
88 Mayhew to P. Gordon-Walker, 22 November 1948, PR1159/23/913G, FO 1110/22, PRO.
89 Adam Watson Minute, 20 December 1948, PR1265/23/913G, FO 1110/22, PRO.
90 US Embassy, London to State Department, 20 May 1949, 841.20200/5-2049, RG 59, NARA.
91 Mayhew to Gordon-Walker, 22 November 1948, PR1159/23/913G, FO 1110/22, PRO.
92 American Embassy, New Delhi to State Department, 22 June 1949, 841.20245/6-2249, RG 59, NARA.
93 Watson, IRD, to W.D. Allen, British Embassy, Washington, 10 February 1949, PR284/65/G, FO 1110/255, PRO.
94 Lucas and Morris, 'A Very British Crusade', p. 101; PUSC(22)Final, 'A Third World Power or Western Consolidation?', 9 May 1949, FO 371/76384, PRO.
95 Lucas and Morris, 'A Very British Crusade', p. 100.

96 Draft circular to certain Information Officers abroad, 24 August 1949, P8128/129/950, FO 953/481; cf., Future Foreign Publicity Policy, CP(48)8, 4 January 1948, CAB 129/23, PRO.

97 Memo by C.P. Mayhew, 28 March 1949, PR795, FO 1110/270, PRO. See also Mayhew, *A War of Words*, p. 33.

98 Anti-Communist Propaganda Policy, Memo by Gladwyn Jebb, 21 June 1949, PR1766/14/G, FO 1110/192, PRO; Mayhew, *A War of Words*, p. 33.

99 Mayhew, *A War of Words*, p. 33.

100 Anti-Communist Propaganda Policy, Memo by Gladwyn Jebb.

101 *Ibid.* The question of control of NATO propaganda reflects later concerns regarding security responsibilities within NATO which were eventually assigned to the British Security Service, MI5. R.J. Aldrich, *The Hidden Hand: Britain, America and Cold War Secret Intelligence* (London: John Murray, 2001), pp. 429–30.

102 'Cooperation with British and other Information Services', 30 December 1949, 741.5200/2-950, RG 59, NARA.

103 'US Views on Capturing Initiative in Psychological Field', Washington, nd [*circa* April 1950], *FRUS, 1950*, vol. 4 (Washington, DC: US GPO), pp. 296–302.

104 'Cooperation with British and other information services', 30 December 1949.

105 The US delegation at the tripartite preparatory meetings to the Secretary of State, 24 April 1950, *FRUS, 1950*, vol. 3, pp. 856–7.

106 *Documents on British Policy Overseas*, series 2, vol. 2, *The London Conferences, Anglo-American Relations and Cold War Strategy January–June 1950* (London: HMSO, 1987), p. 48, quoted in fn 3.

107 Notes on Barrett-Warner talks, first meeting, 20 May 1950, 611.41/5-2650; Memo, action responsibilities on follow-up on London meetings, 'NATO: Tasks of New Central Machinery', 29 May 1950, 611.41/5-2950, RG 59, NARA.

108 Memo from Harriman to Bohlen, 7 February 1950, Records of Charles E. Bohlen, Box no. 5, RG59, NARA; Public Affairs Officer US Embassy in France to the Secretary of Date, 3 February 1950, *FRUS, 1950*, vol. 3, pp. 1357–9.

109 Rough Notes on European Trip, nd [*circa* May 1950], Office Files of Assistant Secretary Edward W. Barrett, 1950–51, Box no. 5, Lot52D432, RG 59, NARA.

110 US delegation Minutes, first session, preliminary conversations for the September Foreign Ministers meeting, Washington, 29 August 1950, *FRUS, 1950*, vol. 3, p. 1,137.

111 *Ibid.*

112 Secretary of State to the Acting Secretary of State, 16 September 1950, *FRUS, 1950*, vol. 3, pp. 308–9.

113 Counter-Propaganda by the NATO Information Service, J.H. Peck, 1 December 1950, PR78/3/51, FO 1110/429, PRO.

114 Views of the Department of State Concerning Programmes and Instrumentalities to Further the Objectives of NATO and MDAP, 23 February 1951, Office Files of Assistant Secretary Edward Barrett, 1950–51, Box no. 5, Lot 52D432, RG 59, NARA.

115 Counter-Propaganda by the NATO Information Service, J.H. Peck, 1 December 1950, PR78/3/51, FO 1110/429, PRO.

116 Minute by Ralph Murray, 19 December 1950, PR78/3/51, FO 1110/429, PRO.

117 NATO Information Services Counter Propaganda, Minute by J.H. Peck, 15 December 1950, PR78/3/51, FO 1110/429, PRO.

118 *Ibid.*

119 *Ibid.*

120 Counter-Propaganda by the NATO Information Service, J.H. Peck, 1 December 1950, PR78/3/51, FO 1110/429, PRO.

121 NATO Information Services Counter Propaganda, Minute by J.H. Peck.

122 Minute by T.S. Tull, 18 August 1952, FO 1110/526, PRO.

123 *See*, for example, D.D. Brown, IRD, to F.D.W. Brown, UK Permanent Delegation to NATO, 23 July 1952, PR117/9, FO 1110/526, PRO.

124 Lord Ismay, *NATO: The First Five Years, 1949–1954* (London: 1954), p. 155.

125 Watson Minute, 1 July 1949, PR1558/9/G, FO 1110/185, PRO.

Photo 1 Ralph Murray, head of the IRD from 1948 to 1951. Murray had previously worked for the BBC and, during the War, in the Political Warfare Executive (source: Foreign and Commonwealth Office).

Photo 2 John Peck, head of the IRD from 1951 to 1954. Peck had been one of Churchill's Private Secretaries during the War and was instrumental in formulating a new strategy of political warfare for Churchill's peacetime administration (source: Foreign and Commonwealth Office).

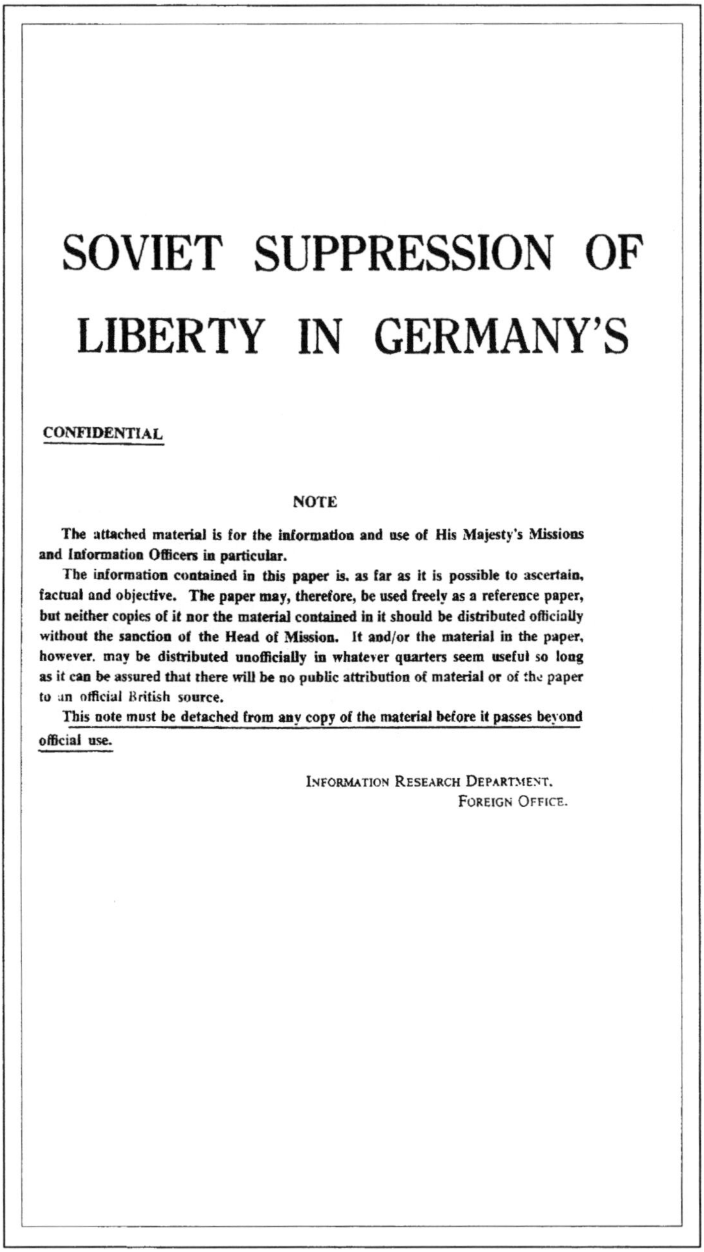

SOVIET SUPPRESSION OF

LIBERTY IN GERMANY'S

NOTE

The attached material is for the information and use of His Majesty's Missions and Information Officers in particular.

The information contained in this paper is, as far as it is possible to ascertain, factual and objective. The paper may, therefore, be used freely as a reference paper, but neither copies of it nor the material contained in it should be distributed officially without the sanction of the Head of Mission. It and/or the material in the paper, however, may be distributed unofficially in whatever quarters seem useful so long as it can be assured that there will be no public attribution of material or of the paper to an official British source.

This note must be detached from any copy of the material before it passes beyond official use.

INFORMATION RESEARCH DEPARTMENT.
FOREIGN OFFICE.

Photo 3 'Soviet Suppression of Liberty in Germany's Eastern Zone.' An IRD basic paper with the removable cover-slip still attached (source: Public Record Office).

'Sez Authority

A Communist Party newspaper reports: "Reinforcement of the Pearl River dykes has been victoriously achieved; the farmlands in Kwangtung Province will be free from inundation during the flood season."

Photo 4 'The unfortunate Chinese victim of communism, Mr Wang.' A regular cartoon in the IRD serial, *Inside Soviet China*. Visual propaganda was a particularly important means of targeting mass opinion and widely used in South-East Asia (source: Public Record Office).

Photo 5 One of the IRD's most successful forays into the field of visual propaganda. The IRD secured the rights to produce a strip-cartoon serialization of Orwell's *Animal Farm* which was published in newspapers around the world (source: Public Record Office).

Photo 6 Edward W. Barrett, US Assistant Secretary of State for Public Affairs, 1950–52. Barrett was a great admirer of British 'grey' propaganda and, in 1950, agreed a policy of 'close and continuous' cooperation with the British on all aspect of information policy (source: Truman Library).

Photo 7 C.D. Jackson, a driving force behind the National Committee for a Free Europe, and Eisenhower's Special Assistant for psychological warfare. The photograph is inscribed, 'To Beedle...' (Walter Bedell Smith, Director of Central Intelligence from 1950–53) (source: Eisenhower Library).

Photo 8 Gordon Gray taking the oath of office as Director of the Psychological Strategy Board in 1951, as President Truman looks on (source: US National Archives).

Photo 9 'An ingenious new instrument devised to aid the Voice of America in carrying the testimony of the Free World to peoples behind the Iron Curtain.' President Truman dedicating the US Coast Guard cutter *Courier*, which was used as a floating radio transmitter as part of the Radio 'Ring Plan' (source: US National Archives).

Photo 10 Truman and Churchill, in the Oval Office in January 1952. To the Americans'
surprise, Churchill raised the subject of psychological warfare against the
communist bloc and facilitated expanded British and US cooperation in the field
(source: US National Archives).

Photo 11 The Winds of Freedom project. Balloons being released to transport Radio Free
Europe leaflets into Czechoslovakia in the early 1950s (source: Radio Free Europe).

Photo 12 In an effort to counter defeatism and neutralism in Europe, parties of foreign journalists were invited to tour British defence institutions. Here, journalists from Norway, Denmark and the Netherlands are given a demonstration on the use of Geiger counters (source: Public Record Office).

Photo 13 The NATO Caravan of Peace in Portugal in 1954. One of a raft of publicity measures introduced following the creation of an Information Policy Working Group to promote the Alliance and provide a forum for consultation on anti-communist propaganda (source: NATO).

4   'Close and continuous liaison'

British and American cooperation, 1950–51

In 1950, two years after Britain launched its anti-communist propaganda policy, the US Government launched its own coordinated global response to communist propaganda entitled the 'Campaign of Truth'. This propaganda offensive was part of a new global strategy for resisting communist expansion and undermining the Soviet monolith. It was the product of a fundamental reassessment of US national security objectives which began in mid-1949. This review was prompted by the Berlin blockade and the Soviet detonation of an atomic bomb, and given added impetus by the communist victory in China and, in 1950, the outbreak of the Korean war. The resulting policy document, NSC-68, recommended a dramatic military rearmament, increased support for America's allies and a programme of psychological warfare and covert action designed to 'roll back' communist power.[1]

The development of this new global strategy had a direct effect on cooperation with Britain in the field of anti-communist propaganda. In late 1949, as part of the review of US strategy, the State Department began to review its overseas propaganda activities, and in particular cooperation with other powers in this field. Just as the British Foreign Office had done in 1948, at the earliest opportunity the State Department canvassed Foreign Office opinion, and proposed expanded cooperation between Britain and the USA in the field of anti-communist propaganda. Their proposals met with qualified enthusiasm. The USA's new commitment to anti-communist propaganda coincided with the British Government's final rejection of the Third Force concept. In October 1949, Bevin presented the Cabinet with a paper arguing for the rejection of the Third Force in favour of 'the closest association with the United States.'[2] Britain's commitment to an alliance with the USA, coupled with the launch of the new US propaganda offensive resulted in increased cooperation in anti-communist propaganda activities. From 1950, although Britain would continue to promote the anti-communist propaganda activities of other Powers, British anti-communist propaganda policy was based increasingly on the premise that 'there are only two governments conducting anti-communist operations on a worldwide scale, the British and the United States Governments.' Success against the communist propaganda machine, it was felt, was dependent on the closest cooperation between these two Powers.[3]

This chapter will examine the expansion of British and US cooperation in anti-communist propaganda in the wake of the USA's new global strategy for responding to communist propaganda. It will begin by assessing the impact of the Campaign of Truth on American strategy for resisting communism. The principal features of the campaign will be examined, and the policy and machinery for overt and covert US

propaganda activities will be outlined. The central section of this chapter will assess
the impact of this new strategy on British and US cooperation in the field of anti-
communist propaganda. As US propaganda activities grew, so did the areas in
which cooperation with Britain was sought. The policy and organizational machinery for cooperation between the two powers, in London and Washington, and in the
field, expanded considerably in 1950. Nevertheless, both nations maintained a distinctive approach to anti-communist propaganda activities, and it will be argued that
– with few exceptions – British and US information staff maintained the policy of
shooting at the same target from different angles. The chapter will conclude with an
assessment of the expansion of Britain's anti-communist propaganda activities in
which it will be argued that in 1951 propaganda was elevated to become a central
feature of Britain's strategy for fighting the Cold War.

The Campaign of Truth and American psychological warfare, 1950–51

In 1950, a fundamental reassessment of US Cold War defences led to a new global
strategy for countering communist propaganda under the banner, 'The Campaign of
Truth'. In April 1950, Edward W. Barrett, the new Assistant Secretary of State for Public
Affairs, produced a memorandum outlining 'proposals for a total information effort
abroad.' Barrett compared the existing information programme with an attempt 'to battle a four-alarm fire with a bucket brigade.' He advocated an urgent strengthening of the
US propaganda apparatus and a reassessment of their objectives. According to Barrett,
if used intelligently, US propaganda could perform two important tasks: strengthen the
free world to resist Soviet imperialism; and expose the people of the Soviet Union and
its satellites to the truth about the peaceful intentions of the free world.[4] Barrett's paper
was passed to President Truman. Later that month, in a speech to the American Society
of Newspaper Editors, Truman launched the Campaign of Truth, in which he promised:

> ...to meet false propaganda with truth all around the globe. Everywhere that
> the propaganda of the Communist totalitarianism is spread, we must meet it and
> overcome it with honest information about freedom and democracy.[5]

The Campaign of Truth marked the revival of US propaganda and the USA's first
organized response to communist propaganda. Up to 1950, the US Government's anti-
communist propaganda had been improvised on a piecemeal basis. The Campaign of
Truth heralded a global counter-offensive which signified a shift to 'long-term strategic planning in American propaganda based on fundamental goals and policies.'[6] It
also marked a new more offensive response to communist propaganda. As George
Kennan observed, this entailed a shift away from the 'full and fair presentation' of the
USA as encapsulated in his original concept of containment, towards the development
of propaganda as a 'major weapon of policy.'[7] Planning for the Campaign of Truth
entailed targeting key regions around the globe with a 'propaganda weapon' designed
to 'win the Cold War.' In this first attempt at long-term strategic planning for propaganda activities the world was divided into four categories: the hard core, comprising
the Soviet Union; the Iron Curtain, including the satellite states, China, North Korea
and Tibet; the crucial periphery, which included Indo-China, Malaya, Greece, Turkey,

West Germany, Yugoslavia, Austria and Japan; and the danger zone, comprising France, Italy, India, Pakistan, Ceylon, Indonesia and the Philippines.[8]

In order to secure additional funding for this global propaganda campaign, the State Department deliberately emphasized its offensive nature. Officials in the State Department stopped referring to US overseas propaganda benignly as 'information activities' and instead began to use the term 'psychological warfare'. Edward Barrett later conceded that the resurrection of the term psychological warfare was to some degree motivated by Congressional considerations:

> I guess, from a purely philosophical standpoint, that I would question the term. I'm afraid it was adopted partly as a means of getting appropriations out of Congress. In those days we found that money for pure information operations, for libraries in neutral areas, for sending American performers abroad, was very hard to come by. If you dressed it up as warfare, money was very easy to come by.[9]

The Campaign of Truth was not, however, simply a device for securing additional funds for the State Department's information programme. It was part of a fundamental reassessment of the Soviet threat and the USA's response which began in 1949 and culminated in a major policy review in 1950. The basic principles underlining the Campaign of Truth were outlined in the influential policy document, NSC-68, through which the Truman administration began to develop a more offensive strategy 'intended to check and to roll back the Kremlin's drive for world domination.'[10] Although NSC-68 was not implemented until September 1950, following the outbreak of the Korean War, its psychological dimension was launched in April when the document was first drafted.[11]

NSC-68 began by stressing that the conflict between the USA and the Soviet Union was essentially a conflict of ideas, 'between the idea of freedom under a government of laws, and the idea of slavery under the grim oligarchy of the Kremlin.' In engaging in this conflict, Soviet power could be resisted when faced with economic strength and military power; it could also be undermined using the USA's psychological weapons.[12] Details of the information programme's objectives were outlined in an Annex to NSC-68 which stated that the USA's global propaganda campaign should aim to: increase the Free World's psychological resistance to Soviet aggression; foster a 'community of interests' in the free world; and create doubt among people in the Soviet dominated countries. To implement the new propaganda offensive it provided for a series of five year appropriations averaging $120,000,000 a year.[13]

At least some of the funding for this new psychological offensive was channelled into the expansion of the State Department's existing propaganda activities. According to the State Department, funding under the Campaign of Truth provided 'improved publications and press facilities, more and better motion pictures, larger libraries, and a greater volume of information materials of all kinds tailored to the needs and understanding of specific audiences.'[14] However, the most ambitious plans were undertaken in the field of international broadcasting. The centrepiece to the psychological operations provided for under NSC-68 was the expansion of broadcasting over the Iron Curtain as part of what became known as the radio 'Ring Plan'.[15]

Soviet jamming of the Voice of America began in 1948, and by 1950 had become increasingly intensive. The State Department had identified 250 Soviet jamming installations, and estimated that a further 1,000 installations were operating inside the Soviet bloc.[16] The 'Ring Plan' aimed to overcome jamming by encircling the Soviet bloc with a ring of high-powered transmitters, strong enough to force an audible signal into the Soviet Union capable of being received on small medium-wave sets. The three-year plan provided for 14 high-powered medium-wave transmitters, which at 1,000 kilowatts each were 20 times more powerful than was legally permitted in the USA. Each medium-wave transmitter was to be accompanied by two medium-powered short-wave transmitters. A further six short-wave feeder stations were to be built in the USA. Initial authority was secured for the first five bases in the Philippines, Munich, Okinawa, Greece and Ceylon.[17] In addition, due to the problem of obtaining and then securing sites for such installations on the Soviet periphery, a further plan, named 'Project Vagabond', was implemented for placing high-powered transmitters on ocean-going vessels. The first 'Project Vagabond' vessel, USS *Courier*, began operating in March 1952, and five more vessels were earmarked for the project. The *Courier* was a reconditioned cargo vessel manned by electronic technicians from the State Department and crewed by the US Coast Guard; it carried a transmitter more powerful than any radio station in the USA. The vessel was dedicated by President Truman who stated that the vessel 'will be carrying a message of hope and friendship to all those who are oppressed by tyranny; it will be carrying a message truth and light to those who are confused by the storm of falsehood that the Communists have loosed on the world'; and it was publicised as, 'an ingenious new instrument devised to aid the Voice of America in carrying the testimony of the Free World to peoples behind the Iron Curtain.'[18]

Allied to this overt global propaganda campaign was a programme of covert action designed to put pressure on the Soviet bloc at certain strategic points. NSC-68 recommended an '[i]ntensification of affirmative and timely measures and operations by covert means in the fields of economic warfare and political and psychological warfare with a view to fomenting and supporting unrest and revolt in selected strategic satellite countries.'[19] Although US covert action had been underway in selected satellites since November 1948, covert operations expanded considerably in the wake of NSC-68.[20] In April 1950, before the final draft of NSC-68 was approved, Robert Joyce, of the Policy Planning Staff, instructed the Office of Policy Coordination (OPC) to begin consideration of 'increased activities.'[21] Between 1949 and 1952, the OPC grew from 302 to 2,812 personnel, with 3,142 overseas contract employees. Its budget increased from $4.7 million to $82 million, and in a significant indication of the global ambition of this covert counter-offensive OPC presence in overseas CIA stations grew from 7 to 47.[22] OPC activities centred around the organization of émigrés from the Soviet Union and the satellites in support of a covert American strategy aimed at the liberation of volatile sections of the Soviet bloc, most notably Albania, the Baltic States and the Ukraine. The OPC provided covert support for paramilitary incursions into the Soviet bloc by groups of émigrés.[23] It also supported anti-communist propaganda activities by a network of private individuals and groups in the USA. This state–private network provided an extensive 'front' for the more offensive and covert aspects of the US Government's attempts to roll back communism.[24]

The most prominent of the private organizations which benefited from the OPC's largesse was the National Committee for a Free Europe (NCFE). The NCFE was established in May 1949. It's board was chaired by former Under-Secretary of State,

Joseph C. Grew, and included Dwight D. Eisenhower, Cecil B. De Mille and OSS veterans such as William Donovan and DeWitt Poole. The NCFE acted as a rallying point for Russian and Eastern European exiles in the USA. It sought, first of all, to put the exiles 'on their feet, materially and spiritually.'[25] When the émigrés were organized, the NCFE aimed to 'put the voices of exiled leaders on the air, addressed to their own peoples, back in Europe, in their own languages, in familiar tones.'[26] In July 1950, the NCFE began broadcasting across the Iron Curtain through Radio Free Europe (RFE). Although covertly funded and guided by the CIA, as an independent broadcaster, RFE enjoyed an operational freedom not available to official national broadcasters. The station's main task was, 'the disintegration of the Soviet Communist regimes, sowing dismay, doubt, defeatism and dissension in the minds of the present usurpers.'[27] An early draft RFE policy directive observed that in pursuing this objective, RFE was not hampered by the restraints under which stations such as the Voice of America and the BBC operated:

> Among the number of other differences are Radio Free Europe's emphasis on subject matter of immediate interest to its audience – an emphasis which is largely if not exclusively dependent on a constant flow of excellent inside information – its acceptance of rumor and gossip as effective weapons of psychological warfare, and especially the informality and intimacy of its contact with its listeners.[28]

In the wake of NSC-68, as propaganda became an increasingly important, and expensive, part of the US armoury, the US Government sponsored a range of academic studies designed to identify the most effective means of wielding the new propaganda weapon. Various studies were undertaken to identify Soviet psychological vulnerabilities, the best means of getting the American message over the Iron Curtain, and the most effective means of undermining Soviet control.[29] The largest of these, entitled 'Project TROY', was launched by Edward Barrett in October 1950. Barrett convened a panel of 21 distinguished academics – scientists, social scientists and historians – to consider the technical problems of overcoming Soviet jamming of the Voice of America.[30] By the time 'Project TROY' reported early in 1951, its remit had extended to consider other means of perforating the Iron Curtain and it had sought to develop a concept of 'political warfare'. 'Project TROY' reported that 'real opportunities for political warfare against Russia exist and have been only barely exploited.' It advocated 'a vigorous unified psychological warfare program,' designed to: consolidate support among allies and neutrals; impair the functioning of the Soviet regime by exploiting fissures in the system; and lay the basis for eventual negotiation by creating possible alternatives to Soviet policies and organizations:

> …leaving the way open for the top leadership to move, under internal pressure, toward one of these alternatives without sacrificing prestige so utterly that they would feel compelled to embark upon an all out war.[31]

For such a policy to be effective, the academics on 'Project TROY' were convinced that political warfare 'should be organized like any form of warfare, with special weapons, strategy, tactics, logistics and training.'[32] The reorganization of the USA's propaganda operations was already being considered by others in the US adminis-tration. By late 1950, propaganda operations were divided uneasily between the State Department, the Defense Department, the Economic Cooperation Administration and the CIA. To solve the organizational problems, on 4 April 1951, following pro-tracted negotiations, and against State Department wishes, President Truman estab-lished a Psychological Strategy Board to provide more effective planning, coordination and conduct of psychological operations.[33] The PSB was composed of senior officials of the three interested agencies – State, Defense and CIA – with an independent director appointed by the President. It was not an operating agency, but was authorized to plan psychological operations at the strategic level, coordinate the implementation of psychological strategy by operating agencies, and evaluate the results of the entire psychological effort in its fulfilment of national policy.[34]

The creation of the PSB was the culmination of a process which began in late 1949, in which propaganda was elevated from being an adjunct to diplomacy to become a major weapon in US strategy for winning the Cold War. The organizational imperative for the creation of the PSB reflected the expansion of the US propaganda apparatus, both overt and covert, in the wake of NSC-68. The location of the PSB within the national security apparatus of the US Government indicates the elevated position that psychological warfare had taken in US planning. According to Dr Edward Lilly's internal study, the major accomplishment of the establishment of the PSB was 'that interdepartmental planning and coordination in the psychological field was raised to a much higher level,' just below the National Security Council and with a link to the President.[35] Gregory Mitrovich later observed, 'so extensive and ambitious was the planning for covert and psychological warfare that it may be con-sidered strategic in nature; that is, the framers of the plans designed them not only to fight, but also to win, the cold war.'[36]

British and American cooperation, 1950–51

In late 1949, as part of the reassessment of the USA's propaganda programme, the State Department reviewed the possibility of 'expanded US–British cooperation in the foreign information field.' Cooperation, the State Department suggested, could be extended beyond the exchange of propaganda material to include an exchange of papers on current and prospective information policy.[37] As part of this review, US missions were asked to comment on current arrangements for cooperation with British information staff in the field, and to make recommendations of areas in which propaganda cooperation might be expanded. In anticipation of additional cooperative measures an informal approach was made to the British Embassy in Washington to determine the procedures for expanding cooperation.[38]

The Foreign Office, however, had been somewhat disappointed with the results of cooperation since 1948. In October 1949, the British Embassy in Washington informed the Foreign Office that the State Department was reviewing its anti-communist prop-aganda. The State Department, they said, had found the exchange of material with IRD of the 'greatest value,' and felt the time had come for a further exchange of views with the Foreign Office.[39] Warner replied that, 'we have not been particularly impressed with the results of [the State Department's] Research Section, nor with the activities of US Information Officers in the field.' Nevertheless, he added, it would be worthwhile to send someone to Washington with a view to finding out 'what their resources are and also to get a better idea than we have at present of how they are using them.'[40]

In January 1950, the IRD's Adam Watson was despatched to Washington. His remit, however, was strictly limited. The IRD was not keen on any division of labour and Watson was merely to report back on US suggestions. He was informed that the Foreign Office was not contemplating any closer coordination in the policy of anti-communist propaganda, and he was instructed that he 'should not discuss this at all.'[41] It is apparent that Foreign Office views of US propaganda had improved little since 1948. Closer coordination of activities 'would be too hampering and prevent our operations being as speedy as is essential.' Watson was also asked to raise, tactfully, the quality of the USA's anti-communist propaganda. Reports from some British missions suggested that 'the general desire of the United States Information Officers put into the field is to be able to report large quantitative results, regardless of whether they have done any good or not.' Watson was asked to pass on the Foreign Office's concern that the large volume of US propaganda material, particularly in South-East Asia, could spoil the market for Britain's anti-communist material. In addition to his meetings in the State Department, Watson was given a wide remit to explore other potential sources or recipients of the IRD's anti-communist material, most notably the newly established National Committee for a Free Europe, about which, the Foreign Office apparently knew little. He also planned to visit a number of research institutes at the Universities of Harvard, Yale, Princeton and Columbia, which, according to Warner, generated a volume of research material on a scale not practicable for the Foreign Office, and 'much of which may be of considerable value as raw material for publicity.'[42]

Despite Foreign Office expectations, Watson's visit to the USA in January 1950 was a success. He spent some time working in the State Department and was able to impress upon senior officials the need for greater subtlety in US anti-communist propaganda. Watson explained at length the IRD's methods for distributing propaganda material unattributably. Citing the example of South-East Asia, he discussed the 'de-Europeanizing' treatment required in the production of propaganda material, he stressed the value of material written by natives, signed feature articles by prominent individuals, and interviews with refugees by prominent local journalists. Where material was sent from home, Watson emphasized the need for accurate translations, and in all output, the importance of propaganda based on facts. Dissemination, Watson said, was best undertaken through, 'native, if necessary obscure and small publishing houses, unsuspected of foreign contacts.' The IRD, he added, had already begun to develop such outlets.[43]

Watson clearly had some success in attempting to explain the value of a more subtle approach to anti-communist propaganda. According to the British Embassy, US officials were particularly interested in Watson's explanation of IRD's tactics:

> They have freely admitted that, in many ways, they consider our publicity techniques in this field superior to their own. For example, I gather that people like Tommy Thompson (Deputy Assistant Secretary of State for European Affairs) and John Davies (of the Policy Planning Staff) have been concerned for some time at the relative lack of sophistication and of selectivity in the State Department's anti-communist publicity. They therefore particularly welcomed Watson's visit, since it enabled them to point out their own deficiencies to their own people.[44]

Observing his terms of reference, Watson was deliberately vague about any future division of labour in the production of propaganda material, suggesting that informal exchanges of information in London and Washington and in the field should be based upon personal relationships. He stuck to the existing Foreign Office line, which allowed a pooling of resource material, designed to enable 'the two services to aim at the same target from different angles.'[45]

Although there was no real change in policy on cooperation, the visit was considered a success on both sides of the Atlantic. In Washington, Thompson felt that Watson's 'penetrating and substantial conclusions based on British experimentation and practice' would serve to increase cooperation around the world and make 'our parallel efforts more effective.'[46] Watson's visit, Thompson declared, 'has brought this initial stage of cooperation to a new and promising level.'[47] In London, Warner noted that Watson had 'evidently done well' in his attempts to influence the Americans.[48] Moreover, both Powers considered such an exchange of views worth repeating. The embassy in Washington thought the cross-fertilization of ideas resulting from such visits was valuable and recommended 'continuing to concert our anti-communist publicity fairly closely with the Americans.'[49] Thompson also considered the visit to be 'eminently worthwhile' and hoped that 'this type of cooperation may be continued and increased in the future.'[50]

The Foreign Office's growing confidence in US anti-communist propaganda was reinforced by the launch of the Campaign of Truth in April 1950. The British were now also keen to expand cooperation. In May 1950, a Foreign Office memorandum regarding priorities in the field of anti-communist propaganda, observed that, 'the State Department and the Foreign Office have now arrived at much the same ideas about the general need for publicity, both overt and covert and for kindred activities, in order to counteract the spread of communism.'[51] Although the Foreign Office appreciated that differences of resources and policy might lead to certain variations of approach, it was felt that

> A frank exchange of opinion about projects, and about the effects of these projects, cannot fail to be beneficial... It may therefore prove valuable in future to extend the collaboration between the State Department and the Foreign Office beyond the existing exchange of material and programme of action, so as to include comment by each Department, on the general strategy of the other, and the results which appear to be obtained, as well as observations on individual projects while these are still at the planning stage.[52]

The Foreign Office was given an early opportunity to discuss these proposals at a series of meetings between British and US officials which followed the Foreign Ministers Conferences held in London in April 1950. Between 20 and 22 May 1950, the most senior officials responsible for the propaganda activities of the Foreign Office and the State Department met at the Foreign Office to discuss the increased coordination of propaganda policies. The British delegation comprised Christopher Warner, Ralph Murray and Adam Watson of the IRD, representatives of the Information Policy Department, and J.B. Clarke of the BBC External Services. The US delegation comprised Edward W. Barrett, Bill Stone, Chairman of the Interdepartmental Foreign Information Staff, and Mallory Browne, Public Affairs Officer at the US Embassy.[53]

Barrett began the meetings by outlining his hopes for extending cooperation in five broad areas: the coordination of policy and ideas; the exchange of propaganda material; cooperation in techniques of distribution; the Voice of America and the BBC; and the consequences in the information field of the North Atlantic Treaty.[54] Barrett described the changing attitude in the USA towards the use of propaganda as a weapon in the Cold War. He emphasized the increase in Congressional support for propaganda activities generated by the Campaign of Truth. Although US plans, Barrett stated, were still in the 'preliminary stage', the USA was devoting considerable resources to the propaganda effort. Barrett informed the meeting in the strictest confidence that estimates were for $78 million for the first year, and $120 million for the second.[55]

As Watson had done in January, Warner and Murray sought to impress upon the Americans the importance of concentrating less on the quantity of propaganda and focus on the need for a more subtle, carefully targeted and indirect campaign. Warner said that the Foreign Office had found that saturation point for directly distributed material was very quickly reached and British information officers devoted much time and effort to developing local contacts who would print British material, or reflect British views in their own writing. In particular, he suggested, there was little value in saturating areas such as South-East Asia and the Middle East with Western-issued anti-communist material which would be automatically distrusted. American officials once again expressed great interest in British methods. Barrett replied that although much could be done through public statements which stressed the 'unity of purpose of the nations of the free world,' he was also interested in developing similar techniques to the British for the use of 'grey' propaganda, particularly in South-East Asia.[56]

One area in which the USA was keen to expand cooperation was broadcasting. One of the problems in the development of the 'Ring Plan' was the fact that with the exception of Alaska, where new transmitters were planned, the USA had no territory near the Soviet bloc. The British, of course, had territory and influence in various strategic locations where the Americans hoped to site new transmitters, most notably in the Middle East and South-East Asia. Although full details of the radio 'Ring Plan' were not revealed to the British at this stage, Barrett described US efforts to overcome Soviet jamming. He also gave a brief account of US plans for broadcasting over RFE, which, he said, would 'take a tougher line than the BBC or even VOA.'

Barrett suggested further technical cooperation to circumvent Soviet jamming. The Voice of America had already begun negotiations with the BBC for relay time on BBC transmitters in Singapore, Malaya and Ceylon, in return for time on US transmitters in Munich and Salonika. Barrett proposed the construction of new transmitters in Ceylon, Singapore and Bahrain to relay BBC and VOA programmes. The State Department also wished to take advantage of the high-powered transmitter at Crowborough in Sussex which, under the codename Aspidistra, had broadcast BBC and 'black' radio transmissions during the War.[57] In early 1950, an American technical team had visited the facility at Crowborough, which was now used by the Diplomatic Wireless Service (DWS), and found that it was not being used to full advantage.[58] The Americans wanted to use the Aspidistra's 650-watt medium-wave transmitter after midnight for broadcasts to the Ukraine. Barrett also offered to provide two additional transmitters for DWS morse code use, releasing two larger short-wave transmitters for further VOA relays. Although the Foreign Office deferred a decision on the use of Aspidistra, they supported the proposals for the BBC and VOA to share facilities, and agreed to approach the governments of Ceylon, Bahrain and Singapore regarding the construction of new transmitters. It was also agreed that technicians from the BBC and the VOA would undertake a joint study of the problems of overcoming jamming.[59]

There were, however, signs that the Foreign Office was somewhat uneasy at the Americans' ambitious broadcasting plans. Warner noted that BBC contracts with Malaya, Singapore and Ceylon included clauses reserving the power of veto over anything carried from transmitters in their territories, and he warned that broadcasts criticizing the Chinese Communist Government might lead to protests.[60] Barrett reassured the Foreign Office that the VOA would 'avoid anything in their relays which might be embarrassing to His Majesty's Government or to the local authorities on whose territory relay transmitters were situated.'[61] The British were also sceptical about RFE. British experience during the War had, Warner said, 'shown that exiles were apt to get out of touch with their own countries surprisingly quickly and to be moved by personal and internal political considerations rather than strictly patriotic considerations.' He made it clear that Britain would not be returning to 'black' broadcasting. Wartime experience had shown such work had to be 'exceptionally brilliantly done,' and it would now be 'prohibitively difficult and expensive.'[62] The British were also concerned that the expansion of American broadcasting in Europe might be provocative and lead to interference in domestic broadcasting. The allocation of long and medium wavelengths in Europe had been agreed by 33 nations, including those from the Soviet bloc, at a conference in Copenhagen in June 1948. Warner stressed that the British Government would be 'averse to anything which might lead to a breakdown in the Copenhagen Plan and broadcasting "war", particularly on medium waves.'[63] The American minutes recorded, 'that the British Government is apprehensive about the European broadcasting situation and will be careful not to take any action which might affect British home services.'[64]

The meetings also revealed significant differences in the target area priorities for British and US anti-communist propaganda. The British gave a higher priority to countries outside the Iron Curtain, particularly those parts of the free world in danger of communist penetration, and in which 'public opinion could still exercise a considerable effect on policy, especially in times of crisis.' First priority was given to France, Italy, Germany and South-East Asia. Secondary priority was given to India, Pakistan and the Middle East. US propaganda, Barrett replied, was principally directed over the Iron Curtain, and most strongly at the Soviet Union itself. British efforts to penetrate the Iron Curtain with propaganda were limited to the overseas services of the BBC. Moreover, the Foreign Office focused greater attention on the satellite states than on the Soviet Union. They considered these countries to be 'less firmly controlled, more recently Sovietised, and more used to listening to foreign broadcasts.'[65]

Despite such differences the talks concluded with a wide-ranging discussion, in which various degrees of cooperation in certain 'critical areas' were agreed. In South-East Asia, Barrett recommended closer liaison in Singapore including an exchange of propaganda material, translations and analysis of the Chinese press. Warner invited the Americans to send a top man or team to work at the British Regional Information Office in Singapore. It was also proposed that reading through the Chinese press could be divided between the British service in Peking and the USIS in Hong Kong. There was a general agreement on cooperation in the Middle East, where Britain and the USA would occasionally pursue joint policies to offset communist charges of disagreement and rivalry. Cooperation was also to be extended in India and Pakistan. In Europe, there was concern at the trend towards neutrality, particularly in France. In an effort to counter this trend and promote the North Atlantic Treaty, it was agreed to 'exchange ideas on all possible common lines of action and give more attention to developing effective slogans.' It was noted that cooperation between British and US information officers in Paris was already very close. The British information officer, it was reported, even passed on, 'insulting remarks about the Americans made to him by Frenchmen.' It was hoped that the Americans would pass on similar remarks made about the British! Finally, there was an agreement to exchange ideas on all output to the satellite states.[66]

In a significant indication of British and US cooperation in covert propaganda activities, it was agreed that 'further study should be given to exploiting the propaganda possibilities in Albania.' In late 1948, the British Government had formulated a policy of subversion aimed at 'detaching' one of the satellites from the Soviet bloc. The proposed target was Albania, and a covert operation was launched in cooperation with the American CIA to infiltrate Albanian resistance fighters into the country to foment unrest. The first team of men had gone ashore at the beginning of October 1949.[67]

In planning, it had been assumed that special operations in Albania would be accompanied by a propaganda offensive.[68] However, the restriction on the Foreign Office conducting subversive propaganda in communist countries was not lifted until December 1949, after the operation had begun.[69] Even then, Britain and the USA had few resources for propaganda in Albania. Neither Britain or the USA had embassies in Tirana, and therefore had no direct contact with the Albanian people or local channels for the dissemination of subversive propaganda. The IRD conducted little direct anti-communist propaganda in Eastern Europe, and relied upon the overseas services of the BBC. The BBC's daily 15-minute Albanian language programme was broadcast 90 minutes before the electricity was switched on in Albanian towns.[70] US broadcasts to Albania via Radio Free Europe and Voice of America did not begin until July 1950 and May 1951 respectively.[71]

Nevertheless, the BBC remained the principal means of directing propaganda at the Albanian people. Albanian resistance leaders were given time on the BBC's Albanian service, and shortly after the first landings the Foreign Office agreed to fund an additional 15-minute Albanian language slot, later in the evening.[72] However, with no representation in Albania, it was difficult to assess the impact of the operation, or acquire new material for broadcasts. At the meetings in May 1950, Warner agreed to ask the French, who had an embassy in Tirana, to provide information on events in Albania which could be broadcast by the BBC and VOA.[73] Barrett said the State Department was also considering 'various suggestions in the "H.G. Wells" category' for penetrating the Iron Curtain, such as the use of balloons.[74] A balloon leaflet drop over Albania was later aborted when the wind changed.[75] The whole Albanian operation eventually collapsed when it was realised that the country was not ripe for revolt. Those émigrés dropped into Albania were betrayed by Kim Philby, the MI6 liaison officer in Washington, and arrested by the Albanian security services.[76]

Although the operation in Albania marked the nadir of Anglo-American covert operations in Eastern Europe, the meetings in London in May 1950 resulted in the expansion of British and US cooperation in the use of propaganda as a weapon in the Cold War. The meetings cemented the close personal ties between those senior British and US officials responsible for anti-communist propaganda, and revealed the extent of common thinking in the Foreign Office and the State Department regarding the use of propaganda. Barrett recorded in his own notes on the trip, that Britain and the USA now agreed 'that informational activity, indeed psychological warfare, is becoming vitally important.'[77] As a result, Britain and the USA agreed to maintain 'close and continuous liaison' on all aspects of information policy.[78]

The most immediate result of the London talks was an increase in cooperation in the field. The State Department and the Foreign Office sent instructions to field missions regarding the talks and the desirability of extended cooperation.[79] Both expressed the importance of maintaining 'freedom of action' in propaganda work, but as the State Department's circular indicated, there was a new policy for the closest possible cooperation short of joint operations:

> While each government will retain complete freedom of action in conducting overseas information, there should be close cooperation wherever possible in support of common objectives. To this end there should be continuous exchange of ideas between the Department and the Foreign Office and between our missions abroad with a view to developing common lines of information policy, planning and conduct of activities. It was agreed, however, that such cooperation should normally stop short of joint information operations.[80]

Despite the restriction on joint operations, it is apparent that in many countries the extent of cooperation in the planning and implementation of propaganda activities was such that joint activity was often undertaken. Indeed, it is difficult to see how information staff could seek to develop common lines in information policy, and the planning and conduct of operations, without becoming involved in joint activity. In practice, rather than avoiding joint operations, British and US information staff in the field took great care to maintain the outward appearance of acting independently. A US review of field comments on cooperation with the British information services in August 1950 found that most posts agreed that, 'no appearance should be given publicly of joint action either in policy formulation or programming.'[81] Information officers were happy to exchange material and consult in private, but there was no question that they would seek to combine the output of their propaganda activities. In each case the State Department found information officers in the field were careful to maintain 'individuality of output.'[82] The one notable exception to this rule was the Middle East. In response to Soviet propaganda, which sought to highlight Anglo-American rivalry, it was agreed, 'to lay on from time to time demonstrations of solidarity between the USA and UK in the Middle East.'[83]

In 1950, the Foreign Office and the State Department both completed reviews of British and US cooperation in propaganda work in the field. Both concluded that British and US information staff generally enjoyed 'cordial relations.'[84] The Foreign Office review, which was concluded after the talks in London, found a significant expansion of cooperation followed the circular instruction outlining the result of the talks:

> Though there has generally been goodwill before the arrival of the circular, and in some cases active cooperation, there is no doubt that it has led to a complete re-examination of what can be done and in many cases to more effective measures for joint consultation and the pooling of ideas and for mutual help in every possible way. As a result, regular discussions between the information staff have been arranged in most posts and the exchange of material and films has been placed on a regular footing.[85]

The degree to which British and US information staff worked together continued to vary from post to post. In several cases cooperation involved a division of labour designed to avoid duplication of effort in, for example, the reading of local press or the translation of propaganda material into local languages.[86] In other cases, British staff provided the benefit of their experience regarding possible channels for the distribution of propaganda material. For example, the US Embassy in Bombay reported that British information officers regularly commented on local editors and 'the editorial policies of Bombay papers.'[87] Similarly, in Hong Kong, British information staff provided information 'relative to subversive activity among local trade unions so that appropriate pamphlets and posters can be more strategically distributed.'[88] In posts where cooperation was even closer, British and US information staff agreed to distribute each others' propaganda material through their own established channels. In Baghdad, the US Embassy reported, 'we have used certain anti-communist squibs from the British in our Kurdish bulletin, they in turn have translated some of our Soviet Affairs Notes material, notably the one on the treatment of Moslems in the USSR.'[89]

One notable example, which serves to illustrate several aspects of liaison, was Venezuela. British and US information officers in Caracas inaugurated weekly meetings in 1950. As a result of these meetings, the US Embassy reported that the British Press Officer had many journalistic acquaintances of long-standing, particularly in the provinces, and 'British press channels are somewhat more effective than ours.' Consequently, it was agreed that anti-communist material would be translated by the US Embassy and given to the British for distribution. Similar arrangements were made for the distribution of material on religious persecution behind the Iron Curtain, which the British passed to Venezuelan parish priests, with whom they had long-established contacts. As a result, the US Embassy reported, this material often appeared in their weekly sermons![90]

One area in which particularly close cooperation developed was South-East Asia. By 1950, British officials concluded that since communism had been held in check in France and Italy, Western Europe was not the weak spot it had been, and South-East Asia was now 'the softest spot in the world picture.'[91] The decline of the communist threat in Western Europe was, British officials believed, due in no small part to the anti-communist propaganda effort. On 1 August 1950, the Russia Committee paid tribute to the:

> ...revolution that has been achieved in the field of publicity...partly by the compulsion of events, but also as a result of a deliberate counter-propaganda campaign, a majority of people, certainly in the English-speaking world and Western Europe and a growing number elsewhere have come to recognise communist aims and methods for what they are... Much remained to be done in the areas more vulnerable to communism, such as South-East Asia.[92]

By 1950, the British already had a well-established organization for countering communism in South-East Asia. The British Government had become concerned about the spread of communism in the region following the outbreak of the Malayan Emergency in 1948. Malcolm MacDonald, the British Commissioner General in South-East Asia, was a powerful proponent of what later became known as the domino theory of communist expansion. The region, he insisted, should be viewed as a whole, the communists planned their actions on a theatre-wide basis and Britain should respond in a similarly coordinated manner.[93]

In late 1948, MacDonald advocated the creation of a regional centre to coordinate anti-communist propaganda activities throughout South-East Asia.[94] In May 1949, the IRD established a Regional Information Office (RIO) at the Commissioner General's headquarters at Phoenix Park in Singapore. Singapore was the centre for British defence forces east of Suez, and the Commissioner General's crowded headquarters at Phoenix Park already hosted local centres for the British intelligence and security services.[95] The RIO served as a central planning and production centre for propaganda, both anti-communist and positive, for South-East Asia. It produced propaganda material 'suitably prepared for Asiatic audiences' and, where necessary, in local languages which was passed to 'local publicists for them to pass on to their own public in their own manner.' It used local contacts in the media, trade unions and youth organizations. It also passed background information on communism and Soviet policy 'not of a secret nature but not normally available through public channels' to governments in the region.[96]

In February 1950, as Britain's involvement in Malaya intensified, further regional coordination was provided by a Joint Information and Propaganda Committee (JIPC) which was established in Singapore. Its role was to coordinate the propaganda activities of all agencies involved in the campaign in Malaya to ensure they all 'speak with one voice,' and organize an effective counter to communist-inspired propaganda throughout the region.[97] In August 1950, following the outbreak of the Korean war, MacDonald also established a high-level committee of British regional governors which held monthly meetings at Bukit Serene to consider 'the Cold War as it affects us here.'[98] The committee devoted considerable time to the discussion of propaganda. One of its first meetings, in December 1950, was attended by Ralph Murray and Angus Malcolm, respectively heads of the Foreign Office's IRD and IPD. The committee informed Murray and Malcolm that British propaganda was 'of great importance in helping maintain stability' in South-East Asia. The committee, they were told, regarded 'all British propaganda here as being anti-communist in effect.' Although purely negative anti-communist propaganda was required, its impact was reinforced by a large volume of positive material, the latter was required 'not only for its own sake, but in order that we may demonstrate how communism is inimical to the alternative way of life we offer.'[99]

The Americans were informed about the plans for the creation of the RIO as early as January 1949.[100] Shortly after the RIO's creation, the IRD's Adam Watson wrote to its director, John Rayner, instructing him to take the Americans on the spot 'fairly fully into your confidence' regarding the functions of the RIO.[101] Rayner got on well with his American colleagues and became a valuable asset to Anglo-American propaganda liaison. Joseph Burkholder Smith, a former CIA representative in Singapore, fondly remembers his first encounter with the somewhat eccentric Rayner:

> Rayner was dressed in a bush jacket and a pair of old white walking shorts that looked as though he had worn them for the past week. He had a sharp, thin face, and a clipped Oxbridge accent, the kind most Americans find mimicking irresistible. The walls of his office were covered with clippings of old headlines. All were examples of editorial slips that produced double entendres, like 'KING FLYS BACK TO FRONT' and dozens and dozens more.[102]

Cooperation between British and US information staff in South-East Asia expanded considerably following the outbreak of the Korean War in June 1950. At talks in Washington, in July, British and US information officials agreed on the importance of coordinating propaganda on Korea to avoid divergences of presentation.[103] Later that month, the State Department despatched special instructions to information officers in South-East Asia on cooperation with the British RIO. These indicated a 'wide area in which cooperation could contribute greatly to the achievement of common objectives.' It inaugurated a regular exchange of all propaganda material, particularly 'special Chinese-language material' and information on groups which could receive locally prepared unattributable material. There was also some division of labour, with the Americans providing the product of their press monitoring service in Hong Kong, in exchange for British translation facilities in those posts maintaining such a service.[104]

The Americans also began to build up their propaganda organization in the region along similar lines to the British RIO. In November 1950, the US Consul General in Singapore recommended that he be kept informed of all USIS activities in the region so that he might be 'in a position to supply RIO with information duplicating on the American side what RIO is receiving on the British side.'[105] On a visit to Washington, in July 1951, Rayner pressed the Americans to establish their own regional information office. Shortly afterwards, a Far East Regional Production Centre, with a similar remit to the British RIO, was established in the US Embassy in Manila.[106] A regional liaison officer, the highly respected Si Nadler, was appointed to keep Rayner informed of US propaganda activities in the region.[107] Early in 1951, British and US information staff also began to hold monthly meetings at Phoenix Park to consider proposals for joint activity.[108] A further level of liaison was established when the CIA opened a small station in Singapore in the early 1950s.[109]

Cooperation in anti-communist propaganda did not, however, extend as far as Korea itself. On the outbreak of war the US Secretary of State, Dean Acheson, activated an interdepartmental information committee chaired by Edward Barrett who immediately turned over all the United States Information Service personnel in Korea to General MacArthur and effectively turned the committee into a psychological strategy board.[110] The handover of the State Department's information work to the army rather cut the British out of psychological warfare in Korea. Although there was a proposal to attach a British representative to the US psychological warfare organization in Korea, the military intelligence section (G-2) of the US 8th Army in Korea, jealously guarded its control of this activity. In June 1951, the IRD's Peter Wilkinson observed that, 'as long as General Willoughby was in charge of G-2 there was little chance of any agreement being reached to British participation in the psychological warfare run by the American military authorities.' Wilkinson added that Willoughby would not even allow the CIA's covert action arm, the OPC, to operate in this theatre.[111] The US military did provide the British with extensive details of their psychological warfare activities in Korea.[112] Moreover, a Foreign Office review of information work in Korea concluded that Britain had no interests in Korea which were not identical with those of the Americans, and any service Britain could offer would be 'hardly better than a poor duplication of the American effort.'[113]

Whilst propaganda in Korea was largely controlled by the US military, the British played an important supporting role in South-East Asia. Through the RIO in Singapore the British monitored the effect of events in Korea on audiences throughout South-East Asia and disseminated replies to communist propaganda through local channels.[114] In July 1950, Paul Gore-Booth, the head of the British Information Service in Washington, told Howland Sargeant, the acting head of the State Department's information programme, that Britain's propaganda aimed to 'nail the main Communist lies': that the South Koreans attacked first; that the United States or South Koreans were premeditating aggression or action of any kind; that the Security Council's action was illegal under the UN Charter; that the action taken by the United States had even less justification; and that the 'peace' campaign can honestly be regarded as a genuine effort towards peace.[115]

British propaganda on the Korean War also had an important secondary aim which was directed at the USA and reflected the desire of the British Government to localize the conflict and to rein in what many in Britain saw as a rising tide of anti-communism in the USA which threatened to extend the conflict to China or even the Soviet Union. The Foreign Office informed Rayner in Singapore that it wanted 'to avoid giving any support to the tendency in some circles in America to regard the United Nations as a body to crusade against communism.'[116] In Washington, Gore-Booth informed Sargeant that although there was 'little doubt [in the public mind] that the Soviet Government is in fact behind the Korean adventure,' British propaganda was based on the premise that 'the Soviet Government should not be explicitly identified with the military aggression committed by North Korea.' They should, he wrote, do nothing which 'would make it difficult for the Soviet Government to retreat from the support of North Korea.'[117] Britain's fears of a wider conflict receded, however, following the beginning of the armistice negotiations in July 1951. In discussions with USIS staff, at the end of July, Rayner now agreed that British propaganda would stress the achievement of the United Nations in 'putting a stop to Russian imperialist penetration in Asia,' and present the armistice as 'a defeat for Stalin and the communist regime.'[118]

From 1950, the British RIO and the US Information Service cooperated closely in the dissemination of anti-communist material in South-East Asia. In 1950, the IRD began production of a South-East Asian version of its unattributable weekly digest consisting of quotations of news and comment from the South-East Asian press and radio.[119] The RIO also distributed a large volume of pamphlets, most of which appeared 'without any publishers' imprints and constitute our "discreet" publications.'[120] One pamphlet, produced by the USIS and distributed by the British RIO, was entitled *When the Communists Came*; it was targeted at the overseas Chinese and contained stories of extortion and suicide among their families in China.[121] Articles for which second rights had been obtained were despatched from London for distribution to the local English press and the vernacular press in Singapore; these included, in December 1950, 12 articles on China from the *Manchester Guardian*, which the RIO turned into a pamphlet in English and Chinese.[122] The USIS and the RIO also distributed cheap imprints of prominent anti-communist literature in local languages. In June 1951, the USIS informed British information staff that their new book translation programme intended to produce 2 Malay and 12–14 Chinese volumes per year. Notable subjects were Richard Crossman's edited volume of revelatory essays *The God that Failed*, and Orwell's *Animal Farm*.[123] The US information officer in Djakarta reported that the editor of the national newspaper, *Keng Po*, had received a copy of *The God that Failed* from the British Information Services. He had subsequently written two front page editorials on the book, and 'pointedly commended it to the Chinese of Djakarta as worthwhile reading for those toying with communism.'[124]

Most of this propaganda material was directed at the educated classes. MacDonald admitted, in 1951, that the Commission-General had no contact with Chinese working classes in South-East Asia, and that more innovative thinking was required to target the less educated.[125] Broadcasting clearly had a key role to play. In the early 1950s, the VOA had only modest medium-wave broadcasts in the region, but the BBC Overseas Service was considered an important branch of overseas propaganda and was kept fully informed by the Foreign Office of the government propaganda line.[126] The British also had important contacts with local broadcasting services. A Director of Broadcasting jointly responsible to the governments of Malaya and Singapore sat on the JIPC. In July 1951, he was provided with the first scripts of interviews with captured communist soldiers.[127] There was also regular consultation regarding propaganda themes between the RIO and government-controlled Radio Malaya. RIO advice was given in particular in connection with weekly series of broadcasts entitled 'World Affairs' and 'This is Communism', broadcast in English and various Chinese dialects.[128]

Various visual formats were also used. The British Government had employed film and newsreel to good effect in Malaya since 1948, and British newsreel coverage of Korea was intensive in the first sixth months of the conflict.[129] In July 1951, the USIS asked Rayner for documentary newsreels showing, through the mouth of a Chinese ex-communist soldier, how the Korean War had been planned in Moscow; the communist defeat; and separate documentaries on each Asian contingent in Korea. The USIS also ran a 'photo review' poster campaign for which they requested photographs of Chinese and Korean POWs.[130]

The use of strip cartoons to illustrate the points made in the printed matter was one of the more innovative developments in targeting mass opinion in South-East Asia. A film and strip cartoon based on the booklet *When the Communists Came* was produced at the US Regional Production Centre in Manila.[131] The RIO produced a weekly booklet, *Inside Soviet China*, which included cartoons depicting the effects of communism in China, together with 'two strip cartoons of our popular Chinese victim of communism, Mr Wang.'[132] In 1950, the IRD secured the overseas rights to produce a strip cartoon version of *Animal Farm* for newspaper serialization. The strip cartoon – which consisted of 90, four-frame strips – was widely published in newspapers across the Far East, Middle East, Latin America, India, Pakistan, Ceylon, Africa, the West Indies and Iceland. The RIO in Singapore was particularly active in promoting the strip and produced translations in Chinese, Malay, Vietnamese and French.[133]

Alongside this considerable propaganda effort British and US authorities also worked together to censor opinion about China and the war in Korea. In December 1950, MacArthur's headquarters introduced direct censorship of military news, and a Press Advisory Commission was established in Tokyo with the full support of the British authorities. In London, the IRD worked with the Foreign Office News Department to brief journalists on the conflict and when *The Daily Worker* ran a piece attacking Rhee's tyranny and implicitly criticizing American policy, the Cabinet toyed with the idea of introducing draconian press laws banning journalism which brought 'aid and comfort to the enemy.'[134] In South-East Asia, British authorities were less chary about wielding their administrative power. In August 1950, the British High Commissioner and the Governor of Singapore claimed to have enough information to bring a case against two pro-communist newspapers in the territory. 'The suppression of both newspapers' they concluded, 'was highly desirable and if possible the timing should be coordinated.'[135] In Singapore, the JIPC considered the control of films, gramophone records and songs from Chinese sources and agreed that films which 'focused the loyalty of the Chinese audience on China,' were 'undesirable and should be banned.'[136]

British and US cooperation in the production and dissemination of anti-communist propaganda in South-East Asia was the primary example of the kind of 'close and continuous liaison' agreed by Barrett and Warner in London in May 1950. Cooperation in the production and dissemination of anti-communist propaganda material was aided by the existence of a large British propaganda organization in Singapore, and by British experience and contacts across the region. It is also apparent that the USA's propaganda organization and methods in South-East Asia were in some degree modelled on the British effort. Both Powers, however, maintained an independent propaganda programme. There were geographical divisions. The British were satisfied to take a back-seat in Korea and the USA limited its propaganda activities in Malaya. Britain also pursued an independent line in its policy and propaganda with regard to the Soviet role in the war in Korea, at least until mid-1951. Most importantly, Britain and the USA were careful to maintain an independent output. 'Though collaborating closely in private,' wrote Rayner in June 1951, 'we continue our propaganda separately, in this way getting the benefit of approaching our target with two separate weapons.'[137]

The coordination of propaganda activities in the field was mirrored by close consultation on the development of anti-communist propaganda policies between

London and Washington. The most important development was the appointment of information liaison officers (ILO) to the British Embassy in Washington and the American Embassy in London. The IRD's Adam Watson was appointed ILO at the British Embassy in Washington, in August 1950. According to Watson, his role was, 'to explore every part of the field as best I could, and to see what could be done to bring American and British operations and long-term planning as much into harmony as possible.'[138] In addition to liaison with the State Department, Watson's post involved a certain amount of work at the United Nations, and liaison with the Voice of America in New York. Watson's counterpart at the US Embassy in London, W.F. Frye, was instructed to liaise with the British Government on 'all aspects of current information activities, including broadcasting and certain special activities.' Both ILO's were also expected to make occasional field trips to attend regional meetings of information officers and maintain a personal knowledge of the operational problems of information work.[139]

Adam Watson was a particularly successful liaison officer and had many influential contacts. Watson was an ideal choice for the post of liaison officer in Washington. He had joined the IRD in 1949 after four years at the British Embassy in Moscow. His detailed firsthand knowledge of Soviet affairs and life behind the Iron Curtain made him a typical recruit for the IRD. When in Moscow he had also established close relations with his counterparts at the American Embassy, most notably George Kennan, John Paton Davies, and the ambassador, Walter Bedell Smith. One of Watson's duties in Moscow was to drive over to Bedell Smith's house with papers and telegrams which the British Ambassador wished to show to the Americans. Bedell Smith was a genial host who would provide Watson with a glass of whisky while he read the reports, and the two became good friends. By 1950, Watson's contacts were back in Washington – Kennan and Davies joined the Policy Planning Staff and Bedell Smith shortly became Director of Central Intelligence. Watson later recalled that when he first visited Washington, in January 1950, he was relieved to find himself, 'among very good friends.' He eschewed the luxury of a Washington hotel and stayed in the homes of his American friends. He was only too pleased to be offered the post of Information Liaison Officer, and his appointment was warmly welcomed in Washington.[140]

Watson began regular meetings at the State Department shortly after arriving in Washington in August 1950.[141] He also quickly established contact with 'certain sections of the CIA,' most notably Frank Wisner of the OPC. Through his contacts with the CIA, Watson met C.D. Jackson, a highly connected psychological warfare veteran, who was a guiding hand behind the NCFE. Jackson went on to become Eisenhower's Special Assistant for psychological operations. He was, Watson wrote, 'warmly anglophile' and the two 'worked very closely together' under Truman and Eisenhower.[142]

In May 1951, Watson established liaison with the Psychological Strategy Board. During a visit to the USA in May 1951, the head of the IRD, John Peck had astutely recognized that the ongoing struggle in Washington for control of psychological operations had implications for cooperation with Britain and instructed Watson to establish contact with the new PSB. Hitherto, Foreign Office cooperation in this field had, for the most part, been with the State Department, whose amenability was, according to Peck, 'probably greater than that of the other governmental agencies concerned with psychological warfare.'[143] Peck observed – and events in Korea supported his view – that if the international situation deteriorated and war became probable, 'the controlling emphasis will shift from the State Department towards the Service Departments,' and Britain's influence would diminish. He was, therefore, keen to seize the initiative and establish close ties with the PSB and accustom them 'to a policy of cooperation with the UK.'[144] In August 1951, Watson met with Gordon Gray, the newly appointed Director of the PSB, to request arrangements for liaison.[145] US officials were in favour of extending cooperation to include the PSB as long as it did not bring similar requests from other governments, and Watson was informed that he should liaise directly with Gray.[146]

In mid-1951, Watson's role became even more important when his counterpart at the American Embassy in London was relieved of his responsibilities. Frye, it seems, had little appetite for propaganda and had failed to establish an effective role in London. Frye was not replaced, and Watson proceeded to handle liaison in both directions. He informed the Foreign Office:

> This means I have been playing the part of a broker: exploring the advantages which cooperation in various fields might bring, and trying to arrange it where desirable. I have been a strictly British broker, of course; but the Americans have not minded this.[147]

From his position in Washington, Watson was well placed to witness the elevation of propaganda in USA's Cold War strategy. Throughout 1950 and 1951, Watson's reports from Washington are littered with references to 'the new concept of influencing public opinion' which was developing among 'the more thoughtful people concerned in the State Department.' He continued:

> More than one of the people concerned here has said to me that we must look on these activities as among the most important in all foreign policy… It was not just a question of 'projecting America' but rather of seeing how public opinion in each country could be influenced so as to incline the Government more towards the policy which the US desired it to adopt and deter it from those policies which the US disliked. In many areas this might involve saying little about the United States itself. I will write more fully about this in the near future: it is a pretty new concept even in Washington and has hardly reached the field. But I will quote one remark of Stone's 'I presume that the Projection of Britain is regarded as old time around Christopher Warner's office too?'[148]

In June 1951, shortly after the creation of the PSB, Watson provided a more detailed overview of American thinking on political warfare. 'The Americans,' he began, 'have accepted "the struggle for men's minds" as a major feature of their general struggle with the Kremlin.' Psychological strategy, he stated, had now been given its due place alongside more traditional means of waging war. The Administration, he observed, was not merely concerned with minimizing communist propaganda and subversion in the free world, Russia was 'the heart of the matter.' Alongside the plans for propaganda advocated in the TROY project, Watson revealed that 'other aspects of promoting and exploiting disorder inside the Soviet Union have been carefully studied.' These plans fitted into a broader American strategic concept on how war against Russia might be waged. The Americans he said were strongly opposed 'to slogging the issue out on the plains of Northern Europe: what they call "rolling our troops down the old European bowling alley."' They were looking at other ways of weakening the Soviet drive in Europe:

> A large proportion of the population of Central Asia and Western Siberia is made up of racial minorities, political exiles, discontented draft labour and forced labour. In war, the Americans seem to think these men could be supplied with arms and built up by radio into a serious, though disconnected, threat to Soviet power and especially communications with the Far East.[149]

The Americans, Watson said, had told him many of the details of these schemes, and were 'anxious for our cooperation not only in the event of war but also now during the preparatory period.'[150]

US officials were particularly keen to encourage British participation in Radio Free Europe. In London, in September 1950, Frank Wisner and Robert Joyce of the OPC met with Christopher Warner, the IRD head, Ralph Murray, and D.P. Reilly of the Permanent Under-Secretary's Department. The Americans wanted the Foreign Office to join with them in organizing Radio Free Europe, and pressed them to organize the large Russian and Eastern European exile groups in London along similar lines to the National Committee for a Free Europe.

The Foreign Office were cautious about the American proposal and deferred their decision pending a closer investigation of the organization and broadcasts of RFE.[151] In Washington, Watson was asked to provide details of the station's programmes and policy but warned to discourage further developments of the idea of cooperation. According to Murray, they had to consider, among other factors, 'the damage we might be doing to ourselves by boosting Radio Free Europe at the expense of the services of the BBC.'[152] As a result of wartime experience, officials in London also remained cautious about getting involved with exile groups. In February 1951, Murray informed Watson that they had 'only just got some way in obtaining authorisation' to organize exiles and establish liaison with them, 'the arrangements envisaged do not go beyond appointing a liaison official and providing some finance.'[153] In a chilling reply, Watson wrote:

> Kim Philby, George Jellicoe and I were all most interested...that you had obtained authorisation to proceed to organise the Eastern European exiles in the United Kingdom and to establish some liaison with them...in spite of a search we do not know anything about this development. Could you therefore please arrange for us to be informed?[154]

While the Americans went ahead with RFE alone, the Foreign Office undertook a detailed review of the service. BBC monitoring reports and a sample of RFE scripts provided by Watson were scrutinized by the Information Policy Department, who found that 'their quality is quite good – most of it has been reasonably sound, dignified and unsensational stuff.'[155] From his contacts in the CIA, Watson also provided information on the general policy of RFE, and the extent of guidance exercized by the US Government. This was, according to Watson 'of a very general kind.' The exiles were allowed to write their own scripts, 'subject to occasional warnings and requests,' but, he reassured the Foreign Office, 'the squabbles and feuds between the various groups of exiles here' did not get on the air.[156]

C.D. Jackson impressed upon Watson the importance of RFE, and in March 1951, following discussions with Paul Gore-Booth, head of the British Information Services in America, Watson urged the Foreign Office not to 'rebuff overtures from an organisation of this calibre to help with cooperation and advice.'[157] Such cooperation, he added, need not be publicly known. There was also, he argued, no reason why RFE should damage the BBC:

> If it is recognised that the BBC and the Voice of America can shoot into the same target from different angles, there must also be a place for a broadcast which is not that of a free western power but of exiles from the country itself who have found refuge abroad. Since the approach is so different, I do not see that we should lose anything in effecting an improvement in the quality of Radio Free Europe broadcasts.[158]

The following month C.D. Jackson called on Warner in London. He described current and planned RFE services, and agreed a programme for cooperation with the British. British missions would be asked for comments on the effectiveness of RFE transmissions, and this information would be passed to Jackson through Watson. In return, Jackson would provide the Foreign Office with RFE policy directives, and details of any Eastern Europeans resident in the UK whom the RFE proposed to employ. The British Government's comments on these individuals, Jackson added, would be welcome. It was agreed that a representative of the RFE's editorial organization in Munich would visit the IRD in London to discuss 'material requirements,' and that an IRD official might visit Munich.[159] At a meeting with Wisner and Jackson, in Washington in July 1951, British officials agreed that the Foreign Office would supply news and 'discreet advice' to a RFE correspondent who was about to be appointed to London. Jackson also asked the Foreign Office to help him to hand-pick people for the new Hungarian and Polish services, as some of 'the best Poles for the purpose' were in London.[160]

British cooperation was, however, to remain strictly confidential. Warner made it clear that any official British connection with RFE, 'must be kept secret and also the British official origin of any material we supply.'[161] Although the offer for the Foreign Office to participate in the RFE remained open, the possibility of putting British representation inside RFE was problematic as long as there was no émigré organization in London to act as a front for Foreign Office involvement. Bernard Burrows, the British Information Officer in Washington observed, in July 1951, that although the CIA assisted the RFE, and even had men in the organization, the NCFE had an independent existence and its own funds. Consequently, the US Government could claim it was an unofficial organization for which they were not responsible:

> If, however, we put someone into Radio Free Europe he would in present circumstances have to be either directly dependent on the Foreign Office or some other government organisation, and if H.M. Government were asked questions in Parliament about it they could probably not say they had nothing to do with it. This would, in the American view, gravely prejudice the whole operation.[162]

The Americans, Burrows said, found the NCFE an 'indispensable buffer' between themselves and the RFE, and pressed the British Government to establish a similar buffer. Although the IRD were keen on the idea, Bevin turned down IRD's recommendation that they should enter into an 'informal relationship' with the East European section of the European Movement, which was headed by Harold Macmillan. The IRD put the suggestion again to Bevin's successor, Herbert Morrison, who was similarly cautious of involvement with exile politics.[163]

Although there was no official Foreign Office involvement in the RFE, informal contact was maintained. Sir Ian Jacob of the BBC Overseas Services met C.D. Jackson in April 1951 and agreed to keep Warner informed of the BBC's contacts with the RFE.[164] IRD representatives visited the RFE in September 1951 and, in February 1952, the veteran British propaganda expert, Robert Bruce-Lockhart, provided the IRD with a detailed account of his own independent tour of the RFE.[165] Some degree of institutional contact was provided in August 1951, when an IRD official named Ramsey was offered a post as a RFE correspondent in Germany. Following discussions with the intelligence section of RFE, it was agreed that Ramsey might also 'serve as an unofficial link between RFE and IRD.' Ramsey, the IRD observed, was keen to accept the position, not least because the pay was over five times what he was earning at the Foreign Office![166]

In addition to support for exile broadcasting, the US Government sought British assistance in the development of the 'Ring Plan'. When Peck visited Washington, in May 1951, he met with representatives of the State Department, the CIA, the PSB and the VOA. In the course of these discussions Peck was given a detailed overview of American offensive psychological operations and the objectives of the 'Ring Plan'. The aim of these operations, he was told, was to 'make things as difficult as possible for the Soviet Government in their relations with their satellites and with their own people.'[167] The objectives of the 'Ring Plan', Peck discovered, went beyond planning for psychological operations in peacetime. It was, he observed, 'an essential part of military preparedness' for war. In addition to fostering discontent in the Soviet bloc, the 'Ring Plan' had three further objectives: to divert Soviet electronic research into seeking means of countering the American operations; and, in the event of war, to create a secure wireless link around the world for use by American and allied armed forces; and to provide a means of establishing contact with the Russian people for psychological warfare purposes. Peck also heard of a plan, 'still in the discussion stage,' to use the ring of transmitters as part of a combined military and psychological warfare operation directed at the 'soft underbelly' of the Soviet Union, those regions east and north-east of the Caspian sea, 'with the aim of detaching the subject peoples of the region from the Soviet Union and virtually cutting it in half.'[168]

The Americans, Peck reported, were quite clear regarding the assistance Britain could provide in developing the 'Ring Plan':

> They frankly look to us for help in negotiating the necessary permission to build radio stations in those parts of the world where we have influence, e.g. India, Pakistan and the Persian Gulf.[169]

Peck, however, was a little taken aback at the wholly offensive nature of the USA's plans for psychological operations. He was surprised that although it was clear that the Americans 'intended to go ahead vigorously, both on political and military grounds with their preparations for offensive psychological warfare,' their approach to defensive operations in the free world were, 'tentative and uncertain.' Moreover, the operations described to Peck, including the 'Ring Plan', revealed a general blurring in US plans between peacetime psychological operations and preparations for war. Although the Americans were anxious to stress that they aimed to avoid any incitement to premature revolt, Peck was concerned that it was not always clear whether US psychological operations were intended to be part of a plan leading up to open warfare, or whether it was hoped they would make war less likely:

> Those that I talked to appeared genuinely anxious to avert another world war, but they certainly do not consider the present situation, in which tens of thousands of Americans have been killed in Korea and a vast effort is being made to defend America and Western Europe, as peace. They have no hesitation in seeking to deploy against Russia in peacetime a psychological warfare effort as vigorous as that being deployed by Russia against the free world. They do not think this effort makes world war any more likely; but they hope that, if war comes, their current PW efforts will have contributed substantially to weakening the Russian war effort and strengthening that of the free world.[170]

Reaction to the 'Ring Plan' in London was decidedly mixed. There was a good deal of scepticism as to whether it would be effective in overcoming Soviet jamming, and opinions differed as to whether the plan was provocative. Paul Falla of the Overseas Planning Section derided the views of those Americans who, 'expect the walls of Jericho to fall down after the first half a dozen blasts or so on the "Coherent Transmitter Array" or whatever their latest engine of psychological warfare is called.'[171] The Permanent Under-Secretary's Department (PUSD) produced a brief on the 'Ring Plan' early in 1951. They doubted that the plan would be successful, but worried that, if it was, the Soviets, 'might feel compelled to take counter-action.' The PUSD brief placed the 'Ring Plan' alongside such clearly provocative measures as the establishment of US bases in Norway.[172]

Foreign Office regional departments also identified local political difficulties regarding the location of broadcasting facilities. The output of stations in the Middle East needed to be carefully monitored to avoid reference to controversial political issues such as Palestine, and Bahrain was felt to be a poor choice because of the need to avoid provoking Persian sovereignty claims over the state.[173] The Foreign Office Eastern Department also rejected the option of Kuwait on the grounds that the regime there was already unstable. They concluded that Anglo-American broadcasting would serve to 'focus upon Kuwait the attentions of all those subversive and communist-inspired elements in the Middle East,' this would not only 'imperil the stability of the present regime but would be likely to put in jeopardy both the oil operations and the station itself.'[174]

The IRD disagreed with the PUSD, and did not believe the plan to be provocative. Notwithstanding local political concerns, the IRD did not object to the 'Ring Plan', and pursued a policy of 'cautious cooperation.'[175] Although they accepted that broadcasts which could not be jammed easily might be seen as 'a good deal more provocative than broadcasts which could be jammed,' IRD officials dismissed the idea that the erection of a ring of transmitters was in itself provocative.[176]

The IRD's policy of cooperation was, however, largely undermined by the Foreign Secretary, Herbert Morrison. In September 1951, Morrison visited Washington and took with him the PUSD brief on the 'Ring Plan'. To the Americans' dismay, Morrison informed Acheson that Britain, 'would regard as provocative any scheme for ringing the Soviet Union with broadcasting transmitters.' Acheson and the State Department were somewhat taken aback by Morrison's assertion. The US Embassy in London reported that the Secretary of State had been 'shocked' by Morrison's statement, not least because the Foreign Office, 'had been kept fully informed of the project for a considerable time and had not raised any objections in principle.'[177]

The IRD were similarly alarmed. They had not been consulted prior to the Foreign Secretary's visit to Washington, and the PUSD brief had not been cleared in draft form by either the IPD or the IRD. The issue was only resolved, to the obvious relief of Acheson and the IRD, by the election of a Conservative Government in October 1951. On 5 November, the Permanent Under-Secretary, John Nicholls, recommended that the State Department be informed that Morrison's remark:

> ...should not be taken as meaning that we were against the project in principle ... [and]...[T]hat the doubts that we had expressed on previous occasions about particular aspects of the scheme (e.g. the proposal for a transmitter in the Persian Gulf) were based solely on practical considerations and were certainly not mere pretexts to conceal any fundamental objection to the scheme; and that, so far as provocation was concerned, it was in our opinion the uses to which the transmitters were put rather than their mere existence which would have to be handled with caution.[178]

British cooperation with the 'Ring Plan' was not the only concern US officials had regarding Britain's commitment to the anti-communist propaganda offensive. While US propaganda activities had expanded, there had been a gradual reduction in British information expenditure since 1947. In September 1950, Foreign Office officials expressed 'grave concern' at the effect of successive cuts in the information budget.[179] Annual cuts since 1947, coupled with rising costs, meant that by 1950 the information services had reached the point at which there were insufficient funds to maintain basic services. At the end of 1950, the Foreign Office information departments, the BBC and the Central Office of Information had no money left for new campaigns. Even if no further cuts were made it would, they claimed, be impossible to carry out work planned for 1950 and 1951. The Foreign Office also pointed out that the US Government was stepping up its propaganda activities around the world. It would, the Foreign Office suggested, 'be difficult to maintain our present close and friendly collaboration' if the USA was left to take the burden of anti-communist propaganda. Moreover, in a phrase which echoed the 1948 Cabinet paper, it claimed:

> It is important in our and common interest that we, as Europeans and with our special knowledge of the Middle East and Far East and South East Asia, should be able to influence United States planning and day-to-day publicity just as we influence United States policy.[180]

The Foreign Office proposed that a reserve fund of £250,000 be created to cover expenses not covered in the previous year's estimates.[181] In support of this proposal officials stressed that Britain had entered an 'acute phase of the struggle against Communism,' in which the Government was obliged to devote large sums to all aspects of the country's defences, including propaganda:

> It is a commonplace that one of the most powerful weapons in the Soviet and Communist armoury is the propaganda weapon... It follows that the publicity arm should be an equally important branch of the defence of the West. The Cabinet recognised this when they laid down their overseas publicity directive in January 1948. Since then the Communist propaganda campaign has been greatly extended and intensified... The burden of our own publicity organs has been correspondingly increased.[182]

The Chancellor of the Exchequer, Hugh Gaitskell, was not convinced, and more drastic cuts were to follow. In January 1951, faced with the burden of contributing forces to the war in Korea, the Cabinet reluctantly approved a massive programme of rearmament amounting to £4,700 million over three years. This was funded by large cuts in government spending, not least in the health services.[183] It also prompted a re-evaluation of Britain's overseas information activities. The cost of the information services was a frequent target for Parliamentary criticism and it was Gaitskell's view that expenditure on propaganda could be dispensed with more easily than other areas of Britain's defence. 'We could afford "no frills" at the present time,' he asserted. Therefore, instead of sanctioning further funding, Gaitskell suggested a cut of £2 million in overall information expenditure, and even proposed dismantling the British Council.[184] Although the eventual cuts in information expenditure for 1951–52 were closer to £1.4 million,[185] and the British Council was saved, the Foreign Office noted with some bitterness that the danger from communist propaganda had been largely ignored: 'The Treasury attitude is "Let us avoid war by all means, provided that it does not cost more than £10.5 million."'[186]

As the Foreign Office suggested, the Americans were indeed concerned about the proposed reductions. The State Department heard of Gaitskell's proposed cuts from Watson early in 1951, and quickly sought to impress upon the British the importance of maintaining their propaganda effort. Barrett suggested that the State Department 'exert a little pressure' to keep the British from cutting their budgets, and also asked the OPC 'to indicate through your channels, the deep concern with which the US Government has heard this news.'[187] In February 1951, Acheson wrote to Frye, instructing him 'to inform Strang personally at first opportunity for informal conversation that all our plans count heavily on British psychological warfare as important part joint defence effort.'[188] Frye replied two days later, after having discussed the matter with Murray and Warner. They had told him that some cuts in the information budget were inevitable, but that although this would result in some paring of staff from anti-communist propaganda activities, the cuts would be targeted at Britain's positive propaganda work. Murray mentioned that Latin American services might be cut down to press offices only, except for Venezuela where the IRD maintained a regional centre. The most drastic cuts would be in British Council support, and the BBC overseas services would be affected. Short-term cuts in Western Europe would only be made if necessary and anti-communist propaganda would be the least affected.[189] When US embassy officials finally spoke to Strang, late in February

1951, he was more forceful in reassuring them that anti-communist activities would not be affected. He repeated that, wherever possible, cuts would be made in the British Council and the BBC and assured the Americans that 'no (repeat no) cuts are planned in direct anti-communist activities and there even may be some expansion in this field.'[190]

'A coordinated anti-communist operation': the convergence of British and American Cold War propaganda

Strang was not being disingenuous. In the course of 1951, whilst stringent cuts were applied to other areas of Britain's information activities, the anti-communist propaganda campaign expanded. Under the financial pressure of rearmament, the Foreign Office was successful in presenting anti-communist propaganda activities as an essential part of Britain's defence. As propaganda work as a whole was pared down, the main focus of Britain's overseas propaganda shifted away from the 'Projection of Britain', and combating communism became the principal function of the British Government's propaganda both at home and abroad.

In May 1951, Patrick Gordon-Walker took over from Morrison as Minister with overall responsibility for the information services. Gordon-Walker was determined that 'all our publicity should be geared to the Cold War.'[191] He chaired two new ministerial committees which were created to deal with the domestic and overseas information services. In July 1951, Gordon-Walker presented the Cabinet with a paper on information policy which called for 'a renewed and vigorous information campaign in this country.' Its principal aim was to counter the 'uncertainty and confusion in the public mind' regarding the basis and economic implications of Britain's foreign policy:

> What therefore we have to do is to bring home to our people with greater emphasis and persistence than has yet been done the true nature of the Soviet regime and the real motives behind Soviet behaviour in international affairs. Only if we successfully bring home to our people the root cause of our policies will they sufficiently accept the need for rearmament and all that it implies.[192]

Gordon-Walker also ordered an enquiry into Britain's overseas propaganda activities. In July 1951, the IRD presented him with a detailed overview of Britain's anti-communist propaganda operations.[193] It documented a substantial propaganda effort by the IRD, and a considerable expansion of the department's work since the launch of the new propaganda policy in 1948.

In January 1948, the Foreign Office had been instructed to conduct propaganda designed: to expose the myth of the Soviet workers' paradise and reveal the real conditions of life under Soviet rule; to promote the virtues of British social democracy; and to encourage resistance to communism in the free world. To these themes, the IRD had added propaganda about: Britain's defence arrangements; the Brussels Treaty and North Atlantic Treaty Organizations; and, in addition to the 'Projection of Britain', propaganda 'about the virtues of the Western way of life.'[194]

The IRD's output had also expanded considerably. By mid-1951, the IRD was producing four main types of propaganda material: detailed 'Basic Papers' for dissemination to opinion-formers; the 'Digest' which was issued in English, French,

Italian, Spanish and Greek, with a total circulation of nearly 2,000 copies per week; specially commissioned or second rights articles; and miscellaneous publications such as *Points at Issue*, a 'handbook of comment on Soviet and communist behaviour and practice', which had gone through five editions since 1949, with a total print run of 32,000.[195]

During 1951, there had also been some interesting additions to the IRD's output. A new 'Defence Digest' was created to provide Ministers with material to sustain public support for rearmament. This interdepartmental production, with contributions from the Treasury and the Ministry of Defence, emerged from the briefing group on rearmament.[196] In November 1951, the IRD launched a fortnightly 'Religious Digest' which illustrated the treatment of religion and religious bodies in communist countries and the communist attitude to religion in the free world. It was intended to cover the communist attitude to all religions, although as most states under communist control had been Catholic, the first editions had a heavy bias towards Catholicism. Although some items in the Digest would, it was felt, be of interest to the press, and the ecclesiastical press in particular, it was chiefly designed for the information of religious leaders for use in their own churches. The Foreign Office had developed particularly close relations with the Church of England, and copies of the Religious Digest were passed to Lambeth Palace through Canon Herbert Waddams, General Secretary of the Church's Council on Foreign Relations, and a former member of the wartime Ministry of Information.[197]

Book publishing became one of the IRD's favoured methods of disseminating information as the Foreign Office believed that the public would more readily accept information which did not emanate from official sources, and that the most effective propaganda was attributable to authoritative or prominent authors. The most notable new project was the first in the series of 'Background Books'. The IRD's early forays into the book market also involved the distribution of existing work such as R.N. Carew-Hunt's *The Theory and Practice of Communism*, which had been written as an in-house guide for the intelligence service,[198] and, most prominently, *Animal Farm* and *1984*.[199] Orwell himself, and subsequently his widow Sonia and publisher Frederic Warburg, had been 'most cooperative' in granting the IRD overseas rights to Orwell's work.[200] However, securing copyright for existing works was often complicated and expensive. By commissioning its own work, the Foreign Office and British missions abroad were free to make local arrangements for the printing, translation and distribution of books.

The 'Background Books' series ran until 1970, and comprised almost 100 titles. They were edited by Stephen Watts, a former MI5 officer, and published by Batchworth Press, Phoenix House and, most widely and stylishly, by Bodley Head. This was to all intents and purposes a Foreign Office venture.[201] It is apparent that in many cases the IRD directly commissioned 'Background Books' from trusted confidential contacts, often with a background in the intelligence service or the Foreign Office – such as Christopher Mayhew, Robert Bruce Lockhart and C.M. Woodhouse.[202] The IRD also drew on the services of a number of prominent intellectuals who received IRD material and occasionally wrote papers for the department, including Leonard Schapiro and Bertrand Russell.[203] Relations between the authors and the IRD was in many cases quite open and, if they wished, authors were able to draw on a large volume of source material available in the department.

Brian Crozier, who later worked as an IRD consultant, has described how, whilst working for *The Economist* in the 1960s, he 'transformed a thick folder of IRD documents into a short book called *Neo-Colonialism*.' Crozier added that books produced in this manner would be vetted by IRD officials to ensure that secret material had been removed.[204] Most importantly, the whole series was financially supported by the IRD which bought up large quantities of each title for distribution abroad.

The series, when published under Batchworth, was clearly not targeted at a sophisticated audience but satisfied the demand for cheap anti-communist literature by recognized authors. The books had a distinctive red cover featuring a large question mark and generally sought to answer big questions of the day. The titles reflected this basic intent: *What is Democracy?*; *What is Peace?*; and *How did the Satellites Happen?* The first volume, *What is Communism?*, by an anonymous 'Student of Affairs', was sent to British posts in February 1951. It was described by the IRD as:

> ...a good light publication... While obviously not a book for experts [it] is well written and we think capable of interesting a wide range of readers. It has the merit of being an anti-communist work written in dispassionate style and therefore more acceptable to waverers and fellow travellers who recant from arguments more trenchantly expressed.[205]

The Foreign Office purchased 5,000 copies for distribution to British posts and the Colonial Office took a further 10,000. Copies were also freely provided to US information staff who were in a position to help with distribution. The American Embassy in Caracas, for example, agreed to print 5,000 copies. It was followed shortly afterwards by *Trade Unions: True or False?* by Victor Feather; *Why Communism Must Fail*, a symposium of essays by Bertrand Russell, Leonard Schapiro, Francis Watson, W.N. Ewer and C.D. Darlington; and *Cooperatives: True or False?*, by J.A. Hough. Posts were asked to seek local publishers for the series, and offer copyright 'as a minor inducement.' The Foreign Office added, 'If a means of publication offers itself which requires financial help within reason, let us know, and we will see what can be done.'[206] Profit was clearly not a consideration.

In addition to its editorial activities, the IRD had also assiduously cultivated recipients for its material. The IRD, Gordon-Walker was told, worked, 'through all available channels to ensure that the facts about Soviet aims and methods are known as widely as possible.'[207] Internally, the IRD briefed British spokesmen, Ministers, and delegations to United Nations' organizations and to international conferences. In 1951, it began to brief all Heads of Missions on their appointment, and close cooperation was developed between Heads of Missions, Labour Attachés and Information Officers.[208] It was also responsible for day-to-day monitoring of Soviet propaganda and for initiating counter-action when necessary, either through the Foreign Office News Department, a Ministerial statement, a question in Parliament, or instructions to British missions abroad. IRD material was disseminated widely to other government departments and British missions. Regional centres for the adaptation and translation of IRD material had been established in Singapore, Cairo, Buenos Aires and Caracas. There was, the IRD reported, 'a growing tendency' for foreign governments to cooperate with British missions in anti-communist activities.[209]

There had, however, been a significant, if predictable, change in the IRD's methods since 1948. Mayhew and Bevin's instruction that British propaganda should be directed at the broad masses of workers and peasants in Europe and Asia had been dropped. Officials in the Foreign Office, who were more accustomed to directing information at opinion forming élites, had always been sceptical about this policy. In practice, since 1948, the IRD had gradually reverted back to the entrenched Foreign Office view that, 'it is better to influence those that can influence others than to attempt a direct appeal to the mass of the population.'[210] The paper drafted for Gordon-Walker gave the clearest summation of Foreign Office thinking on this subject:

> [I]n any organised community there are certain leaders on whom the general public depends for a large part of its thinking. These leaders and the confidence reposed in them by the public are the key to any campaign of indoctrination. By working through them, the appearance of official propaganda is avoided. In a western state the greater part fall into the following categories:- ministers and members of parliament, trade union leaders, churchmen, editors and journalists, certain professors and teachers, and leading public figures... To conduct an indoctrination campaign effectively and economically it is necessary to impress upon these groups the importance and urgency of the operation, to enlist their cooperation, and provide them with all necessary material facts and arguments.[211]

In January 1952, British diplomats were informed that combating communism was no longer simply a publicity task and should not be left to Information Officers. 'The task is one in which all the principal members of a Mission have a duty to participate.' The greater part of the IRD material was no longer designed for dissemination to the general public, but rather aimed to 'enable or assist recognised leaders of public opinion...to influence their own following.' As all diplomatic staff had access to local opinion formers, they should all work to ensure the widespread dissemination of IRD material. These contacts, it was suggested, should be encouraged to turn to them for 'reliable and accurate advice on the technical and general aspects of enlightening public opinion about Communism.'[212]

The IRD had developed contacts with many of these leaders of opinion, at home and abroad, including: the Labour and Conservative party headquarters;[213] the TUC – and through them the International Confederation of Free Trade Unions; the British Council of Churches; the Quakers; the National Peace Council; and 'certain selected scientists.' The purpose of these contacts was to ensure that those individuals and organizations who wished to combat communism had the necessary factual material, 'which they can work on in their own way to make acceptable and comprehensible to their particular target audience.' In certain cases – the trade unions, for example – IRD sought to provide material which 'may induce leaders to take administrative action against Communists.'[214]

Most significantly, since the launch of the new propaganda policy in 1948, there had been a shift in Foreign Office thinking regarding the role of propaganda in fighting the Cold War. The expansion of the IRD's activities reveals how important propaganda had become in Britain's Cold War strategy. As the IRD's role had expanded the Foreign Office had also developed a more expansive definition of the role of propaganda in British foreign policy. The traditional view of propaganda as a useful tool of diplomacy had been transformed as the Foreign Office began to embrace political warfare. British overseas propaganda was no longer simply used to publicise British achievements, and counter communist misrepresentations. By mid-1951 the Foreign Office, and the IRD in particular, advocated a strategy which elevated propaganda alongside diplomacy and military power as part of a coordinated political warfare offensive. Propaganda was no longer simply an adjunct to British foreign policy but an essential and indivisible part of a combined strategy for combating global communism, to be used 'hand in hand' with diplomacy and military power.

The phrase 'anti-communist propaganda', the IRD argued, was now an 'incomplete and in some respects misleading' description of the department's activities. Firstly, it was not communism they were seeking to counter but the aggressive aims of the Soviet Government, which operated through communist parties and communist-controlled organizations. Communism was 'merely a technique of political agitation' used by the Soviet Government, alongside other rallying cries, such as 'peace', it merely served as 'a convenient umbrella for such diverse activities as sabotage and fomenting disunity in the West.' Secondly, as political, military and propaganda activities were interconnected in the Soviet strategy of political warfare, it was necessary to respond with a similarly coordinated counter-offensive. Propaganda alone was insufficient, 'propaganda and diplomacy must go hand in hand and the Soviet military threat must be counterbalanced.' The IRD recommended an ambitious programme of political warfare which combined: 'a worldwide operation of factual indoctrination'; sufficient military strength to deter aggression; internal security and 'democratic vigilance' to prevent subversion at home; and economic improvement to promote 'an understanding and enthusiasm for the democratic way of life.'[215]

As the Foreign Office was clearly aware, this new concept of political warfare brought the British much closer to the US position regarding the role of propaganda as an offensive weapon in the Cold War. A similar review of US anti-communist operations in Washington, reveals that by the end of 1951, British and US thinking was converging regarding both the concept of political warfare and the conduct of such activities.

Having served the two years he had agreed to devote to the job, Assistant Secretary of State, Edward W. Barrett, resigned at the beginning of 1952. Barrett left behind a reorganization plan designed to strengthen the US information programme by providing greater integration of propaganda with the formulation and conduct of US foreign policy. Barrett's plan was implemented on 16 January with the establishment of a new International Information Administration (IIA) within the State Department. The creation of this semi-autonomous agency within the State Department was ostensibly a further effort to centralize responsibility for overseas propaganda activities. It was also an attempt by the State Department to head off calls for the creation of an independent information agency. The IIA was headed by Wilson Compton, a Republican with 26 years experience in the US timber industry and the President of the State College of Washington, but with little experience of propaganda work. Compton reported directly to the new Assistant Secretary of State, Howland Sargeant. Sargeant, who had been Barrett's deputy and later went on to become Director of

Radio Liberty, had more impressive credentials in the propaganda field and brought the added glamour of being married to the Hollywood actress, Myrna Loy.[216]

Before leaving his post, Barrett reviewed the progress of US overseas propaganda since the launch of the 'Campaign of Truth'. A review which revealed a remarkable convergence of British and US thinking regarding anti-communist propaganda operations. Since the launch of the Campaign of Truth, Barrett claimed the USA had learnt, 'that psychological factors must be taken into account when policy is being formulated – not just when it is being announced and publicized.' In words that closely echoed those used by IRD officials, Barrett described how the USA had defined a new role for international propaganda operations in the two years since the launch of the Campaign of Truth:

> This meant ceasing to consider the psychological as just a minor but necessary adjunct to the handling of international affairs; it meant considering the psychological as one of the four major arms of government in the world field – the political (or diplomatic), the economic, the psychological and the military.[217]

Just as British and US concepts of offensive political warfare were converging, it is clear from Barrett's review that the Americans had embraced British methods in the conduct of anti-communist propaganda. Barrett described a marked shift in emphasis in US propaganda – a shift which was testament to the efforts of British officials to persuade the USA to tone down its anti-communist propaganda and to adopt a more carefully targeted and discreet approach. Over the previous two years, Barrett observed:

> ...we have begun to learn much more about the potentialities of overseas propaganda... We have learnt that often subtlety pays off in terms of long range ends far more than direct, sledge-hammer techniques... We have learned that, to be truly effective, the media must be carefully tailored to meet the individual problems of each target area and each target group.[218]

Like the British, Barrett placed considerable emphasis on the role played by posts abroad in tailoring propaganda to local requirements. Barrett asserted that propaganda was too important to be left to information staff, and his proposals for reorganization in the field closely paralleled British plans. Overseas information activities were no longer to be the sole preserve of hard-pressed Public Affairs Officers in US Embassies. To ensure the integration of propaganda with the conduct of foreign relations, responsibility for propaganda activities was to reside with the ambassador. Ambassadors were to be supported by a 'Cold War staff or strategy board', comprising the chief political officer, the chief economic officer, the chief information officer and a military liaison officer. Like the British, Barrett also suggested that wherever possible propaganda material should be distributed through local channels, even though this 'may mean, on occasion, that we let local authorities take the major share of credit for some US aid.'[219]

This more subtle approach was not without its drawbacks. Acheson observed, in 1952, that 'in view of the need to impress Congress with solid evidence of wise and effective stewardship' the increased use of 'indigenous' sources to wage the anti-communist battle 'has not always been without its handicaps and frustrations.'[220]

The departing Barrett, who left, by his own admission, 'in the doghouse' with the appropriations subcommittee,[221] was somewhat less restrained in his assessment:

> Chowderheads continually come back from abroad and announce that our program is ineffective because they have not seen USIE clearly identified with some of the most effective free-world propaganda in the areas they visited. Some of them have even contrasted our open efforts unfavourably with local-group efforts which we actually inspired and engineered.[222]

Nevertheless, 'indigenous operations' were now at the heart of the USA's anti-communist propaganda policy. This was in contrast to the position in May 1950, when Barrett had informed British officials that US propaganda was driven by public statements and that the US Government conducted little 'grey' propaganda. By November 1951, Barrett was advocating that, 'a major share of US funds in this field should go into grey and covert operations that we have found to pay off so importantly.' Even large-scale propaganda operations such as the 'Radio Ring' plan, which had been heralded in public speeches by the President, Barrett suggested, should in future 'be so handled as to produce a minimum of fanfare and debate.'[223]

The objectives of US propaganda had also sharpened. Since 1950, when the US had begun to combat communist misrepresentations through the 'Campaign of Truth', US propaganda had focused increasingly on the task of undermining communism itself. Although Barrett recommended that the USA continue 'a modest world-wide program of combating misrepresentations' and presenting a 'full and fair picture of America', from 1952, US propaganda, like the British, was to be focused almost wholly on the negative anti-communist aspect. Barrett recommended that the major share of manpower and funds be devoted to a psychological campaign aimed at 'undermining communist regimes in some areas, strengthening anti-communist political forces in another, bolstering anti-communist labor groups in a third, inducing the regime in another to make major economic adjustments.'[224] In developing a psychological counter-offensive against the Soviet bloc, the USA did, of course, wish to go somewhat further than the British. In January 1952, the last major propaganda directive issued to US missions by the Truman administration asserted the importance of multiplying and intensifying 'psychological deterrents to aggression by Soviet Communism.' Within the Soviet bloc, it asserted, the subject peoples needed to be addressed in such a manner that they maintained their identification with the non-communist world and sustained 'hope for ultimate liberation.'[225]

Conclusion

Cooperation between Britain and the USA in the field of anti-communist propaganda expanded dramatically in the two years from January 1950 to the end of 1951. In 1948, British officials had been keen to inform the USA of Britain's new propaganda policy. They had not, however, been impressed with the endproduct of cooperation between January 1948 and January 1950. In 1950, the willingness of US officials to seek British advice and experience regarding the most effective methods of conducting anti-communist propaganda, coupled with the launch of the 'Campaign of Truth', restored British faith in US anti-communist propaganda policy.

Cooperation was formalized in a series of meetings between senior officials from the Foreign Office and the State Department early in 1950. Instructions to British and US missions following these talks prompted information officers in the field to do what to many came naturally: cooperate with their opposite numbers. Relations were particularly close in South-East Asia, where the propaganda effort was in many respects combined. Both nations, however, were careful to maintain 'individuality of output.' The policy of 'shooting at the same target from different angles' remained the guiding principle for cooperation in the field.

The most important development was the appointment of Adam Watson as Information Liaison Officer at the British Embassy in Washington. Watson was a vital link in developing British and US cooperation in anti-communist propaganda. He was well known to many prominent figures in Washington and assiduously cultivated contacts with the most senior officials. By the end of 1951, Watson had established close and regular liaison with all the principal agencies responsible for US psychological operations, both overt and covert. After only eight months in Washington, Watson claimed to know more about American anti-communist propaganda than he did about British policy.[226]

To be sure, US hospitality was not entirely benign. It is clear that the US Government was keen to elicit British support for many of their psychological operations. In particular, in organizing Soviet and Eastern European émigrés and developing Radio Free Europe. The State Department was also dependent on British facilities to expand VOA broadcasting through the 'Ring Plan'. The extent to which US plans for anti-communist propaganda depended upon British cooperation are revealed by the US Government's reaction to British cuts in spending on propaganda activities; Acheson urgently sought to impress upon the Foreign Office that, 'all our plans count heavily on British psychological warfare as important part joint defence effort.'[227]

However, while cuts in spending led to dramatic reductions in Britain's positive propaganda activities, anti-communist propaganda expanded considerably. By 1951, all of Britain's propaganda activities at home and abroad were geared towards the Cold War. The IRD's editorial output was increasing and the department had established contacts with a great number of prominent opinion formers. Moreover, the IRD had begun to develop a more expansive definition of Britain's anti-communist propaganda policy which, by the end of 1951, brought the IRD closely in line with the US strategy of political warfare.

Notes

1 A Report to the National Security Council by the Executive Secretary, NSC-68, 14 April 1950, *FRUS, 1950*, vol. 1, pp. 234–92.
2 European Policy, Memo by the Secretary of State for Foreign Affairs, 18 October 1949, CP(49)208, CAB 129/37, PRO. For a more detailed examination of the decline of the Third Force concept, see Kent and Young, 'British Policy Overseas: The Third Force and the Origins of NATO', pp. 41–61.
3 Anti-Communist Propaganda Operations, 27 July 1951, CAB 127/296, PRO.
4 Proposals for a Total Information Effort Abroad, Edward W. Barrett, enclosure with Memo for the President from D.Acheson, 3 April 1950, WHCF:CF Box no. 41, Truman Papers, Truman Library.
5 Address to American Society of Newspaper Editors, 20 April 1950, *Public Papers of the Presidents: Harry S. Truman, 1950*, pp. 260–4.

6 The Development of American Psychological Operations, 1945–51, by Edward P. Lilly, 19 December 1951, pp. 82–4, SMOF: PSB Files; Box no. 22, Truman Papers, Truman Library. Recent scholarship has sought to reassert the importance of the Campaign of Truth in US Cold War strategy; see G.D. Rawnsley, 'The Campaign of Truth: a Populist Propaganda', in G.D. Rawnsley (ed.), *Cold War Propaganda in the 1950s*, pp. 31–46; S. Lucas, *Freedom's War: The American Crusade Against the Soviet Union* (New York: New York University Press, 1999), ch. 6; W.L. Hixson, *Parting the Curtain: Propaganda, Culture and the Cold War 1945–61* (London: Macmillan, 1998), ch. 1.

7 Quoted in Lucas, 'Beyond Diplomacy', p. 19.

8 Memo by Acting Secretary of State to Executive Secretary of National Security Council, 26 May 1950, *FRUS, 1950*, vol. 4, pp. 311–13.

9 Edward W. Barrett, Oral History, Truman Library. See also Hixson, *Parting the Curtain*, pp. 13–16.

10 A Report to the National Security Council by the Executive Secretary, NSC-68, 14 April 1950, *FRUS, 1950*, vol. 1, pp. 234–92. On NSC-68, see, E.R. May (ed.), *American Cold War Strategy: Interpreting NSC-68* (London: Macmillan, 1993); B. Heuser, 'NSC-68 and the Soviet Threat: A New Perspective on Western Threat Perception and Policy-Making', *Review of International Studies*, 17 (1991), pp. 17–40.

11 On the importance of NSC-68 to US psychological strategy, see Lucas, 'Beyond Diplomacy' pp. 19–20; *ibid*. 'Campaigns of Truth: The Psychological Strategy Board and American Ideology, 1951–1953', *International History Review*, 18 (1996), pp. 279–302.

12 A Report to the National Security Council by the Executive Secretary, NSC-68, 14 April 1950, *FRUS, 1950*, vol. 1, pp. 234–92.

13 Annex 5 to NSC 68/1, 21 September 1950, quoted in The Development of American Psychological Operations, 1945–51, by Edward P. Lilly, 19 December 1951, pp. 82–4, SMOF: PSB Files, Box no. 22, Truman Papers, Truman Library.

14 International Information Program of US Department of State, The Campaign of Truth, Memo, nd [*circa* 1950], Box no. 4, papers of Howland Sargeant, Truman Library.

15 The 'Ring Plan' gains little attention in the literature. For a detailed account, see R.W. Pirsein, *The Voice of America: An History of the International Broadcasting Activities of the United States Government, 1940–1962* (New York: Arno Press, 1979), pp. 160–97. Pirsein suggested that the 'Ring Plan' grew out of Project TROY. More recently, Aldrich has revealed that the plan was in fact outlined in an Annex to NSC-68 only recently declassified: Aldrich, *The Hidden Hand*, p. 320.

16 International Information Program of US Department of State, The Campaign of Truth.

17 Memo, Radio 'Ring Plan', 12 September 1951, 511.004/9-1251, RG 59, NARA; International Information Program of US Department of State, The Campaign of Truth.

18 Address broadcast from the Voice of America floating radio transmitter, USS *Courier*, 4 March 1952: *Public Papers of the Presidents: Harry S. Truman 1952* (Washington DC: US GPO, 1952), pp. 54–5. Information and Policy Guidance, Operation Vagabond Try-Out Cruise, 10 March 1952, 511.004/3–1052, RG 59 NARA. Memo, Project Vagabond, 1 February 1951, 511.004/2–151, RG 59, NARA. On USS *Courier*, see also Pirsein, *The Voice of America*, pp. 170–5; Rawnsley, 'The Campaign of Truth: a Populist Propaganda', pp. 41–2.

19 A Report to the National Security Council by the Executive Secretary, NSC-68, 14 April 1950, *FRUS, 1950*, vol. 1, pp. 234–92.

20 Mitrovich argues that NSC 20/4 of November 1948, and not NSC 68, was the origin and the definitive statement of the Truman administration's policy of 'roll back.' G. Mitrovich, *Undermining the Kremlin: America's Strategy to Subvert the Soviet Bloc, 1947–1956* (Ithaca, NY: Cornell University Press, 2000), pp. 34–6.

21 Memo for the Record, Policy Guidance, 19 April 1950, in M. Warner (ed.), *The CIA Under Harry Truman* (Washington, DC: CIA History Staff, Center for the Study of Intelligence, 1994), p. 323.

22 Aldrich, *The Hidden Hand*, p. 315; D.F. Rudgers, 'The Origins of Covert Action', *Journal of Contemporary History*, 35, 2 (2000), pp. 249–62.

23 See, in particular, Aldrich, *The Hidden Hand; also* H. Rostizke, *The CIA's Secret Operations* (Boulder, CO: Westview, 1988).
24 See, in particular, S. Lucas *Freedom's War*, pp. 93–106.
25 NCFE recruitment leaflet, 'To Halt Communism and Save Freedom', June 1950; C.D. Jackson Papers, 1931–1967, Box no. 90, Eisenhower Library.
26 S. Lucas, *Freedom's War*, p. 67.
27 'Radio Free Europe: Nature, Purpose and Goals', Memo from Radio Free Europe to C.D. Jackson, 26 June 1950, C.D. Jackson Papers, Box no. 90, Eisenhower Library. There is now an extensive literature on NCFE and Radio Free Europe: see, in particular, R. Holt, *Radio Free Europe* (Minneapolis, MN: University of Minnesota Press, 1958); S. Mickelson, *America's Other Voice: The Story of Radio Free Europe and Radio Liberty* (New York: Praeger, 1983); M. Nelson, *War of the Black Heavens: The Battles of Western Broadcasting in the Cold War* (London: Brassey's, 1997).
28 Draft of an Overall Directive for Radio Free Europe, 1950; C.D. Jackson Papers, 1931–1967, Box no. 90, Eisenhower Library.
29 C. Simpson, *Science of Coercion: Communication Research and Psychological Warfare, 1945–1960*, (Oxford: Oxford University Press, 1994).
30 A.A. Needell, ' "Truth is Our Weapon": Project TROY, Political Warfare, and Government–Academic Relations in the National Security State', *Diplomatic History*, 17, 3 (1993), pp. 399–420; S. Lucas, *Freedom's War*, pp. 99–100.
31 W.A. Curtin, Memo for Director of PSB, Project TROY, 9 October 1951, SMOF: PSB Files, 1951–1953, Box no. 1, Truman Papers, Truman Library.
32 Needell, ' "Truth is Our Weapon" ', p. 399.
33 Directive establishing the Psychological Strategy Board, 20 June 1951, *Public Papers of the President*, pp. 128–9; The Development of American Psychological Operations, 1945–1951, by Edward P.Lilly, p. 94, SMOF: PSB Files, Box no. 22, Truman Papers, Truman Library.
34 The literature on the PSB is scarce but growing: see, S. Lucas, 'Campaigns of Truth: The Psychological Strategy Board and American Ideology, 1951–1953', *International History Review*, 18, 2 (1996), pp. 253–304; J. Prados, *Keepers of the Keys: A History of the National Security Council from Truman to Bush* (New York: William Morrow, 1991), pp. 50–7; Mitrovich, *Undermining the Kremlin*, pp. 59–82.
35 The Development of American Psychological Operations, 1945–1951, by Edward P. Lilly, p. 94, SMOF: PSB Files, Box no. 22, Truman Papers, Truman Library.
36 G. Mitrovich, *Undermining the Kremlin*, p. 59.
37 Office of Assistant Secretary of State for Public Affairs, Memo, 'Cooperation with British and other Information Services', 30 December 1949, 741.5200/2-950, RG 59, NARA.
38 *Ibid.*; Circular Airgram, Cooperation with the British Information Services, 28 February 1950, 741.5200/2-2850, RG 59, NARA.
39 Allen, British Embassy, Washington, to Warner, 8 October 1949, PR3128/46/913, FO 1110/236, PRO.
40 Warner to Allen, British Embassy, Washington, 3 November 1949, PR3128/46/913, FO 1110/236, PRO.
41 Warner to Hoyer-Millar, British Embassy, Washington, 31 December 1949, PR4078/46/913, FO 1110/236, PRO.
42 *Ibid.*
43 Meeting with Adam Watson of the IRD, 16 January 1950, 611.41/1-1650, RG 59, NARA.
44 Hoyer-Millar, British Embassy, Washington to Warner, 13 February 1950, PR30/31, FO 1110/305, PRO.
45 Meeting with Adam Watson of the IRD, 16 January 1950, 611.41/1-1650, RG 59, NARA.
46 Llewellyn E. Thompson, State Department, to Hoyer Millar, 20 February 1950, 511.6141/2-2050, RG 59, NARA.
47 *Ibid.*

48 Warner Note on Hoyer Millar to Warner, 13 February 1950, PR30/31, FO 1110/305, PRO.
49 Hoyer Millar, British Embassy, Washington to Warner, 13 February 1950, PR30/31, FO 1110/305, PRO.
50 Llewellyn E. Thompson, State Department, to Hoyer Millar, 20 February 1950, 511.6141/2-2050, RG 59, NARA. On British enthusiasm for further meetings, see Warner to Edward W. Barrett, 28 February 1950, Office Files of Assistant Secretary of State Edward W. Barrett, 1950–51, Box no. 3, Lot52D423, RG 59, NARA.
51 Priorities in publicity and similar activities designed to counter communism, 16 May 1950, P1013/33, FO 953/629, PRO.
52 *Ibid.*
53 The British and American Minutes for these meetings are available: Anglo-American Cooperation in Information Work, May 1950, P1013/33, FO 953/629, PRO; Notes on the First Meeting Between Christopher Warner and Edward Barrett at London, Saturday, 20 May 1950; Notes on the Second Meeting Between Christopher Warner and Edward Barrett at London, Monday, 22 May 1950, *FRUS, 1950*, vol. 3, *Western Europe*, pp. 1,641–8. Barrett's own personal notes on the meetings may be found in: Rough Notes on European Trip, nd [*circa* May 1950], Office Files of Assistant Secretary of State Edward W. Barrett 1950–51, Box no. 5, Lot52D432, RG 59, NARA. See also Agreed Anglo-American Report, Continued Consultation on and Coordination of Policy, 6 May 1950, *Documents on British Policy Overseas,* series 2, vol. 2, no. 67, pp. 242–4. There is an administrative anomaly in the various accounts in that the British Minutes refer to three meetings whereas the US Minutes refer to only two. This is merely due to the fact that the Americans lump the Minutes for the two meetings held in the morning and the afternoon of 22 May together as one, and both sets of Minutes cover the same discussions. Both sets of Minutes have been used and quotes are referenced to individual sets of Minutes.
54 Anglo-American Cooperation in Information Work, Note of first meeting held in Warner's Room, 20 May 1950, P1013/33, FO 953/629, PRO. The Foreign Office gave the Americans a copy of the paper, 'Priorities in Publicity and Similar Activities Designed to Counter Communism', 16 May 1950. Foreign Office paper given to Barrett during talks with Christopher Warner, 611.41/5-2650, RG 59, NARA.
55 Note of First Meeting between Warner and Barrett, 20 May 1950, *FRUS, 1950*, vol. 3, p. 1,642.
56 Anglo-American Cooperation in Information Work, Note of First Meeting Held in Mr Warner's Room, 20 May 1950, P1013/33, FO 953/629, PRO; Notes on First Meeting between Warner and Barrett, 20 May 1950 and Notes on Second Meeting between Warner and Barrett, London, 22 May 1950, *FRUS, 1950*, vol. 3, pp. 1,641–8.
57 Anglo-American Cooperation in Information Work, Notes of Second Meeting, 22 May 1950, P1013/33, FO 953/629, PRO; Notes on the Second Meeting between Warner and Barrett, 22 May 1950, *FRUS, 1950,* vol. 3, pp. 1,644–8. On the Aspidistra in the Second World War, see M. Kenyon, 'Black Propaganda', *After the Battle,* 72 (1992), pp. 8–31.
58 Douglas, US Embassy, London, to Secretary of State, 22 May 1950, 511.414/5-2250, RG 59, NARA.
59 Anglo-American Cooperation in Information Work, Notes of Second Meeting, 22 May 1950, P1013/33, FO 953/629, PRO; Notes on the Second Meeting between Warner and Barrett, 22 May 1950, *FRUS, 1950*, vol. 3, pp. 1,644–8.
60 Notes on Second Meeting between Warner and Barrett, 22 May 1950, *FRUS, 1950*, vol. 3, p. 1,645.
61 Anglo-American Cooperation in Overseas Information Work, May 1950, P1013/33, FO 953/229, PRO.
62 *Ibid.*
63 *Ibid.*
64 Notes on Second Meeting between Warner and Barrett, 22 May 1950, *FRUS, 1950,* vol. 3, p. 1,646.

65 Anglo-American Cooperation in Information Work, May 1950, P1013/33, FO 953/629, PRO; Notes on First Meeting between Warner and Barrett, London, 20 May 1950, *FRUS, 1950*, vol. 3, pp. 1,641–4.
66 *Ibid.*
67 On the Albanian operation, see B. Heuser, 'Covert Action within British and American Concepts of Containment, 1948–51', in R.J. Aldrich (ed.), *British Intelligence, Strategy and the Cold War, 1945–51* (London: Routledge, 1992), pp. 65–84; N. Bethell, *The Great Betrayal: The Untold Story of Kim Philby's Greatest Coup* (London: Coronet Edition, 1986); Aldrich, *The Hidden Hand*, pp. 152–4, 160–6.
68 See, in particular, Minutes of Russia Committee meeting, 25 November 1948, N13016/765/G38, FO 371/71687, PRO. See also Lucas and Morris, 'A Very British Crusade', pp. 85–110.
69 Anti-Communist Propaganda, third meeting, 19 December 1949, GEN 231, CAB 130/37, PRO.
70 Bethell, *The Great Betrayal*, p. 108.
71 E. Mainland, M. Pomar and K. Carlson, 'The Voice Present and Future: VOA, the USSR and Communist Europe', in K.R.M. Short (ed.), *Western Broadcasting over the Iron Curtain* (London: Croom Helm, 1986), p. 130; Mickelson, *America's Other Voice*, pp. 26–7.
72 Bethell, *The Great Betrayal*, pp. 108–9.
73 Anglo-American Cooperation in Information Work, May 1950, P1013/33, FO 953/629, PRO. Heuser describes how the French provided valuable insights into the situation in Albania, 'Covert Action within British and American Concepts of Containment', pp. 71, 76–80.
74 Notes on Second Meeting between Warner and Barrett, London, 22 May 1950, *FRUS, 1950*, vol. 3, pp. 1644–8.
75 Bethell, *The Great Betrayal*, pp. 140–2.
76 Heuser, 'Covert Action within British and American Concepts of Containment'; Bethell, *The Great Betrayal*.
77 Rough Notes on European Trip, nd [*circa* May 1950], Office Files of Assistant Secretary of State Edward W. Barrett 1950–51, Box no. 5, Lot52D432, RG 59, NARA.
78 Notes on First Meeting between Warner and Barrett, London, 20 May 1950, *FRUS, 1950*, vol. 3, pp. 1641–4.
79 Circular airgram, Secretary of State to Certain Diplomatic and Consular Offices, 15 July 1950, *FRUS, 1950*, vol. 4, pp. 318–19; Circular no. 079, Cooperation with United States Information Services, 7 July 1950, P1013/33/G, FO 953/629, PRO. See also Department of State to HICOG, 18 July, 741.5200/7-1850, RG 59, NARA.
80 Circular airgram, Secretary of State to Certain Diplomatic and Consular Offices, 15 July 1950, *FRUS, 1950*, vol. 4, pp. 318–19.
81 Review of Field Comments on Cooperation with the British Information Services, 28 August 1950, 611.41/8-2850, RG 59, NARA.
82 *Ibid.*
83 Warner Minute, 15 May 1950, P1013/30, FO 953/628, PRO. See also Browne, US Embassy, London, to State Department, 'Anglo-American Rivalry in ME', 16 March 1950, 511.90/3-1650, RG 59, NARA.
84 Review of Field Comments on Cooperation with the British Information Service, 28 August 1950, 611.41/8-2850, RG 59, NARA; Anglo-US Cooperation in Information Work, J.C. Moberly, 18 December 1950, P1013/158, FO 953/640, PRO.
85 Anglo-US Cooperation in Information Work, J.C. Moberly, 18 December 1950, P1013/158, FO 953/640, PRO.
86 American Embassy, Budapest, to State Department, 12 April 1950, 741.5200/4-1250; American Embassy, Bangkok, to State Department, 19 April 1950, 741.5282/4-1950, RG 59, NARA.
87 American Consulate, Bombay, to State Department, 31 August 1950, 741.5291/8-1350, RG 59, NARA.
88 American Embassy, Hong Kong, to State Department, 24 March 1950, 741.5246G/3-2450, RG 59, NARA.

89 American Embassy, Baghdad, to State Department, 20 May 1950, 741.5287/5-2050, RG 59, NARA.

90 Caracas 741.5200/5-2351. Other examples include: Burma, where USIS agreed to assist in the distribution of an anti-communist text, *Buddhism and the Personal Life*. The British Embassy ordered 7,000 copies translated into Burmese but could not order any more for lack of funds and the USIS agreed to order an extra 10,000 copies, 741.5290B/5-1650; see also US Embassy, San Salvador, to State Department, 31 August 1950, 741.5216/8-3150, RG 59, NARA.

91 Record of First Bipartite Official Meeting, 24 April 1950, *DBPO*, series 2, vol. 2, no. 29, pp. 90–4.

92 Western Measures to Counter Soviet Expansion Together with some Indication of their Effect, 1 August 1950, NS1052/79, FO 371/86757, PRO.

93 R. Ovendale, 'Britain, the United States, and the Cold War in South East Asia, 1949–1950', *International Affairs*, 58, 3 (1982), pp. 447–64.

94 A.J. Gardener to J.D.K. Beighton, Treasury, PR1203/953/G, FO 1110/143, PRO.

95 R. Deacon, *'C': A Biography of Sir Maurice Oldfield* (London: Futura, 1985) pp. 88–91; R.J. Aldrich, ' "The Value of Residual Empire": Anglo-American Intelligence Co-operation in Asia after 1945', in R.J. Aldrich and M.F. Hopkins (eds), *Intelligence, Defence and Diplomacy: British Policy in the Postwar World* (London: Frank Cass, 1994), pp. 226–58.

96 'The Regional Information Office, Singapore', 16 May 1949, PR1243/9/G, FO 1110/185, PRO.

97 Joint Information and Propaganda Committee, terms of reference, J.C.C.29, 21/6/21, Malcolm MacDonald Papers, University of Durham. On the British propaganda campaign in Malaya, see S.L. Carruthers, *Winning Hearts and Minds: British Governments, the Media and Colonial Counter-Insurgency, 1944–1960* (Leicester: Leicester University Press, 1995), pp. 72–117; On IRD relations with intelligence and security services at Singapore, see file, FO 1110/184, PRO.

98 Singapore to Foreign Office, 29 August 1950, 18/3/3, MacDonald papers, Durham University; C. Sanger, *Malcolm MacDonald: Bringing an End to Empire* (Liverpool: Liverpool University Press, 1995), pp. 360–2.

99 Singapore to Foreign Office, 13 December 1950, 18/3/17, MacDonald Papers, Durham University.

100 Extract from letter dated 6 January 1949 from Head of IRD to British Embassy, 'handed by Mr Frames? of British Embassy to Mr Langdon', 10 January 1949, 841.202046D/1-1049, RG 59, NARA.

101 A. Watson to J.R. Rayner (Singapore), 10 August 1949, PR 2144/9/G, FO 1110/186, PRO.

102 J.B. Smith, *Portrait of a Cold Warrior* (New York: Ballantine Books, 1976), p. 158.

103 T. Shaw, 'The Information Research Department of the British Foreign Office and the Korean War, 1950–53', *Journal of Contemporary History*, 34, 2 (1999), p. 275.

104 'Cooperation with the British in Southeast Asia', Department of State to certain missions, 27 July 1950, 611.41/7-2750, RG 59, NARA. On the British side, see Publicity in, and about, South East Asia and the Far East: Liaison with the State Department, August 1950, PR30/72, FO 1110/305, PRO.

105 Langdon, US Embassy, Singapore, to State Department, 10 November 1950, 511.41/11-1050, RG 59, NARA.

106 Watson, British Embassy, Washington, to Peck, 6 July 1951, PR24/119/G, FO 1110/386, PRO. E.J. Wilson, 'The Far East Regional Production Center', in W.E. Daugherty and M. Janowitz, *A Psychological Warfare Casebook* (Baltimore, MD: John Hopkins University Press, 1958), pp. 150–3. Although US officials conceded that Singapore was the obvious location for such a centre, it was felt the Singapore consulate was unlikely to carry the authority or prestige to coordinate US propaganda throughout the region.

107 J.H.A. Watson, British Embassy, Washington, to J. Peck, IRD, 6 July 1951, PR24/119/G, FO 1110/386, PRO. On Nadler's good relations with the British, see also S.I. Nadler, Oral History, Foreign Affairs Oral History Program (FAOH), Georgetown University.

108 Minutes of sixth meeting of United States and British Information Officers in Malaya, held at Phoenix Park, Singapore, 29 June 1951, P10622/9, FO 953/1200, PRO.

109 Smith, *Portrait of a Cold Warrior*, pp. 135–7; Aldrich, ' "The Value of Residual Empire," ' pp. 236–7.
110 Barrett, *Truth is Our Weapon*, p. 94; S. Pease, *Psywar: Psychological Warfare in Korea 1950–1953* (Harrisburg, PA: Stackpole Books, 1992), pp. 164–6.
111 Wilkinson Minute, 29 June 1951, PR47/7, FO 1110/405. On proposals for attaching British team to USIS in Korea, see Watson, Washington, to Murray, 31 October 1950, PR44/38, FO 1110/317, PRO.
112 Watson, Washington, to Murray, 31 October 1950, PR44/38, FO 1110/317; Military Aspects of Psychological Warfare, US Department of the Army, Training Circular no. 17, 12 December 1950, WO 216/425, PRO.
113 Information Work in Korea, H. Vere Redman, 11 April 1951, FO 953/1138, PRO.
114 Shaw, 'The IRD and the Korean War', pp. 263–81.
115 Gore-Booth, British Embassy, Washington to Howland Sargeant, 7 July 1950, 611.41/7-750, RG 59, NARA.
116 D. MacFarlane, Foreign Office to J. Rayner, Singapore, P1622/12, FO 953/1200, PRO.
117 Gore-Booth, British Embassy, Washington to Howland Sargeant, 7 July 1950, 611.41/7-750, RG 59, NARA.
118 Minutes of seventh meeting of United States and British information officers in Malaya, 27 July 1951, P10622/10G, FO 953/1200, PRO.
119 The Use of IRD Material: A Note for the Guidance of Information Officers and Chanceries, January 1953, PR101/2/G, FO 1110/532; A Report on the Regional Information Office and its Activities during the First Three Quarters of 1952, 10 November 1952, PR, FO 1110/499, PRO.
120 A Report on the Regional Information Office and its Activities during the First Three Quarters of 1952.
121 Minutes of sixth meeting between United States and British information officers in Malaya, 29 June 1951, P8071/53/51, FO 953/1200, PRO.
122 JIPC minutes of twentieth meeting 29 December 1950, PR24/6, FO 1110/386; A Report on the Regional Information Office and its Activities during the First Three Quarters of 1952.
123 Eighth and ninth meetings; Minutes of sixth meeting between United States and British information officers in Malaya, 29 June 1951.
124 US Embassy, Djakarta, to State Department, 27 June 1950, 511.90/6-2750, RG 59, NARA.
125 Meeting held at Foreign Office on 11 October to discuss publicity and propaganda policy in South-East Asia, FZ1681/2, FO 371/84681, PRO.
126 Carruthers, *Winning Hearts and Minds*, p. 102.
127 A Report on the Regional Information Office and its Activities during the First Three Quarters of 1952, 10 November 1952; Minutes of seventh meeting of United States and British Information Officers in Malaya, 27 July 1951.
128 A Report on the Regional Information Office and its Activities during the First Three Quarters of 1952.
129 On British film and newsreels coverage of Malaya, see Carruthers, *Winning Hearts and Minds*, pp. 102–16; on Korea, see H. Smith, 'BBC Television Newsreel and the Korean War', *Historical Journal of Film, Radio and Television*, 8, 3 (1988), pp. 227–52; J. Bourne and S. Lucas, *The Korean War 1950–1953*, Inter-University History Film Consortium Archive Series, no. 5 (IUHFC, 1992).
130 Minutes of seventh meeting of United States and British Information Officers in Malaya, 27 July 1951.
131 Minutes of sixth meeting of United States and British Information Officers in Malaya, 29 June 1951; Minutes of seventh meeting, 27 July 1951; Minutes of ninth meeting, October 1951, P10622/16, FO 953/1200, PRO.
132 A Report on the Regional Information Office and its Activities during the First Three Quarters of 1952.
133 IRD to Information Officers, 25 April 1951, PR32/41/51; 'Animal Farm' Strip Cartoon SITREP, 19 June 1951, PR32/89/G, FO 1110/392, PRO.

134 Shaw, 'The IRD and the Korean War', p. 269.
135 Bukit Serene Conference, 22 August 1950, 18/9/38, MacDonald Papers, Durham University.
136 A Report on the Regional Information Office and its Activities during the First Three Quarters of 1952.
137 Rayner to Peck, IRD, 8 June 1951, P10622/8, FO 953/1200, PRO.
138 Watson to Murray, IRD, 19 October 1950, PR30/31, FO 1110/305, PRO.
139 Notes on First Meeting Between Warner and Barrett, 20 May 1950, *FRUS, 1950*, vol. 3, p. 1,644. On the appointments and functions of the ILO, see Warner to Sir Oliver Franks, 11 August 1950, PR30/31, FO 1110/305, PRO; Memo of Conversation by the Chairman of the Interdepartmental Foreign Information Staff (Stone), Participants, Stone and Frye, State Department and Adam Watson, Foreign Office, 18 October 1950, *FRUS, 1950*, vol. 3, pp. 1,683–4.
140 Adam Watson, telephone interview with author, August 2003.
141 Watson to Murray, 27 October 1950, PR30/102, FO 1110/305, PRO.
142 Watson to Murray, 1 March 1951, PR9/21/51G, FO 1110/374, PRO. On Watson's relations with C.D. Jackson, see F. Stonor Saunders, *Who Paid the Piper? The CIA and the Cultural Cold War* (London: Granta, 1999), pp. 151–2; Log, Box no. 68; Correspondence, Box no. 111; C.D. Jackson Records, 1953–54, Eisenhower Library. On C.D. Jackson, see B.W. Cook, 'First Comes the Lie: C.D. Jackson and Political Warfare', *Radical History Review*, 31 (1984), pp. 42–70; D. Haight, 'The Papers of C.D. Jackson: A Glimpse at President Eisenhower's Psychological Warfare Expert', *Manuscripts*, 27 (1976), pp. 27–37.
143 J.H. Peck Minute, 31 May 1951, PR33/105G, FO 1110/393, PRO.
144 *Ibid.*
145 Memo of Conversation, Adam Watson, Howland Sargeant, Walter Schwinn, 16 August 1951 SMOF: PSB Files, Box no. 7, Truman Papers, Truman Library.
146 Memo to Mr Webb from Mr Raynor, PSB Liaison with the British, 24 October 1951, Box no. 1, Lot File no. 62D333 Executive Secretariat, Psychological Strategy Board Working File, 1951–1953, RG 59, NARA; J.B.Phillips to Gordon Gray, PSB Liaison with the British, 11 October 1951, SMOF: PSB Files, Box no. 7, Truman Papers, Truman Library; Memo of Conversation, Adam Watson, Joseph B. Phillips, 27 November 1951, SMOF: PSB Files, Box no. 7, Truman Papers, Truman Library.
147 Watson to Warner, 6 June 1951, PR9/51, FO 1110/374, PRO.
148 Watson, British Embassy, Washington to Murray, IRD, 19 October 1950, PR30/96, FO 1110/305, PRO.
149 Watson to Warner, 6 June 1951, and enclosure, PR 9/51, FO 1110/374, PRO.
150 *Ibid.*
151 B.A.B. Burrows, British Embassy, Washington, to D.P. Reilly, PUSD, 25 July 1951, PR33/64, FO 1110/393; Murray to Watson, 21 February 1951, PR9/15, FO 1110/374, PRO.
152 Murray to Watson, 21 February 1951, PR9/15, FO 1110/374, PRO.
153 *Ibid.*
154 Watson to Murray, 1 March 1951, PR9/21/51G, FO 1110/374, PRO. Philby later wrote at some length of British and American involvement with émigré groups, in *My Silent War* (London: Grafton, 1990), pp. 214–25.
155 Radio Free Europe, Minute by K.S. Butler, 12 March 1951 PR9/21/51G, Murray to Watson, 21 February 1951 PR9/15/51G, FO 1110/374, PRO.
156 Watson to Murray, 1 March 1951, PR9/21, FO 1110/374, PRO.
157 *Ibid.*
158 *Ibid.*
159 Radio Free Europe, Minute by P.A. Wilkinson, 25 April 1951, P.A. Wilkinson to Watson, 10 May 1951, PR9/21/51G, FO 1110/374, PRO.
160 B.A.B. Burrows to D.P. Reilly, PUSD, 25 July 1951, PR33/64, FO 1110/393, PRO.
161 Radio Free Europe, Minute by P.A. Wilkinson, 25 April 1951, P.A. Wilkinson to Watson, 10 May 1951, PR9/21/51G, FO 1110/374, PRO.
162 B.A.B. Burrows to D.P. Reilly, PUSD, 25 July 1951, PR33/64, FO 1110/393, PRO.

163 Wilkinson to Watson, 10 May 1951, PR9/21/51G, FO 1110/374, PRO. The European Movement received significant financial support from the CIA in the early 1950s, see R.J. Aldrich's groundbreaking work including: 'European Integration: an American Intelligence Connection', in A. Deighton (ed.), *Building Postwar Europe: National Decision-Makers and European Institutions, 1948–63* (London: Macmillan, 1995); *ibid.*, 'OSS, CIA and European Unity: the American Committee on United Europe, 1948–1960', *Diplomacy and Statecraft*, 8, 1 (1997), pp. 184–227; *ibid.*, *The Hidden Hand*, pp. 342–70.

164 B.Ruthven-Murray Minute and Warner Minute, 27 April 1951, PR9/21/51G, FO 1110/374, PRO.

165 Radio Free Europe, Munich, F.C. Stacey, Minute, 4 September 1951, PR33/81/G, FO 1110/393; R.H. Bruce-Lockhart to J.H. Peck, 18 February 1952; Report on Radio Free Europe, Munich by Sir Robert Bruce Lockhart, copies also sent to Sir Pierson Dixon and Sir Ian Jacob, PR94/8, FO 1110/518, PRO.

166 P.A. Wilkinson Minute; 15 August 1951, PR33/64/G, FO 1110/393, PRO.

167 J.H. Peck Minute, 31 May 1951, PR33/105, FO 1110/393, PRO.

168 *Ibid.*

169 *Ibid.*

170 *Ibid.*

171 Falla Minute, 3 April 1952, N51052/30/G, FO 371/100842, PRO, quoted in Aldrich, *The Hidden Hand*, p. 321.

172 Aldrich, *The Hidden Hand*, p. 321; J.W. Nicholls Minute, 5 November 1951, PR33/106, FO 1110/393, PRO.

173 Warner Minute, 15 May 1950, P1013/30, FO 953/628, PRO.

174 Establishment of Voice of America Relay Broadcasting Station at Kuwait, A.C.E. Malcolm, 26 May 1952, Aide-Memoiré, [1951], PB1046/11, FO 953/1275, PRO.

175 J.W. Nicholls Minute, 5 November 1951, PR33/106, FO 1110/393, PRO.

176 *Ibid.*; Murray Minute, 7 November 1951, PR33/106, FO 1110/393, PRO.

177 Scrivener Minute, 8 January 1952, PB1046/1, FO 953/1275, PRO; J.W. Nicholls, Minute, 5 November 1951, PR33/106, FO 1110/393, PRO.

178 J.W. Nicholls Minute, 5 November 1951, PR33/106, FO 1110/393, PRO. In his memoirs, Acheson was far from complimentary in his descriptions of Morrison and recalls the 'great and signal improvement' brought about by the Conservative victory and the replacement of Morrison by Anthony Eden: D. Acheson, *Present at the Creation: My Years in the State Department* (New York: Norton, 1969), pp. 505, 510–11.

179 'The Case for a New Approach to Overseas Information Expenditure', September 1950, P10125/39, FO 953/666, PRO.

180 *Ibid.*

181 *Ibid.*

182 *Ibid.*

183 K.O. Morgan, *Labour in Power 1945–1951* (Oxford: Oxford University Press, 1984), p. 433; E. Shinwell, *Conflict Without Malice: An Autobiography* (London: Odhams Press, 1955), pp. 217–25.

184 Gaitskell to Attlee, 15 September 1950, P10125/39, FO 953/666; Overseas Information Expenditure, Memo by Parliamentary Under-Secretary for Foreign Affairs, 16 November 1950, P10125/55, FO 953/667, PRO.

185 Cmnd.8267, *Government Information Services Statement Showing Estimated Expenditure 1951–1952* (London: HMSO, 1951).

186 Overseas Information Expenditure, Brief for the Parliamentary Under-Secretary of State for Foreign Affairs, P10125/39(II), FO 953/666, PRO.

187 Memo, Barrett to Macknight, 12 February 1951, Box no. 5; Memo, Barrett to Joe Frank, OPC, 22 February 1951, Box no. 6; Lot 52D432, Bureau of Public Affairs, Office files of Assistant Secretary of State, Edward W. Barrett, 1950–51, RG 59, NARA.

188 Acheson to Frye, 6 February 1951, 541.00/2-651, RG 59, NARA.

189 Frye to State Department, 8 February 1951, 511.41/2-851, RG 59, NARA.

190 Gifford to Barrett, 26 February 1951, 541.00/2-2651, RG 59, NARA.

191 Shaw, 'The IRD and the Korean War', p. 272.

192 Information Policy, 26 June 1951, CP(51)179, CAB 129/46, PRO.

193 Anti-Communist Propaganda Operations, 27 July 1951, CAB 127/296. A copy may also be found in: PR126/5, FO 1110/460, PRO.

194 Anti-Communist Propaganda Operations, 27 July 1951, CAB 127/296, PRO.

195 *Ibid., Points at Issue: This is a Handbook of Comment on Soviet and Communist Behaviour and Propaganda*, 4th edn (1951). The booklet carries no information regarding printer or publisher. I am grateful to Lord Mayhew for providing me with a copy of this booklet. Details of *Points at Issue* may be found in the files, FO 1110/199, FO 1110/372, PRO.

196 Sir P. Dixon Minute, PR68/180, FO 1110/423; F.C. Mason, Foreign Office, to A. Greenhough, Ministry of Labour, 18 October 1951, O229/951, LAB 13/697, PRO. Copies of the *Defence Digest* were also passed to the US State Department. In November 1951, Barrett requested additional copies: Memo, Barrett to Schwinn, 27 November 1951, Bureau of Public Affairs, Office Files of Assistant Secretary of State Edward W. Barrett 1950–51, Lot 52D432, Box 6, RG 59, NARA.

197 The use of IRD material, A Note for the Guidance of Information Officers and Chanceries, 10 January 1953, PR 101/2/G, FO 1110/532; L. Sheridan Minute, 18 October 1951, PR/20/87, J.H. Peck to Rev. H.M. Waddams, 6 November 1951, FO 1110/382, PRO. On Foreign Office relations with the Church of England, see D. Kirby, *Church, State and Propaganda: The Archbishop of York and International Relations, a political study of Cyrill Forster Garbett, 1942–1955* (Hull: University of Hull Press, 1999).

198 Aldrich, *The Hidden Hand*, p. 458; N.West (ed.), *The Faber Book of Espionage* (London: Faber & Faber, 1993), p. 268; Minutes, and Circular no. 023, Theory and Practice of Communism, 4 March 1949, N1739/1015/38, FO 371/77563, PRO.

199 Aldrich, *The Hidden Hand*, p. 133; P. Deery, 'Confronting the Cominform: George Orwell and the Cold War Offensive of the Information Research Department, 1948–1950', *Labour History*, 73 (November 1997), pp. 219–25.

200 Murray to Rayner, 24 February 1951, PR24/34/51, FO 1110/386, PRO.

201 The best account of the 'Background Books' venture is in: L. Smith, 'Covert British Propaganda: The Information Research Department: 1947–1977', *Millennium: Journal of International Studies*, 9, 1 (1980), pp. 67–83.

202 Aldrich, *The Hidden Hand*, p. 458.

203 For Russell's links to IRD, see Rusell to John Peck, 15 November 1951; Peck to Russell, 14 July 1952; D.C. Hopson to Russell, 13 August 1953, Russell Papers, MacMaster University Library.

204 B. Crozier, *Free Agent: The Unseen War 1941–1991* (London: Harper Collins, 1993), pp. 51–2.

205 IRD Circular to Information Officers, 15 February 1951, PR97/1/51G, FO 1110/444, PRO. This file does not indicate the author of this first 'Background Book', although reference in another file is made to 'Elisabeth Barker's paper, "What is Communism?" for which she was paid 95 guineas', C.F. Maclaren Minute, 4 January 1951, PR92/1/51, FO 1110/439, PRO. I am grateful to Margaret Bryan of the FCO Library and Records Department for drawing my attention to this latter file.

206 IRD Circular to Information Officers, 13 April 1951, PR97/1/51G, FO 1110/444, PRO.

207 Anti-Communist Propaganda Operations, 27 July 1951, CAB 127/296, PRO.

208 Minutes of Western European Information Officers Conference, 12–14 September 1951, PR121/7, FO 1110/458, PRO.

209 Anti-Communist Propaganda Operations, 27 July 1951, CAB 127/296, PRO.

210 P.M. Taylor, *British Propaganda in the Twentieth Century: Selling Democracy* (Edinburgh: Edinburgh University Press, 1999), p. 27, quoting Foreign Office correspondence from 1914.

211 Anti-Communist Propaganda Operations, 27 July 1951, CAB 127/296, PRO.

212 Circular to British Missions, William Strang, 30 January 1952, PR89/3, FO 1110/516, PRO.

213 The IRD contact at Conservative Central Office was Henry Hopkinson and, from 1952, Michael Fraser. Peck Minute, 12 January 1952, PR89/8, FO 1110/516, PRO.

214 Anti-Communist Propaganda Operations, 27 July 1951, CAB 127/296, PRO.
215 *Ibid.*
216 Establishment of the United States International Information Administration, 16 January 1952, *FRUS, 1952–1954*, vol. 2, pp. 1,591–5; Barrett, *Truth is Our Weapon* pp. 97–8; (New York: J.W. Henderson), *The United States Information Agency* (New York: Praeger, 1969), p. 47. Along with other luminaries, such as Cecil B. De Mille, Myrna Loy had attended meetings at the State Department in 1950 to discuss how Hollywood might contribute to the 'Campaign of Truth': Minutes of meeting held on 1 August 1950, 511.004/10-2650, RG 59, NARA.
217 Memo by Assistant Secretary of State for Public Affairs, Barrett, 13 November 1951, *FRUS, 1951*, vol. 1, pp. 957–61.
218 *Ibid.*
219 *Ibid.*
220 Acheson to American Embassy, London, 3 June 1952, 541.00/2-2952, RG 59, NARA.
221 Subcommittee of Committee on Appropriations, *Objectives of the United States Information Program: Reply to Questions asked by Honorable Pat McCarran*, September 13 1951, 82nd Congress, 2nd sess. (Washington, DC: US Government Printing Office, 1952); Edward W. Barrett, Oral History Interview, Truman Library, pp. 61–3.
222 Notes Regarding Indigenous Operations, Edward W. Barrett, 4 February 1952, Lot File no. 52D 432, Bureau of Public Affairs, Office files of Assistant Secretary Edward W. Barrett, 1950–51, RG 59, NARA.
223 Memo by Assistant Secretary of State for Public Affairs, Barrett, 13 November 1951, *FRUS, 1951*, vol. 1, pp. 957–61.
224 *Ibid.*
225 N.O. Wood, 'Strategic Psychological Warfare of the Truman Administration: A study of National Psychological Warfare Aims, Objectives and Effectiveness,' PhD thesis, University of Oklahoma, 1982.
226 Watson to Warner, 6 June 1951, PR9/51, FO 1110/374, PRO.
227 Acheson to Frye, 6 February 1951, 541.00/2-651, RG 59, NARA.

5 A global propaganda offensive

Churchill and the revival of political warfare

In October 1951, Winston Churchill led the Conservative Party back into Downing Street. Although Churchill's enthusiasm for covert activities has been well documented, his attitude towards the use of propaganda is less well known. The historian, Philip M. Taylor, has only recently corrected the long accepted assertion, made by Duff Cooper, a somewhat hapless wartime Minister of Information, that Churchill was not interested in propaganda.[1] Taylor asserts that during the Second World War, Churchill played a central role in the elevation of propaganda as an instrument of government. Churchill's well-known appetite for covert operations, Taylor observes, certainly encompassed propaganda and disinformation. It was on Churchill's initiative that the Special Operations Executive was established to 'set Europe ablaze,' with a brief which included covert propaganda as well as sabotage and subversion. Moreover, Taylor reveals, it was Churchill who set in motion the reorganization of government machinery which led, in 1946, to the establishment of the Central Office of Information.[2] Indeed, as a politician, writer and former war correspondent renowned for his own rhetorical skill, Churchill was perhaps more acutely aware than most of the impact of propaganda. According to Sir Ian Jacob, who served under Churchill in war and peace, he was certainly aware of the potential dangers. He was, Jacob found, suspicious of broadcasting in all its forms, 'he thought it was a dangerous development, because out of that box in the Englishman's sitting room came things over which he had no control.'[3]

Perhaps as a result, Churchill was careful to ensure that responsibility for such activities was in the hands of his most trusted advisers. Cooper was followed as Minister of Information by Churchill's confidante, Brendan Bracken, who held the post almost until the end of the War. When Churchill returned to power in 1951, he was fortunate to find several of his closest wartime advisers in prominent positions in Britain's propaganda machinery. Sir Ian Jacob, who had advised Churchill on defence matters, had moved, in 1946, to head the BBC external services. Although Churchill summoned Jacob in 1952 to assist the new Minister of Defence, after six months Jacob returned to the BBC as Director-General. Lord Ismay, a former Chief of Staff, became Secretary-General of NATO in 1952, and did much to expand the propaganda activities of the alliance. Most notably, John Peck, who had served from 1939 to 1946 as one of Churchill's esteemed Private Secretaries, became head of the IRD in 1951.[4] Such relationships were particularly important during Churchill's second term in Downing Street. Even if he was not always inclined to listen to the Foreign Office, Churchill relied heavily on those relationships forged in the cauldron of war.[5]

British anti-communist propaganda activities expanded considerably under Churchill. In marked contrast to the Labour Government's reluctance to return to wartime propaganda methods, Churchill positively embraced them. Unlike Bevin and Attlee, Churchill was not shy of using terms such as 'political warfare' to describe British anti-communist propaganda. Activities which had been consistently resisted by the Labour Government, most notably the organization of Eastern European exiles, were allowed to grow under Churchill. Although Churchill held a deep-seated belief that Cold War tensions could be eased by negotiation at the highest level with the Soviet leadership, as the prospects of a summit with Stalin receded he embraced the idea of using propaganda to make direct appeals to the people behind the Iron Curtain. To be sure, senior officials in the Foreign Office, and the IRD in particular, were already moving towards a more offensive policy of intensified psychological operations against the Communist bloc. Nevertheless, Churchill's endorsement of these activities was a powerful engine behind them. Churchill's advocacy of such operations was also influential in facilitating expanded Anglo-American cooperation in this field. At a time when US officials were beginning to doubt Britain's commitment to offensive anti-communist activities, particularly in the Communist bloc, Churchill raised the subject at his first meeting with Truman, in January 1952, and ensured continued consultation between Britain and the USA.

Indeed, the expansion of anti-communist propaganda activities under Churchill was partly directed at the USA. Just as British propaganda activities were expanding, the US Government was also expanding its covert propaganda operations around the globe. The scale of these activities renewed concerns in the Foreign Office regarding the tone and the conspicuousness of US propaganda. British officials continued to express concern about the dangers of provoking premature unrest in the Communist bloc. Elsewhere, there was some unease at the expansion of US propaganda activities in areas of traditional British interest such as India, South-East Asia and even Britain. It was feared that the obvious hand of the USA behind a range of anti-communist activities might jeopardise established, and more subtle, British operations. Consequently, British anti-communist propaganda policy behind the Iron Curtain and in the free world was increasingly characterized by an attempt to exert a restraining influence on US policy. In order to achieve this, Britain actively sought increased involvement in US operations in order to be in a stronger position to make suggestions and criticisms of US policy from the inside. This was an expressed intention of Foreign Office proposals for a more forward policy in the Communist bloc. An examination of British and US cooperation in the free world, indicates that a similar policy was also in operation there.

'Intensified psychological operations': Britain, America and anti-communist propaganda behind the Iron Curtain

Churchill's attempt to re-establish close relations with Britain's wartime allies dominated the foreign policy of his second administration. In a bad-tempered election campaign, Churchill derided the Labour Party's handling of international affairs. He castigated Labour for neglecting the 'special relationship' with the USA and squandering Britain's colonial possessions. Churchill was determined to renew the intimacies of the wartime relationship with the US Administration as a key to resolving the tensions of the Cold War. In marked contrast to Attlee who had visited Washington only once, late in his term in office, and specifically to ensure consultation over the use of atomic weapons, Churchill was eager for an early meeting with Truman for informal discussions on a whole range of issues.[6] Less than two weeks after his election, Churchill informed Washington of his hopes for a meeting with the President. Churchill's objective, as he explained to Truman, was that 'we should reach a good understanding of each other's point of view over the whole field, so that we can work together easily and intimately at the different levels as we used to.'[7] Although US officials were somewhat taken aback both by Churchill's eagerness to visit at such short notice, and reluctance to draft a detailed agenda for the talks, the first meeting between the Churchill and Truman was scheduled to begin on 5 January 1952.

The renewal of the special relationship with the USA was central to Churchill's hopes of achieving a negotiated settlement with Britain's other wartime ally, the Soviet Union. Churchill advocated a policy of firmness towards the Soviet Union based on the Anglo-American alliance and military power, including US, and ultimately British, nuclear weapons. During the General Election campaign Labour had sought to label Churchill as a warmonger. Labour Ministers argued that Churchill's return to power would make a third world war almost inevitable, and the Conservative majority was damaged by press articles which posed the question, 'Whose finger do you want on the trigger?' However, as John Young has observed, Churchill was 'no simple Cold Warrior bent on an anti-Communist crusade.'[8] Despite the warmonger charges, throughout the election campaigns of 1950 and 1951, Churchill had made it clear that he believed world tension could be relaxed, and war avoided, by seeking a negotiated settlement with the Soviet Union on a range of issues. Most dramatically, in a speech in Edinburgh, in February 1950, Churchill had called for 'a supreme effort' to bridge the gulf between East and West, and proposed a 'summit' meeting between the leaders of the major powers.[9] Churchill returned to this theme in his first major statement on foreign policy after taking office. In a speech to the House of Commons, on 6 November 1951, Churchill once again called for 'a supreme effort to bridge the gulf between the two worlds.' He suggested that he was prepared to overlook ideological differences and Soviet control of Eastern Europe, in order to ease international tensions. It ought to be possible, he claimed, to achieve an abatement in the Cold War, 'by negotiation at the highest level' from a position of strength.[10]

Stalin, however, was not receptive to Churchill's appeals to wartime fraternity, and shortly after taking office Churchill was forced to concede that a early summit was unlikely. On 8 November, two days after Churchill's foreign policy statement in the Commons, Soviet Foreign Minister, Andrei Vyshinsky, launched a violent and abusive tirade against Western disarmament proposals at the United Nations. Vyshinksy's speech was consistent with hostile Soviet propaganda at the United Nations since 1947 and dashed Churchill's hopes of an imminent easing of international tension. Eden later told the Commons that there 'did not appear to be a chink open in [Vyshinsky's] mind' to accept an appeal from others, and Churchill began to adopt a more cautious tone in public regarding his hopes for an eventual meeting.[11] Nevertheless, in the face of consistent opposition from Eden and the Foreign Office, Churchill remained committed to achieving a summit with the Soviet leadership.

According to John Young, Churchill's hopes of achieving such a high-level conference, 'provided the main rationalization for clinging to office, despite illness and old age, until the Spring of 1955.'[12]

Churchill's enthusiasm for a summit to ease international tensions presented a problem for the Foreign Office, which by the end of 1951, was moving towards a more offensive strategy for undermining the Soviet leadership through intensified psychological warfare. Almost immediately on taking office, Churchill was presented with a detailed review of British policy towards the Soviet Union prepared by the Permanent Under-Secretary's Committee (PUSC) of the Foreign Office. This review sought to dampen Churchill's enthusiasm for a high-level summit by arguing that the West was not yet in a position to 'negotiate from strength.' Western leaders would not be able to talk on terms of relative equality with the Soviet leaders, it argued, until there was a balance of strength in conventional forces, and until there was a balance of psychological strength. That was until, 'the peoples of the free world…no longer fear being overrun as a result of external military aggression or intimidated by subversive Communist activity at home.' Such a balance of military and psychological power, it argued, could not be obtained without a fundamental change in the nature of the Soviet regime.[13]

In examining how such a change might be brought about, the PUSC reviewed the thorny question of liberating the satellites which had preoccupied British Cold War planners since 1948. There had never been widespread enthusiasm for liberation operations in the Foreign Office, and support had waned further with the unsuccessful operations in Albania. In December 1951, the SIS and the CIA, whose joint covert action had hitherto been at the forefront of these operations, held a crisis meeting in London at which the SIS was forced to concede that it was now only interested in intelligence gathering and not subversion in Eastern Europe.[14] The SIS stance reflected a shift in the British approach to liberation which was to place a greater emphasis on propaganda rather than covert action. The PUSC concluded that although there remained powerful arguments in favour of a policy aimed at detaching a satellite by promoting a series of ostensibly spontaneous uprisings, such operations, 'are impracticable and would involve unacceptable risks.' The Committee suggested a new policy designed to bring about change through a process of evolution rather than revolution. Moreover, this policy was to be directed at the Soviet Union as well as the satellites.

Like all revolutionary regimes, it observed, the Soviet regime was inherently unstable and liable to change if the 'rhythm of revolutionary expansion could be checked.'[15] The PUSC believed:

> This may come about by a process of evolution, or cracks may appear in the apparently monolithic structure and the whole system, carrying within itself the seeds of its own destruction, may disintegrate. It follows that if the West can do anything to hasten this process the attainment of a genuine settlement will be brought nearer.[16]

Although the PUSC did not reject the use of positive action designed to 'compress and disrupt' the Soviet bloc, it eschewed the blunt and unpredictable instrument of mass uprisings in favour of a more carefully targeted programme of psychological warfare designed to open up fissures in the heart of the Soviet system. 'Intensified psychological warfare operations,' were now placed at the cutting edge of Britain's Soviet policy. Such operations, the Committee recommended, should be designed to highlight 'known weaknesses and contradictions in the Soviet fabric.' These included: potential unrest in the armed forces outside Russia; the extremes of wealth and poverty, and the small size of the ruling political class; the unpopularity of the collective system; potential unrest among the nationalities; and the fact that the whole system was held together by force. The principal targets were to be the communist government machinery in the orbit countries and the Soviet Union itself and the above all the Red Army.[17]

Such targets reflected the Foreign Office's long-held view that the most effective propaganda was that which targeted ruling élites, this dictum was perhaps most true in the case of dictatorships in which the general population had very little influence on the conduct of everyday life, let alone the conduct of government. Whereas mass uprising might be easily quelled by the use of force, disruption within the Red Army and within or between the communist governments themselves could be less easily purged without fundamentally damaging the Soviet system.

Above all, the PUSC strategy was predicated on the need to maintain control of subversive activities in order to avoid provoking Soviet military counter-action. British planners had long been concerned about the dangers of provoking premature unrest in Eastern Europe. In contrast to 'revolutionary operations,' which could easily run out of control, British planners believed they could exercise greater control over the conduct of propaganda within the Soviet bloc and more clearly define its intent. This represented a marked shift in Foreign Office thinking regarding the extent to which propaganda directed towards the Soviet Union might be viewed as provocative. Although British policymakers remained concerned about the dangers of provocation they were now less inclined to view propaganda alone as unduly provocative. An assessment of Soviet 'sore spots,' completed by the Russia Committee in January 1952, concluded that the West could exert considerable pressure on the Soviets in a number of areas without provoking a violent response. In particular, it concluded that it was 'unlikely that any measure of propaganda would by itself elicit a Soviet military reaction.'[18] As a result more aggressive psychological operations, which had previously caused consternation, were now embraced by Whitehall planners. In January 1952, the Russia Committee concluded that the US 'Ring Plan' offered the best hope of overcoming Soviet jamming and recommended that Britain and the USA 'make full use of radio for enlightening the Soviet people about the true state of affairs.'[19]

The strategy proposed by the PUSC, coupled with SIS's withdrawal from such activities, placed the IRD at the forefront of Britain's new approach to liberation. It would, however, require a redirection of Britain's propaganda resources from countering communism in the free world towards the Soviet bloc itself. Fortunately, by the end of 1951, officials within the IRD were already considering a redirection of priorities for Britain's anti-communist propaganda. In December 1951, the IRD produced a revised version of the memorandum which had been drafted for Gordon-Walker in July. It questioned whether British propaganda should be more offensive. There was, it argued, a certain dualism in British propaganda policy, in that it attacked communism but was not concerned with the internal regimes of the Soviet

Union and other communist-dominated countries. Presumably, it suggested, 'we should like to see Russia pushed back to her real frontiers in Europe' and failing a disappearance of the Stalinist regime in the Soviet Union, at least the renunciation of communism as an instrument of foreign policy. Britain, it argued, should no longer be content to attack communist subversion in the free world, but should 'attack communist regimes wherever they are found.' British propaganda should be based on the assumption that Soviet communism was 'a wicked system', and should hold out some hope of bringing about a 'fundamental change in the Soviet Union…and that the peoples of the satellite countries need not endlessly suffer under their present regimes.' In deference to Churchill's hopes for a high-level meeting, it conceded that this would not necessarily mean that British propaganda should be constantly attacking the Soviet Government:

> It would mean that the aim of our propaganda to communist countries should be to weaken the existing regimes and that subject to the policy considerations of the moment, we should openly in our propaganda to the Soviet Union and the satellite countries adopt the line that they live under a tyranny from which we wish to see them free themselves.[20]

The adoption of such a policy, the IRD observed, would also prevent a 'widening divergence' between Britain and the USA in the field of propaganda. It would allow Britain to agree with the general US approach to 'psychological operations' whilst exerting a restraining influence over US operations, 'to ensure that they were well planned and well worked and did not by rashness, blatant inaccuracy, and lack of constant adaptation, do more harm than good.'[21]

Richard Aldrich has suggested that Whitehall's more cautious approach to liberation was directed as much towards the USA as the Soviet Union. Certainly, by the end of 1951, British officials were increasingly concerned about the implications of the US strategy of liberation. The PUSC predicted that the Americans would 'wish to go faster and further than ourselves.' The USA, it observed, rated the possibility of detaching satellite states by subversion, 'a good deal higher than we do,' yet they warned, the Americans appeared to have little clear idea as to what the outcome of such a policy might be. There were evident risks that such activities might get out of control. In a prescient passage, the PUSC predicted that the West could be faced with the choice of providing armed support for the revolutionary movements, or abandoning them to their fate, 'an alternative which would inevitably lead to a strengthening of the Soviet hold over the whole of the Soviet Empire and the liquidation of all potential supporters of the West.'[22]

However, rather than simply withdrawing from such operations, the more controlled strategy of intensified psychological operations advocated by the IRD and the PUSC, would, it was hoped, allow Britain to continue to exert 'a moderating influence' on US policy. The PUSC concluded:

> [T]he United States Government may be reluctant to pay much heed to British criticisms which seem to be only obstructive and negative. They might be more ready to listen if the United Kingdom was able to indicate agreement in principle to study the possibilities of a more forward policy aimed not at fomenting revolt

in the satellites but at weakening the whole fabric of the Soviet empire; and was then in a position to put forward suggestions and criticisms from the inside. The course then would clearly involve the United Kingdom in going some way with the Americans towards a more active policy.[23]

The accuracy of the PUSC's assessment of the likely US attitude towards an apparently obstructive British policy is revealed in US preparations for the Churchill–Truman talks, in 1952. Briefs prepared in advance of the talks indicate that the Americans were unimpressed with Britain's reluctance to engage in propaganda against the Soviet bloc, and it was decided that the question of propaganda against the Soviet bloc would not be discussed with the British unless it was raised by Churchill himself. A brief prepared for Truman, predicted that if the subject were raised, the British would 'tend to question the necessity or desirability of political warfare operations.' The brief continued:

> They are inclined to accept the present *status quo* in Eastern Europe and do not desire to engage in activities which they consider not only will be calculated to increase East–West tension but which might even provoke the Kremlin to acts of aggression. The British, in short, appear to believe that the immediate dangers of provocation overbalance the long-range deterrent results of political warfare carried on within Moscow's own orbit.[24]

Contrary to American expectations, Churchill did raise the subject of propaganda against the Soviet bloc when he met Truman in January 1952, and even hinted that Britain was prepared to adopt a more active policy in this field. Throughout the Washington talks, Churchill sought to reassure Truman about British policy towards the Soviet Union. He informed Truman that he believed a summit was unlikely at present and conceded that Truman, as the most powerful Western leader, should take the lead in dealing with the Soviets. Significantly, Churchill added, if a summit meeting were held and ended in failure he would like to see an intensification of the Cold War. The democracies, he said, should make an 'intensive effort to bring home to all people behind the Iron Curtain the true facts of the world situation – by broadcasting, by dropping leaflets and by all other methods of propaganda which were open to them.' The Kremlin, Churchill suggested, would fear 'such a revelation of truth' and under the pressure of intense propaganda be forced back to the conference table. Churchill suggested that details of the methods for conducting such a campaign might be studied in advance by Britain and the USA. Truman, clearly unprepared for such a proposal, replied that he was, 'in principle in favour of spreading knowledge of the truth among the people behind the Iron Curtain,' and agreed that the subject should be studied further in consultation with the British.[25]

This brief exchange between Truman and Churchill marked a significant development in British and US cooperation in the field of anti-communist propaganda. This was the first occasion on which cooperation in the field of anti-communist propaganda was discussed at the executive level and is an indication of how important propaganda had become in the Cold War strategies of both countries. Churchill's powerful advocacy of psychological operations to undermine the Soviet leadership is further evidence, if any were needed, to undermine Duff Cooper's assertion that Churchill was not interested in propaganda. It also suggests that Foreign Office thinking had some influence on the Prime Minister's view of the Soviet Union. Most significantly, the Washington talks revealed an unexpected convergence in British and US approaches to propaganda against the Soviet bloc. Churchill's support for such activities came as something of a relief to officials in Washington and, as the PUSC had hoped, ensured that US officials were prepared to listen to British views on the subject. Churchill heralded a new strategy of intensified psychological operations against the Soviet bloc which brought British and US strategies closely into line, and was to be developed in close consultation with the Americans in the years ahead.

More substantial discussions followed, in May 1952, when John Nicholls, Foreign Office Permanent Under-Secretary responsible for information activities, led a delegation to Washington for a series of meetings with representatives of US propaganda agencies. The visit allowed Nicholls to establish contact with the new heads of the IIA, Compton and Sargeant, and took in the State Department and the headquarters of Radio Free Europe. The most pressing subject was the conduct of Western propaganda against the Soviet bloc. These talks illustrated the success of the Foreign Office policy of agreeing in principle with a more aggressive policy towards the Soviet bloc whilst seeking to exert a restraining influence 'from the inside.' US officials who, in January, had suggested that anti-communist propaganda activities in the communist bloc should not be discussed with the British at all, now laid out their plans in detail before the Foreign Office delegation. In light of Britain's new found commitment to intensified psychological operations, Nicholls was asked to comment on US plans for propaganda towards communist satellite states and the Soviet Union. He expressed the Foreign Office's satisfaction with the plans but questioned 'how far we are justified in taking open encouragement as our main theme to the satellites.' The British, he said, were concerned that undue encouragement might lead the people in these countries to lose hope. It was, Adam Watson added, 'unwise to keep on repeating that "the Campbells are coming tomorrow", lest either premature action or cynical apathy result.' Nicholls also urged caution in the use of material generated by émigré groups, whom the Americans conceded, were 'always "beating the gong" about hope.' It was best, Nicholls suggested, to report their statements as straight news rather than something that was endorsed by Britain or the USA. Rather than exciting hopes of liberation, Nicholls suggested that the West might use other themes to a greater extent in its propaganda to the satellites, such as: the vitality and variety of the West; the 'community of thought' that linked the satellites to the West; and the national traditions of the satellite countries. They should not, Nicholls said, eliminate the hope theme, but merely ensure that it was not emphasized to the exclusion of others. 'We must,' he concluded, 'tell the satellite peoples those things that will make them hope without actually using the word hope.' Nicholls's comments were well received and Compton recommended that they be incorporated into the State Department's propaganda plan for the satellites.[26]

Considerable time was devoted to the discussion of broadcasting as the principal means of directing Western propaganda over the Iron Curtain. Nicholls took the opportunity to explain the background to Morrison's comments the previous year on the 'Ring Plan', and reassured the Americans that current British policy no longer viewed the erection of a ring of transmitters as unduly provocative. The Americans reviewed the progress of the 'Ring Plan', and provided the results of the first broadcasts from the Vagabond vessel, USS *Courier*, which was being tested with broadcasts to Latin America from the Caribbean before proceeding to its station off the island of Rhodes.[27] The Americans reaffirmed their commitment that the West should retain the upper hand in the field of broadcasting, and expressed concern about the well-publicized cuts in British spending on overseas broadcasting. The BBC had also recently fallen into third place behind the Soviets and the VOA in terms of hours of overseas broadcasting per week.[28] Nicholls sought to reassure the Americans that the size of the BBC budget was such that in order to maintain broadcasting output some of its activities could be added to other budgets. Nevertheless, he was concerned about Soviet plans for a new transmitter in Berlin. The USA, Nicholls was informed, 'would not be willing to accept a stalemate in Europe on broadcasting,' and it was clear that in the event of such developments Britain would need to rely on US technical capabilities. If there was a likelihood of the Soviets developing too much transmitting power, Nicholls was informed, US plans would be revised accordingly.[29]

Nicholls sought to reassure the Americans that the BBC's importance as an instrument of British Cold War propaganda was out of proportion to its size. While the scale of BBC broadcasting was not comparable with the combined output of the VOA, Radio Free Europe and Radio Liberty, the BBC had an unparalleled reputation even amongst communists. A Foreign Office review, in 1952, concluded that the BBC retained a high reputation for truthfulness and British missions reported that, 'even convinced communists tend to turn to the BBC for information whenever a major international event occurs.'[30] Moreover, Nicholls informed the Americans, that the BBC 'proves very amenable to Foreign Office "advice," with regular contact at the working level.'[31] Representatives of Central and Eastern European Services attended monthly meetings with the IRD. The IRD also supplied the BBC with information from British Missions in the Soviet orbit. These despatches often contained material too trivial for normal Foreign Office reporting, such as accounts of visits to shops, markets, theatres and exhibitions or any 'titbits of local gossip or current political jokes which have been picked up.' This liaison, the IRD reported, 'helps to ensure that the BBC keeps in line with H.M. Government's policy towards the Soviet satellites, and also means that they are kept up to date on conditions in these countries and not led astray by the spate of Communist propaganda.'[32]

Although the BBC adopted a more cautious tone than US stations, and any broadcasts which might stimulate revolt were strictly prohibited, one theme which was pursued with vigour, in cooperation with the US, was the encouragement of defection. Exploitation of Soviet and satellite defectors was one of the most promising methods of discrediting communist propaganda and undermining the legitimacy of the Soviet regime. Defectors provided useful intelligence on conditions inside the Soviet bloc, and evidence on the impact of Western propaganda. They also provided a ready pool of personnel for use in propaganda broadcasts, press campaigns and covert operations within the Soviet bloc.

By 1952, the Americans were committing substantial resources to the utilization of defectors for intelligence and propaganda purposes as US officials believed that they could do real damage to the Soviet regime by encouraging defection. A report submitted to the State Department in 1950 by the Soviet Studies' specialist Frederick Barghoorn – based on extensive interviews with defectors and refugees – concluded that the Soviet leadership viewed defection as a grave threat to its authority. In 1951, the National Security Council approved NSC 86/1, 'United States Policy on Soviet-Satellite Defectors', which recommended that defectors should be used to further the aims of US policy 'by placing the maximum strain on the Soviet structure of power through threatening the regime's control of its population.' It was essential, Barghoorn warned, for the USA, through its broadcasts, to provide disgruntled Soviet officials with the hope that a better life awaited them if they defected.[33] In addition, $100,000,000 was made available under the Mutual Security Act for the resettlement and utilization of defectors from the Soviet bloc. The distribution of this so-called 'Hundred Million Dollar Fund' was coordinated by the Psychological Strategy Board. The PSB drafted an ambitious programme, which included the use of defectors for intelligence, propaganda and the formation of military units. The plan for military units developed rapidly under Eisenhower into the Volunteer Freedom Corps, was to be built up from residual escapees from the Second World War and based on the wartime Polish Army of Liberation under General Anders.[34]

The British had fewer resources to devote to the defector programme. Indeed, General Anders left London for Washington, in 1950, disillusioned with the small scale of British operations.[35] Nevertheless, the Foreign Office believed it could inflict substantial damage on the Soviet regime by encouraging high-level defections. The BBC's reputation meant that it was vital tool in promoting such defections. Refugee interrogations revealed that three-quarters of the radio listeners from satellite states who passed through the reception centres had listened to the BBC; and BBC research indicated that, in the Soviet Union, the BBC's audience consisted largely of technicians, officers in the armed forces, executives, senior officials and intellectuals.[36] The Russia Committee recommended that broadcasts should carefully target these groups with propaganda designed to encourage defection. In particular, it suggested, the Soviet atomic programme might be damaged by encouraging Soviet scientists to defect.[37] The IRD also developed propaganda directed specifically at Soviet military personnel stationed abroad. One of the IRD's first operations was the handling of a Soviet lieutenant-colonel, Grigori Tokaev, who defected in 1948. The publicity following Tokaev's defection was handled by the IRD and included prominent coverage in *The Times*, a series of articles for the *Sunday Express*, and a series of BBC radio talks. In the 1950s, the IRD helped Tokaev to publish three volumes of polemical anti-Soviet memoirs.[38]

There was considerable cooperation with the Americans in this field. In 1952, the IRD's Peter Wilkinson informed the Americans that the BBC was broadcasting a programme each week featuring two defectors telling of their escape and their asylum, and that he was gratified that the VOA had recently started a similar type of broadcast. Foreign Office research indicated that these broadcasts were very important tools in the encouragement of defection and it was agreed that there should be an exchange of scripts.[39] There was also cooperation in handling the rapidly increasing flow of defectors passing through the Iron Curtain, which by 1951 had reached around 500 a month. It was with some relief that Allen Dulles, then deputy director of Central Intelligence, reported to the National Security Council, in December 1951, that he had a copy of a paper shortly to be presented to the British Cabinet which recommended that the British accept all Soviet defectors and all high-level defectors from elsewhere.[40] In 1952, it was agreed that there should be 'a full exchange of information' on the interrogation of defectors, although progress with this was evidently slow. At the beginning of 1953, following a tour of reception centres in Berlin, the IRD complained that coordination with the Americans on the ground was limited. Although, it was observed, this was not surprising, as individual US agencies often found it impossible to work with each other![41]

The IRD, of course, also enjoyed a close and productive relationship with the more offensive arms of the US anti-communist broadcasting effort, most notably Radio Free Europe. Although this relationship remained confidential, it expanded in the 1950s as the RFE expanded and allowed the IRD a direct input into psychological operations which openly advocated liberation. It is clear that the IRD was not unduly concerned about the tone of RFE broadcasts, and they were certainly reassured by Robert Bruce Lockhart's review of the station's operations in February 1952. Although Lockhart cautioned that the 'political tempo has been too fast and should be moderated to a pace more in keeping with the indefinite time factor,' he praised the great progress the station had made in a short time, and the ambition and enthusiasm with which it was managed.[42] After visiting the State Department, in April 1952, Nicholls called on C.D. Jackson at the New York offices of the NCFE. Nicholls said that he believed that the RFE, 'was not in fact stirring up revolution, but rather keeping alive the memory of freedom.' Cooperation between the IRD and the RFE, Nicholls found, was now 'on a satisfactory basis,' and a considerable quantity of intelligence and 'other aid' was flowing.[43]

Indeed, by 1952, the IRD's relationship with the RFE extended some way beyond the exchange of propaganda material. What emerged, in the early 1950s, was a close and informal relationship whereby British and US broadcasting policies, and in some cases operations, were closely coordinated. The novelist Fay Weldon, recalls that whilst working in the IRD, in 1952, she 'wrote pamphlets for RFE to be dropped over Poland by air and distributed there by Boy Scouts.'[44] In January 1953, the IRD agreed to a proposal from Allan Michie, the RFE's London representative, for a monthly gathering at his flat to which he would invite representatives from the BBC, the Foreign Office and the VOA. These meetings would be 'quite informal over a glass of whisky in order to discuss lines of publicity to be taken in broadcasting to Eastern Europe and various subjects of immediate interest.' As the meetings were informal it was not felt necessary to inform the Minister, Anthony Nutting, 'except to give general blessing.'[45]

In addition to relations with the US-sponsored RFE, in 1952 the Foreign Office began to organize its own contacts with exile groups. In a move which had been resisted by Bevin and Morrison, Eden gave approval for the provision of substantial support and assistance to an ostensibly independent committee of exiles along the lines of the NCFE. The vehicle chosen for this support was the Central-Eastern European Committee of the European Movement.[46] The Foreign Office's appropriation of the Central-Eastern European Committee is an intriguing episode in European exile politics and one cannot fail to see the hand of Churchill behind it. The European Movement had been established in the aftermath of the war to promote the cause of European unity. While in opposition Churchill had been a leading light in the Movement's creation, and his son-in-law, Duncan Sandys was the Movement's President in 1949 and 1950. Under Sandys leadership the Movement had avoided collapse by accepting substantial financial support from the CIA, channelled through the American Committee for a United Europe (ACUE). Churchill, with his extensive contacts in Washington and the US intelligence community, had acted as an important link between the ACUE and the European Movement. However, British influence in the Movement waned in 1950 as, under American pressure, Sandys was replaced by the more pro-Federalist Paul Henri Spaak, and following his return to office Churchill had also backed away from federalist ideas.[47] Although British influence in the movement receded, the British still retained an interest in the Eastern European arm of the movement. A Central-Eastern European Commission had been established in the European Movement in the late 1940s by the Conservative MP Harold Macmillan and Joseph Retinger the European Movement's first Secretary General. It comprised exiles from Eastern Europe and the Baltic States, and was designed to 'unite all the exiled politicians and democratic groups in the fight against Communism and for the liberation of their subjugated countries.'[48] The CIA's largesse had not extended to the Central-Eastern European Commission. In 1951, the Commission had approached the NCFE for approval and material support to establish itself as an independent organization. Following consultation with the State Department the NCFE turned down this proposal on the grounds that it was likely to undermine the work of the NCFE and lead to further schisms in the already fragmented world of exile politics.[49]

In 1952, the Foreign Office stepped into the breach, and provide the necessary financial support to enable the Commission to establish itself as 'a completely independent group.' The Committee's president was Richard Law, the Conservative MP for Haltemprice, the secretary general was Sir David Kelly, former British ambassador to the USSR, and the vice-president was Paul de Auer, the former Hungarian ambassador to France. The Committee aimed to organize exiles in Western Europe and undertake psychological operations against the captive nations of Eastern Europe. In January 1953, US officials reported, there were, 'ambitious plans' to enlarge its operations in the field of publications, exile activities and information gathering, 'all under the exclusive supervision, and for the benefit, of the Foreign Office.'[50] The Committee gave the Foreign Office an important influence over the activities of Soviet bloc exiles in Europe, and one might discern in this move an attempt to exert a restraining influence on the US policy of liberation. The Foreign Office encouraged the Committee to adopt a more restrained attitude towards the prospects of liberation. While advocating liberation as an aspiration the Committee ruled out the idea of a fighting force of Eastern European exiles, and concentrated its activities in the field of propaganda.[51]

The British move certainly caused some consternation in Washington. Despite the fact that US officials had been encouraging the Foreign Office to establish its own exile committee since the establishment of the NCFE in 1949, 'Under these circumstances,' it was observed, without coordination of activities and some knowledge of, and influence on, British plans for the Central-Eastern European Committee, 'our psychological warfare efforts in this region... would be considerably weakened.' It was also noted that the British, and indeed the French, had 'more and better qualified exile-experts' than the USA, and there was clearly some concern that the USA would fall behind in this field. In an effort to reassert US influence it was decided that they should seek to add two or three American vice-presidents to the Committee, and that the Committee should be encouraged to establish a branch office in Washington. The ultimate objective would be 'to coordinate long-range activities of the Committee with that of its American opposite-numbers.'[52] There is no evidence to suggest that the Foreign Office was not prepared to coordinate activities, indeed, quite the contrary. Nevertheless, British control of the Central-Eastern European Committee gave the Foreign Office another important level of influence over US-led activities in Eastern Europe.

Fundamental differences remained in the British and US approaches. British plans were, if anything, more ambitious and focused on long-term change in the Soviet system rather than merely detaching satellites from the Soviet bloc. British and US propaganda was also to be targeted at different groups within the Soviet bloc. Whilst the British hoped to open up fissures at the heart of the Soviet system, US psychological operations were designed to 'form the political bases and the operational nuclei for resistance groups.'[53] The British sought to break the Soviet system by exploiting weaknesses at the top, whilst the Americans sought to undermine the system by creating popular unrest. Nevertheless, although the British remained sceptical about US chances of success, they were prepared to go some way with the Americans towards a more forward policy of psychological warfare against the Soviet bloc. The *de-facto* division of labour, whereby British anti-communist propaganda was directed largely at the free world whilst the US concentrated on the Soviet bloc, was now over. Britain and America would henceforth seek to coordinate their propaganda activities around the globe.

Combating communism in the free world

The IRD's growing interest in anti-communist activities behind the Iron Curtain in no way diminished the importance of, or the resources devoted to, anti-communist work in the free world. In January 1952, Permanent Under-Secretary William Strang circulated British missions with a new memorandum on combating communism in the free world. He began by reassuring them that Churchill's much-publicized plans for an accommodation with the Soviet leadership did not mean that 'we have felt able to revise our basic assumption' regarding the long-term aims of the Stalinist regime. Nor, he wrote, should the recent cuts in information budgets give rise to the impression that the Government was relaxing its efforts to counter Soviet political warfare. '[S]o far from curtailing their activities in this field,' Strang wrote, 'the Government are resolved to continue their efforts to the highest possible degree.'[54]

It was, Strang wrote, almost four years since British missions had been informed of the new propaganda policy and the establishment of the IRD, yet the communist threat to the free world was, if anything, even greater than it had been in 1948. Consequently, the objectives of British anti-communist propaganda had changed. British overseas propaganda was no longer guided by a dual policy of promoting Western values and exposing the truth about life under communism, but had a more pressing and offensive aspect designed to counter communist infiltration of the free world. The campaign, Strang conceded, was now concentrated 'wholly on the negative, anti-Communist, anti-Soviet aspect.'[55] Although British propaganda would continue in its attempt to disabuse people of their misperceptions about the true nature of the communist regime, it was directed increasingly at exposing and undermining communist tactics in the free world.

The main concern no longer lay in the overt appeal of communism and the activities of communist parties. Communist parties it was felt, could achieve little on their own, a more insidious threat was posed by communist 'front' activities, such as the Peace Campaign, in which communist influence was partly or wholly concealed. 'Their function,' Strang warned, 'is to lead public opinion via any local mass move-ment or agitation that they can exploit, to an acceptance of the Soviet thesis, or to act in accordance with Soviet interests.' Although British propaganda would continue to 'chip pieces off the hard core of Communists in each country,' the principal effort would be directed at dispersing the fellow-travellers and sympathizers with which the hard core surrounded itself, and ensuring there was 'as little public sup-port as possible for any ostensibly non-Communist activity if it is in fact being run by Communists.'[56]

Insofar as there was a positive message in Britain's new programme for combat-ing communism in the free world, it was a defensive message designed to counter a rising tide of neutralism and defeatism in the free world. British propaganda was no longer concerned with projecting a positive alternative to communism, but had a more urgent theme aimed at convincing people that it was possible to resist the tide of communism. It was, Strang asserted, necessary to mobilize leaders of public opin-ion to convince people that Western institutions were, *'worth defending,'* and most importantly, 'that they are *capable of being* defended against military attack,' [emphasis in original]. Strang conceded that efforts to motivate anti-communist activities among most of Britain's allies had largely resulted in failure and, as a result, the need for Britain to take a leading role in combating communism in the free world was even greater than it had been in 1948. 'The half-heartedness of a few of our associates, and the lack of means of most of the remainder,' he wrote, were all the more reason for Britain to make the fullest use of its resources and experience. With the notable exception of the US Government, Britain remained, 'virtually the only Government which has made a worldwide study of the problem and has the organisation to carry out counter-measures on a scale in any way comparable to that of the Soviet Government.'[57]

Under the direction of John Peck, the IRD developed an ambitious strategy to mobilize opinion and actively combat communism in the institutions of the free world. Peck proposed the creation of anti-communist cells by securing the services of individuals in all walks of life, 'whose principal claim to attention is not their anti-communism but the respect that they engender for their pre-eminence in something else – history, science, trade-unionism.' By presenting such leaders of public opin-ion around the globe with a series of stark choices, the IRD aimed to convert and recruit them to the anti-communist cause. Once recruited, such individuals, it was hoped, would play a central and discreet role in keeping their own institutions 'free from infection.' As John Peck stated:

> As I see it we want to recruit them in all the key organisations of a free society – trade unions, press, universities etc. – we want them to be well informed about the aims and methods of Soviet foreign policy; to detect the form which Soviet political warfare is taking in their own society and to take the necessary counter-measures to frustrate it. We also want them to ensure that the public in each country is well supplied with accurate information about what the Soviet Union and Communism really are, and to expose and nail all the lies of the other side. The immediate and practical application of these principles is that in the West

they should support the rearmament programme, and attack the neutralist and defeatist positions in their own way. In the Middle East and South-East Asia we want them to recognise the incompatibility of their own nationalism with Communism, the impossibility of remaining neutral in the present alignment of forces, and the realisation that their best hope of survival is to cooperate with the rest of the free world.[58]

The Foreign Office had, of course, been actively seeking to counter communist influence in international organizations since 1945. Following the launch of the new propaganda policy in 1948, the work of the Cultural Relations Department (CRD) in this sphere had gradually passed to the IRD and the department became Whitehall's principal weapon in the battle against communist front activities. A role which drew the Foreign Office increasingly into anti-communist activities on the home front. One of the IRD's first operations, in 1948, involved a covert subsidy for an anti-communist action group within the TUC entitled *Freedom First* which was instrumental in manoeuvring the TUC to split from the communist-dominated World Federation of Trade Unions. The following year the IRD collaborated with the TUC in an effort to expose communist penetration of the National Council for Civil Liberties (NCCL). The IRD also worked with the CRD to disseminate information on communist persecution of students to representatives of the NUS proposing to attend the World Festival of Youth in Budapest in 1949. By 1950, the department was leading British efforts to counter the communist peace campaign and was instrumental in undermining plans by the World Peace Council to hold its second international congress in Sheffield, in November 1950.[59]

The Sheffield congress was significant as it allowed the IRD to develop a programme of action for countering international conferences which was adapted for future conferences and presented to Britain's NATO allies as an effective model for coordinated action. Faced with the Cabinet's reluctance to ban the congress outright, the Foreign Office sought to 'reduce it to a fiasco by placing every obstacle in the way of undesirable delegates attending.'[60] The IRD suggested that, if entry visas were refused to individuals wishing to attend the congress, the organizers would be forced to relocate to a more amenable location, preferably behind the Iron Curtain, where the congress's claim to widespread popular appeal in the free world would be greatly diminished. In August 1950, Ralph Murray drafted detailed plans in which he urged the Home Secretary to exercise his full powers to withhold visas from persons known or suspected of coming to the congress.[61] Later, when Murray learnt that the Home Office definition of undesirable participants did not include leading members of the World Peace Council, he pressed the Foreign Secretary to adopt a more stringent policy of exclusion which included all members of the World Peace Council, and any members of four other international organizations: the World Federation of Trade Unions; the World Federation of Democratic Youth; the World Federation of Scientific Workers; and the Women's International Democratic Federation.[62] In the event that such actions might lead to adverse public reaction at home and abroad, the IRD produced a wealth of material on the communist peace campaign, much of which was distributed through Denis Healey in the Labour Party's International Department.[63]

The IRD's efforts to 'cripple the congress' were considered a great success. Delegates to the congress were turned away at Dover, and at the last minute the

World Peace Council announced that the congress would be relocated to Warsaw. Public reaction in Britain was largely confined to the *Manchester Guardian*, and in Parliament, where the aborted congress provoked a lively debate, there was general agreement on the need to control the entry of people attending communist-controlled meetings. A post-congress analysis in Downing Street observed that attacks on the Government's policy were quickly exhausted and 'passed with little or no notice.'[64] The combination of control over visas, pressure on individuals proposing to attend international congresses and an active programme of counter-propaganda was to become an established IRD strategy.

The IRD's success against the Sheffield Peace Congress established the department as Whitehall's central collection point for information on communist front activities at home and abroad. In preparing for the Sheffield congress, IRD established a close working relationship with the MI5.[65] The MI5's veteran anti-communist, Milicent Bagot, began to provide the IRD with a steady stream of detailed briefs on forthcoming congresses.[66] At a meeting with the MI5, in May 1952, the IRD provided detailed requirements for intelligence on international organizations which not only included information on forthcoming international conferences but on any preparatory meetings in Britain, 'whether or not they are attended by foreign delegates or observers.' The IRD also requested information on prominent communist or 'near communist' personalities visiting Britain privately, and private visits abroad by certain British individuals, such as 'red or pink Trade-Union officials.'[67] Such information was then passed to any sponsoring body in the hope that it might 'induce leaders to take administrative action' against such individuals.[68] The Labour Party banned individuals from attending conferences of an extreme left-wing complexion and, in the 1950s, pursued a rigorous policy of expulsions of individuals involved in such organizations. Briefs were also produced for internal Whitehall consumption and for use by Ministers and officials when warning organizations proposing to send delegates to international conferences. The IRD's John Cloake recalls how the strategy worked:

> We tried to identify some sensible or reliable people among the invitees and give them some advance briefing, either directly or through a cut-out. On one occasion the Astronomer Royal had accepted an invitation to such a meeting. I was detailed to make contact with him and give him a thorough briefing before he set off. I got a good dinner at the Athenaeum out of it and the Astronomer Royal did not make a fool of himself at the meeting.[69]

The IRD's efforts to counter communist front activities led the department into greater cooperation with its counterparts in the US Government. US activities in this arena were boosted in 1951 by the creation of the CIA's International Organisations Division (IOD). Headed by the OSS veteran, Thomas Braden, the IOD was designed to cut across the CIA's established divisions of regional responsibility and enable the agency to fight communist front activities on an international level. Like the IRD, the IOD acted as a central collection point for information on communist front activities and the leading agency in efforts to counter communist influence. By providing covert assistance to a host of voluntary and private organizations, the IOD sought to reach beyond the realm of conventional government propaganda and elicit support for US policies in the widest and most diverse circles. Under Braden's direction, the IOD adopted an imaginative approach to countering communism by providing covert funding for a host of organizations ranging across the fields of labour, student and cultural affairs. Most significantly, the IOD provided extensive funding for organizations on the non-communist left which could not hope to attain overt support under the gaze of the right-wing American Congress. Beneficiaries of the IOD's largesse included the American Federation of Labour, the Congress of Industrial Organizations, the National Student Association, the Museum of Modern Art and the Congress for Cultural Freedom. The IOD also took over responsibility for the CIA's links with Radio Free Europe and Radio Liberty. Whilst some of these larger operations have been well documented, scholars have only recently begun to investigate the multitude of smaller campaigns sponsored by the IOD.[70] However, the sheer scale of the IOD's covert subsidies eventually led to their exposure. In the late 1960s, a series of press reports revealed CIA contacts with US youth and labour organizations and led to a damaging Congressional investigation which revealed 'massive' CIA funding of private organizations. The resulting fall-out saw the collapse of the Congress for Cultural Freedom, and the enforced independence of Radio Free Europe.

By the time of the next major congress – the World Youth and Student Festival in Berlin 1951 – the IRD and the US authorities had organized an aggressive programme of counter-action. Special Branch and the FBI were asked to check the identities of citizens involved, and 'special approaches' were made to organizations proposing to send delegates to the festival. British youth and student organizations – such as the Boy Scouts, the Labour League of Youth, and the Student Christian Association – were approached directly by officials from the Foreign Office and the Ministry of Education, who warned them about the nature of the festival and pressed them not to get involved. The IRD also sponsored a small committee of prominent students to issue a denunciation of the festival. IRD basic papers on the peace campaign and communist oppression of youth and students were circulated to British missions, and British representatives were asked to approach local youth and student groups, 'to make them aware of the position, to stir them to action and to brief them.' The British and American Governments instituted administrative obstructions by refusing passports and visas for those wishing to cross into the Federal Republic, and the British, American and French authorities refused to allow trains bound for the festival to pass through their respective zones of Germany. For those who made it to Berlin, the State Department lavished considerable resources on a counter-propaganda campaign in West Berlin which involved free entry to cinemas and theatres, a pavilion devoted to the European Recovery Programme, broadcasts on the RFE and the distribution of over two million pamphlets and booklets.[71]

By the time British officials visited Washington, in May 1952, British and US efforts to counter communist front activities were closely coordinated and British and US officials congratulated themselves that the Soviet peace campaign in Europe had been effectively exposed. The British, Nicholls reported, had passed all relevant information on communist front organizations to the USA. Adam Watson had begun to exchange biographical data with the Americans in order to establish the continuities of personnel in the controlling directorates of many of these groups, and it was agreed that British and US officials would pool information on forthcoming conferences and coordinate assessments of what communist front groups said, and their methods of operation. US officials had been particularly impressed with Britain's policy of withholding visas and received British support for plans to ban a front meeting in the American zone of Vienna. Nicholls reported that there had been a slight shift in British policy, in that communists were allowed to enter Britain to attend meetings that were openly acknowledged as communist, but were not prepared to let them attend front meetings, 'which might fool the people.' 'It was best,' Nicholls said, 'to show such meetings for what they are and make them meet in the Russian zone.' Although this policy had not been made public, it had the merit of being 'surprisingly acceptable to the British public, even the Liberals.'[72]

Whilst Britain and the USA scored some notable successes against communist front organizations, it soon became clear that, if communist-controlled international congresses were to be effectively undermined, Britain and the USA would need to coordinate their activities more widely with their other allies. Although the IRD had effectively stymied the conduct of communist-controlled meetings in British territory, communist front organizations were able to operate with relative freedom in other Western countries. In preparing for the Sheffield Peace Congress, in 1950, Ralph Murray stressed that if such congresses were to be truly driven behind the Iron Curtain it would be necessary to closely coordinate policy with Britain's NATO allies.[73] By late 1951, senior officials in the Foreign Office were pressing for a wider distribution of anti-communist material with Britain's allies. The Permanent Under-Secretary, William Strang, stressed that 'strengthening morale in the free world,' was an obligation of the North Atlantic Treaty, and Murray's successor, John Peck, told a meeting of Western European information officers, in September 1951, that the IRD should take 'slightly more risks' in disseminating material to the NATO countries.[74]

In January 1952, Strang instructed British missions that attempts to involve other friendly governments in the anti-communist campaign were now to be stepped up. Although British anti-communist propaganda had been operating in a number of countries, 'originally without the knowledge of any of the governments concerned,' information staff were now instructed to work, 'wherever possible, in close association with the appropriate government agency.' The need to operate discreetly, however, remained paramount.

> The matter is of extreme delicacy, since it is vital to the success of the operation that His Majesty's Government should not overtly appear to be conducting a world-wide anti-Communist campaign, and we must in no circumstances appear to be interfering in the domestic affairs of friendly nations. On the other hand, it is greatly to our interest that governments should come to regard us, even tacitly, as the chief providers of information material on this subject and of guidance on general tactics on whom they can rely, and I hope that you will do what you can, as opportunity offers, discreetly to encourage this idea.[75]

The obvious forum for expanding international cooperation in the field of anti-communist propaganda was the North Atlantic Treaty Organisation. The IRD, however, while keen to see an increase in anti-communist activities by Britain's allies in Europe, remained cautious about a multilateral approach to anti-communist propaganda. In particular, they did not wish to cede the initiative in anti-communist activities in

Western Europe either to the USA or a strengthened NATO information service (NATIS). IRD officials still felt that it was up to Britain to give a lead to the forces of anti-communism in Europe. The IRD's T.S. Tull observed that Britain had made the running in developing techniques for countering communism in Western Europe.

> Governments tend to look to us for advice... It is I think important that we rather than the Americans should take the lead in these discussions since the problems which European countries face are all very similar, particularly on the home front and since British initiative is likely to be less suspect.[76]

Before putting any proposals to the European allies, the expansion of NATO propaganda activities was discussed with the USA during Nicholls visit to Washington. The USA had pressed for a more active NATO propaganda policy and machinery since the establishment of the NATIS in 1950. In early 1951, the State Department observed that it was becoming, 'fairly generally recognised that the psychological field is the one area in which Western Europe is even more poorly prepared than in the military.'[77] A review of NATIS activities undertaken on behalf of the Psychological Strategy Board, in 1952, concluded that whatever anti-communist propaganda had been issued by NATIS, and there were few examples, 'has been more by accident than design, and has caused some amount of unhappiness as being contrary to the essentially defensive purposes of NATO.'[78] Yet, US officials complained, with a staff of only six, NATIS was up to the limit of what it might achieve in the field, and they pressed for a substantial reorganization of NATO information machinery. In place of an information service made up of seconded members paid by their own national governments and operating only through the governments of the member states, the State Department recommended an independent NATO information service, with its own operating budget, responsible to NATO itself. Such an information service, it was argued, would not be subject to the whims and resources of the member states but would, 'speak with one voice and use its influence to get the member countries to work toward a common end.'[79]

Despite a glut of US studies on the subject, it is apparent that the British led the discussions both in Washington and Paris regarding the reform of NATO propaganda machinery. Although Nicholls agreed with the US advocacy of a more active NATO information service, he stressed that Britain and the USA should keep their own propaganda machinery 'closely coordinated and in our own control.' Nicholls supported US proposals for placing NATIS within NATO machinery, but went somewhat further than recommending the creation of a substantial propaganda machinery within NATO. It is clear that, following the elevation of propaganda as an integrated part of British foreign policy, what Nicholls suggested was a similarly integrated approach to the handling of propaganda activities within NATO. The main problem, Nicholls said, was not merely one of organization and resources, but one of political guidance. Little thought, he claimed, had been given to the link between propaganda and policy within NATO, and NATIS merely operated as a tool for the promotion of NATO. NATIS, Nicholls said, was well equipped to handle news handouts and publicity for events such as the NATO anniversary but there was no means whereby the propaganda implications of NATO decisions might be considered in advance. Nicholls suggested that a group might be established to act as a link between the

Council of Deputies and NATIS, which could concentrate on the problem of giving policy guidance on a long-range basis.[80]

The proposals outlined by Nicholls in Washington were driven forward at NATO headquarters in Paris by the appointment, in April 1952, of Lord Ismay as NATO Secretary General. Ismay who had been Churchill's wartime Chief of Staff had a keen appreciation of the value of publicity. He came to NATO after publicizing British achievements as Chairman of the Council for the Festival of Britain in 1951. Ismay enthusiastically set about 'spreading the gospel of NATO,' in the press, on the radio and within NATO itself. In September 1952, he told a conference on the Atlantic Community that on taking up the appointment as Secretary General he had little idea of how the organization worked, or why it was important:

> If I, who have followed public affairs pretty closely for many years, know so little about NATO, how must it be with what I may call, the average man and woman in the NATO countries – the workers on the farm and in the factory, the housewives, the soldiers in the ranks, the clerks and so forth. The success or failure of the movement clearly depends upon the wholehearted support of these men and women: and no one will support a project unless he or she fully understands it and is convinced that it is worthwhile.[81]

Moreover, Ismay added, in seeking to educate the public about NATO they were not merely battling against ignorance but also the 'shrill warnings' of communists, on both sides of the Iron Curtain, who derided NATO as an instrument of US aggression. As a result, Ismay reported one of his first tasks on taking office had been to launch a 'crusade against popular ignorance and apathy.'[82]

In June 1952, under Ismay's direction, an Information Policy Working Group (IPWG) was established within NATO. It was chaired by Ismay's energetic Assistant Secretary-General for Political Affairs, the Italian Sergio Fenoaltea, and comprised representatives from all the NATO countries. The IPWG was initially tasked with advising the Council of Deputies on 'the ideas which should be brought home to the peoples of the Atlantic community and the methods by which they might be accomplished.' At its first meeting these terms of reference were extended and the Working Group was also designated as, 'the forum for consultation and exchange of views on problems of countering communist propaganda.' Fenoaltea also persuaded the Council to provide a financial contribution enabling NATO to develop information projects without the need to rely on the support and resources of the member nations. This contribution was modest, and NATO remained largely dependent on the willingness of the information services of member governments to work in cooperation with NATIS. Nevertheless, the IPWG helped to raise the profile of propaganda activities with member governments, and provided a direct link to the Council of Deputies.[83]

Under Ismay and the IPWG, NATO propaganda expanded considerably. A wide range of activities were instituted to stimulate interest in the alliance, many of which are still in operation today. The Secretary-General began to hold fortnightly press conferences and, in one of the first projects organized by the IPWG, tours were organized for groups of journalists to visit NATO and SHAPE and to tour other member countries. The production of printed matter was also increased. A second edition of the NATO handbook was issued in 1953, for the first time in French and

English. By the time of the third edition, timed for NATO's fifth anniversary in 1954, 100,000 copies of the handbook were being distributed. In 1953, a periodical, *NATO Letter*, was launched with a monthly run of 10,000 copies. With the assistance of the US Information Service, a series of short films on NATO themes were produced, with such titles as, *The Atlantic Community – Know Your Allies* and *Alliance for Peace*. In 1953, the Secretary-General himself starred in a short documentary made for troop information purposes. Other schemes to raise the profile of the alliance included the adoption of a NATO flag and the issue of NATO stamps by member governments. Most successfully, a NATO Peace Caravan began to tour member countries with a mobile 'Atlantic Exhibition.' Following tours of Italy, Greece and Turkey, it toured French cities. In May 1954, at Rennes, the exhibition welcomed its millionth visitor – a plumber![84]

Anti-communist propaganda activities, however, were more problematic. In December 1952, Ismay conceded that progress in this field 'must necessarily be slow in view of the differences in the national approaches to the problem.'[85] Although some NATO members were in favour of extending the anti-communist work of NATIS – most notably the Italians and the Greeks – others felt that such activities were contrary to the defensive nature of the alliance. Ironically, it was Britain, the main supplier of anti-communist material to the alliance, which was the most significant brake on a high-profile NATO anti-communist propaganda campaign. By 1952, most IRD publications were sent to NATIS, and some, such as the fortnightly 'Trends of Communist Propaganda,' were distributed to member governments under the NATIS imprint.[86] However, even within NATIS, the existence of the IRD and its methods was not widely known. Only the director of NATIS, Theodore Newton, and his British deputy, William Newton, knew of the IRD's work. However, even they received IRD material in a plain brown envelope from the British delegation with the IRD cover-slip removed, as it revealed 'considerably more of IRD's activities than we want NATIS to know.'[87] Although the IRD was happy to provide material to NATIS, it was reluctant to allow its activities to be discussed within NATO, and they opposed any suggestion that NATIS should be built up as an agency for overt anti-communist propaganda. NATIS was to be used to distribute anti-communist material to member governments, but, the IRD argued, the wider dissemination of such material was best conducted on an unattributable basis, and 'most efficiently performed by member governments rather than by NATO as a whole.'[88] In their new-found enthusiasm for unattributable, 'indigenous operations,' the USA now concurred with the British view. The Psychological Strategy Board observed that propaganda with regard to NATO, 'must be managed with exceptional tact, finesse and indirection.' Although NATIS could be used to stimulate, advise and service the anti-communist activities of member governments, it was felt that national domestic information agencies were better placed, 'to get material into the hands of indigenous agencies for exploitation and distribution.'[89]

IRD officials were particularly concerned about discussing the IRD's methods in a multilateral forum whilst Britain was actively conducting anti-communist propaganda within many of the NATO countries. Before revealing British anti-communist activities to the IPWG, heads of British missions in the NATO capitals were asked to estimate the reaction of their host governments to a description of the IRD's methods. In particular, they were asked to comment on whether they would expect the government to which they were accredited, 'to raise objections to activities on behalf of IRD by members of your staff.'[90] The replies revealed such a complex array of bilateral relations between the IRD and the foreign ministries of Britain's NATO allies that it was decided 'not to indicate the extent of HMG's activities in this field in any given foreign country, or that any of the other NATO Governments are aware of such activities.'[91] This was despite the fact that the IRD had established fruitful relationships with the governments of the Netherlands, Luxembourg, Belgium, France, Italy, Greece, Sweden, Norway, Canada and the USA. These relationships had, however, been established on 'a bilateral and very discreet basis,' and most significantly, not all were aware of the extent of IRD activities within their own territories, most notably the French and the Dutch. These governments, along with those NATO allies that had been given no information about the IRD or its activities, (Iceland, Turkey and Portugal) would, it was felt, 'greatly deprecate' discussion of such activities within the IPWG. These complicated arrangements undoubtedly left the UK representative to the IPWG in an uncomfortable position, alleviated only a little by the instruction that if the existence or work of the IRD was revealed by one of his colleagues in the IPWG, 'he need not deny it.'[92]

Despite these difficulties, the British delegation was instructed to 'guide' the IPWG towards performing, 'a useful counter-propaganda role, in spreading our own ideas on the subject, in arousing a greater sense of urgency among some of the NATO powers, and in facilitating the exchange of information.'[93] In particular, the IRD sought to use the IPWG to coordinate action against communist front activities in Western Europe. The IRD suggested that one of the first objectives of the IPWG, 'should be the exchange of information designed to expose, and the coordination of proposals designed to frustrate, the communist stooge organisations around the world.'[94] In 1953, the IRD provided the British delegation to the IPWG with a list of nine communist front organizations, the names of citizens of NATO countries who held leading posts in these organizations, and a list of 'forthcoming attractions' planned by these organizations in NATO countries. The Dutch, Danish and Norwegian Governments were pressed to take urgent action against imminent meetings of the World Federation of Democratic Youth in their territories. Most significantly, the British delegation to the IPWG proposed that control over entry visas might provide a convenient basis for concerted action by the other NATO allies.[95] The IRD's proposal became NATO policy in January 1954 when the NATO Council approved a recommendation of the IPWG that, 'member governments should take all action open to them to make it impossible for International Communist Front Organisations to hold conferences in NATO countries.' The measures to be adopted were left to individual governments, although various options were suggested, including the refusal of entry to foreigners wishing to attend such conferences and various other forms of 'administrative action' such as refusal of authorization to hold conferences and delay in the issue of visas. No publicity was given to the decision, and member governments were asked to treat it as 'strictly confidential.'[96]

While the IRD sought to guide allied governments towards adopting a more aggressive response to communist propaganda, the department continued to exert a restraining influence on the burgeoning anti-communist propaganda activities of the US Government. The efforts of the CIA's International Organisations Division to counter communism in the free world expanded rapidly in the early 1950s, and the

IRD was closely involved with many of these projects. Senior officials in the IRD were, however, growing increasingly concerned at the overt anti-communism of some of the IOD's operations. As early as February 1952, the IRD head, John Peck, observed that it was 'now little more than polite convention to suggest that certain international organisations – such as Paix et Liberté, the Congress for Cultural Freedom, the World Veterans' Federation, and the Free Journalists – are not American financed and directed.' The IRD's activities were targeted principally at non-communists, and such individuals, the IRD had found, were not readily influenced by anything which was too obviously anti-communist. The Americans, Peck warned, were in danger of building up:

> …a body of enthusiastic but unscientific anti-Communists whose aim and methods will fail to attract – and may even push into the wrong camp – the large body of intellectuals, waverers, neutralists and others which we regard as the most important target for our efforts.[97]

In this context the IRD involvement with IOD operations not only provided important new outlets for IRD material, it also provided the Foreign Office with opportunities to exert a moderating influence on an area of covert action which they considered required the utmost discretion.

In particular, the IRD took a leading role in the development of the intellectual magazine *Encounter*, which was launched in 1953. *Encounter* became one of the most prominent intellectual periodicals of the latter half of the twentieth century and, like many of the IOD's fronts, enjoyed a life which continued after covert funding was withdrawn. *Encounter* was an Anglo-American venture from the start. It was conceived in 1951 by T.R. Fyvel, a freelance journalist, who was a leading British representative of the CIA-financed Congress for Cultural Freedom. During the War, Fyvel had worked on British psychological warfare and had been seconded to work for the American Psychological Warfare Division in North Africa and Italy. After the War, Fyvel worked on the left-wing periodical *Tribune*, and – as a leading member of the British Society for Cultural Freedom and a freelance writer for the IRD – continued to act as a link between British and US propaganda. Fyvel made his suggestion for a new 'Anglo-American left-of-centre publication' to a US information officer in London, and the idea was embraced by the CCF and its CIA backers. When Fyvel's ideas came to fruition, in *Encounter*, it was edited in London jointly by the British intellectual, Stephen Spender, and the Executive Director of the American Committee for Cultural Freedom, Irving Kristol, and financed by the CIA and the IRD.[98]

Although supported by the British and American Governments and produced by a British and American editorial team, *Encounter* was not directed primarily at readers in Britain or the USA. As the CCF's American Secretary, Michael Josselson, observed, 'a communist or neutralist problem does not exist in those two countries,' and *Encounter*, initially at least, was aimed at those parts of the free world, in Europe and the Far East, 'where neutralism is the strongest force.'[99] The Foreign Office, in particular, was keen to use the magazine to combat neutralism in Europe, and to stimulate anti-communism among intellectuals in Asia, India and the Far East. Although the main financial support for *Encounter* was provided by the CIA, the

IRD's contribution was not insignificant. The IRD provided a small financial subsidy which, to avoid the impropriety of the CIA remunerating British subjects, was earmarked for the salaries of the British editor, Stephen Spender, and his secretary. The IRD also agreed to buy a specified number of copies for distribution abroad.[100]

The decision to publish *Encounter* from London also provided the IRD with an opportunity to exert an influence on the organization and content of the magazine. The IRD established a small semi-autonomous office in London, run by the SIS veteran, C.M. Woodhouse. The CCF agreed to consult with Woodhouse through the CIA representative in London, on 'operational' procedures relating to *Encounter*. Woodhouse also acted as a link with the magazine's British publisher, Secker & Warburg, who had already proved accommodating in granting the IRD overseas rights to George Orwell's work. The IRD later established a more direct line of contact, when Margot Walmsley left the IRD to become office manager and later managing editor of the magazine.[101] In addition to these administrative ties, *Encounter* drew heavily on a coterie of British writers and intellectuals, many of whom had close relations with the IRD. Although Stephen Spender later claimed to have been unaware of any covert subsidy for *Encounter*, he was aware of the IRD's activities. Other early contributors – such as Fyvel, Malcolm Muggeridge, Richard Crossman and Robert Conquest – had backgrounds in British intelligence and propaganda and had already produced material for the IRD. Others – such as Bertrand Russell and Isaiah Berlin, who were perhaps less likely to produce material at the behest of the US Administration – regularly received IRD material and had readily written pieces for the department.

The IRD's relationship with *Encounter* can not, however, be explained simply by the magazine's anti-communist credentials. By the time *Encounter* was launched in 1953, the CCF already had something of a reputation as a vehicle for US anti-communist propaganda and the IRD's involvement with *Encounter* is consistent with Foreign Office attempts to exert a restraining influence over US anti-communist propaganda; and, as the IRD had often found, this influence was best exerted from within. In what was a typical example of the IRD's handling of US covert operations, direct contact with *Encounter* in London allowed the IRD to oversee developments at the operational level whilst, in Washington, Adam Watson was instructed to impress upon his contacts in the State Department and the CIA the need to take 'very great pains' to conceal the anti-communist nature of their organizations. 'They then have a much better chance of appealing to all sections of the community, and the anti-communist treatment can be applied naturally and unobtrusively.'[102]

The IRD's attempts to exert a restraining influence over the USA's burgeoning anti-communist propaganda operations in the free world were particularly evident in those regions where British influence had traditionally been dominant, most notably in India and South-East Asia. In 1951, the CCF made a considerable effort to establish itself in India, opening offices in New Delhi, Bombay and Calcutta, and calling for an Indian Congress for Cultural Freedom to be held in New Delhi. Nehru, however, was inclined to view the congress as an American front, and the Indian Government refused to authorize the New Delhi event. The organizers were forced to relocate to Bombay where the CCF secured the assistance of the mayor, Minoo Masani, a leading opposition figure in the Indian Parliament, who was stridently anti-communist and anti-British. Masani was a prime candidate for CCF support, he had lived in the USA, studied at the University of Wisconsin, and was an associate of the legendary anti-communist American trade union leader, Jay Lovestone. The Bombay conference, however, was far from successful. Several speakers took the opportunity to launch vocal attacks on the West, and the USA in particular. Attacks on the communists, in contrast, were treated with indifference. Western observers were disillusioned by Indian attitudes: the *New York Times*, described several speakers as 'anti-totalitarian fellow-travellers.' Although the energetic Masani continued to organize meetings, seminars and distribute anti-communist books and pamphlets, India proved to be increasingly hostile territory for the CCF.[103]

The IRD, in contrast, had enjoyed considerable discreet success in India, both in placing anti-communist material in the Indian press and, to a lesser degree, in impressing the nature of the communist threat upon Nehru. IRD officials were dismayed at the US handling of events in India. They were particularly concerned at US attempts to marginalize, the admittedly difficult, Nehru. It was, the IRD claimed, 'most dangerous to imagine that Nehru does not represent leading opinion in India...wherever he thought it desirable to make the effort, Nehru *is* leading opinion in India;' and the IRD had invested considerable time in stimulating Nehru's efforts. The widely recognised link between the CCF and the US Administration was also problematic. British officials observed that the obvious US interest in the Bombay conference, 'was largely responsible for the rough handling it received in the Indian press.'[104] Anti-Americanism was rife in India and the situation was not helped by the fact that the US Congress was withholding grain exports to the famine-stricken country in protest at their pro-Chinese policies. Two American delegates to the Bombay conference cabled the Speaker of the House of Representatives: 'Prompt dispatch of wheat imperative for American good name in Asia.'[105] Observers in the Foreign Office were concerned that the Americans appeared to think, 'that Indian dislike of them is largely due to ignorance of and not distaste for their way of life.' IRD officials argued that what was required was not more information about the USA – 'the more Indians see of Americans the less they like them' – but a more subtle campaign.[106]

Although it is apparent that some in the IRD greeted American difficulties in India with a certain degree of *schadenfreude*, the CCF's problems in India placed the Foreign Office in an invidious position. India was a primary target for the IRD's anti-communist propaganda, and there were grave fears that British efforts would suffer by association. The Foreign Office also had high hopes for the impact of *Encounter* in India, and hostility to the CCF could seriously undermine this Anglo-American venture. Adam Watson cautioned that it was 'very bad for us to be pulled two separate ways by this hostility,' and suggested that the IRD should do what it could to lessen the mutual hostility between India and the USA. Following the Bombay conference, US officials approached Watson for advice, and he tactfully outlined the IRD's criticisms of US methods in India, stressing in particular, 'that in their new nationalism Indians strongly resent superiority and condescension.' This advice, Watson reported, 'was well received,'[107] and following its own internal investigation, the CCF adopted a new 'constructive' and pro-Nehru policy in India. In 1953, recognizing that Nehru was the leading liberal alternative to Chinese communism in Asia, the CCF sidelined Masani. New offices were opened in New Delhi and a new literary and arts programme was launched which was less stridently anti-communist.

The CCF began to open libraries and information centres across the country and directed its efforts at the gradual erosion of fellow-travelling in India. While this less confrontational approach enjoyed some success, India continued to prove a frustrating target for CCF activities. When Sidney Hook visited India on behalf of the CCF in 1958, he was amazed at the 'almost limitless credulity' of the Indians with regard to the USSR and China, and was somewhat taken aback by the proliferation of neon signs which lit the night sky with the message, 'Read Soviet Books!'[108]

The CCF's activities in India were part of a broad expansion of US support for anti-communism in Asia. This programme was led by the establishment, in early 1951, of a Committee for Free Asia (CFA), modelled on the National Committee for a Free Europe. Like the NCFE, the CFA had a board which comprised prominent industrialists, intellectuals and former intelligence officers, and received advice and guidance from the CIA. The President, Robert Blum, was formerly in charge of the Economic Cooperation Administration in Vietnam, Laos and Cambodia, and the board including the presidents of the universities of California and Stanford, the president of Standard Oil and the writer, James A. Michener. From its headquarters in San Francisco, the CFA directed Radio Free Asia, which began broadcasting from Manila in May 1951. The CFA, however, had a much a broader remit than broadcasting and differed from the NCFE in that its activities were directed primarily at the free countries of Asia rather than the communist bloc. The committee sought 'to develop in Asia a community of interest in resisting communism, and to encourage and promote native leadership of activities which will strengthen freedom.' Its wide-ranging projects included support for the National League for Free Elections in the Philippines, a Chinese bookstore in Hong Kong, and a well-financed programme of travel grants and scholarships for Asian students wishing to study in Taiwan or the USA. It also provided a front for US support for the Asian operations of a host of international organizations such as the World Assembly of Youth and the International Confederation of Free Trade Unions.[109]

As with the NCFE, the British were informed at an early stage about plans for the CFA. There was general sympathy for the CFA's objectives in London and at Phoenix Park in Singapore. There were, however, potential conflicts of interest in South-East Asia which mitigated against the kind of close cooperation which existed between the Foreign Office and the NCFE, notably the colonial conflict in Malaya and the divergence in British and US policy towards China. In December 1951, before the CFA had established a presence in Asia, the Committee's Director of Asian Operations, James L. Stewart, toured South-East Asia and took the opportunity to brief Malcolm MacDonald and John Rayner about the CFA's plans. MacDonald took care to receive assurances that the CFA would, 'avoid any strong taint of K.M.T. influence' and would play down the theme of liberation from Western colonialism. He also ensured that the CFA would not begin any activities in Malaya 'without full prior discussion.'[110] Six months later, Robert Sheeks, the Committee's representative in Malaya, visited the RIO prior to taking up his post. Sheeks provided a detailed list of the kind of projects the CFA planned in Malaya, including: a project for bringing anti-communist newspapers into Malaya; a scholarship programme to enable students to visit the USA and the UK; reception tests for RFA broadcasts from the Philippines; and a project to 'present Malaya to the United States,' in order to improve the US public's appreciation of the Emergency and the British point of view.

Sheeks also agreed that any further projects would only be submitted to the CFA following approval by the Federation authorities. However, in a revealing conclusion, which must have struck a nerve with the cash-starved officials in the British RIO, Sheeks observed that 'the possibilities were limitless as the Committee had plenty of funds and ample facilities for getting support in the United States.'[111]

The CFA, however, did not enjoy an auspicious beginning. Radio Free Asia possessed weaker transmitting facilities than its European counterparts and it was soon found that listening to the radio was extremely limited in communist China – a CIA survey indicated that in mainland China the audience was limited to government officials and those specifically authorized to listen to short-wave broadcasts. Although the station had a small audience amongst the overseas Chinese in South-East Asia, these could equally well be reached by the Voice of America and, in 1954, RFA broadcasts were discontinued.[112] There were also some concerns that the committee's name risked alienating the vast majority of its target audience who did not live under communism. In 1953, the CFA changed its name to the Asia Foundation which, according to one CIA official, had some chance of looking 'less frighteningly ours to a neutralist Burmese or Indonesian.'[113]

British officials in Singapore remained sceptical about CFA activities. In December 1952, at the monthly meeting of British regional governors at Bukit Serene, MacDonald observed that 'much of the good in American policy and actions is often vitiated by the clumsiness of their methods.' 'It is important,' MacDonald concluded, 'that we should do what we can both to mitigate the effects of such propaganda and to exercise a restraining influence where possible on American representatives.'[114] Joseph Burkholder Smith, the CIA representative in Singapore, later wrote that British officials were particularly concerned when the CFA opened an office in Singapore. Although it had obviously been agreed in London and Washington, Smith observed, 'the MI6 and IRD people on the ground evidently had been overruled when this agreement had been reached.' British regional governors sought to take advantage of the CFA's early administrative problems to obtain the same oversight of CFA operations throughout the region as the Americans had conceded in Malaya. According to Smith, this led to a certain degree of horse-trading before the CFA agreed to monthly meetings with Rayner at the British RIO. At these meetings, also attended by a CIA representative, the CFA would provide the British with a general overview of their operations across the region and provide names of any individuals they proposed to use, or offer, scholarships or other financial assistance. This bureaucratic routine, it seems, functioned well and according to Smith the RIO was soon operating as a second level of monitoring alongside the CIA's own Far East division.[115]

If British officials had reservations about the expansion of US anti-communist propaganda activities in Asia, perhaps the most sensitive target for US propaganda was Britain itself. The Truman administration had long been concerned about communist influence in Britain, and the neutralist or openly anti-American stance of the Bevanite left wing of the Labour Party. Even following Churchill's election, in October 1951, the US Embassy in London reported that, 'communism is not declining rapidly in Britain [and] the anti-American feeling must be watched and dealt with carefully.'[116] In 1952, the US Information Service (USIS) Country Plan for Britain stated that the inherent pacifism of 'Bevanism' remained an 'increasingly disturbing' factor in British public opinion.[117] Although the communists made no electoral gains in 1951, the US Embassy reported that communists still had considerable influence in the UK. It was with some dismay that US officials reported that civil servants still sat on the editorial board of the *Daily Worker*, and that communists controlled key positions in the unions which staffed the nation's power industries.[118] US officials in London were also concerned about the widespread availability of communist propaganda material in the UK.

> Communist propaganda is carried on through many media, with great reliance on the spoken word in workers' groups, 'front' groups, rallies, etc. 'Front' groups also distribute propaganda booklets through advertising in the press, and maintain bookshops. Free direct distribution of pro-Communist, anti-American literature is made to newspapers, writers and correspondents and individuals.[119]

In response, in the early 1950s, the US Embassy launched an expansive information programme in Britain, designed to undermine communist influence and counter anti-American sentiment. By 1953, the operating budget for the US Information Service (USIS) in Britain was exceeded only by those for Italy and France, where the communist parties held significant electoral power.[120] The programme in Britain involved a considerable expansion of both overt and indirect information activities. A Regional Production Centre, like the one in Manila, was opened in London, and new posts were created in London for a Labour Information Officer and a Women's Affairs Officer. Additional information offices were opened in Edinburgh and Manchester to service Britain's industrial heartlands.[121] The campaign was targeted primarily at leaders of public opinion: MPs; journalists; intellectuals; organized labour; and youth groups. In Britain, it was observed, 'policy is still framed and opinion formed primarily from the top down.'[122] US Embassy staff were encouraged to establish close personal contact with influential and like-minded journalists, MPs and trade unionists. Documents on US foreign policy and anti-communist material were widely distributed and, in 1950, a new fortnightly bulletin, *Labor News from the US*, was launched. The mailing list of 1,200 comprised Labour MPs, socialist and trade union newspapers and periodicals, workers education officers and industrial correspondents.[123] Individuals were encouraged to use any material they were provided but without attribution to official US sources. The information office in Edinburgh was particularly successful in persuading Scottish trade unionists to write letters to the editors of socialist dailies answering communist charges.[124]

While indirect dissemination of US views through opinion formers was a priority, USIS went to considerable lengths to directly target a mass audience with films, exhibitions and television. During the Second World War, the US Office of War Information had stockpiled in Britain documentaries and motion pictures extolling the American way of life. These films were gradually replaced by films from the Marshall Plan's European Film Unit.[125] This programme was accelerated in the early 1950s and USIS developed an ambitious film programme in cooperation with the Economic Cooperation Administration (ECA). In 1952, a film vault was constructed at the US Embassy, a USIS cinema was opened in London, and a film van was purchased for use in the provinces.[126] Mobile exhibitions aroused considerable interest in the provincial cities and reportedly took advantage of 'the peculiar British propensity for standing in queues.' In 1952, USIS staged the Northern Productivity Exhibition in Newcastle, which attracted an audience of more than 9,000 factory workers, plant managers, technical students and trade union officials. The following year a mobile 'USA Today' exhibition attracted 48,000 visitors in Edinburgh and 23,000 in Newcastle. Most significantly, the advent of mass television viewing in the early 1950s presented the greatest potential audience. Several USIS-ECA films were shown on BBC television. In 1953, when the television broadcast of the Coronation of Queen Elizabeth II led to a dramatic rise in British television viewing, USIS reported staggering six-monthly audience figures for USIS television programmes of 100,000,000.[127]

USIS also fought an aggressive campaign to counter the growing volume of pro-communist literature available in Britain. In the last sixth months of 1950, USIS distributed 19,000 pamphlets in Britain. This, they claimed, was 'dangerously inadequate' when compared with circulation of the *Daily Worker* and the huge number of communist booklets advertised in the left-wing press. In early 1951, USIS produced its first mass circulation pamphlet entitled *Our Foreign Policy*. An initial print run of 100,000 copies were distributed to, among others, national and provincial newspapers and 6,000 Church of England vicars. It was quickly followed by An *Outline of American History* and *Communist Lies about America*, the latter of which was privately published.[128] Great efforts were made to publish pamphlets without an official imprint and Americans studying in Britain were encouraged to publish material under their own names explaining US policy and institutions.[129] The most important material, however, was written by prominent British writers. In July 1951, the US Labour Information Officer (LIO) reported that Fred Douglas, a Scottish ex-communist and former correspondent on the *Daily Worker*, had agreed to write a series of pamphlets on *British Agents of the Cominform*, to be published without US identification. Douglas secured a contract for the mass sale of the pamphlets at news-stands and was prepared to set up a dummy publishing house to print the pamphlets. Following a security check by the embassy, the LIO reported that, 'besides consultation and the furnishing of our regular Cold War materials, our only possible commitment would be in paying him an advance to work the project up.'[130]

The US Government went to considerable lengths to influence intellectual opinion in Britain. In 1951, the US Embassy reported that, next to the communists, intellectual socialists were, 'the most vociferous anti-American, anti-rearmament collection of individuals in the UK.'[131] While the IRD viewed *Encounter* primarily as a means of stimulating anti-communist opinion in Europe and Asia, for the US Government the magazine was also part of a concerted effort to counter communist influence and anti-Americanism among intellectuals in the UK. In 1952, following a major reorganization, the British Society for Cultural Freedom entered the most active period of its existence. A new executive board was elected comprising Malcolm Muggeridge as chairman, Frederic Warburg as treasurer, Michael Goodwin as secretary and John Clews in the new post of national organizer. Under their direction, the BSCF became more uncompromising in its anti-communism and more overtly pro-American. Clews and Goodwin were active in monitoring communist, and suspected communist, front organizations in Britain. The society also distributed thousands of copies of pamphlets written by Clews, a former NUS president, exposing communist infiltration of the International Union of Students, and rebutting communist claims about the US use of germ warfare in Korea.[132] Goodwin, who was editor of the journal *The Twentieth Century*, received substantial financial support from the CCF on the understanding that the journal would actively refute the positions espoused in the magazine, *New Statesman and Nation*. In 1952, he reported that *The Twentieth Century* had kept up 'a running fire of comment upon a variety of subjects which amounts in total to a systematic critical destruction of their position.' He added that the journal was also preparing to undermine the Glasgow University periodical, *Soviet Studies*, which he observed, 'is probably the chief source of Stalinist apologetics in this country.'[133]

Officials at the US Embassy in London were also active in their efforts to counter the pro-Soviet leanings of British academics working in the field of Soviet Studies. In 1951 and 1952 the embassy was particularly agitated by the publication of the first two volumes of E.H. Carr's, *The Bolshevik Revolution, 1917–1923*.[134] In a robust review for the State Department, it reported that Carr's work presented:

> [A] Lenin of breadth and tolerance of view, of prophetic understanding, of inspired and incisive purpose and a revolution which might have painlessly reached a millennium, had it not been forced to react to the opposition of its enemies and steer round the obstructions of its more stupid supporters. Even at that, so little does Professor Carr indicate that any flaws of human character such as hate, greed, pride, ambition or stupidity entered into the high direction of the revolution, that in his book it seems to advance teleologically, from one inspired manoeuvre to another, to a point beyond which, the reader is surely induced to believe, must lie only in the best of all possible worlds... But the most noxious aspect of Professor Carr's book is that in fact it leaves practically no ground for conclusions of any other order.[135]

Carr's work, it was reported, 'cannot but do harm in this country,' not least because it reinforced views regarding 'American hysteria' about communism, which, it was claimed, were widely held, particularly by members of the Labour Party. The embassy's concerns were exacerbated by the fact that Carr's book had not received any unfavourable reviews in the British press, and that Carr proposed to publish further volumes on the subject. It recommended that the State Department 'see what it can do about counteracting the influence of Professor Carr's books.'[136]

Carr's book was passed to Dr Sergius Yakobson of the Library of Congress who was an authority on Russian history, and was 'well acquainted with scholarly activity in the UK.' The London Embassy was asked to suggest someone to review Carr's work and, recognizing the embassy's 'delicate situation,' the State Department agreed to arrange for Dr Yakobson to approach the author concerned. The first choice of Isaiah Berlin was rejected when it was found that he had written a positive review of the first volume of Carr's history, but it was agreed that Professor Michael Florinsky of Columbia, who had offered a less favourable review of the first volume, might be approached to write a further review for a British journal.[137] The embassy also suggested that the State Department might arrange for the publication of books in the UK to counter Carr's work. In particular, it recommended Bertram Wolfe's *Three Who Made a Revolution*, which had not been published in the UK. Wolfe's book, it was claimed, covered the same period as Carr's work, 'and in the treatment of it, more comprehensive and penetrating than Carr's, should go far to counteract effectively the influence of *The Bolshevik Revolution*.'[138] At a time when Macarthyite purges were seeing the removal of books on communism from USIS libraries around the world, the embassy had some trouble convincing the State Department of the value of Wolfe's work, but it eventually agreed to find a British publisher for the book.[139] Books about the USA were less problematic and Denis Brogan was paid $1,000 to update his book, *American Character*, and financial arrangements were made with Brogan's publisher Knopf to reissue the book in the UK.[140]

It is not clear how far the IRD cooperated with US information activities in Britain. The IRD certainly had its own channels for the distribution of anti-communist material to those groups of opinion-formers in Britain whom the Americans wished to target, and the US Embassy observed that British officials were disposed to help distribute USIS literature, 'when it is convenient, economical and politic for them to do so.'[141] The IRD worked closely with the State Department on a global campaign to refute communist allegations about germ warfare in Korea. The IRD ensured that the issue received wide coverage in Britain by commissioning articles, arranging parliamentary questions, and ensuring that the diplomatic editor of the BBC was 'specially briefed' about the situation.[142] The IRD also had close links with those individuals involved in US propaganda activities in Britain. Malcolm Muggeridge and John Clews both wrote material for the IRD. Clews, in particular, actively distributed IRD material within the CCF and used his position to place leading intellectuals in contact with the Foreign Office. Michael Goodwin also worked closely with the IRD and, in 1954, edited a series of booklets, published and distributed with Foreign Office support.[143]

However, evidence of direct IRD support for US information activities in Britain is limited. Indeed, following the removal of the information liaison officer from the American Embassy in London in 1951, contact between the embassy and the IRD was allowed to languish until it was re-established in 1954. Close relations were, of course, maintained in Washington and, in 1952, the State Department agreed to show British officials unexpurgated copies of information guidance bulletins sent to London.[144] Given that US propaganda was targeted so heavily at the Labour Party, the timing of this decision may be explained by the election of the Conservative Government. However, it is clear that the US Government did not seek the support of the IRD in information activities in Britain. Whilst this may be explained by US sensitivities about the scale of their operations in Britain, it is also evident that in so far as US information activities were designed to promote US policy, State Department officials conceded, it was, 'not the responsibility of the British Government to explain American policy, or to correct the communist distortions and misrepresentations of American policy.'[145]

Indeed, far from supporting US propaganda activities in Britain, the IRD actively sought to calm US fears about communism in Britain. Access to US information guidance bulletins seems to have raised concerns in the Foreign Office regarding US overestimations of the communist threat in Britain. This became particularly pressing following the Republican victory in the presidential elections of November 1952. In January 1953, Paul Gore-Booth, the head of the British Information Service in the

United States, observed that:

> [I]n the past we have not actively given publicity in this country either to the strength of anti-communist feeling in the UK (and especially in the Labour Party, which is still widely believed to be vaguely sympathetic to the Russians) or the extent of our activities at home and overseas to combat Communism. It has been in the Republican ranks that we have found some of our severest critics. The critics now have greater power of good and evil over our fortunes, if they continue to believe we are not so anti-communist as we really are, or that we are soft towards communism we shall suffer.[146]

Gore-Booth did not propose that the Foreign Office should spread anti-communist propaganda among the American people, 'who are in process of being over-indoctrinated in this respect.' British information staff in the USA also operated under far greater restrictions than those faced by the US Information Service in London.[147] Nevertheless, Gore-Booth did suggest that more publicity should be given to anti-communist views expressed within the UK. They should, he suggested, continue to give as much publicity as possible to ministerial statements and provide evidence of hostility to communism in the Labour Party and the trade unions. Facing one particular American *bête noire* head on, Gore-Booth observed, 'on occasion, it is useful to be able to show our critics that even Nye Bevan, whatever his views on other matters, is hostile to the Kremlin.'[148]

The IRD was tasked with combating US misperceptions about communism in Britain. The department agreed to provide a periodical summary of extracts from articles, speeches and letters to the press which illustrated the nature of resistance to communism in the UK. They also agreed that official lecturers sent to the US would be briefed to say more on the British way of dealing with the communist threat, and suggested that the next group of lecturers might include an expert on communism – such as Victor Feather or Leonard Schapiro – to speak on 'Britain and the Cold War.' In keeping with the IRD's long established policy of exerting a moderating influence on US policy-makers, it was made clear that, 'the object would not be to show that we are gradually adopting the "tough" American line on this subject but rather to suggest that in the UK a more flexible and subtle method of attacking the problem produces results.'[149]

Conclusion

British anti-communist propaganda activities around the globe expanded considerably following Winston Churchill's return to Downing Street. Despite cuts in information budgets, and Churchill's publicly stated hope of achieving a negotiated settlement with the Soviet leadership, the new Conservative Government was committed to continuing anti-communist propaganda activities, 'to the highest possible degree.' The IRD expanded its operations targeted at communist front activities in the free world and manoeuvred the NATO information apparatus into providing a more effective response to communist propaganda. The Foreign Office continued to work closely with the Americans, who were also expanding their activities in this field, particularly in the arena of international organizations. British and US officials continued to exchange propaganda material and to consult over the planning and conduct of operations, and the IRD continued to urge the Americans towards greater subtlety. Indeed, as US propaganda activities expanded, British policy was increasingly driven by the desire to exercise restraint rather than encouragement for US activities. This was particularly evident in those regions of traditional British influence such as India and South-East Asia, where conspicuous US operations threatened to undermine British efforts.

However, despite some obvious Foreign Office concerns about US encroachment into areas of British interest, there is little evidence to suggest that the USA was seeking to supplant the work of the IRD. Although the State Department and the CIA were clearly anxious to expand their anti-communist propaganda activities around the globe, British officials were informed of US plans at the earliest opportunities and routinely informed of new developments. US officials in Washington and in the field were generally happy to seek British advice in regions in which Britain had considerable experience, and as Adam Watson made clear, welcomed 'any comments or suggestions about the general conduct' of their political warfare campaign. For the benefit of his self-assured colleagues at home, the Information Liaison Officer in Washington added:

> We offer the Americans advice pretty freely. Often it is good advice; and even if not, they accept it with some eagerness as a useful outside view. We are far more cocksure about their advice to us.[150]

It is also clear that in areas of particular British interest, such as Malaya, the USA was prepared to defer to British wishes and subject its activities to British approval. Consultation between British and US information staff, allowed the IRD to ensure that US plans did not threaten existing IRD operations and, more importantly, placed the IRD in a strong position to pursue their policy of urging the Americans towards greater subtlety and, where necessary, restraint. It would be churlish to suggest that Britain did not benefit from the increasingly vast resources the USA was prepared to commit to anti-communist propaganda. As the kind of international front activities pioneered by the Foreign Office in the 1940s expanded into global enterprises, the IRD had neither the financial resources nor the manpower to retain control of such activities. Nevertheless, by maintaining close cooperation with the USA, the IRD continued to exert an influence over them. British influence was particularly important in the formative years of US front activities. At a time when operations such as the Congress for Cultural Freedom and the Committee for Free Asia were widely recognized as thinly veiled fronts for the US administration, British officials were well placed to press for a more discreet approach.

British attempts to exert a moderating influence over US policy were most evident in propaganda behind the Iron Curtain. The emergence of a strategy for intensified psychological operations against the communist bloc was the most significant development in British anti-communist propaganda since the launch of the new propaganda policy in 1948. Up to this point, British offensive operations against the communist bloc had been limited to covert infiltration of agents into countries, most notably Albania, in the vain hope of fomenting popular unrest. These subversive operations had received little propaganda support. The IRD's operations had been principally directed at the free world. The failure of the Albanian operation and the withdrawal of the SIS from such operations, led to the development of a new strategy for offensive operations against the Soviet bloc. The development of this strategy began in 1952 and placed propaganda at its heart. British offensive operations would no longer be targeted at the satellite countries; the IRD began to develop a new strategy designed to open fractures in the Soviet leadership in Moscow. This strategy was, at once, less risky yet also more ambitious than liberation operations in the satellite countries, and was designed to exploit the inherent weaknesses of the Soviet regime and bring about evolutionary rather than revolutionary change in the communist bloc. Although it differed considerably from US policy, which continued to hold out the hope of popular unrest behind the Iron Curtain, an important objective of this more forward policy was the extension of British influence over US operations; this was to become a particularly pressing issue following the Republican victory in the US presidential election of late 1952.

Notes

1   D. Cooper, *Old Men Forget* (London: Rupert Hart Davis, 1955), p. 279; P.M. Taylor, 'Power, Propaganda and Public Opinion: The British Information Services and the Cold War, 1945–57,' in E.Di Nolfo (ed.), *Power in Europe*, vol. 2, *Great Britain, France, Germany and Italy and the Origins of the EEC, 1952–1957* (Berlin: Walter de Gruyter, 1992), pp. 445–61.
2   *Ibid;* Taylor, *British Propaganda in the Twentieth Century*, pp. 208–11; see also D.J. Wenden, 'Churchill, Radio and Cinema', in R. Blake and W.R. Louis (eds), *Churchill* (Oxford: Oxford University Press, 1994), pp. 215–39.
3   C. Richardson, *From Churchill's Secret Circle to the BBC: The Biography of Lieutenant-General Sir Ian Jacob* (London: Brassey's, 1991), p. 225.
4   Richardson, *From Churchill's Secret Circle*. On Peck's enduring relationship, see the chapter on Private Secretaries in: M. Gilbert, *In Search of Churchill* (London: Harper Collins, 1994).
5   J. Wheeler-Bennett (ed.), *Action This Day: Working with Churchill* (London: Macmillan, 1968); see, in particular, Jacob's chapter, pp. 158–217.
6   The best account of Churchill's foreign policy in this period is: J.W. Young, *Winston Churchill's Last Campaign: Britain and the Cold War, 1951–1955* (Oxford: Oxford University Press, 1996).
7   A.P. Dobson, 'Informally Special? The Churchill–Truman talks of January 1952 and the state of Anglo-American relations', *Review of International Studies* (1997) 23, pp. 27–47.
8   Young, *Winston Churchill's Last Campaign*, p. 40.
9   *Ibid.*, pp. 28–33; R.R. James, *Churchill Speaks: Winston S. Churchill in Peace and War, Collected Speeches, 1897–1963* (Leicester: Windward, 1980), p. 924.
10 James (ed.), *Churchill Speaks*, pp. 944–7.
11 *Parliamentary Debates: Commons*, 19 November 1951; A. Eden, *Full Circle* (London: Cassell, 1960), pp. 9–11.
12 Young, *Winston Churchill's Last Campaign*, pp. 28–40.
13 PUSC (51) 16 (Final), Future Policy Towards Soviet Russia, 17 January 1952, FO 371/125002/4, PRO. J. Young, *The British Foreign Office and Cold War Fighting in the Early 1950s: PUSC(51)16 and the 1952 'Sore Spots' Memorandum*, Leicester University Discussion Papers in Politics, no. P95/2, (Leicester: Leicester University Press, 1995).
14 Aldrich, *The Hidden Hand*, pp. 323–4.
15 PUSC (51) 16 (Final), Future Policy Towards Soviet Russia, 17 January 1952, FO 371/125002/4, PRO.
16 *Ibid.*

17 PUSC (51) 16 (Final), Future Policy Towards Soviet Russia, 17 January 1952, FO 371/125002/4, PRO.
18 Soviet Reactions to Western Pressure on 'Sore Spots', February 1952, N51052/G/G, FO 371/100840, PRO.
19 *Ibid.*
20 Anti-Communist Propaganda Operations: Revised Memo, 18 December 1951, PR126/9, FO 1110/460, PRO.
21 *Ibid.*
22 Aldrich, *The Hidden Hand*, pp. 324–5; PUSC (51) 16 (Final), Future Policy Towards Soviet Russia, 17 January 1952, FO 371/125002/4, PRO.
23 PUSC (51) 16 (Final), Future Policy Towards Soviet Russia, 17 January 1952, FO 371/125002/4, PRO.
24 Basic US and UK policy towards the USSR with particular reference to political warfare activities against the USSR, 16 January 1952, TCT D-1/5a, President's Secretary's Files, General File – Churchill Truman Meetings, Box no. 116, Truman Papers, Truman Library.
25 Minutes of fifth Plenary session, 18 January 1952, CAB 21/3058; Minutes of Meeting of Truman and Churchill, 18 January 1952, *FRUS, 1952–1954*, vol. 6, pp. 846–9. For background to this meeting, see M. Gilbert, *Never Despair: Winston S. Churchill 1945–1965* (London: Minerva, 1990), pp. 690–2; Young, *Winston Churchill's Last Campaign*, p. 85. Young suggests that Churchill's comments did not indicate a sophisticated grasp of Western psychological warfare capabilities, 'since he placed considerable emphasis on leaflet dropping, a rather old-fashioned tool for propagandists though one still useful for overcoming Soviet "jamming" of radio broadcasts.' Churchill, however, may well have been speaking from the most recent information. The first US-sponsored operation to disseminate propaganda leaflets over the Iron Curtain by balloon, the so-called 'Winds of Freedom' project, only began in August 1951, with the launch of 15,000 balloons over Czechoslovakia and Poland. Memo by Deputy Assistant Secretary of State for Public Affairs to Under-Secretary of State, 17 August 1951; Memo by Assistant Secretary of State for Public Affairs, 20 November 1951, *FRUS, 1951*, vol. 4, pp. 1,270–1, 1,311; R.H. Cummings, 'Balloons over East Europe: The Cold War Leaflet Campaign of Radio Free Europe', *The Falling Leaf*, 166 (Autumn 1999), pp. 97–110.
26 Minutes of US–UK Meetings on Information Activities, 28 April 1952, PR63/55, FO 1110/505, PRO.
27 Operation Vagabond Try-Out Cruise, 10 March 1952, 511.004/3-1052, RG 59, NARA.
28 Chiefs of Staff Committee, The Overseas Services of the BBC, Memo by Sir Ian Jacob, 7 December 1951, COS(51)728, PREM 11/184, PRO; G.Mansell, *Let Truth Be Told: Fifty Years of BBC External Broadcasting* (London: Weidenfeld & Nicolson, 1982), pp. 221–4.
29 Minutes of US–UK Meetings on Information Activities, 28 April 1952, PR63/55, FO 1110/505, PRO.
30 Committee of Enquiry into Overseas Information Services, Survey of United Kingdom Publicity in Foreign Countries, 30 July 1952, GEN407/15, CAB 130/75, PRO.
31 Minutes of US–UK Meetings on Information Activities, 30 April 1952, PR63/55, FO 1110/505, PRO.
32 Liaison with the BBC Eastern and Central European Services, nd [*circa* January 1953], PRG106/8, FO 1110/618, PRO.
33 G. Mitrovich, *Undermining the Kremlin: America's Strategy to Subvert the Soviet Bloc, 1947–1956* (Ithaca, NY: Cornell, 2000), pp. 78–80.
34 PSB D-18, Memo by W.H.Gedel, The role of PSB in the use of the 'Defector Funds' authorized in the Mutual Security Act, 1951, 19 October 1951; PSB D-18a, A National Psychological Program with Respect to Escapees from the Soviet Orbit, 15 January 1953, Box no. 2, Lot File no. 62D333, Executive Secretariat, PSB Working File 1951–53, RG 59, NARA.
35 Aldrich, *The Hidden Hand*, p. 166.
36 Overseas Information Services: Report of the Drogheda Committee, 13 November 1953, C(53)305, PREM 11/691, PRO.
37 Minutes of Russia Committee meeting, 1 March 1949, N2190/1052/38G, FO 371/77623, PRO.

38 W.K. Wark, 'Coming in from the Cold: British Propaganda and Red Army Defectors 1945–1952', *International History Review*, 9, 4 (1987), pp. 59–61; Lucas and Morris, 'A Very British Crusade', pp. 85–110.
39 Minutes of US–UK Meetings on Information Activities, 30 April 1952, PR63/55, FO 1110/505, PRO.
40 NSC Senior Staff Meeting, 4 December 1951, George M. Elsey Papers, Truman Library.
41 Impressions gathered during a visit to Berlin, W.Klatt, 15 February 1953, Minute by C.W. Wiggin, 24 March 1953, PRG18/67, FO 1110/567, PRO.
42 Report on Radio Free Europe, Munich by Sir Robert Bruce Lockhart, 17 February 1952, PR94/8, FO 1110/518, PRO.
43 Record of meeting at the headquarters of the NCFE, 5 May 1952, PR63/35, FO 1110/505, PRO.
44 Weldon, *Auto da Fay*, p. 242.
45 D.C. Hopson Minute, 27 January 1953, Nicholls Minute, 30 January 1953, PR 134/12, FO 1110/543, PRO.
46 Paul Fabry to Oswald Lord, re: Central-Eastern European Committee, 27 January 1953, Box no. 1, US President's Committee on International Information Activities (Jackson Committee), Records 1950–1953, Eisenhower Library.
47 Aldrich, *The Hidden Hand*, pp. 342–70.
48 S. Dorril, *MI6: Fifty Years of Special Operations* (London: Fourth Estate, 2000), pp. 439–40; Memorandum on the Establishment of the Central Eastern European Committee, nd, Box no. 1,738, WHCF: OF, Truman Library.
49 Memorandum for Averell Harriman, 28 February 1951, Box no. 1,738, WHCF: OF, Truman Library.
50 Fabry to Lord, re: Central-Eastern European Committee, 27 January 1953.
51 Dorril, *MI6*, p. 440.
52 Fabry to Lord, re: Central-Eastern European Committee, 27 January 1953.
53 Basic US and UK policy towards the USSR with particular reference to political warfare activities against the USSR, 16 January 1952, TCT D-1/5a, President's Secretary's Files, General File – Churchill Truman Meetings, Box 116, Truman Papers, Truman Library.
54 Circular to Missions, William Strang, 30 January 1952, PR 89/3G, FO 1110/516, PRO.
55 *Ibid.*
56 *Ibid.*
57 *Ibid.*
58 J.H. Peck to Adam Watson, 7 February 1952, PR89/49, FO 1110/516, PRO.
59 P. Weiler, *British Labour and the Cold War* (Stanford, CA: Stanford University Press, 1988), pp. 213–19; A. Carew, 'The Schism Within the World Federation of Trade Unions: Government and Trade Union Diplomacy', *International Review of Social History*, 29, 3 (1984), pp. 297–335; H. Wilford, 'The Information Research Department: Britain's Secret Cold War Weapon Revealed', *Review of International Studies*, 24 (1998), pp. 353–69; J. Kotek, *Students and the Cold War* (London: Macmillan, 1996); Cultural Relations Department to British Embassy, Budapest, 11 August 1949, PR2984/78/913, FO 1110/262; P. Deery, 'The Dove Flies East: Whitehall, Warsaw and the 1950 World Peace Congress', *Australian Journal of Politics and History*, 48, 4 (2002), pp. 449–68.
60 CM(50) 56th Conclusions, 6th September 1950, PR87/116; Minutes of meeting held in Home Office, 8 September 1950, PR87/119, FO 1110/347, PRO.
61 Second World Congress of Peace, R. Murray, 31 August 1950, PR87/119, FO 1110/347, PRO.
62 GEN341/1, Bevin to Attlee, 27 October 1950, PR87/52, FO 1110/348, PRO.
63 See, for example, J.H. Peck to D. Healey, 10 November 1950, encloses, The Sheffield Peace Congress, November 1950, Box – Peace and Propaganda, 1949–1953, International Department papers, Labour Party Archive, NMLH.
64 Deery, 'The Dove Flies East', p. 460.
65 See MI5's letter of appreciation, Bagot, MI5 to Peck, January 1951, PR5/28, FO 1110/370, PRO.

66 Bagot worked in that section of MI5's F Division responsible for monitoring international communism; see C.M. Andrew (ed.), *The Security Service 1908–1945: The Official History* (London: PRO), pp. 250–1, 358.

67 R.M. Frewen Minute, 23 May 1952, FO 1110/516, PRO.

68 Anti-communist propaganda operations, 30 July 1951, PR126/5, FO 1110/460, PRO.

69 John Cloake, letter to author, October 2002.

70 The standard accounts of the IOD by the first two heads of the department are: T. Braden, 'The Birth of the CIA', *American Heritage*, 28 (1977), pp. 4–13; C. Meyer, *Facing Reality: From World Federalism to the CIA* (New York: Harper Row, 1980). For recent scholarship, see Aldrich, *The Hidden Hand*, pp. 342–70; Kotek, *Students and the Cold War*, pp. 200–9; G. Scott-Smith, *The Politics of Apolitical Culture: The Congress for Cultural Freedom and the Political Economy of American Hegemony, 1945–1955* (London: Routledge, 1991); M. Warner, 'Sophisticated Spies: CIA's Links to Liberal Anti-Communists, 1949–1967', *International Journal of Intelligence and Counter-Intelligence*, 9, 4 (1996), pp. 425–33; H. Laville, 'The Committee of Correspondence: CIA Funding of Women's Groups, 1952–67', *Intelligence and National Security*, 12, 1 (1997), pp. 104–21.

71 Kotek, *Students and the Cold War*, pp. 192–5; Action on World Youth and Students Festival Berlin 5–15 August 1951, R. Conquest, PR48/23/51; Circular World Youth and Students Festival, 21 April 1951, PR 48/23, FO 1110, 406, PRO.

72 Minutes of US–UK Meetings on Information Activities, 28 April 1952, PR63/55, FO 1110/505, PRO.

73 Second World Congress of Peace, R. Murray, 31 August 1950, PR87/119, FO 1110/347, PRO.

74 Circular to Missions, William Strang, 30 January 1952, PR 89/3G, FO 1110/516; Minutes of Western European Information Officers Conference, 12–14 September 1951, PR121/7, FO 1110/458, PRO.

75 Circular to Missions, William Strang, 30 January 1952, PR 89/3G, FO 1110/516, PRO.

76 T.S. Tull Minute, 18 August 1952, PR119/9, FO 1110/526, PRO.

77 Views of the Department of State concerning programs and instrumentalities to further the objectives of NATO and MDAP, nd [*circa* February 1951], Box no. 5, Lot file no. 52 D432, Office Files of Assistant Secretary of State Edward W. Barrett, 1950–51, RG 59, NARA.

78 Report on European Trip, 22 August–8 September 1952, Charles Norberg, Box no. 11, SMOF: PSB Files, Truman Papers, Truman Library.

79 Views of the Department of State concerning programs and instrumentalities to further the objectives of NATO and MDAP.

80 Minutes of US–UK meeting on information activities, 30 April 1952.

81 'Towards a Better Understanding of the North Atlantic Treaty', text of speech by Lord Ismay, 8 September 1952, III/13/20a, Ismay Papers, Liddell Hart Centre for Military Archives (LHCMA).

82 *Ibid.*

83 Information Policy Working Group, Report by the Chairman, 18 April 1953, III/21/2a, Ismay Papers, LHCMA; Report on European Trip, 22 August–8 September 1952, Charles Norberg, Box no. 11, SMOF: PSB Files, Truman Papers, Truman Library.

84 Information Policy Working Group, Report by the Chairman, 18 April 1953 Report by the Secretary General of Progress during 17 April 1953–3, December 1953, III/21/3a; Report by the Secretary-General of Progress during the period 3 December 1953–7, December 1954, III/21/5a, Ismay papers, LHCMA; Lord Ismay, *NATO: The First Five Years, 1949–1954* (London, Paris: NATO, 1954), pp. 153–157.

85 Report by the Secretary General of Progress during the period 4 April 1952–30 November 1952, III/21/1a, Ismay papers, LHCMA.

86 D.D. Brown, IRD to F.D.W. Brown, UK delegation to NATO, 27 August 1952, PR117/10, FO 1110/526, PRO; Information Policy Working Group, Report by the Chairman, 18 April 1953, III/21/2k, Ismay papers, LHCMA.

87 D.D. Brown Minute, 23 September 1952, PR117/21, FO 1110/526, PRO.

88 D.D. Brown to F.D.W. Brown, 23 July 1952, PR117/9, FO 1110/526, PRO.
89 NATO Information Group, NATO Information Activities, 5 April 1951, Box no. 23, SMOF: PSB Files, Truman Papers, Truman Library.
90 Circular no. 483, 29 July 1952, PR117/6, FO 1110/526, PRO.
91 D.D. Brown to Watson, 19 September 1952, PR117/7, FO 1110/526, PRO.
92 T.S. Tull Minute, 18 August 1952, PR117/9; D.D. Brown to Watson, 19 September 1952, PR117/7, FO 1110/526, PRO.
93 D.D. Brown to Watson, 19 September 1952, PR117/7, FO 1110/526, PRO.
94 D.D. Brown to F.D.W. Brown, 23 July 1952, PR117/9, FO 1110/526, PRO.
95 D.D. Brown to F.D.W. Brown, 23 July 1952, PR117/9, FO 1110/526; Memo for Mr Brown, UK Report on Activities in Countering Anti-NATO Propaganda, 22 January 1953, PR142/4; draft proposal to be circulated at NATO Information Conference by UK delegation, PR142/11, FO 1110/546, PRO.
96 Conferences held by Communist Front Organisations, Report and Recommendations by the Committee on Information and Cultural Relations, 19 January 1954, PR142/6, FO 11110/629, PRO.
97 Peck to Watson, 7 February 1952, PR89/49, FO 1110/516, PRO.
98 On *Encounter*, see P. Coleman, *The Liberal Conspiracy: The Congress for Cultural Freedom and the Struggle for the Mind of Postwar Europe* (New York: Free Press, 1989), pp. 59–79; Saunders, *Who Paid the Piper?*, pp. 165–89; *Aldrich, The Hidden Hand*, pp. 449–50. On Fyvel, see T.R. Fyvel, *And There My Trouble Began: Uncollected Writings, 1945–85* (London: Weidenfeld & Nicolson, 1986).
99 Coleman, *The Liberal Conspiracy*, pp. 60–61.
100 Saunders, *Who Paid the Piper?*, pp. 176–7.
101 *Ibid.* p. 169.
102 Peck to Watson, 7 February 1952, PR89/49, FO 1110/516, PRO.
103 Coleman, *Liberal Conspiracy*, pp. 149–53; Scott-Smith, *The Politics of Apolitical Culture.*
104 USIS Activities in the Commonwealth, Allott, 9 May 1951; Bozman Minute, 10 May 1951, PR63/66, FO 1110/418, PRO.
105 Coleman, *The Liberal Conspiracy*, p. 151.
106 USIS Activities in the Commonwealth, Allott, 9 May 1951; Bozman Minute, 10 May 1951, PR63/66, FO 1110/418, PRO.
107 Watson minute, nd, 1951, PR63/66, FO 1110/418, PRO.
108 Coleman, *The Liberal Conspiracy*, p. 152.
109 Report of the President's Committee on International Information Activities, 30 June 1953, *FRUS, 1952–1954*, vol. 2, pp. 1,828–9, 1834; Letter to Richard M. Nixon from Allen Dulles re: Committee for Free Asia, 6 April 1954, CIA FOIA Electronic Reading Room. In contrast to the RFE, the literature on the CFA and RFA is scarce, see Lucas, *Freedom's War*, pp. 109–231; Kotek, *Students and the Cold War*, pp. 210, 265.
110 J.L. Stewart Committee for Free Asia, to Malcolm MacDonald, 23 May 1952; MacDonald to D.C. MacGillivray, Federation of Malaya, 26 June 1952, PR122/8, FO 1110/527, PRO.
111 Meeting with Mr Robert Sheeks, 25 June 1952, PR122/8, FO 1110/527, PRO.
112 Report of the President's Committee on International Information Activities, 30 June 1953, *FRUS, 1952–1954*, vol. 2, pp. 1,828–9, 1834.
113 Smith, *Portrait of a Cold Warrior*, p. 155; Lucas, *Freedom's War*, p. 231.
114 MacDonald to Foreign Office, Bukit Serene Conference, 8 December 1952, 18/5/18, Macdonald Papers, University of Durham.
115 Smith, *Portrait of a Cold Warrior*, pp. 158–9.
116 Semi-Annual Evaluation Report 1 June–30 November 1951, 511.41/1–2152, RG 59, NARA.
117 USIE Country Plan – United Kingdom, June 1952, 511.41/10-2852, RG 59, NARA.
118 Semi-Annual Evaluation Report 1 June–30 November 1951, 511.41/1-2152, RG 59, NARA.
119 American Embassy, London, IE: Semi-Annual Evaluation Report, 1 December–31 May 1951, 511.41/7-2751, RG 59, NARA.

120 IIA:6–17 Summary of Positions and Total Operating Expenses, 1953–1954, Box no. 14, US President's Committee on International Information Activities, Records, 1950–53, Eisenhower Library.

121 IIA: Semi-Annual Report 1 June–30 November 1952, 511.41/2-1853; Semi-Annual Evaluation Report, 1 September 1952–30 May 1953, 511.41/9-353, RG 59, NARA.

122 Country Paper – USIE in Great Britain, 3 November 1950, 511.41/11-350, RG 59, NARA.

123 Progress Report on Labor Information Activities, 25 July 1951, 511.41/7-2651, RG 59, NARA.

124 IIA: Semi-Annual Report 1 June–30 November 1952, 511.41/2-1853, RG 59, NARA.

125 Albert E. Hemsing interview, FAOH Program, Georgetown University; A. Hemsing, 'The Marshall Plan's European Film Unit, 1948–1955: A Memoir and Filmography', *Historical Journal of Film, Radio and Television*, 14, 3 (1994), pp. 269–98.

126 Semi-Annual Evaluation Report, 1 June–30 November 1951, 21 January 1952, 511.41/1-2152, RG 59, NARA.

127 Semi-Annual Evaluation Report, 1 December 1952–30 May 1953, 511.41/9-353, RG 59, NARA.

128 American Embassy, London, Semi-Annual Report for Press Section, 1 July–31 December 1950, 511.41/3-151; American Embassy, London, IE: Semi-Annual Evaluation Report, 1 December–31 May 1951, 511.41/7-2751; American Embassy, London, IIA: Semi-Annual Report, 1 June–30 November 1952, 511.41/2-1853, RG 59, NARA.

129 American Embassy, London, IIA: Semi-Annual Report, 1 June–30 November 1952, 511.41/2-1853, RG 59, NARA.

130 Aldrich, *The Hidden Hand*, p. 449; Progress Report on Labor Information Activities, Britain, 25 July 1951, 511.41/7-2651, RG 59, NARA.

131 Semi-Annual Evaluation Report, 1 September–31 May 1951, 27 July 1951, 511.41/7-2751, RG 59, NARA.

132 H. Wilford, ' "Unwitting Assets?": British Intellectuals and the Congress for Cultural Freedom', *Twentieth Century British History*, 11, 1 (2000), pp. 47–9.

133 Saunders, *Who Paid the Piper?*, p. 110.

134 American Embassy, London, to State Department, 20 March 1951, 511.4121/3-2051; American Embassy, London, to State Department, 10 April 1952, 511.412/4-1052, RG 59, NARA.

135 American Embassy, London, to State Department, 10 April 1951, 511.412/4-1052, RG 59, NARA.

136 American Embassy, London, to State Department, 10 April 1951, 511.412/4-1052, RG 59, NARA.

137 State Department to American Embassy, London, 23 May 1952, 511.412/4-1052; American Embassy, London, to State Department, 13 June 1952, RG 59, NARA.

138 American Embassy, London to State Department, 20 March 1951, 511.4121/3-2051, RG 59, NARA.

139 Secretary of State to Certain Diplomatic Posts, 17 March 1953, *FRUS, 1952–1954*, vol. 2, pp. 1,686–7; American Embassy, London, to State Department, Books by Communist Authors Removed from USIS Information Center, 21 April 1953, 511.4121/4-2153; American Embassy, London, to State Department, 10 August 1951, 511.4121/8-1051, RG 59, NARA.

140 American Embassy, London, to State Department, 19 October 1950, 511.4121/10-1950, RG 59, NARA.

141 Semi-Annual Evaluation Report, 1 December–31 May 1951, 27 July 1951, 511.41/7-2751, RG 59, NARA.

142 Bacteriological Warfare, T.S. Tull Minute, 25 March 1952, PR41/81, Memo by J.H. Peck, 2 April 1952, PR41/68, FO 1110/494, PRO.

143 Wilford, ' "Unwitting Assets?" ', pp. 48–9; IRD Circular, 18 August 1955, PR 121/299, FO 1110/738, PRO.

144 Department of State Instruction, 29 January 1954, 511.41/1-2954; State Department to American Embassy, London, 6 August 1952, 511.41/8-652, RG 59, NARA.

145 American Embassy, London, Semi-Annual Evaluation Report of Press Section, 1 July–31 December 1950, 511.41/3-151; American Embassy, London, IE: Semi-Annual Evaluation Report, 1 December–31 May 1951, 511.41/7-2751, RG 59, NARA.
146 P.H. Gore-Booth to A. Malcolm, IPD, 6 January 1953, PRG45/6, FO 1110/586, PRO.
147 There was some consternation in the IRD when a newspaper in Ohio quoted extensively from an IRD bulletin entitled, 'British Answers to Communism'. Watson to Hopson, 20 January 1954, PR1045/9, FO 1110/684, PRO.
148 Gore-Booth to Malcolm, IPD, 6 January 1953, PRG45/6, FO 1110/586, PRO.
149 Peck to Gore-Booth, 9 April 1953, PRG45/6, FO 1110/586, PRO.
150 Watson Minute, nd, 1951, PR63/66, FO 1110/418, PRO.

6   A new strategy of political warfare

On 24 March 1953, Jack Nicholls, Permanent Under-Secretary in the Foreign Office with overall responsibility for information activities, observed that the moment was opportune for a fundamental review of British Cold War propaganda policy.[1] Earlier that month the Kremlin had announced the death of Joseph Stalin. Almost immediately Stalin's successor, Georgi Malenkov, launched a peace offensive designed to improve relations with the West. On 15 March, Malenkov declared that there were no disputes between Moscow and Washington, 'that cannot be decided by peaceful means, on the basis of mutual understanding.' By the end of the month the communists in Korea had announced their willingness to exchange sick and wounded POWs and suggested that truce talks be reopened.[2] Although officials in the Foreign Office were predictably sanguine about the prospect that Stalin's death would usher in an era of détente, Nicholls conceded, that 'something like a stabilisation of the Cold War front can at the moment be said to exist.' The local war fronts, Nicholls observed, were 'static,' there was equilibrium in the defence field, 'and in the realm of ideas the Soviet political warfare offensive is by and large not gaining ground.'[3]

At least as important to British Cold War propaganda, was the election of the new Republican administration in the USA. In November 1952, barely a year after Churchill's election, Dwight D. Eisenhower was elected US President. The arrival of new administrations in Downing Street and the White House, prompted the first major post-War reviews of the overseas information activities of both Britain and the USA. In Britain, after years of financial stringency and parliamentary criticism, a series of official and independent committees of enquiry sought to assess the value of overseas propaganda and to make recommendations for future policy. These reviews informed Foreign Office thinking regarding the future conduct of anti-communist propaganda policy. In a process which was begun by the Permanent Under-Secretary's Committee, in 1952, senior officials in the Foreign Office began to recast British propaganda policy to reflect a more forward policy towards the communist bloc. This review culminated in 1953 with the formulation of a new strategy of political warfare, which marked the most fundamental reorientation of British propaganda since the launch of the new propaganda policy in 1948. From a policy designed to oppose the inroads of communism in Europe and Asia, officials in the IRD devised a new long-term strategy designed ultimately to bring an end to communism behind the Iron Curtain. In the USA, Eisenhower's election was characterized by a wave of anti-communist rhetoric. Statements by Eisenhower and, more particularly, the new Secretary of State, John Foster Dulles, projected bold hopes for the 'liberation' of Eastern Europe. On assuming office, Eisenhower set in motion a process of review and reorganization designed to formulate a coordinated psychological strategy to support these hopes. This led to a far-reaching reform of the US propaganda apparatus and, in particular, the elevation of the more covert and offensive aspects of anti-communist propaganda.

Although conducted on either side of the Atlantic these reviews did not take place in isolation. British officials, in particular, were acutely aware of the review being undertaken in Washington, and were keen to have some input on the process. Nicholls pressed his case for a review of British anti-communist propaganda in the spring of 1953, on the grounds that the new US Administration was in the process of formulating its own policy in the field of political warfare, 'and will inevitably seek to make changes if it can.'[4] The British were anxious to ensure that consultation and cooperation should continue and were quick to impress upon the new administration the extent of British anti-communist propaganda activities. It is also apparent that the new strategy of political warfare being devised in the IRD was directed in part at the US Administration. Britain's new strategy of political warfare was placed before US officials at the earliest opportunity in the hope that British views would be taken into account by those reviewing the US propaganda apparatus. This strategy went some way towards embracing US hopes for the possibility of using offensive propaganda to bring an end to the Cold War. However, it stopped short of the aggressive calls for liberation emanating from Washington. The British strategy for political warfare presented to the Americans in 1953 was unequivocal in its rejection of the possibility of liberation in Eastern Europe in favour of a long-term strategy designed to bring about more fundamental evolutionary change in the communist bloc. British officials were hopeful that the new US Administration should adopt a similarly restrained posture.

Eisenhower and the reorganisation of the American propaganda apparatus

Like Churchill, Eisenhower was convinced of the value of propaganda by his experiences in the Second World War. As Supreme Allied Commander, Eisenhower had paid tribute to the work of the Office of War Information, proclaiming, 'the expenditure of men and money in wielding the spoken and written word was an important contributing factor in undermining the enemies will to resist and supporting the fighting morale of our potential allies.' Edward Barrett and Theodore Streibert, who, respectively, headed US information agencies under Truman and Eisenhower, both paid tribute to Eisenhower's appreciation of the importance of propaganda in war and peace.[5] Eisenhower's election, like Churchill's, also saw the return of a number of wartime aides to key positions in the US propaganda organization. Walter Bedell Smith, who had been Eisenhower's wartime Chief of Staff, had been Director of Central Intelligence since 1950. In February 1953, Bedell Smith was appointed Under-Secretary of State and was replaced at the CIA by Allen Dulles, another advocate of psychological operations and brother of the Secretary of State, John Foster Dulles, the most vocal proponent of liberation. The most significant proponent of psychological operations was C.D. Jackson. Eisenhower had been responsible for appointing Jackson as head of the Psychological Warfare Division in 1943. More recently, Jackson had been Eisenhower's speech writer in the election campaign, and had also kept Eisenhower informed about the USA's overseas propaganda activities. An unabashed enthusiast of psychological warfare, and a leading light in Radio Free Europe, Jackson had impressed upon the President-elect the importance of psychological warfare in fighting the Cold War. Shortly after Eisenhower took office, C.D. Jackson was appointed White House special advisor on psychological warfare.[6]

Eisenhower's election led to the most fundamental reorganization of American overseas propaganda since 1945. The reorganization plan, bequeathed by Edward Barrett in 1951, had failed to elevate the status of the US information programme. In December 1952, Barrett's successor, Wilson Compton, declared that, 'as a nation, we are not really trying to win the Cold War.' Expenditure on armaments, he warned, might win a hot war, but US facilities for winning the 'war of ideas' remained inadequate.[7] Overseas propaganda was still viewed with a certain degree of distaste by many professional diplomats in the State Department, and was consistently attacked in Congress as an unquantifiable waste of money.[8] The PSB had also failed to resolve the organizational rivalry which characterized US psychological warfare and provide effective coordination. In December 1952, C.D. Jackson informed Eisenhower that psychological warfare was conducted by the State Department, the CIA, the Department of the Army and the Air Force. These organizations, Jackson wrote, were 'highly competitive, in fact to the point of sabotage.' The reason for this 'fratricidal warfare,' Jackson suggested was not mutual dislike or empire building but the realisation that the US Government, 'has neither policy nor plan for conducting the Cold War.'[9] Although overseas propaganda activities had, without doubt, expanded considerably under Truman, Eisenhower's election provided another irresistible opportunity for a reorganisation of the US information programme.

A reorganization of the US propaganda instrument was presaged by Republican rhetoric in the presidential election campaign of 1952. The Republicans vehemently attacked the Truman Administration's handling of the Soviets, and openly advocated a strategy of liberation as an alternative to the reactive containment of the Truman Administration. Eisenhower publicly stated his refusal to write off the loss of Eastern Europe. In August 1952, he declared, 'never shall we desist in our aid to every man and woman of those shackled lands...who is dedicated to the liberation of his fellows.' Secretary of State John Foster Dulles went even further, publicly advocating the use of propaganda and 'freedom fighters' to 'try to split the satellites away from ... Moscow,' and threatening to unleash the Chinese Nationalist leader, Chiang Kai-Shek, so that he might launch raids against the Chinese mainland.[10] Although widespread concern in Europe prompted Eisenhower to press Dulles to tone down his rhetoric, Eisenhower himself was strongly committed to the use of the USA's psychological weapons to bring an end to the Cold War and, in his inaugural address, emphasized the need to 'make more effective, all activities of the government-related international information programs.'[11]

In January 1953, Eisenhower announced the formation of two committees whose work would shape the organization and policy of the administration's overseas propaganda activities. The Advisory Committee on Government Organization was established on 19 January 1953. Headed by the Republican businessman, Nelson Rockefeller, it was asked to make recommendations on the bureaucratic structure of the executive branch. Five days later, Eisenhower announced the establishment of the

President's Committee on International Information Activities. The Committee was chaired by William Jackson, a former Deputy Director of the CIA, and included C.D. Jackson, Gordon Gray, National Security Advisor Robert Cutler and Deputy Secretary of Defence Roger Keyes. Ostensibly tasked with making 'a survey and evaluation' of US information activities, the Jackson Committee in effect analysed, 'the entire range of national Cold War policies covert as well as overt.'[12]

Following a sixth-month investigation, which ranged across US official propaganda activities and the work of a host private organizations and individuals, the Jackson Committee presented its report to the President in June 1953. Of its 50 recommendations, the central conclusion was that psychological warfare should be integrated with policy on an equal standing with political, economic, and military initiatives. The Committee reiterated the conclusions of NSC-68 that the primary threat posed by the Soviet Union was not military but propaganda and subversion. The US, it concluded, would need to adopt similar methods to counter this threat, and considerations of propaganda should be integrated into all aspects of policy.[13] In the past, the White House press secretary James Hagerty explained ' "psychological strategy" somehow existed apart from official policies and actions and could be dealt with independently by experts in the field.' The Jackson Committee, Hagerty observed, believed 'a psychological aspect or implication [existed for] every diplomatic, economic or military policy and action.'[14]

Although the integration of propaganda on an equal basis with other aspects of policy had been a premise of US information programme since the time of Edward Barrett's departure, the Jackson Committee was highly critical of the coordination of information activities under Truman and recommended a fundamental reorganization of the US information apparatus. It asserted that, 'opportunities had been missed to take the offensive in global propaganda campaigns' and that US propaganda was too defensive and suffered from a lack of coordination resulting in the 'haphazard projection of too many and too diffuse propaganda themes.' In an effort to elevate the importance of propaganda and provide a more coherent programme, the Committee called for greater direction from the President and the centralization of control of propaganda operations under the National Security Council. It recommended the dissolution of the Psychological Strategy Board, which 'possessed neither sufficient power to exercise effective coordination nor the techniques adequate to produce meaningful evaluations.' On the Committee's recommendation, Eisenhower replaced the PSB with a new Operations Coordinating Board (OCB) which operated under the remit of the National Security Council (NSC). The OCB was mandated to coordinate propaganda policy across the range of overt and covert activities, and under the protection of the NSC, operated with greater authority than the PSB.[15]

The most significant change wrought by the Jackson Committee involved the removal of the overseas information programme from the State Department, and the creation of the United States Information Agency (USIA). The location of propaganda activities within the State Department had long been a contentious issue, both within and without the Foreign Service, and the creation of a separate agency responsible for information activities had been considered at various stages since 1945. Shortly before the Jackson Committee submitted its report, the Rockefeller Committee on Government Organization recommended 'a new foreign information agency' to absorb programmes spread across the federal government.[16] The Jackson Committee recognized the 'antagonism on the part of political officers in the State Department toward the entire information effort and personnel engaged in it,' and acquiesced in Rockefeller's findings, recognizing that 'there are strong arguments in favour of taking the information programme out of the State Department.'[17] Eisenhower himself felt that few diplomats were suited to propaganda work and was convinced that what was needed was an organization of experts like those who had staffed the Office of War Information.[18] On 1 June 1953, Eisenhower announced the creation of the USIA. The new agency assumed control of information programmes formerly under the State Department, including Voice of America, overseas libraries and information centres, the motion picture service and press and publications agencies. The agency had a director and assistant director appointed by the President, would implement plans approved by the OCB, and reported directly to the President and the NSC. Its guiding principle was 'to submit persuasive evidence to peoples of other nations by means of communications techniques that their own aspirations for freedom, progress and peace are supported by the objectives and policies of the United States.'[19]

Although some have argued that the separation of the information programme from the State Department ensured a certain marginalization of the propaganda programme,[20] those involved testify to the elevation of propaganda considerations in the policy-making of the Eisenhower Administration. Abbott Washburn, the USIA's first Assistant Director, witnessed Eisenhower's personal commitment, and the change in attitudes which saw the USIA become an active participant in policy-making:

> [T]he Agency reported directly to the President, who took a keen interest in its operations. He wanted to see us on a regular basis, whether or not we had particular problems to discuss with him. Often Ted [Streibert] would take other agency officials over to the White House for these meetings. You can imagine what this did for morale!... The President also wanted the world opinion factor to be cranked in to NSC meetings when decision-options were being discussed. He put us at the table at the NSC where we could speak up without being first asked what we thought or what data we had. Previously, [as the I IA] in the back row as observers, we could not do this.[21]

While the Jackson Committee led to a fundamental reorganization of the information apparatus established under Truman, it enshrined those methods for conducting unattributable anti-communist propaganda most strongly advocated by Truman's information chief, Edward Barrett. The growing enthusiasm for unattributable activities amongst officials involved in the US propaganda apparatus was due, in no small part, to the extraordinary and frequent exchange of ideas with British officials since 1950. 'Propaganda,' the committee recommended, 'should be attributed to the United States only when such attribution is an asset. A much greater percentage of the information program should be unattributed.' Like the British before them, US officials had discovered that 'saturation point' for official propaganda was quickly reached and found 'the sheer volume of material bearing the American label harmful.' Three years after British officials had first impressed upon the State Department 'the importance attached...to the use of local channels for the dissemination of anti-communist propaganda,' the Jackson Committee concluded that 'insofar as possible, information and propaganda should be prepared locally to meet local needs.'[22]

The committee went so far as to recommend substantial cuts in official propaganda, including the replacement of American information staff overseas with 'qualified local nationals,' the curtailment of short-wave broadcasts in some areas, and a reduction in the distribution of pamphlets, magazines and films bearing the US imprint.[23] The commitment to unattributable propaganda was, in contrast, wide ranging. While covert propaganda was to be centralized in the CIA, the USIA was also authorized 'to communicate with its audiences without attribution to the United States Government on matters for which attribution could be assumed by the Government if necessary.'[24] Although the Committee accepted that the Voice of America and US Information Centres abroad continued to fill an important informational and cultural need, it strongly advocated the exploitation of a diverse range of unofficial channels for the purposes of political warfare. While the VOA 'should concentrate on objective factual news reporting,' the Committee recommended that 'all material intended for purposes of political warfare...be diverted to Radio Liberation or other non-official stations.' The Committee also suggested that more use could be made of personal contacts in 'influencing the attitudes of important local individuals,' and in another move which closely reflected British efforts, it recommended that unattributable publications could be more widely employed. In particular, the committee suggested, the Government should cooperate with the commercial publishing industry and 'subsidize its efforts when necessary to combat the flood of inexpensive communist books in the free world.'[25]

The Jackson Committee had far-reaching consequences for the long-term shape of the US information programme. Following a multitude of investigations and reorganizations in the period since 1945, the creation of the USIA provided a permanent bureaucratic foundation for the US information programme. A secure home for those committed individuals convinced of the central role of propaganda in modern diplomacy. Alongside the elevation of the USIA, the Eisenhower Administration's commitment to the expansion of unattributable operations meant that US overseas propaganda was increasingly driven by those agencies responsible for directing covert propaganda, the CIA, the OCB and the NSC. In both cases, the real locus for control of psychological warfare under the Eisenhower administration was the White House, and to an ever increasing degree the office of the President's special advisor on psychological warfare, C.D. Jackson.

Britain, America and the re-establishment of close and continuous liaison

Eisenhower's election received a mixed reception in London. It was warmly welcomed by Churchill. The Prime Minister was pleased to find another wartime ally in the White House and promptly sent his congratulations, expressing his hopes for 'a renewal of our comradeship and of our work together for the same causes of peace and freedom as in the past.' Eisenhower's election reinvigorated Churchill. Although he privately conceded that it made 'war much more probable,' the prospect of a close working relationship with the White House once again enthused Churchill with the hope of bringing together the USA and the Soviet Union.[26] Eisenhower's victory inspired less enthusiasm in the Foreign Office. Eden's Private Secretary, Evelyn Shuckburgh, recorded the 'great disappointment' with which the news was greeted in the Foreign Office, and Under-Secretary Roger Makins warned it would, 'make great difficulties for us in the immediate future, especially if Dulles became Secretary of State.'[27] British officials were particularly concerned about the belligerent anti-communist rhetoric of the presidential election campaign. Dulles's public statements advocating the 'liberation' of Soviet satellites, including proposals for the use of propaganda and support for paramilitary 'freedom fighters', renewed concern about the provocative nature of US policy. Relations were further strained by Eisenhower's announcement in February that the US 7th Fleet was to be removed from its posting protecting the Chinese mainland. The removal of the fleet, which inhibited raids on the Chinese mainland by the Chinese Nationalist leader, Chiang Kai-Shek, was seen by many in Britain as a dangerous escalation of the Cold War in Asia. British concerns peaked following the uprising of workers in East Berlin in June 1953. While Soviet tanks restored order, there was considerable concern among the British and French authorities in Berlin and subsequently in London, that the US-sponsored radio station, Radio-in-the-American-Sector (RIAS), had contributed to the unrest by broadcasting the workers' demands across the Eastern Zone. Churchill was 'deeply worried' by events in Berlin, and the Foreign Office sought to 'resist any American attempts...to take an unduly tough line.' Although the Americans, like the British were surprised by the uprising and ill-equipped to provide real support, they sought to keep up the pressure with a programme of food aid to East Germany designed to humiliate the communists.[28] In July 1953, Lord Salisbury, the Secretary of State for Commonwealth Relations, who stood in as Foreign Secretary in Eden's absences, informed the Cabinet of 'a new and more dangerous American tendency, which has its roots in the Republican election campaign.' The Americans, he said, interpreted the situation behind the Iron Curtain as, 'very shaky and therefore advocate, new, although unspecified, measures to promote the early liberation of the satellite countries.' British policy, he said, should 'resist American pressure for new initiatives of this kind.'[29]

British officials were also concerned that the new administration had little appreciation of the anti-communist policies of the British Government. Paul Gore-Booth, head of the British Information Service in the USA, warned of the widespread feeling in Republican ranks, that Britain was 'soft on communism.'[30] The head of the IRD John Peck, who welcomed the fact that the new administration was 'clearly interested in all aspects of Cold War policy,' was nevertheless concerned at 'signs of criticism in America of an alleged British softness towards the problems of communism in Britain and abroad.'[31] Coupled with concerns regarding the reorganization of the US propaganda apparatus which was likely to arise from the Jackson Committee, in particular the removal of information activities from the State Department, this led to real fears of a fundamental breach in British and US cooperation in anti-communist propaganda.[32]

In early 1953, British policy-makers and officials set about laying Britain's anti-communist credentials before the new administration. In January, Churchill visited Eisenhower in order to impress upon the President 'the vital importance of a common Anglo-American front' against communism. Churchill continued to advocate a return to political warfare in the absence of a negotiated settlement with the Soviet Union, and believed he would find a willing partner in Eisenhower. Churchill's private secretary, Jock Colville, recalled overhearing a conversation between Churchill and Eisenhower, in which the Prime Minister proclaimed, 'I think you and I are agreed that it is not only important to discover the truth but to know how to present the truth.'[33] The following month, a visit to London by John Foster Dulles and Harold Stassen, the new head of the Mutual Security Administration, provided the Foreign Office with the opportunity to outline the British approach to presenting the truth about communism. In preparation for the visit, Peck drafted a brief for Eden on the British attitudes to political warfare. Perhaps more than anyone in the Foreign Office, John Peck appreciated the efforts made to convince the Americans to adopt a more subtle approach to anti-communist propaganda, and the dangers of reverting back to a more openly uncompromising stance. After years trying to encourage the Americans to adopt a more subtle approach there were signs of some exasperation in the IRD at the prospect of beginning this process again. In contrasting British policy with the aggressive rhetoric of the new US administration, Peck stressed that:

> We make no emotional appeals to those already converted, and we regard propaganda issued by right-wing elements designed to appeal only to other right-wing elements as dangerous to us and helpful to the enemy ... Our policy being to obtain as many allies as possible on the ideological front, we feel that great damage is done to our cause by ill-judged statements in Congress and elsewhere which suggest that the United States is the sole effective opponent of communism while all other powers, Britain included are to some extent in league with the enemy.[34]

In a thinly veiled attack on the Macarthyite purges underway in the USA, Peck added that, 'we regard the quest for perfection in security and for the ideological purity of public opinion, as unattainable and greatly favouring communist interests.' The net result, he warned, was to make enemies of those individuals and groups whom the Soviets hoped to split off from the USA. British policy, in contrast, aimed to drive a wedge between the hardcore of Stalinist communists and those on the non-communist left. This was most effectively implemented through non-governmental organizations such as political parties, the trades unions, the Churches and the press. Government activity he added, 'should be confined to discreet behind-the-scenes advice, informal passing of relevant information etc.' Most importantly, however, Peck was concerned that the close and continuous liaison established under Truman should be continued under the new administration. Peck wished for Eden to impress upon the new Secretary of State agreements made with the previous administration that there should be 'close cooperation on all political warfare matters.' 'We have greatly valued this cooperation,' Peck affirmed, 'and hope that it may be continued and extended.'[35]

It is not clear whether Eden raised the subject of anti-communist propaganda in the course of his meeting with Dulles in February 1953. He certainly did at their next meeting in Washington in March, but the subject was quickly brushed aside by Dulles. Eden stated that it was his understanding that the USA was 'developing a new set-up to handle political warfare,' and asked whether the Secretary of State wished to discuss the matter. Dulles replied that the matter was still being studied and a new organization had not yet been put into operation and he briskly moved onto the next subject.[36] While Dulles was dismissive, it is clear that at least some US officials, were aware of a growing gap between Britain and the USA in the direction of anti-communist propaganda. Charles Norberg, a psychological warfare expert in the US Air Force, observed that the removal of the 7th Fleet was 'an essentially psychological warfare move.' The psychological impact, however, had been invalidated by not warning the USA's allies about the move. During the War, Norberg observed, the US Government had a joint psychological warfare board with the British through the Office of War Information. 'If we are going to continue to make major moves on the international psychological chessboard,' he warned, 'we will not only be doing ourselves harm but we will be failing to gain the positive good which can accrue to us in these essentially psychological manoeuvres,' if US allies were not made aware of their significance beforehand.[37]

By the time of Stalin's death at the beginning of March, British officials were growing increasingly concerned that the USA might take unilateral action in the psychological warfare field. The Eisenhower Administration was eager to take advantage of the death of Stalin. On 4th of March, on hearing news that the Soviet premier was gravely ill, the subject was discussed at a hastily convened meeting between the President, the CIA Director, Allen Dulles, C.D. Jackson and others. Jackson in particular was eager to exploit the situation by seeking to 'overload the enemy at the precise moment when he is least capable of bearing even his normal load.' This was a prime opportunity, Jackson argued, to 'advance the real disintegration of the Soviet Empire.' He even suggest the resurrection of plans for 'an Albanian *coup d'état.*' Remarkably, it was Foster Dulles who reined in Jackson's plans at a meeting of the National Security Council later that day, in which he noted that it would be unwise to make a direct appeal to the Soviet people to rise up at a time when Stalin was regarded more reverentially than normal.[38] Eisenhower was persuaded to make a brief statement asking God to watch over the Russian people and bring them the, 'opportunity to live their lives in a world where all men and women and children dwell in peace and comradeship.'[39]

If Eisenhower's words brought comfort to the Russian people, they did little to ease concerns in the Foreign Office. British officials were not inclined to think that Stalin's death would bring about any change in Soviet internal or external policy. If anything, the Foreign Office Russia Committee suggested, the new Soviet leadership would seek to strengthen its internal control over the Soviet Union and the communist bloc, and be no less tough and uncompromising towards the West than it was under Stalin. The Western world, the Russia Committee concluded, 'should continue the policy of building up their defensive strength and of avoiding unnecessary provocation.'[40] However, speculation in the US media about the future of Russia and, in particular, the Soviet hold on the satellites, prompted fears among British officials about US intentions and suggestions that the US Government was conducting its psychological strategy in the press. On the same day the Kremlin announced Stalin's death, the British Embassy in Washington contacted the office of the Assistant Secretary of State for Public Affairs, McCardle, indicating their wish for an urgent meeting to discuss the propaganda implications of Stalin's death.

The State Department recorded:

> There is apparently reason to believe that the British are gravely concerned at
> the way in which these matters are being discussed in the US press and on the
> radio. It was even suggested, not entirely humorously, that maybe the British
> would take the same secretive attitude toward us on this issue we have taken
> toward them on the atomic issue.[41]

Once again, however, it was Adam Watson who served to ease the strains in
Anglo-American relations. While British officials in London and Washington worried about the breakdown of British and US cooperation in the propaganda field,
Watson used his contacts to establish a working relationship with the new administration. Watson's influential position in Washington ensured an important element of
continuity in Anglo-American relations. Watson already enjoyed particularly close
relations with some of the most important advocates of psychological warfare in
the Eisenhower Administration such as Walter Bedell Smith, Gordon Gray and
C.D. Jackson. Gray and Jackson sat on the President's Committee on International
Information Activities and through Jackson, Watson established contact with the
chairman of Eisenhower's Advisory Committee on Government Organisation,
Nelson Rockefeller. Watson and Rockefeller became good friends and the American
would speak warmly of Watson as 'a pioneer in the field of psychological operations,' who brought to the Americans many techniques of propaganda with which
they were unfamiliar. In 1954, Rockefeller succeeded Jackson as the President's
Advisor on Psychological Warfare, and went on to become Vice-President under
Gerald Ford. Following his elevation to White House Special Advisor, C.D. Jackson
was Watson's most important contact in this transitional period. Watson described
Jackson as 'a jovial extrovert, who sometimes overdid it.'[42] His tendency to launch
into operations without consideration for the consequences, is illustrated by a suggestion to Watson in July 1953, that the Kremlin was so anxious for a truce in Korea,
'that we could get even better terms by going on with the fighting for a bit.'[43]
Nevertheless, Jackson had the ear of the President, his enthusiasm for psychological
warfare was legendary and as a result he 'got a lot done.'

Watson's friendship with Jackson served to smooth Anglo-American relations in
the transition to the Eisenhower Administration, and it ensured that as control of US
psychological operations shifted from the State Department to the Executive Branch,
the primary locus for liaison with the British also shifted to the White House. On
30 March 1953, Watson visited Jackson in his office in the White House. According
to Jackson, Watson displayed his 'customary genuine willingness to cooperate with
the Americans.' More particularly, to Jackson's obvious relief, Watson agreed with
him on, 'practically all points on implications of Stalin's death.'[44] Watson and Jackson
met on almost a monthly basis throughout 1953. Watson used the meetings to reassure
the Americans about British policy. He showed Jackson 'certain interesting documents' designed to impress the Americans, 'with the fact that British officialdom was
not as bloody-minded about India or Communist China as US headlines would
indicate,' and reassured Jackson of 'the virtual unanimity FO position with respect to
Germany and a Four Power Conference on our side rather than Churchill's.'[45]

Despite obvious British misgivings it is clear that Jackson used the meetings to probe Watson for British views on liberation. Although the records of Jackson's discussions with Watson on this subject are incomplete, it is clear from Jackson's log and the recollections of Adam Watson that the two discussed the possibility of detaching Albania in some detail on several occasions in 1953.[46] Jackson was particularly interested in Watson's report of Tito's visit to London in March 1953. Tito's impressions of the future of Russia following the death of Stalin supported US hopes for liberation in Eastern Europe. The new regime, Tito stated, would not want war any more than the old one. Although Tito cautioned against provocative propaganda, there would, he observed, be uncertainty at home and a weakening of Moscow's influence over the satellites. This interpretation came as a welcome surprise to Jackson who passed it on to the CIA.[47] In October 1953, Jackson discussed the Albanian situation with Watson and the visiting Conservative MPs, Tufton Beamish and Julian Amery. Amery had been involved in special operations in Albania in the Second World War, and had acted as an advisor to the British Government and a link with the Albanian exile community at the time of the first Albanian infiltrations in 1949. Amery was enthusiastic about reviving the Albanian operation, although his views were clearly not reflected in London. At his next meeting with Watson, Jackson was dismayed to learn of Amery's 'unfortunate blurbing to Eden' about the plans. Jackson's reaction suggests that he did not have great hopes of securing material support from the British. Although, Jackson informed Watson, the plans were 'back on the rails,' Watson had learnt from London that senior figures were not happy about Amery's activities and he decided it would be prudent to back away from the Albanian operation.[48] Jackson pressed on regardless. At the beginning of 1954, his enthusiasm undimmed by the failed uprising in Berlin, Jackson wrote to the CIA's Frank Wisner that, 'the chances of provoking the Soviets into a military reaction are as low as they have been since the War.' Jackson offered a list of possible targets for probing Soviet vulnerability including: Berlin; East Germany; widespread passive resistance in the satellites; and the detachment of 'country X' [Albania].[49]

The degree of liaison between Jackson and Watson suggests that British officials, and possibly even the Foreign Secretary, were fully conversant with the details of the more offensive aspects of the US liberation strategy. Jackson, it seems, was entirely candid in laying before Watson, US aspirations and plans for the detachment of Albania, and freely sought the advice of those, such as Watson and Amery, who had experience of the first Albanian operations in the late 1940s. Jackson was not unaware of serious British concerns regarding the US approach to liberation. Lord Salisbury set out the British position at a meeting of foreign ministers in Washington in July, and Watson provided Jackson with a document on the IRD position which stated that there was 'no prospect of any Eastern European nation detaching itself from the Soviet bloc until the strength and unity of the Soviet Union have declined to a point beyond anything that seems likely in the foreseeable future.'[50] Nevertheless, there is no evidence to suggest that this information caused Jackson to be any less candid in his relations with Watson. Although Jackson did, on occasion, privately express his annoyance at British attitudes and the popular perception of a gung ho US foreign policy, he remained warmly anglophile. Following criticism from the British and the French over the US aid programme to East Germany,

Jackson vented his frustration in a letter to Bedell Smith:

> It is an irony of history and a triumph of British international public relations that they have the reputation for politeness and we have the reputation for doing silly things off the top of the head, when as a matter of fact we are internationally polite to the point of dangerous timidity, whereas they are constantly barging around doing silly things in the Imperial sunset. I still love them dearly but I don't see why we have to ask their gracious permission every time we want to blow our nose.[51]

Despite continued tensions in the British and US approaches to liberation, close and continuous liaison was firmly re-established shortly after Eisenhower's election. British concerns regarding a breakdown in Anglo-American liaison in the field of anti-communist propaganda proved unfounded: individuals such as C.D. Jackson, Frank Wisner and Bedell Smith were as amenable to British cooperation as they had been under the Truman Administration. Through them, British officials had direct access to the review process underway in Washington and arrangements were soon made to institute cooperation with the new US propaganda apparatus. In reviewing propaganda operations in the wake of the Jackson Committee Report, the State Department recorded that, 'at the present time only the United Kingdom among the nations of the free world has capabilities approaching those of the United States.'[52] The British information liaison officer, Adam Watson, provided an important element of continuity. Watson's office and personal contacts ensured the maintenance of formal and informal ties. Watson was in a strong position to continue the British policy of exerting a 'moderating influence' over US policy at a time when the British were deeply concerned about the provocative nature of the new administration's policy towards the communist bloc. While Jackson expressed frustration at British restraint, he was not, it seemed, inclined to take unilateral action without at least informing the British. Certainly the discussions regarding Albania, suggest that if the Eisenhower Administration was to move unilaterally on Albania, they would do so with the full knowledge of the British Government. The extent to which Jackson was prepared to heed British calls for restraint is of course questionable, nevertheless, the Jackson–Watson axis ensured that the British were at least in a strong position to apply such pressure. Moreover, Watson continued to provide the Americans with details of the British approach to anti-communist propaganda, which in 1953 was also evolving a more offensive strategy of political warfare designed to bring about fundamental change in the communist bloc. In keeping with British plans since early 1952, this new strategy was directed at least in part at the USA.

A new strategy of political warfare

At the same time as the Jackson Committee was scrutinizing the US information programme, the first major post-War evaluation of the British propaganda was already underway in London. Although British overseas propaganda had not suffered from the kind of bureaucratic wrangling endemic in Washington, British propagandists, like their counterparts in the USA, had struggled to justify spending on propaganda activities in the face of an obvious military threat from the Soviet bloc, particularly when other policy areas, such as health, were forced to make concessions to pay for rearmament.

By the early 1950s, as a result of successive cuts in funding, the British propaganda apparatus was in a precarious situation. Following Churchill's election, the Foreign Office had been asked to make further cuts of £500,000 in overseas information expenditure. After years of trying to assuage Gaitskell's calls for a 'no-frills' defence policy, the Foreign Office offered a bleak response to this new demand for economy. 'Terms such as "pruning" and "cutting off the frills" no longer have any meaning,' it warned; the only remaining way to save money would be to stop large quantities of information work altogether.[53] In December 1951, the Foreign Office produced a lengthy paper on 'Information, Propaganda and the Cold War', which stressed that the Cold War was 'a struggle for men's minds.' In this struggle only the continuous and widespread employment of propaganda would persuade those wavering between East and West, that Western institutions offered them 'a better and surer hope of realising their dreams of social justice, material progress and national freedom.' Successive reductions in information expenditure had, it was claimed, severely damaged Britain's propaganda apparatus. Highly qualified individuals had left the information services for positions with greater job security, and the cuts had damaged British prestige abroad as the disappearance of services suggested that Britain was either bankrupt or had written off large areas of the globe. Any further cuts, it was argued, would ultimately lead to the breakdown of the constituent parts of the British information apparatus. The government information services, it was suggested, were like a car which could not be expected to 'go on running with less and less oil and petrol each year.'[54]

In an effort to satisfy the House of Commons that the information services provided value for money, in April 1952 a small committee of senior officials was assembled to assess the value of the overseas information services. Under the chairmanship of John Nicholls, the Foreign Office Under-Secretary responsible for information activities, the committee comprised officials from the Foreign Office, the Commonwealth Relations and Colonial Offices, the Ministry of Defence, the Chiefs of Staff, the Board of Trade, the Central Office of Information, the British Council and the BBC. The Nicholls Committee ranged widely across British overt and covert propaganda activities, in an effort to show 'what the information services did and where and in what media it performed.'[55]

The Nicholls Committee produced the most detailed account of British anti-communist propaganda since the launch of the new propaganda policy in 1948. It found that, 'considerable results' had been achieved particularly in the field of anti-communist propaganda. Reports from British Missions, it found, 'produced excellent evidence of the value of the work of the Information Research Department.' The committee's account continued:

> Her Majesty's Ambassador in Tokyo, for example, considers that this work has helped to make the Japanese conscious of the Soviet menace. Again in Finland we have secured a considerable audience among the various political parties and Trades Unions, in Syria IRD material is widely published and in Siam it provides the basis for a weekly broadcast from Radio Bangkok ... The Holy See, for example, find our material useful. In Burma, Indo-China and Egypt much of our material is used by the official Information Services and in one major European country large passages of the Prime Minister's speeches during the last two years have been lifted bodily from IRD publications.[56]

The committee struggled to isolate the strategic benefits of information work from the political ones, but did find examples of successful British efforts to counter neutralism and defeatism in the face of the Soviet threat. In France, for example, the British Ambassador reported that publicity given to the British defence effort had 'undoubtedly been a factor in reconciling the French to their rearming also.' Similarly, a tour of the United Kingdom by the public relations officer of the Italian Ministry of Defence, had resulted in a return invitation to Home Office experts and the setting up of the Italian Civil Defence organization on the British model. In Germany, Ivone Kirkpatrick reported, that if British and US information services had not made a considerable effort in the information field, German public opinion 'would be more unstable, more confused and more intractable than it is.' Even in the Middle East, where xenophobia was rife, the information services were, 'consolidating good relations where they exist, and working to lessen anti-British feeling'; and in some countries, 'a more favourable disposition' towards a Middle East defence pact had been achieved.[57]

Although reports of IRD's work were generally positive, the Nicholls Committee also revealed some enduring concerns about the complexion of British anti-communist propaganda. Significantly, these concerns differed little from those voiced by some British diplomats shortly after the launch of the new propaganda policy in 1948. A number of heads of mission were concerned to stress 'the importance of keeping a careful balance between material exposing Communism and material offering a constructive alternative.' It is also clear that the Foreign Office still struggled to produce propaganda material tailored to a mass audience. Although the creation of regional information offices in South-East Asia and the Middle East, had helped to tailor material to local tastes, and in many countries, it was reported, IRD material satisfied a need which was not met by local resources. Some IRD material, particularly in the Far East and the Middle East, still appeared to have 'gone over the heads of local audiences.' Despite these difficulties, in general the Nicholls Committee testified not only to the quality of the IRD's output but also the scale of its work. Whilst the US Government was seeking to step up unattributable activities in the face of a market saturated with official propaganda, the Nicholls Committee cautioned that the IRD's coverage was such that the market for its unattributable material was, 'in places nearing saturation.'[58]

The Nicholls Committee concluded that the international situation: 'the Communist ideological onslaught on the free world'; the need to right the balance of payments; and the maintenance of Commonwealth relations demanded, 'an intensification of overseas information work and a measure of continuity in its financing.' Most significantly, the committee identified the Cold War as the defining influence on British overseas propaganda policy. Historically, the main peacetime role of the British overseas information services had been to promote trade. Although this had clearly changed with the launch of the new propaganda policy in 1948, the findings of the Nicholls Committee provided the clearest indication to date that anti-communist propaganda was the central role of the British overseas information services. In contrast to the marked achievements in the field of anti-communist propaganda, the Committee found only 'limited' evidence of achievements in the commercial sphere.[59] These senior officials, however, were reluctant to make judgements regarding what proportion of national resources should be committed to these activities. Although the Nicholls

Committee was clearly convinced of the value of British overseas propaganda, it concluded that a committee comprising officials closely involved in information work was unlikely to satisfy the House of Commons. It suggested the creation of a small independent committee of eminent people, was a more appropriate means to convince the House of Commons, that 'the expenditure involved was in fact laid out to the best advantage.'[60]

In July 1952, the Foreign Office Minister, Anthony Nutting, announced the appointment of an independent committee drawn from Outside government service to 'assess the value, actual and potential' of the government's overseas information services, and make recommendations for future policy. The committee was chaired by the Earl of Drogheda, who had been Director-General of the wartime Ministry of Economic Warfare (MEW), and comprised eminent personalities including Victor Feather of the TUC, Donald Maclachlan foreign editor of *The Economist*, Gervase Huxley, another veteran of the MEW and a specialist on Colonial Affairs and J.L. Heyworth a director of Lever Brothers. Sir Robert Bruce Lockhart was forced to resign early due to illness. The Drogheda Committee conducted an exhaustive survey. After 67 twice-weekly meetings in London, the committee broke up and travelled the globe to view the work of overseas information services on the ground, in Europe, the USA, Asia and Africa. Lord Drogheda himself undertook a six-week trip which encompassed Lebanon, Syria, Pakistan, Ceylon, Malaya, Singapore, Calcutta, Delhi, Cairo and Rome.[61]

When the Drogheda Committee presented its report to the Prime Minister in November 1953, it was harshly critical of the consistent under investment in information activities. 'Since the war,' it observed:

> ...the Overseas Information Services have lived in the worst of all possible worlds. Reluctantly accepted as being necessary in the post-war era they have nevertheless been steadily whittled down. So far as we can judge this has not been done in accordance with any plan which took into account the needs of the country for propaganda abroad, but by a series of annual cuts in which the total amount available for all overseas information work was reduced by a more or less arbitrary figure.[62]

The committee asserted that the Overseas Information Services played, 'an important and indeed essential role in support of our Foreign, Commonwealth and Colonial policies.' This work, they stressed, should be 'done well, continuously and on an adequate basis,' and as a result more money would undoubtedly need to be spent. The committee recommended a substantial expansion in spending over a three- to five-year period, designed to place the information services back on stable long-term footing. Unlike the Jackson Committee, Drogheda did not recommend any major organizational changes to the information apparatus, but it did call for a considerable expansion of information staff overseas most notably in the Middle East, South-East Asia and the Commonwealth, and the restoration of recently cut services in Europe and Latin America. It also concluded that the time had come to establish new information offices in Africa. To support these overseas activities, the Committee recommended an expansion in the technical services in London, most notably the London Press Service and the feature articles and the film production services of the Central

Office of Information. The Committee also recommended increased facilities in the UK for handling foreign journalists. Significantly the Committee praised the Foreign Office practice of employing a proportion of non-career experts as information specialists and recommended an expansion of this practice.[63]

The committee paid particular attention to the overseas services of the BBC. Budgetary cuts combined with the increasing cost of counteracting Soviet jamming meant that the reception of BBC programmes around the world had steadily weakened between 1946 and 1952. The committee was unequivocal in its presentation of the BBC external services as a vital instrument of Cold War propaganda. It called for the restoration of recently cut services to Latin America and an expansion of the Arabic service, although it acquiesced in cuts to the Western European an services on the grounds that, 'the burden of what is essentially an Allied operation of political warfare should be shared equitably between the NATO powers.'[64] Greatest emphasis was put on those services directed over the Iron Curtain. In an unpublished section of the report, the committee asserted that the BBC services to Russia and its satellites, 'are of much the same nature and have much the same purpose as had the services to Germany and the occupied countries during the last war.' As broadcasting was in many respects the only means of reaching behind the Iron Curtain, these services were, 'required for the purposes of political warfare.' There was, the committee stressed, 'no alternative but for the BBC to continue to make every effort to play their part in this propaganda battle.' The committee was careful to stress that the popularity of the BBC was dependent above all 'on its high reputation for objective and honest news reporting.' This, the committee claimed, was a 'priceless asset' to be maintained at all costs. Nevertheless, in a passage, all the more remarkable because it appeared in the published version of the report, the committee clearly defined the Cold War role of the BBC external services:

> [W]e would deplore any attempt to use the British Broadcasting Corporation for anything in the way of *direct propaganda of the obvious kind*. This is not to suggest that the British Broadcasting Corporation External Services are not in fact a weapon of propaganda. The best and most effective propaganda to many countries consists of a factual presentation of the news and British views concerning the news. [emphasis added][65]

Aside from its detailed examination of the role of the BBC, the Drogheda Committee, unlike its predecessor, did not offer any detailed review of British anti-communist propaganda activities. Although its exhaustive survey took into account the value of covert operations, the Committee operated under the assumption that 'any report should be so drafted as to be suitable for publication.'[66] Nevertheless, the Drogheda Committee did confirm the role of propaganda as the most potent weapon in Britain's Cold War arsenal. Like the Nicholls Committee, it relegated commercial considerations to a secondary role. The principal consideration in the future development of the British information services was to be the Cold War. Echoing the words of the Foreign Office, the Drogheda Committee concluded, 'this is essentially a struggle for men's minds – a war of propaganda which is likely to continue for some time to come.' Whilst making no reference to the IRD, an unpublished section of the Committee's report set out a new global commitment to anti-communist propaganda which encompassed propaganda directed over the Iron Curtain. This ambitious programme marked a return to the defensive-offensive strategy advocated by senior officials in period before 1948. Britain's Cold War propaganda, the Drogheda Committee concluded, had to do three things:

> First, we have to encourage our friends and weaken our enemies behind the Iron Curtain; we cannot escape from this responsibility. Secondly, we must somehow keep on our side and strengthen the morale of all those countries, particularly in Asia, which are poor, weak, suspicious, highly nationalistic and inclined to be apathetic about the cold war. Thirdly, the United Kingdom forms part of a great defensive alliance of free nations with which we see eye to eye on broad principles but with which in our day-to-day relations there is plenty of room for misunderstanding. Of particular importance and delicacy are our relations with the United States of America.[67]

The broad generalities of the Drogheda Report masked a more detailed review of British anti-communist propaganda which had begun in the spring of 1953. The more forward policy in propaganda towards the communist bloc, which senior officials in the IRD and the PUSC had been advocating since early 1952, was given added impetus by the public calls for liberation emanating from the USA in the run-up to Eisenhower's election. There had even been some debate in the British press, albeit more restrained, advocating a more offensive policy towards the communist bloc.[68] Even before the Drogheda Committee reported, senior officials in the Foreign Office had begun to recast British anti-communist propaganda policy to reflect its new global role, and in particular a new more offensive policy designed to bring an end to communism behind the Iron Curtain. In a clear indication of how far thinking had developed since the launch of the new propaganda policy in 1948, officials now referred openly to 'a new strategy of political warfare.'

In March 1953, Nicholls suggested that enlightenment propaganda, on which British anti-communist propaganda policy had been based since 1948, was reaching the limits of its usefulness. Nicholls argued that the present stabilization of the Cold War, was due in no small part to the conscious efforts of governments, 'primarily our own,' to 'expose Soviet/communist activities in the free world and to shed the light of truth on the facts of existence in Communist states.' Although recognition of the communist menace would certainly help to prevent further communist penetration of the free world, Nicholls argued it offered, 'no solution of the fundamental conflict between East and West.' Such a policy could prevent a non-communist from becoming a communist, but it was 'not likely to convert any significant number of Communists into non-Communists – much less to bring any of the present satellites into the Western camp.' The fact that British propaganda held out no hope of an end to the Cold War was of little consequence when the principal task was to open peoples eyes about communism. However, Nicholls argued, it became crucially important once the existence of the 'communist menace' was accepted and the question in the public mind was 'whether and for how long the cost and burden of confronting it can be sustained.' This stage, Nicholls suggested, had been reached in Europe and the USA. Alternately, it was just as important when a people or government shut its eyes to the menace 'because it is unwilling to recognise a danger to which it can see no end.' This, Nicholls added, was the prevalent position in Asia, and much of the rest of the free world:

> Under either of these sets of conditions, a political warfare policy which does not in fact offer, or which cannot plausibly pretend to offer, a reasonable ultimate solution begins to defeat its own objects. One type of mind swings towards neutralism or appeasement, and a second towards demands for a military solution; and as each movement gains strength it reinforces the other. From this point on – and I think we are approaching it – propaganda based solely on enlightenment will be of diminishing value... Indeed, at that stage there is a risk that the arguments which are necessary to demonstrate the existence and the scale of the Soviet menace will work to our disadvantage by making the prospect of an eventual end to the Cold War seem all the more remote.[69]

An ambitious programme designed to address with the problems outlined by Nicholls, and set out a new policy of political warfare, was drafted in early 1953 by the IRD head, John Peck. The new policy was the product of a long period of re-evaluation within the IRD, which had begun shortly after Peck took over as head of department. Peck had conducted a detailed review of British anti-communist propaganda operations in July 1951, in response Patrick Gordon-Walker's call for all British propaganda be geared toward the Cold War. This paper had been redrafted a year later following Churchill's election, and the PUSC re-evaluation of British Soviet policy. The new policy for political warfare was the culmination of this process but was also markedly different. The most striking feature of the new policy was the central role of propaganda directed over the Iron Curtain and aimed directly at the transformation of the Soviet regime. What had previously been a sideshow to the IRD's attempts to combat communism in the free world, was now the central tenet of British anti-communist propaganda policy. This policy was, of course, informed by a detailed study of communist methods and tactics and internal conditions within the Soviet Union. However, one can also detect in Peck's drafting a cautious response to American psychological warfare planning. Peck prefaced his memorandum with a clear statement that it was, 'a fundamental feature of the proposed operation that it can be conducted in a non-provocative manner.'[70]

The central premise of the new policy was that the Soviet system held the seeds of its own destruction. The Soviet regime, it asserted, could only be held together by 'force and fraud.' This created a constant state of tension and suspicion inside the administration particularly at the higher levels. British political warfare would seek to exploit these tensions. The principal cohesive factor in the higher levels of the Communist Party of the Soviet Union was the belief in the 'dynamic, expansionist doctrine of Soviet communism.' That was: a fundamental belief that the structures of the Soviet state were growing stronger; that loyalty to the regime was growing at home; and that communism would eventually be embraced by the whole world. If western political warfare could sow seeds of doubt regarding these fundamental assumptions within the minds of the ruling class in the Soviet Union, it was argued:

> It could create a crisis of confidence in the Presidium of the Communist Party itself, leading either to an internal revolution or a general paralysis of the machine, a loss of the momentum on which dictatorship depends, and the gradual disintegration of the centralised control.[71]

The new policy was dependent on 'reaching the minds of the ruling class in the Soviet Union.' There was, the IRD felt, little point in directing propaganda at the masses in the Soviet Union, or the satellite states. So long as the regime retained a strong centre, the possibility of a successful popular revolution was limited. Similarly, the possibility of detaching a satellite was slight so long as the power of Moscow prevailed. The greatest hope of bringing an end to the Cold War lay in the exploitation of existing and demonstrable tensions at the heart of the Soviet regime, which, it was hoped, would eventually lead, either by paralysis or reform, to a fundamental reconfiguration of the Soviet regime. Purges, arrests and tightening of discipline within the Soviet Union provided evidence to support this premise, both by indicating that seeds of doubt existed within the Soviet leadership and by illustrating the social and political decay which resulted. This policy did not, however, hold out hope of rapid change; it was a long-term plan, which Peck later conceded, 'might take decades to produce an effect.'[72] It did, however, have significant advantages. Most notably, by exploiting existing weaknesses inherent in the system it sought to transform the regime peacefully without resorting to provocative measures or military force and, by targeting the regime in Moscow, avoided the 'dilemma of fostering resistance in Eastern Europe without promoting premature results.'[73]

In an effort to create a 'crisis of confidence' or, more accurately, crises of confidence, in the higher reaches of the Soviet regime, British political warfare would seek to demonstrate that Soviet communism was in decline and that the free world, by contrast, was progressive, resilient and prosperous. This policy was dependent upon new ideas and evidence of their effectiveness reaching the minds of the Soviet leadership and 'generating an interest in a more convincing and more satisfactory alternative.' It would stress that, far from being embraced by the world, communism was steadily being rejected by increasing numbers of people around the world, and was far from popular in the Soviet bloc. At the same time it would seek to increase 'confidence, unity and efficiency' in the free world, and in an effort to counteract defeatism and neutralism, 'a consciousness of its own superiority.' Above all, the ultimate collapse of tyrannical regimes such as existed in the communist bloc, was to be presented as 'inevitable.' The fundamental objective was the:

> ...assiduous universal propagation with supporting evidence of the idea that throughout the world people want the Soviet tyranny to come to an end, that the number of such people is increasing, that if enough people throughout the world want it to come to an end it will come to an end, that this can happen without the use of force against Russia, and can happen by peaceful transformation without a bloodbath inside Russia; that this chain of events is the only way in which the world can evolve into a peaceful and united organisation capable of dealing with the problems of food and population which threaten it.[74]

Central to the new policy was an intensive campaign, covert as necessary, to instil these ideas into all Soviet subjects in contact with non-Soviet ideas, including: Soviet missions abroad; Soviet military intelligence officers; armed forces in Germany and Austria; postal censors and radio monitors; Soviet delegations to the UN; and listeners to the BBC. A similar campaign was to be carried out in the free world to disrupt and confuse the communist-controlled international front

organizations. The positive elements of the programme were also to be widely prop-
agated in the free world. In the Middle East and South-East Asia, propaganda was to
be used to enlist the support of nationalist and progressive elements. In Western
Europe, an additional programme was to be launched to counter the Soviet peace
campaign by explaining the real conditions of peace: freedom of access to Russian
peoples; government by consensus; and also the defensive purpose of armaments
and the conditions for disarmament. The programme also involved a new emphasis
on the merits and possibilities of the UN charter.[75]

The programme, it was stated, involved three levels of activity: a covert and overt
propaganda operation; government policy; and the discreet presentation of the project to other governments in order to enlist their support. The principal method was
to be, 'the covert propagation, on the widest possible scale of this positive doctrine
as a non-governmental movement.' Although the British Government, it was suggested, should offer implicit acceptance of the new programme, in particular by
accepting the 'ultimate inevitability' theory, the degree of overt endorsement was to
be dependent on the 'degree of provocation it would represent.' This, of course,
would change over time dependent on the relative strength of the two blocs, but
would not at that time entail any modifications in policy aside from periodical references in ministerial speeches and, if possible, 'enlisting the secret support of
the Opposition front bench.' The only other action would involve providing appropriate instructions to the BBC external services, and the application of 'such discreet
pressure as can be brought to bear on the Home Services.'[76]

The policy would continue to entail efforts to involve other governments in the
anti-communist propaganda battle – most notably the Indian Government and the
NATO allies. However, as in 1948, the new policy was first presented to the USA. In
July 1953, Watson passed Jackson a memorandum outlining Britain's new strategy
of political warfare. The sharing of such a complete outline of British psychological
warfare policy was, according to Watson, 'an absolutely unique and unprecedented
action on HMG's part.'[77] This was not entirely true, the Foreign Office had been similarly candid in setting Britain's new propaganda policy before the Americans in
1948. Moreover, as in 1948, the criticism of US propaganda which appeared in an
earlier draft had been removed.[78] Nevertheless, the document was clearly designed
to influence US policy and was drafted with the intention of setting out the British
approach for the benefit of the Jackson Committee. Following in the wake of the
Berlin uprising this was a timely annunciation of British policy and a powerful argument in favour of policies designed to bring about evolutionary rather than revolutionary change in the communist bloc. Although it marked a fundamental change in
British propaganda policy towards the communist bloc, it was consistent with that
aspect of British anti-communist propaganda policy which, since 1948, had urged
the USA towards greater discretion and restraint.

On 19 February 1954, almost exactly six years since British Missions had been
informed about the new anti-communist propaganda policy, the Foreign Office
issued a directive outlining the new strategy of political warfare. The new directive,
it was claimed, marked the end of the period of enlightenment propaganda which had
characterized British anti-communist propaganda policy since 1948 and heralded a
new era of political warfare. Enlightenment propaganda, it stated, had been essentially defensive and negative and suffered from the major defect of not offering any

prospect of an end to the Cold War. Although British propaganda would continue to expose the nature and threats of communism, it would also seek to convince people that the collapse of communism was inevitable. Moreover, the policy which was originally conceived and designed to appeal to the broad masses of workers and peasants in Europe and Asia was now directed at opinion-forming élites on both sides of the Iron Curtain. IRD material, it reported, was being received by ministers or high officials of more than 50 governments, and 'non-official leaders and shapers of public opinion' in 60 countries. These individuals, 'from Asian nationalists to European Trade Unionists,' were to be mobilized to convince their counterparts in the Soviet Union, that 'the true future of Russia lies in the free contact of Russian peoples with those of the rest of the world.' The ultimate hope was that 'the Russian people, and especially the managerial and technical classes,' would come to realize that as the fundamental doctrines of communism were false the rule of the Communist Party of the Soviet Union had no foundation or justification.[79] The *raison d'être* of British propaganda was no longer to interpret communism, the point was to change it.

Notes

1 'Cold War Policy and Propaganda,' 24 March 1953, PR101/116, FO 1110/532, PRO.
2 V. Zubok and C. Pleshakov, *Inside the Kremlin's Cold War: From Stalin to Khrushchev* (Cambridge, MA: Harvard University Press, 1996), pp. 154–6.
3 'Cold War Policy and Propaganda'. On Foreign office reactions to Stalin's death, see J.W. Young, *Winston Churchill's Last Campaign: Britain and the Cold War, 1951–1955* (Oxford: Oxford University Press, 1996), pp. 135–8.
4 'Cold War Policy and Propaganda,' 24 March 1953, PR101/116, FO 1110/532, PRO.
5 J.W. Henderson, *The United States Information Agency* (London, Praeger, 1969), pp. 34–5; W.L. Hixson, *Parting the Curtain: Propaganda, Culture and the Cold War, 1945–1961* (London: Macmillan, 1998), p. 21; F. Green, *American Propaganda Abroad* (New York: Hippocrene Books, 1988), pp. 28–9.
6 Hixson, *Parting the Curtain*, p. 23; D. Haight, 'The Papers of C.D. Jackson: A Glimpse of President Eisenhower's Psychological Warfare Expert', *Manuscripts*, 27 (1976), pp. 27–37.
7 Extract from a Report on International Information Administration – 1952, to the Secretary of State from the Administrator, Compton, 31 December 1952, *FRUS, 1952–1954*, vol. 2, p. 1,645.
8 Hixson, *Parting the Curtain*, pp. 19–21.
9 C.D. Jackson to Eisenhower, 17 December 1952, Box no. 50, C.D. Jackson papers, Eisenhower Library.
10 S. Lucas, *Freedom's War: The American Crusade Against the Soviet Union* (New York: New York University Press, 1999), pp. 163–6; Young, *Winston Churchill's Last Campaign*, pp. 104–9.
11 Hixson, *Parting the Curtain*, p. 23.
12 D.D. Eisenhower to J. Lay, establishing President's Committee on International Information Activities, 24 January 1953, Jackson Committee, Records, 1950–1953, Box no. 1, Eisenhower Library; Hixson, *Parting the Curtain*, pp. 23–4.
13 Report to the President by the President's Committee on International Information Activities, 30 June 1953, *FRUS, 1952–1954*, vol. 2, pp. 1,795–875.
14 S.J. Parry-Giles, 'Exporting America's Cold War Message: The Debate over America's First Peacetime Propaganda Program, 1947–1953', PhD thesis, Indiana University, 1992, pp. 222–3.
15 Hixson, *Parting the Curtain*, pp. 25–6; G. Mitrovich, *Undermining the Kremlin: America's Strategy to Subvert the Soviet Bloc, 1947–1956* (New York: Cornell, 2000), pp. 124–5.

16 Memo for the President by the President's Advisory Committee on Government Organization, 7 April 1953, *FRUS, 1952–1954*, vol. 2, pp. 1,691–7.
17 Hixson, *Parting the Curtain*, pp. 25–6.
18 Abbott Washburn, Ike and the USIA: A Symposium, Foreign Affairs Oral History Program (FAOH), Georgetown University, Washington, DC, 1990.
19 Special Message to the Congress on Organization of Executive Branch for Conduct of Foreign Affairs, 1 June 1953, *Public Papers of the Presidents, Dwight D. Eisenhower, 1953* (Washington, DC: US GPO), pp. 342–50; NSC 165, Note by the Executive Secretary to the NSC, Mission of the United States Information Agency, 9 October 1953, National Security Council Papers, RG 273, NARA.
20 Hixson, *Parting the Curtain*, p. 27.
21 Abbott Washburn, Ike and the USIA, FAOH.
22 Notes of First Meeting between Warner and Barrett, at London, 20 May 1950, *FRUS, 1950*, vol. 3, pp.1641–44; Report to the President by the President's Committee on International Information Activities, 30 June 1953, *FRUS, 1952–1954*, vol. 2, pp. 1,871–2.
23 Report to the President by the President's Committee on International Information Activities, 30 June 1953.
24 NSC 165, Note by the Executive Secretary to the NSC, Mission of the United States Information Agency, 9 October 1953, National Security Council Papers, RG 273, NARA.
25 Report to the President by the President's Committee on International Information Activities, 30 June 1953.
26 Young, *Winston Churchill's Last Campaign*, pp. 110–11; M. Gilbert, *Never Despair*, pp. 773–4.
27 E. Shuckburgh, *Descent to Suez: Diaries 1951–56* (London: Weidenfeld & Nicolson, 1986), p. 47.
28 M.S. Fish, 'After Stalin's Death: The Anglo-American Debate Over the New Cold War', *Diplomatic History*, 10, 4 (1986), pp. 340–1; Young, *Winston Churchill's Last Campaign*, pp. 176–9; 'Churchill "Betrayed East German Rising"', *The Guardian*, 17 June 2003.
29 Fish, 'After Stalin's Death', p. 343.
30 Gore-Booth to Malcolm, IPD, 6 January 1953, PRG45/6, FO 1110/586, PRO.
31 Brief for discussion with Dulles and Stassen, Political Warfare, 28 January 1953, PR102/8/G, FO 1110/533, PRO.
32 Marshall, for Watson, British Embassy Washington, to Hopson, IRD, 27 May 1953, PRG45/75, FO 1110/587; Brief for discussion with Dulles and Stassen, Political Warfare, 28 January 1953, PR102/8/G, FO 1110/533, PRO.
33 J. Colville, *The Fringes of Power: Downing Street Diaries*, vol. 2, *1941–April 1955* (London: Hodder & Stoughton, 1987), p. 318.
34 Brief for discussion with Dulles and Stassen, Political Warfare, 28 January 1953.
35 *Ibid.*
36 Minutes of Second Meeting of Secretary of State Dulles and Foreign Secretary Eden, 6 March 1953, *FRUS, 1952–1954*, vol. 6, p. 907.
37 Coordinated US–UK Psychological Warfare, Charles Norburg, 19 February 1953, Box no. 13, PSB Central File Series, White House Office, NSC Staff papers, 1953–1961, Eisenhower Library.
38 Lucas, *Freedom's War*, pp. 169–70; Memo of discussion, NSC, 4 March 1953, *FRUS, 1952–1954*, vol. 8, pp. 1,091–5.
39 Statement by the President, 4 March 1953, *FRUS, 1952–1954*, vol. 8, p. 1,085; D.D. Eisenhower, *Mandate for Change, 1953–1956* (New York: Doubleday, 1963), p. 144.
40 Memo: The Death of Stalin, nd, NS1023/14, FO 371/106529, PRO; Young, *Winston Churchill's Last Campaign*, pp. 135–8.
41 Memo State Department Meeting, 6 March 1953, Box no. 8, PSB Central Files Series, White House Office, NSC Staff, Papers 1953–61, Eisenhower Library.
42 Adam Watson, telephone interview with author, August 2003.
43 Watson to Nicholls, 17 July 1953, PRG45/122, FO 1110/587, PRO.

44 C.D. Jackson Log 1953, Box no. 68, C.D. Jackson Papers, 1931–1967, Eisenhower Library.

45 *Ibid.*

46 *Ibid.* Adam Watson, telephone interview with author, October 2003. On leaving his post as White House Advisor, Jackson sent a highly classified letter, discussing Tito's visit and Albania, to Frank Wisner, for his disposal: Jackson to Wisner, 26 March 1954, Box no. 6, C.D. Jackson Records, 1953–54, Eisenhower Library.

47 Shuckburgh, *Descent to Suez*, pp. 80–1; Jackson Log, April 9 1953, C.D. Jackson Papers, 1931–1967, Eisenhower Library.

48 Jackson Log, October, November 1953, C.D. Jackson Papers, 1931–1967, Eisenhower Library; Adam Watson, telephone interview with author, October 2003.

49 Jackson to Wisner, 27 February 1954, Box no. 111, C.D. Jackson Papers, Eisenhower Library.

50 Fish, 'After Stalin's Death'; The Strategy of Political Warfare, 25 June 1953, PRG45/110, FO 1110/587, PRO.

51 Jackson to Bedell Smith, 18 August 1953, Box no. 6, C.D. Jackson Records, 1953–54, Eisenhower Library.

52 Report of the State Department on Implementation of Jackson Committee Report, October 1953, *FRUS, 1952–54*, vol. 2, pp. 1,887–8.

53 Economy in Overseas Information, Memo by Parliamentary Under-Secretary of State, 11 December 1951, GEN395/2, CAB 130/72, PRO.

54 'Information, Propaganda and the Cold War', 10 December 1951, P1011/94, FO 953/1051, PRO.

55 Committee of Enquiry into Overseas Information Services, first Meeting, 21 April 1952, GEN 407, CAB 130/75, PRO.

56 Committee of Enquiry into Overseas Information Services, Survey of United Kingdom Publicity in Foreign Countries, 30 July 1952, GEN 407/15, CAB 130/75, PRO.

57 *Ibid.*

58 *Ibid.*

59 Committee of Enquiry into Overseas Information Services, Report, 18 July 1952, GEN 407/14, CAB 130/75, PRO.

60 Committee of Enquiry into Overseas Information Services, first Meeting, 21 April 1952; Committee of Enquiry into Overseas Information Services, Report, 18 July 1952; Cmnd.9138, *Summary of the Report of the Independent Committee of Enquiry into the Overseas Information Services, April 1954* (London: HMSO), p. 5.

61 Cmnd.9138, *Summary of the Report of the Independent Committee of Enquiry into the Overseas Information Services, April 1954*; F. Donaldson, *The British Council: The First Fifty Years* (London: Johnathan Cape, 1984) pp. 178–93; Sir Robert Marett, *Through the Back Door: An Inside View of Britain's Overseas Information Services* (London: Pergamon Press, 1968), pp. 153–69.

62 Cmnd.9138, *Summary of the Report of the Independent Committee of Enquiry into the Overseas Information Services, April 1954*, p. 5. The full report may be found in: Overseas Information Services, Report of the Drogheda Committee, 13 November 1953, C(53) 305, PREM 11/691, PRO.

63 Cmnd.9138, *Summary of the Report of the Independent Committee of Enquiry into the Overseas Information Services, April 1954*.

64 Overseas Information Services, Report of the Drogheda Committee, 13 November 1953; Cmnd.9138, *Summary of the Report of the Independent Committee of Enquiry into the Overseas Information Services, April 1954*.

65 Cmnd.9138, *Summary of the Report of the Independent Committee of Enquiry into the Overseas Information Services, April 1954*, p. 44.

66 Committee of Enquiry into Overseas Information Services, first Meeting, 21 April 1952.

67 Overseas Information Services, Report of the Drogheda Committee, 13 November 1953.

68 Young, *Winston Churchill's Last Campaign*, pp. 107–8; 'Containment Plus', *The Economist*, 26 April 1952, pp. 205–7.

69 'Cold War Policy and Propaganda', J.W. Nicholls, 24 March 1953, PR101/117, FO 1110/532, PRO.

70 'Political Warfare: A New Policy', J.H. Peck, PR101/116, FO 1110/532, PRO.
71 *Ibid.*
72 'The Strategy of Political Warfare', 25 June 1953, PRG45/110, FO 1110/587, PRO.
73 'Political Warfare: A New Policy'.
74 *Ibid.*
75 *Ibid.*
76 *Ibid.*
77 Log 1953, Box no. 68, C.D. Jackson Papers, 1931–1967, Eisenhower Library. The paper was 'The Strategy of Political Warfare'.
78 'Political Warfare: A New Policy'.
79 Anti-Communist Policy, 19 February 1954, PR1011/14, FO 1110/636, PRO.

Conclusion

It was with some reluctance that the British Government embarked on a new anti-communist propaganda policy in January 1948. The post-War Labour Government was not averse to the use of propaganda. Although wartime propaganda agencies, such as the Ministry of Information and the Political Warfare Executive, were dismantled, substantial elements of the propaganda apparatus were retained within the Foreign Office and in a new Central Office of Information. Moreover, the Labour Government was ready to use propaganda to explain British policies abroad and, in the face of declining power, to advertise British achievements. Bevin in particular was keen that Britain should not 'hide its light under a bushel.'[1] Given such enthusiasm, it was perhaps inevitable that propaganda would once again be used in an offensive capacity. However, faced with an increasingly hostile barrage of anti-British propaganda from the Soviet Union and communists around the world, Bevin initially resisted calls from senior officials in the Foreign Office to respond with offensive propaganda. Events at the end of 1947 – most notably the creation of the Cominform and the breakdown of the Council of Foreign Ministers meetings in London – prompted Bevin to reconsider this position. He was persuaded to adopt a new propaganda policy when his Parliamentary Under-Secretary, Christopher Mayhew, combined the Foreign Office's call for a propaganda offensive with the promotion of Bevin's own strategy for 'Third Force' defence.

The new propaganda policy was an uneasy compromise between Foreign Office thinking, and the desire of Bevin and the Labour Government to promote a British led 'Third Force.' The new propaganda policy had several radical features. It was to be based upon the 'vital ideas of British Social Democracy' and attack by comparison the 'principles and practice of communism, and also the inefficiency, social injustice and moral weakness of unrestrained capitalism.' Moreover, British propaganda was to be directed at the 'broad mass of workers and peasants.'[2] Although the new propaganda policy was designed to take the offensive against communism, Bevin was quite clear as to how far that offensive would be allowed to go. He firmly resisted a return to wartime methods of political warfare. In contrast with the Second World War, British propaganda was not directed at the enemy, but was designed to consolidate democracy in the free world. Bevin resisted calls to embark upon a campaign of 'political warfare' against the Soviet Union and pressure from the Services for a more offensive propaganda policy and organization. Very little propaganda was directed at the Soviet Union or the satellite states, and propaganda which aimed to incite unrest in the communist bloc was, until December 1949, strictly prohibited.

Britain's new propaganda apparatus was not modelled on the wartime Political Warfare Executive, and Bevin forbade the use of the phrase 'political warfare,' even within Whitehall, to describe Britain's propaganda activities.[3] Moreover, in contrast to wartime arrangements, all overseas propaganda activities were the responsibility of the Foreign Office, where the new Information Research Department, the IRD, was located.

It has been suggested that the Labour Government was hoodwinked into supporting an anti-communist propaganda campaign by hardline elements in the Foreign Office.[4] However, it was the Labour Minister, Christopher Mayhew, who suggested the inclusion of anti-capitalist propaganda as a device to sell the new propaganda policy to sceptical colleagues in the Cabinet. This anti-capitalist device has been confused with Bevin's genuine hopes for a 'Third Force' in international affairs, in an effort to present the new propaganda policy as traditional Foreign office anti-communism wrapped up in a progressive agenda. In fact the 'Third Force' was integral part of the new policy and Bevin's wider hopes for the direction of British foreign policy at this particular time. Indeed, officials in the Foreign Office were far from happy with the 'Third Force' concept but its inclusion was testament to the irresistible force of the Foreign Secretary. It is also clear that senior Labour Ministers took a close interest in both the creation, and the conduct, of the new propaganda policy. Bevin acted as a significant brake on plans proposed by senior officials in the Foreign Office before 1948, and the Foreign Secretary was closely involved in the development and conduct of anti-communist propaganda policy after the launch. The degree to which Bevin confined discussions of the more offensive aspects of British propaganda to a small informal group of Ministers reflected real divisions in the Labour Party and the Cabinet regarding British policy towards the Soviet bloc. However, it is also evident that views in Cabinet hardened significantly following the Czech coup of April 1948, and suggestions in Cabinet for political warfare against the Soviet Union went some way beyond what Bevin was prepared to sanction at that time. Moreover, one of the notable features of Britain's anti-communist propaganda policy was the extent to which senior politicians were actively involved. The campaign was launched in a series of speeches by Attlee, Morrison and Bevin, and Attlee in particular was 'glad to lend all the assistance in my power' to the anti-communist propaganda campaign.[5] The Foreign Office Minister, Christopher Mayhew, took a close interest in the new propaganda policy and was instrumental in formulating plans for a coordinated counter-offensive with Britain's European allies; and, from 1951, Patrick Gordon Walker, the Secretary of State for Commonwealth Relations, presided over plans for 'a renewed and vigorous information campaign.' Churchill, of course, had a legendary appetite for covert activity, and covert propaganda was no exception. Churchill's wartime Private Secretary, John Peck, was head of the IRD from 1951, and even fairly lowly officials in the IRD have testified to Churchill's personal interest in their work.[6] Churchill's own appreciation of the role of propaganda in international affairs was strongly rooted in his wartime experience and he was more willing to embrace offensive methods than his Labour predecessors.

It is also clear that, irrespective of the views of senior official in Whitehall, the new propaganda policy was driven forward by a series of Cold War crises. The immediate trigger for the adoption of the new propaganda policy was the creation of the Cominform and the breakdown of the Council of Foreign Ministers meetings in

London in 1947. The Czech coup had a profound impact on opinion in the Labour Party and prompted a sea change of opinion in the Cabinet. The Berlin blockade heralded the end of 'Third Force' propaganda, and the adoption of a more Atlanticist approach to anti-communist propaganda. Most significantly, the Korean War hangs over the period from 1950 to 1953. The war in Korea, coupled with the problems of British Imperial decline in India and Malaya, prompted an expansive British anti-communist campaign in Asia and increased British cooperation with the USA. The Korean War also led to a dramatic increase in British defence spending, and corresponding cuts in other areas of government expenditure, including overseas information activities. Faced with difficult choices over spending priorities, issues of national security were naturally given precedence and, from 1951, all British overseas propaganda was geared towards the Cold War.

Beyond these defining factors, officials did, of course, play a central role in the day-to-day conduct of British anti-communist propaganda. The IRD's methods were informed by Foreign Office experience of propaganda in two World Wars. This experience dictated that the most effective propaganda was the truth and that propaganda of any kind was most likely to be believed if it was not seen to emanate from an official source. Consequently, the IRD's work was well researched and authoritative. It was also disseminated on a discreet basis, to be used unattributably. The Foreign Office, however, was uncomfortable with certain aspects of the new propaganda policy and the policy was gradually modified to reflect Foreign Office experience. The idea of attacking capitalism was never a sensible proposition and officials in the Foreign Office had few qualms about dismissing it in practice. More significant was the shift from targeting mass opinion towards a propaganda campaign directed at opinion-formers. The Foreign Office was more accustomed to targeting élite opinion, according to the principle that, 'it is better to influence those who can influence others than to attempt a direct appeal to the mass of the population.'[7] From the beginning, the IRD's output was a little too detailed and scholarly to appeal to mass opinion. Although genuine and imaginative attempts were made to develop propaganda with mass appeal, most notably in the Middle East and South-East Asia, the Foreign Office gradually shifted back to its traditional position of targeting leaders of opinion.

It is also clear that officials in the Foreign Office had few reservations about directing anti-communist activities at home. In the aftermath of the War there was growing concern in Whitehall about the depth of pro-Soviet sentiment in Britain, and the Foreign Office Russia Committee made a number of suggestions to counter this trend. The new propaganda policy was effectively launched in a series of ministerial speeches in Britain, and IRD material was from the start distributed to selected Ministers, MPs and leading figures in the trades union and cooperative movement in Britain. However, it is clear that the material which passed through these channels was primarily directed towards an international audience. At an early stage, Christopher Mayhew grasped that statements made by prominent parliamentarians in Britain were quickly reported around the world. The IRD's primary contact in the Labour Party, Denis Healey, was Secretary of the Party's International Department, and was expected to distribute IRD material to his contacts on the left across Europe. Similarly, the IRD's early contacts with the TUC were primarily intended to counter communist influence in the international trade union movement. Indeed, it was in seeking to counter communist influence in international organizations that the IRD became most closely involved in the domestic arena. As the department sought to counter communist influence among certain specific groups – trades unions, intellectuals, youth and students – the lines between domestic and international propaganda became blurred. The department undoubtedly established links with a large number of individuals and groups in Britain, whom the IRD sought to help in keeping their own institutions 'free from infection.'[8] The IRD also sought to make life difficult for those who knowingly accepted invitations to communist conferences abroad. However, while the IRD sought to counter reactionary views, there is no evidence of a coordinated campaign primarily directed at the manufacture of public opinion in Britain. Officials in the Foreign Office had no wish to preside over some kind of British Macarthyism. The IRD positively avoided support for right-wing groups and the IRD head, John Peck, was harshly critical of the quest by some elements in the USA for 'ideological purity of public opinion...'[9] Indeed, far from seeking to undermine the left in Britain, the IRD actively worked to convince the USA that the British Left was not susceptible to communist influence.

The Foreign Office also found the positive side of the new propaganda policy problematic. The positive aspect of the new propaganda policy was treated separately from its negative anti-communist aspect. The IRD was tasked with coordinating anti-communist propaganda and was never asked to produce positive propaganda. This is a significant point, because the IRD has often been castigated for ignoring the positive side of the new propaganda policy. The positive projection of British values and the merits of a British-led 'Third Force' were the responsibility of a new Foreign Office working party on the 'spiritual aspects of the Western Union.' This work continued alongside, but independently from, the anti-communist work of the IRD. Although the idea of a British-led 'Third Force,' independent of the USA, ultimately proved untenable, perhaps the biggest blow to Britain's positive propaganda work was financial. Budgetary constraints led to severe cuts in Britain's overseas propaganda work, and positive propaganda bore the brunt of these cuts. As the Cold War intensified only direct anti-communist propaganda was considered essential. By 1951, all British propaganda, both at home and abroad was directed towards fighting the Cold War.

In one important respect, however, the IRD did seek to promote a 'Third Force' propaganda campaign. Although the department was not concerned with the positive projection of the 'Western Union' it did seek to give a lead to the forces of anti-communism in Europe and Asia by providing an arsenal of anti-communist propaganda for Britain's allies. The IRD established a complex series of arrangements for cooperating with foreign governments in the field of anti-communist propaganda. It also provided a vast amount of anti-communist material to individuals and organizations in friendly countries sometimes with the knowledge of the host government. If this campaign was not always conducted independently of the USA, it was certainly led by Britain. While the USA launched campaigns to counter-communism in key crisis points such as Italy, France and Korea, the IRD's campaign to counter communism in the free world was global, highly organized, and coordinated. If there was, in any sense, a 'Third Force' propaganda campaign, this was it.

Nevertheless, perhaps the most remarkable aspect of Britain's anti-communist propaganda policy was the extent of cooperation with the USA. In this, as in the creation of the policy itself, the driving force was not official opinion in Whitehall, but a combination of interests, precedent and circumstance. In his masterly study of

Anglo-American code-breaking in the Second World War, Bradley F. Smith observes that the extension of Britain's secret special relationship with the USA into the post-war years:

> ... was not the result of any secret tricks played on the people or governments of the two countries by shadowy figures who huddled in dark doorways practicing the arts of secret chicanery... The important cause-and-effect relations that operate in clandestine secret politics do not differ much from those that operate 'above the line.' Invisible men, with or without trenchcoats, did not create the postwar secret special relationship that continues to bind together Britain and the United States, for the documentary record shows that the combination of governmental self-interest, wartime precedent, and the force of circumstance came together at just the right moment to offer the secret special relationship the opportunity for an extended life.[10]

The same may be said of British and US cooperation in the field of propaganda. Even before the end of the War, Britain and the USA were exchanging plans for the post-War organization of their respective information apparatus. This exchange revealed fundamental differences of approach to the continued use of propaganda. However, faced with a sustained assault by communist propagandists, Britain and the USA developed complementary perceptions of the threat from communist propaganda and subversion and were already working together to respond to that threat in some areas prior to 1948. Given these precedents, the continuation of cooperation after 1948 is perhaps not surprising. Nevertheless, it is also clear that the same important factors which led to the decline of Bevin's hopes for a British-led 'Third Force' in international affairs, and the creation of NATO, also led to closer Anglo-American cooperation in the field of propaganda. Britain's attempts to lead a coordinated counter-offensive to communist propaganda ultimately foundered because none of Britain's allies in Europe or Asia had a propaganda apparatus comparable with that of Britain, or capable of responding to the Soviet propaganda machine. Only the USA had the inclination and the resources to pursue a similar policy for responding to communist propaganda.

However, as Smith adds, 'once the massive and powerful general factors had done their work... then new circumstances were created in which invisible men could ply their trade in ways the public at large, and most government leaders could not see or understand.'[11] Similarly, British and US officials developed an extensive network of formal and informal arrangements for cooperation in the field of anti-communist propaganda which was far greater than has previously been appreciated. It is extraordinary that only days after the Cabinet approved a Memo which stated that it was up to Britain, 'not the Americans,' to give the lead to the forces of anti-communism, and which openly criticised US propaganda, the same document was being shown to American information staff in both London and Washington.[12] Moreover, cooperation in the field began almost immediately, in Italy, in March 1948. In contrast with cooperation with other powers, British cooperation with the USA involved the formal exchange of propaganda material between London and Washington and a great deal of close and informal contact between information staff in British and US missions around the world. The USA was keen to involve Britain in some of their own more ambitious projects, most notably Radio Free Europe and the radio 'Ring Plan'. The policy for cooperation developed at a regular meetings between senior officials from the Foreign Office and US propaganda agencies, which took place in February 1948, October 1948, January 1950, May 1950, May 1951 and April 1952. In between these high-level summits there were numerous trips between London and Washington by representatives of the Foreign Office, the State Department, the CIA, the VOA and the RFE. Cooperation expanded considerably in 1950, following the launch of the American 'Campaign of Truth'. Information liaison officers were appointed to the British and US Embassies in Washington and London, and a policy of 'close and continuous liaison' was agreed with a view to developing, 'common lines of information policy, planning and conduct of operations.'[13]

Perhaps the most remarkable manifestation of this cooperation was the work of Adam Watson, the British Information Liaison Officer in Washington. Watson was one of those officials, like Sir John Dill or Oliver Franks, who seem to embody the 'Special Relationship' between Britain and the USA. Watson was the linchpin of British and US cooperation in the field of anti-communist propaganda. He assiduously cultivated contacts in the State Department, the CIA, the VOA, the RFE and, ultimately, the White House. The extent of Watson's contacts may be illustrated by one, not untypical, letter to the Foreign Office from July 1953, in the course of which Watson referred to a telephone call from George Kennan, a ride from the airport with the US Ambassador to Moscow, Chip Bohlen, dinner with Walter Bedell Smith, a conference at the State Department with John Foster Dulles and C.D. Jackson, and a further encounter with Bohlen over dinner at Dulles's house.[14] Under both Truman and Eisenhower, every aspect of US propaganda, overt and covert, was discussed with Watson. If anything, Watson's influence expanded under the Eisenhower Administration, when his friends C.D. Jackson and Nelson Rockefeller rose to prominent positions in the new administration. Watson provided an important element of continuity at a time when officials in the Foreign Office, and in the IRD in particular, were growing increasingly concerned at the complexion of US psychological warfare; and it is clear that senior US officials were happy to discuss matters with Watson which they would not be prepared to broach in conversation with representatives of the British government.

It has been generally assumed that Britain's anti-communist propaganda effort was soon eclipsed by the greater resources of the USA, and that British propaganda was redirected against other 'anti-British' targets.[15] It is now clear that although Britain clearly took the lead in providing a coordinated global response to communist propaganda in 1948, it did not merely hand the baton to the USA in the 1950s. Britain retained and expanded its anti-communist propaganda policy and machinery, and expanded cooperation with the USA. In many respects, British and US approaches to anti-communist propaganda were complementary. Initially, although this was not intentional, Britain and the USA effectively divided the world between them for the purposes of conducting anti-communist propaganda. Although the anti-communist propaganda policies of both nations was global in scale, Britain concentrated its effort on countering communism in the free world while the principal focus of US propaganda was the Soviet Union and the Iron Curtain countries.

Similarly, although Britain and the USA adopted quite different methods, these methods were often combined to good effect. Britain favoured a discreet approach, whereas US propaganda was often more overt, or at least more prominent, conducted through large broadcasting operations such as Radio Free Europe. It has been suggested that the IRD could not compete with the din of the CIA's 'mighty Wurlitzer.'[16] However, as officials in the Foreign Office were keenly aware, the scale of the output did not necessarily guarantee its impact, and there were benefits in both approaches. Britain's more discreet approach was more appropriate for countering communism in the free world. The more bold propaganda of the Americans was more suited to bolstering resistance behind the Iron Curtain. Moreover, the two approaches were not mutually exclusive. A Foreign Office review of British and US cooperation completed in 1950 observed:

> It seems that our general approach is often somewhat different from that of the Americans and, on the whole, the discreet and personal approach of our Information Officers gets more material effectively placed than the American reliance on volume of output. The rather aggressive portrayal of the American way of life is not always welcome and may be self-defeating. In any case it is preferable to maintain the two independent lines of approach, since both together certainly cover more ground than either could hope to do working alone.[17]

It has not been the purpose of this book to assess the effectiveness of the IRD's campaign. Nevertheless, the evidence suggests that, through its discreet approach, the IRD achieved some remarkable successes. The department's first set-piece campaign, the publication of documents and a series of ministerial speeches to publicize the use of forced labour in the Soviet Union, received widespread coverage in the press around the world, and in every national newspaper in Britain. *The Daily Telegraph*, the IRD recorded, 'splashed on page 1 a story from its Vienna Correspondent giving details of life in forced labour camps allegedly told by people who have escaped, but in fact all based on various IRD papers.'[18] Numerous examples of a similar use of IRD material may be found in the IRD's day-to-day work. In June 1949, the British information service in Karachi reported that it had been able to place in the local media 100 per cent of everything issued by the IRD.[19] The department also commissioned and distributed material on Soviet affairs by some of the most prominent commentators of the day, including Harold Laski, A.J.P. Taylor, Bertrand Russell, Woodrow Wyatt, R.H.S. Crossman and Leonard Schapiro.[20] Perhaps most remarkable, was the Nicholls Committee's finding that, 'in one major European country large passages of the Prime Minister's speeches during the last two years have been lifted bodily from IRD publications.'[21]

The British were also particularly good at concealing the existence of their anti-communist propaganda policy and operations. Given the scale of its activities, it is remarkable that the IRD's existence was not more widely known. The restriction forbidding disclosure of the fact that Britain was distributing anti-communist material through official channels was lifted in December 1949, but there had been no change in the IRD's methods.[22] In 1951, the IRD proudly boasted that 'during the three years since it was set up the fact that His Majesty's Government is conducting anti-communist publicity operations has been successfully concealed from the public at home and abroad.'[23] This was not entirely true: references to the British anti-communist propaganda campaign had appeared in the Eastern European press in 1948. More remarkably, Barrett's trip to London, in May 1950, had been prominently featured in the *New York Times*, and was followed by an article in *Pravda*.[24] In September 1951, the IRD head, John Peck, told a meeting of European information officers, 'the communists themselves were aware of what we were doing.' The department's origins were certainly revealed to the Russians by Guy Burgess and, unbeknown to Peck, Kim Philby was fully apprised of the extensive arrangement for cooperation in Washington.[25] Nevertheless, Peck added, 'it was essential to avoid public discussion at home or abroad of H.M.G.'s anti-communist work.'[26] The Foreign Office remained committed to a discreet strategy based on the assumption that, 'the public has a tendency to react against officially issued information,' and the IRD's methods remained unchanged throughout the department's existence.[27]

British and US officials were keenly aware of the value of each others anti-communist propaganda, although the Americans were a good deal more complimentary about the IRD's work than British officials were about US propaganda. Both also recognized the value of maintaining their own independent propaganda campaigns. The policy for cooperation was characterized in a Foreign Office circular to British missions in May 1948, as 'shooting into the same target from rather different angles.'[28] This aphorism was used frequently to describe the relationship between British and US propaganda throughout the period. By maintaining 'individuality of output' in anti-communist propaganda, Britain and the USA sought to concentrate their fire along as broad a front as possible. The policy had the added advantage of presenting the communists two targets to aim at in response.

Finally, rather than shifting its focus to 'anti-anti-British' operations, through its cooperation with the USA, the IRD was drawn towards a more offensive anti-communist propaganda policy. British anti-communist propaganda policy was both informed by, and reactive to, US plans. By 1952, the IRD had begun to develop a strategy for offensive political warfare and was advocating an increase in British propaganda directed over the Iron Curtain. These proposals were motivated, at least in part, by the desire to exert a restraining influence over some of the USA's more provocative plans. Nevertheless, it is clear that, in the 1950s, Britain went some way with the USA in the development of a more offensive strategy for the use of propaganda to bring an end to communism in the Soviet bloc. The British strategy of political warfare was, however, at the same time more ambitious, and less provocative, than US psychological warfare planning. Well into the 1950s, the Americans held out the hope of detaching a satellite state, while British propaganda sought the collapse of communism in the Soviet Union itself. While the Americans sought to bolster the forces of resistance which might stimulate revolution in the Communist bloc, British propaganda sought a fundamental evolution of the regime from above.

This study has traced the origins of Britain's anti-communist propaganda policy. It has established the organization and the methods of Britain's principal Cold War propaganda agency, the Information Research Department, and it has stressed the importance of cooperation between Britain and the USA in the field of anti-communist propaganda. The evolution of Britain's propaganda policy throughout the Cold War must be the subject of further studies. In 1953, the Drogheda enquiry concluded that the 'struggle for men's minds' was likely to continue for some time, and it is clear that propaganda remained a central and increasingly important feature of

British foreign policy throughout the Cold War.[29] In 1964, the Plowden Committee on overseas representation concluded that it was 'in the general interest that Britain's voice should continue to be heard and to carry weight in the world.' Moreover, it added, the 'spread of communism' had put upon Britain's 'representational services a new range of activities and problems on a world scale.'[30] The IRD was dissolved in 1977, at the height of *détente*, by the Labour Government on the instructions of Foreign Secretary, David Owen, because its operational style, 'got out of step with our more open democracy.'[31] However, it is evident that significant elements of the department survived in the Foreign Office and the SIS.[32] *Détente*, moreover, was short lived and British and US anti-communist propaganda enjoyed a revival, along with Anglo-American relations, under Margaret Thatcher and Ronald Reagan. In May 1980, in the wake of the Soviet invasion of Afghanistan, Thatcher said that, because modern weapons were so hideous, she did not think that Soviet action justified taking the world to the brink of war. The West, she proposed, should concentrate on methods short of war. It was time, she said, for 'a massive propaganda campaign of a kind we have never mounted yet.'[33] Two years later, in a speech before the British Houses of Parliament, President Reagan called for a new 'crusade for freedom.'[34] British and US cooperation in the field of anti-communist propaganda may well prove to have been as close at the end of the Cold War as it was at its start.

Notes

1. Central Office of Information, Overseas Production Conference (OP46)1, 30 April 1946, GN1/5 Part A, INF12/61, PRO.
2. Future Foreign Publicity Policy, 4 January 1948, CP(48)8, CAB 129/23, PRO.
3. Anti-Communist Propaganda, Minutes of meeting held on 12 March 1948, CAB 21/2745, PRO.
4. S. Dorril, 'The Puppet Masters', *The Guardian*, 18 August 1995; S. Jenkins, 'Spies Bungling for Britain', *The Times*, 19 August 1995; P. Weiler, *British Labour and the Cold War* (Stanford, CA: Stanford University Press, 1988).
5. Attlee to Mayhew, 20 July 1948, PR45/142/913G, FO 1110/41, PRO.
6. Weldon, *Auto Da Fay*, p. 243.
7. Taylor, *British Propaganda in the Twentieth Century*, p. 27.
8. Peck to Watson, 7 February 1952, PR89/49, FO 1110/516, PRO.
9. Brief for discussion with Dulles and Stassen, Political Warfare, 28 January 1953.
10. B.F. Smith, *The Ultra-Magic Deals and the Most Secret Special Relationship, 1940–1946* (Novato, CA: Presido Press, 1993), p. 227.
11. *Ibid.*
12. Future Foreign Publicity Policy, 4 January 1948, CP(48)8, CAB 129/23, PRO.
13. Notes on the First Meeting between Warner and Barrett at London, May 20, 1950, *FRUS, 1950*, vol. 3, *Western Europe*, p. 1,644; Circular airgram, Secretary of State to Certain Diplomatic and Consular Offices, 15 July 1950, *FRUS, 1950*, vol. 4, p. 318.
14. Watson to Nicholls, 17 July 1953, PRG45/122, FO 1110/587, PRO.
15. Lucas and Morris, 'A Very British Crusade', pp. 85–110; Wilford, 'The Information Research Department', pp. 353–69; T. Barnes, 'Democratic Deception: American Covert Operations in Postwar Europe', in D.A. Charters and M.A.J. Tugwell, *Deception Operations: Studies in the East–West Context* (London: Brassey's, 1990).
16. Barnes, 'Democratic Deception'; Wark, 'Coming in from the Cold: British Propaganda and Red Army Defectors, 1945–1952', *International History Review*, 9, 1 (1987), p. 53.
17. Anglo–US Cooperation in Information Work, J.C. Moberly, 18 December 1950, P1013/98G, FO 953/640, PRO.
18. Reports on Publicity about Forced Labour Codex, July 1949, FO 1110/277, PRO.

19 Progress Report: Information Research Department, 1st January to 31st July, 1949, FO 1110/277, PRO.
20 *Ibid.*
21 Survey of United Kingdom Publicity in Foreign Countries, Memo by the Foreign Office, 30 July 1952, GEN407/15, CAB 130/75, PRO.
22 GEN231/third meeting, Confidential Annex, 19 December 1949, Anti-Communist Propaganda, Policy and Machinery, CAB 130/37, PRO.
23 Anti-Communist Propaganda Operations, 27 July 1951, CAB 127/296, PRO.
24 See ch. 2 above; *Soviet Monitor*, 7 April 1948, AN1614, FO 371/68068, PRO; Burrows, Washington, to Warner, 15 May 1950, enclosure, '100 Voices Beamed at Soviet Planned by US and Britain', *New York Times*, 14 May 1950, P1013/25, FO 953/628, PRO; Moscow to State Department, 12 June 1950, full text of *Pravda*, 8 June 1950, 'The Mission of Edward Barrett,' 511.614/6-1250, Decimal File, State Department Central Files, 1950–1954, RG 59, NARA.
25 Adam Watson, telephone interview with author, October 2003.
26 Minutes of Western European Information Officers Conference, 12–14 September 1951, PR121/7, FO 1110/458, PRO.
27 Anti-Communist Propaganda Operations, 27 July 1951, CAB 127/296, PRO.
28 Foreign Office circular letter, 12 May 1948, PR229/1/G, FO 1110/6, PRO.
29 Overseas Information Services, Report of The Drogheda Committee, C(53)305, 13 November 1953, PREM 11/691, PRO.
30 Cmnd.2276, *Report of the Committee on Representational Services Overseas, 1962–63* (London: HMSO, February 1964).
31 D. Owen, *Time to Declare* (London: Michael Joseph, 1991), pp. 347–8. Owen disputes Brian Crozier's claim that the decision to dissolve the IRD was based on concerns in the Labour Party regarding the right-wing complexion of some of the IRD's contacts: see B. Crozier, *Free Agent: The Unseen War 1941–1991* (London: Harper Collins, 1993), pp. 119–21; Lord Owen letter to author, 7 October 1996.
32 Lord Owen, letter to author, 7 October 1996; J. Bloch and P. Fitzgerald, *British Intelligence and Covert Action* (London: Junction Books, 1983), pp. 100–1.
33 *The Times*, 5 May 1980, p. 1. The parallels with the creation of the IRD were not lost on the press, 'Flaws Seen in Propaganda Idea', *The Times*, 6 May 1980; D. Leigh, 'The PM's Aerial Manoeuvres', *The Guardian*, 6 May 1980; P. Hennessy, 'Revival of Political Warfare', *The Times*, 1 March 1983.
34 Address to Member of the British Parliament, 8 June 1982, *Public Papers of the Presidents: Administration of Ronald Reagan, 1982*, vol. 1 (Washington, DC: US GPO), pp. 742–8. For Thatcher's reaction, see M. Thatcher, *The Downing Street Years* (London: Harper Collins, 1993), pp. 257–8. For the implications for American propaganda, see L. Alexandre, *The Voice of America: From Detente to the Reagan Doctrine* (Norwood, NJ: Ablex Publishing, 1988).

Bibliography

Unpublished documents

Public Record Office, Ruskin Avenue, Kew, Surrey, UK

CAB 21 Cabinet Office: Registered Files
CAB 102 Cabinet Office: Official Histories
CAB 127 Cabinet Office: Private Papers: Lord Gordon-Walker
CAB 128 Cabinet: Minutes
CAB 129 Cabinet: Memoranda
CAB 130 Cabinet Committees
CO 537 Colonial Office: Correspondence
DO 35 Commonwealth Relations Office: Correspondence
DEFE 5 Ministry of Defence: Chiefs of Staff Committee, Memoranda
DEFE 11 Ministry of Defence: Chiefs of Staff Committee, Registered Files
FO 366 Foreign Office: Chief Clerk's Department Papers
FO 370 Foreign Office: Research Department Memoranda
FO 371 Foreign Office: General Correspondence
FO 800 Foreign Office: Private Offices: Bevin Papers; Morrison Papers
FO 817 Foreign Office: Embassy Files, Czechoslovakia
FO 898 Political Warfare Executive Files
FO 924 Foreign Office: Cultural Relations Department Papers
FO 930 Foreign Office: Records of Information Departments, 1945–1947
FO 953 Foreign Office: Records of Information Departments, 1947–1954
FO 975 Foreign Office: IRD, Information Reports
FO 1059 Foreign Office: IRD 'Interpreter' Briefs
FO 1110 Foreign Office: Records of the Information Research Department
INF 12 Central Office of Information, Registered Files
LAB 13 Ministry of Labour, Overseas Department Papers
PREM 8 Prime Minister's Office Correspondence and Papers, 1945–51
PREM 11 Prime Minister's Office Correspondence and Papers, 1951–1964
WO 216 War Office: Chief of Imperial General Staff, Papers

Labour Party Archives, National Museum of Labour History, Princess street, Manchester, UK

Labour Party International Department Papers
Labour Party General Election Manifestos and Miscellaneous Pamphlets

Liddell Hart Centre for Military Archives, King's College, London, UK

US Document Collection on Microfilm
Records of the Joint Chiefs of Staff, 1946–53
Documents of the National Security Council, 1947–1954

US National Archive and Record Administration, College Park, MD, USA

RG 59 Department of State Central Files, 1945–1954
RG 59 Records of Charles E. Bohlen, 1942–1952
RG 59 Lot File No. 52 D342 Bureau of Public Affairs, Office Files of Assistant Secretary Edward W. Barrett, 1950–51
RG 59 Lot File No. 62 D333 Executive Secretariat, Psychological Strategy Board Working File, 1951–53
RG 59 Lot File No. 62 D430 Records of State Department Participation in the Operations Coordinating Board and national Security Council, 1947–1963
RG 263 CIA 'Studies in Intelligence'
RG 273 National Security Council Papers

Harry S. Truman Library, Independence, MO, USA

President's Secretary's Files (PSF), 1945–53
White House Central Files (WHCF), 1945–53
    Official File (OF)
    Confidential File (CF)
Staff Member and Office Files (SMOF)
    Psychological Strategy Board (PSB) Files, 1951–53
    National Security Council (NSC) Files, 1947–53
    Naval Aide to the President Files, 1945–53
    Charles W. Jackson Files
Oral History Collection
Vertical File: Clippings Collection

Dwight D. Eisenhower Library, Abilene, KS, USA

Dwight D. Eisenhower: Papers as President, 1953–61 (Ann Whitman File)
Dwight D. Eisenhower: Records as President, White House Central Files (WHCF), 1953–61
White House Office, National Security Council Staff papers, 1948–61
    Psychological Strategy Board Central File Series
    Operations Coordinating Board Central File Series
    Operations Coordinating Board Secretariat Series
    National Security Council Registry Series, 1947–62
    Executive Secretary's Subject File Series
President's Committee on International Information Activities (Jackson Committee): Records, 1950–53
C.D. Jackson: Records, 1953–54
Oral History Collection

Lauinger Library, *Georgetown University, Washington, DC, USA*

Foreign Affairs Oral History Program

Private papers

Dean Acheson Papers, Harry S. Truman Library
John Foster Dulles Papers, Dwight D. Eisenhower Library
George M. Elsey Papers, Harry S. Truman Library
G.E.R. Gedye Papers, Imperial War Museum, London
Gordon Gray Papers, Harry S. Truman Library
Charles Hulten Papers, Harry S. Truman Library
Ismay papers, Liddell Hart Centre, King's College, London
C.D. Jackson Papers, Dwight D. Eisenhower Library
Robert F. Kelley Papers, Georgetown University, Washington, DC
Malcolm MacDonald Papers, Durham University
Morgan Phillips Papers, National Museum of Labour History, Manchester
Bertrand Russell Papers, MacMaster University Library
Howland H. Sargeant Papers, Harry S. Truman Library
Charles W. Thayer Papers, Harry S. Truman Library
C.M. Woodhouse Papers, Liddell Hart Centre for Military Archives, King's College London

Published documents

UK Parliamentary papers

House of Commons: Debates.
House of Lords: Debates.
Cmnd.6852, *White Paper on Broadcasting* (London: HMSO, 1946).
Cmnd.6975, *Copy of Licence and Agreement between HM Postmaster General and the BBC* (London: HMSO, 1946).
Cmnd.7567, *Central Office of Information (COI) Annual Report 1947–48* (London: HMSO, 1948).
Cmnd.7616, *Report of the Tribunal Appointed to Inquire into Allegations Reflecting on the Official Conduct of Ministers of the Crown and other Public Servants*, 'The Lynskey Tribunal' (London: HMSO, January 1949).
Cmnd.7830, *COI Annual Report, 1948–49* (London: HMSO, 1949).
Cmnd.7836, *Cost of Home Information Services*, 'The French Committee' (London: HMSO, 1949).
Cmnd.7974 *Broadcasting from Ceylon* (London: HMSO, 1950).
Cmnd.8081, *COI Annual Report, 1949–50* (London: HMSO, 1950).
Cmnd.8116, *Report of the Broadcasting Committee 1949* (London: HMSO, 1951).
Cmnd.8267, *Government Information Services: Estimated Expenditure, 1951–52* (London: HMSO, June 1951).
Cmnd.8578, *Government Information Services: Estimated Expenditure, 1952–53* (London: HMSO, 1952).
Cmnd.8872, *The Festival of Britain 1951* (London: HMSO, 1953).
Cmnd.8949, *Government Information Services: Estimated Expenditure, 1953–54* (London: HMSO, 1953).
Cmnd.9138, *Summary of the Report of the Independent Committee of Enquiry into the Overseas Information Services*, 'The Drogheda Report' (London: HMSO, 1954).

Cmnd.9192, *Government Information Services: Estimated Expenditure, 1954–55* (London: HMSO, 1954).
Cmnd.225, *White Paper on Overseas Information* (London: HMSO, 1957).
Cmnd.685, *Overseas Information Services* (London: HMSO, 1959).
Cmnd.2276, *Report of Committee on Overseas Representation, 1962–63* (London: HMSO, 1964).
Cmnd.4107, *Report of the Review Commission on Overseas Representation 1968/69*, 'The Duncan Report' (London: HMSO, 1969).
Cmnd.2290, *White Paper on Open Government* (London: HMSO, 1993).
Fourth Report from the Expenditure Committee (Defence and External Affairs Sub-Committee): The Central Policy Review Staff Review of Overseas Representation, Session 1977–78, Parliamentary Paper 286–1, lxxix.

UK non-parliamentary official publications

The Foreign Office List and Diplomatic and Consular Yearbook (London: Harrison & Sons Ltd, 1950–1964).
Diplomatic Service List (London: HMSO, 1965–1978).
The Lord Chancellor's Advisory Council on Public Records, *Review of Security Service Selection Criteria* (December 1998).

US Congressional papers

Committee on Foreign Affairs, *The United States Information and Educational Exchange Program of 1948*, 80th Congress, 2nd Session, H. Rept. 3342, 1948 (Washington, DC: Government Printing Office, 1948).
Committee on Foreign Affairs, *The United States Information Service in Europe*, Report of the Special Mundt Subcommittee, 80th Congress, 2nd Session, 1948 (Washington, DC: Government Printing Office, 1948).
Select Committee on Intelligence, Subcommittee on Oversight, *The CIA and the Media*, 95th Congress, 1st & 2nd Sessions, 1978 (Washington, DC: Government Printing Office, 1978).
Subcommittee on Foreign Relations, *Expanded International Information and Education Program*, 81st Congress, 2nd Session, S. Rept. 243, 1950 (Washington, DC: Government Printing Office, 1950).
Committee on Government Operations, *Establishing USIA*, 82nd Congress, 1st Session, 1952 (Washington, DC: Government Printing Office, 1953).
Committee on Appropriations, *The Objectives of the United States Information Program*, 82nd Congress, 2nd Session, 1952 (Washington, DC: Government Printing Office, 1952).
Select Committee to Study Governmental Operations with Respect to Intelligence, *Final Report [Book 1: Foreign and Military Intelligence; Book 4: Supplementary Detailed Staff Reports on Foreign and Military Intelligence; Book 6: Supplementary Reports on Intelligence Activities]*, 'The Church Committee', 94th Congress, 2nd Session, 1976 (Washington, DC: Government Printing Office, 1976).

Published documentary collections

Andrew, C.M. (ed.), *The Security Service, 1908–1945: The Official History* (London: PRO, 2001).
Aldrich, R.J. (ed.), *Espionage, Security and Intelligence in Britain, 1945–1970* (Manchester: Manchester University Press, 1998).
Bullen, R. and Pelly, M.E. (eds), *Documents on British Policy Overseas:* series 1, vol. 4, *Britain and America: Atomic Energy, Bases and Food, 12 December 1945–31 July 1946* (London: HMSO, 1987).

Bullen, R. and Pelly, M.E. (eds), *Documents on British Policy Overseas:* series 2, vol. 2, *The London Conferences: Anglo-American Relations and Cold War Strategy, January–June 1950* (London: HMSO, 1987).

Department of State Bulletin, various volumes, 1948–1953 (Washington, DC: Government Printing Office, 1948–53).

Etzold, T.H. and Gaddis, J.L. (eds), *Containment: Documents on American Foreign Policy and Strategy, 1945–50* (New York: Columbia University Press, 1978).

Foreign Relations of the United States (FRUS), various volumes, 1945–1957 (Washington, DC: Government Printing Office, 1969–1987).

Koch, S.A. (ed.), *CIA Cold War Records: Selected Estimates on the Soviet Union, 1950–1959* (Washington, DC: Center for the Study of Intelligence, 1993).

Kuhns, W.J. (ed.), *Assessing the Soviet Threat: The Early Cold War Years* (Washington, DC: Center for the Study of Intelligence, 1997).

Nelson, A.K. (ed.), *The State Department Policy Planning Staff Papers, 1947–1949*, 3 vols, (New York: Garland Publishing, Inc., 1983).

Pelly, M.E., Yasamee, H.J. and Hamilton, K.A. (eds), *Documents on British Policy Overseas*: series 1, vol. 6, *Eastern Europe, August 1945–April 1946* (London: HMSO, 1991).

Public Papers of the President: Harry S. Truman, 1946–1953, 7 vols (Washington, DC: Government Printing Office, 1961–66).

Public Papers of the President: Dwight D. Eisenhower, 1953–54, 2 vols (Washington, DC: Government Printing Office, 1960).

Public Papers of the Presidents: Administrations of Ronald Reagan 1982, vol. 1 (Washington, DC: Government Printing Office, 1982).

Warner, M. (ed.), *CIA Cold War Records: The CIA Under Harry Truman* (Washington, DC: CIA Center for the Study of Intelligence, 1994).

Yasamee, H.J. and Hamilton, K.A. (eds), *Documents on British Policy Overseas*: series I, vol. 7, *The United Nations: Iran, Cold War and World Organisation, 1946–1947* (London: HMSO, 1995).

Yasamee, H.J. and Hamilton, K.A. (eds), *Documents on British Policy Overseas:* series 2, vol. 4, *Korea June 1950–April 1951* (London: HMSO, 1991).

Newspapers and periodicals

The Daily Express
The Daily Telegraph
The Sunday Express
The Economist
Keesing's Contemporary Archive
The Guardian
The Independent
The Independent on Sunday
The Nation
New Statesman
The New York Times
The Observer
Public Opinion Quarterly
Spectator
The Sunday Times
The Times

Memoirs, autobiographies, diaries and letters

Acheson, D., *Present at the Creation: My Years in the State Department* (New York: Norton 1969).

Amis, K., *Memoirs* (London: Hutchinson, 1991).

Beeston, R., *Looking for Trouble: The Life and Times of a Foreign Correspondent* (London: Brassey's, 1997).

Benn, T., *Conflicts of Interest, Diaries, 1977–1980* (London: Hutchinson, 1990).

Bohlen, C., *Witness to History 1929–1969* (New York: Norton, 1973).

Cavendish, A., *Inside Intelligence* (London: Collins, 1990).

Colby, W. and Forbath, P., *Honorable Men: My Life in the CIA* (London: Hutchinson, 1978).

Colville, J., *The Fringes of Power: Downing Street Diaries 1939–1955* (London: Hodder & Stoughton, 1955).

Critchlow, J., *Radio Hole in the Head/Radio Liberty: An Insider's Story of Cold War Broadcasting* (Washington, DC: American University Press, 1995).

Crozier, B., *Free Agent: The Unseen War, 1941–1991 – The Autobiography of an International Activist* (London: Harper Collins, 1993).

Davison, P. (ed.), *The Complete Works of George Orwell,* vol. 20 (London: Secker & Warburg, 1998).

Eden, A., *Full Circle* (London: Cassell, 1960).

Eisenhower, D.D., *The White House Years, 1953–1956: Mandate for Change* (New York: Doubleday, 1963).

Fyvel, T.R., *And There My Trouble Began: Uncollected Writings, 1945–85* (London: Weidenfeld & Nicolson, 1986).

Gladwyn, Lord, *The Memoirs of Lord Gladwyn* (London: Weidenfeld & Nicolson, 1972).

Gore-Booth, P., *With Great Truth and Respect* (London: Constable, 1974).

Gouzenko, I., *This Was My Choice* (London: Eyre & Spottiswoode, 1948).

Healey, D., *The Time of My Life* (London: Michael Joseph, 1989).

——, *When Shrimps Learn to Whistle* (London: Michael Joseph, 1990).

Ismay, Lord, *The Memoirs of Lord Ismay* (London: Heinemann, 1960).

James, R.R. (ed.), *Churchill Speaks: Winston S. Churchill in Peace and War, Collected Speeches, 1897–1963* (Leicester: Windward, 1980).

Kennan, G.F., *Memoirs 1925–1950* (New York: Pantheon Books, 1967).

——, *Memoirs 1950–1963* (New York: Pantheon Books, 1983).

Kirkpatrick, I., *The Inner Circle* (London: Macmillan, 1959).

Kravchenko, V., *I Chose Freedom: The Personal and Political Life of a Soviet Official* (London: Robert Hale, 1949).

Marett, R., *Through the Back Door: An Inside View of Britain's Overseas Information Service* (London: Pergamon Press, 1968).

Mayhew, C., *Time to Explain: An Autobiography* (London: Hutchinson, 1987).

——, *Party Games* (London: Hutchinson, 1969).

——, *A War of Words: A Cold War Witness* (London: I.B. Tauris, 1998).

Meyer, C., *Facing Reality: From World Federalism to the CIA* (New York: Harper Row, 1980).

Modin, Y., *My Five Cambridge Friends* (London: Headline, 1994).

Morrison, H., *Herbert Morrison: An Autobiography* (London: Odhams Press, 1960).

Nitze, P.H., *From Hiroshima to Glasnost: At the Centre of Decision – A Memoir* (London: Weidenfeld & Nicolson, 1989).

Owen, D., *Time to Declare* (London: Michael Joseph, 1991).

Parrott, C., *The Serpent and the Nightingale* (London: Faber & Faber, 1977).

Philby, K., *My Silent War* (London: MacGibbon & Kee, 1968).

Rimington, S., *Open Secret* (London: Hutchinson, 2001).

Schuckburgh, E., *Descent to Suez: Diaries, 1951–1956* (London: Weidenfeld & Nicolson, 1986).

Shinwell, E., *Conflict without Malice: An Autobiography* (London: Odhams Press, 1955).

Simpson, J., *Strange Places, Questionable People* (London: Macmillan, 1998).

Smith, J.B., *Portrait of a Cold Warrior* (New York: Putnam, 1976).

Smith, R.J., *The Unknown CIA: My Three Decades With The Agency* (New York: Pergamon-Brassey's, 1989).

Strong, K., *Intelligence at the Top: The Recollections of an Intelligence Officer* (London: Cassell, 1968).

Taylor, A.J.P., *A Personal History* (London: Hamish Hamilton, 1983).

Thatcher, M., *The Downing Street Years* (London: Harper Collins, 1993).

Tokaev, G.A., *Comrade X* (London: Harvill Press, 1956).

Truman, H.S., *Years of Trial and Hope: Memoirs, 1946–1952* (New York: Doubleday, 1956).

Urban, G.R., *Radio Free Europe and the Pursuit of Democracy: My War Within the Cold War* (London: Yale University Press, 1998).

Walden, G., *Lucky George: Memoirs of an Anti-Politician* (London: Allen Lane, 1999).

Weldon, F., *Auto Da Fay* (London: Flamingo, 2002).

Wheeler-Bennett, J. (ed.), *Action This Day: Working with Churchill* (London: Macmillan, 1968).

Williams, F. (ed.), *A Prime Minister Remembers: The War and Post War Memoirs of the Right Honourable Earl Attlee* (London: Heinemann, 1961).

Woodhouse, C.M., *Something Ventured* (London: Granada, 1982).

Worsthorne, P., *Tricks of Memory: An Autobiography* (London: Weidenfeld & Nicolson, 1993).

Young, K. (ed.), *The Diaries of Sir Robert Bruce Lockhart:* vol. 2, *1939–65* (London: Macmillan, 1980).

Secondary works

Articles

Adamthwaite, A., 'Britain and the World 1945–9: The View from the Foreign Office', *International Affairs*, 61, 2 (1985), pp. 223–35.

——, ' "Nation Shall Speak Peace Unto Nation": The BBC's Response to Peace and Defence Issues, 1945–58', *Contemporary Record*, 7, 3 (1993), pp. 557–77.

Adler, L. and Paterson, T., 'Red Fascism: The Merger of Nazi Germany and Soviet Russia in the American Image of Totalitarianism', *American Historical Review*, 75 (1970), p. 1,046.

Aldrich, R. 'OSS, CIA and European Unity: The American Committee on United Europe, 1948–1960', *Diplomacy and Statecraft*, 8, 1 (1997), pp. 184–227.

——, 'British Intelligence and the Anglo-American "Special Relationship" during the Cold War', *Review of International Studies*, 24 (1998), pp. 331–51.

——, 'Never-Never Land and Wonderland? British and American Policy on Intelligence Archives', *Contemporary Record*, 8, 1 (1994), pp. 133–52.

——, 'The Waldegrave Initiative and Secret Service Archives: New Materials and New Policies', *Intelligence and National Security*, 10, 1 (1995), pp. 192–7.

——, 'Did Waldegrave Work? The Impact of Open Government Upon British History', *Twentieth Century British History*, 9, 1 (1998), pp. 111–26.

——, ' "Grow Your Own" Cold War Intelligence and History Supermarkets', *Intelligence and National Security*, 17, 1 (2002), pp. 135–52.

Anderson, E.E., 'The Security Dilemma and Covert Action: The Truman Years', *International Journal of Intelligence and Counterintelligence*, 11, 4 (1998–99), pp. 403–27.

Andrew, C.M., 'Whitehall, Washington and the Intelligence Services', *International Affairs*, 53, 3 (1977), pp. 390–404.

Anstey, C., 'The Projection of British Socialism: Foreign Office Publicity and American Opinion 1945–50', *Journal of Contemporary History*, 19 (1984), pp. 417–51.

Attlee, C.R., 'Britain and America: Common Sense, Different Opinions', *Foreign Affairs*, 32 (1954), pp. 190–202.

Barnes, T., 'The Secret Cold War: The CIA and American Foreign Policy in Europe, 1946–56. Part I', *Historical Journal*, 24 (1981) pp. 399–415.

——, 'The Secret Cold War. Part II', *Historical Journal*, 25 (1982), pp. 649–70.

Baylis, J., 'Britain, the Brussels Pact and the Continental Commitment', *International Affairs*, 60, 4 (1984), pp. 615–30.

Baylis J. and Macmillan, A., 'The British Global Strategy Paper of 1952', *The Journal of Strategic Studies*, 16, 2 (1993), pp. 200–26.

Becker, H., 'The Nature and Consequences of Black Propaganda', *American Sociological Review*, 14 (1949), pp. 221–35.

Beloff, M., 'The Projection of Britain Abroad', *International Affairs*, 47, 3 (1965), pp. 478–89.

Bernhard, N.E., 'Clearer than Truth: Public Affairs Television and the State Department's Domestic Information Campaigns, 1947–1952', *Diplomatic History*, 21, 4 (1997), pp. 545–67.

Boehling, R., 'The Role of Culture in American Relations with Europe: The Case of the United States's Occupation of Germany', *Diplomatic History*, 23, 1 (1999), pp. 57–69.

Bogart, L., 'A Study of the Operating Assumptions of the US Information Agency', *Public Opinion Quarterly*, 19, 4 (1955–56), pp. 369–79.

Borhi, L., 'Rollback, Liberation, Containment or Inaction? US Policy and Eastern Europe in the 1950s', *Journal of Cold War Studies*, 1, 3 (1999), pp. 67–110.

Boyle, P.G., 'The British Foreign Office and American Foreign Policy, 1947–8', *Journal of American Studies*, 16, 3 (1982), pp. 373–89.

——, 'The British Foreign Office View of Soviet–American Relations, 1945–46', *Diplomatic History*, 3 (1979), pp. 307–20.

Braden, T., 'The Birth of the CIA', *American Heritage*, 28 (February 1977), pp. 4–13.

Browne, D.R., 'R.I.A.S. [East] Berlin: A Case Study of a Cold War Broadcast Operation', *Journal of Broadcasting*, 10 (1966), pp. 119–35.

Campbell, D. and Thomas, A., 'The BBC's Trade Secrets', *New Statesman* (4 July 1980), pp. 13–14.

——, 'The FO and the Eggheads', *New Statesman* (27 February 1981), pp. 13–14.

Carew, A., 'The Schism Within the World Federation of Trade Unions: Government and Trade Union Diplomacy', *International Review of Social History*, 29, 3 (1984), pp. 297–335.

——, 'The American Labour Movement in Fizzland: The Free Trade Union Committee and the CIA', *Labour History*, 39, 1 (1998), pp. 125–38.

Carruthers, S., 'A Red Under Every Bed?: Anti-Communist Propaganda and Britain's Response to Colonial Insurgency', *Contemporary Record*, 9, 2 (1995), pp. 294–318.

——, 'Not like the US? Europeans and the Spread of American Culture', *International Affairs* 74, 4 (1998), pp. 883–92.

Catlin, G.E.G., 'Propaganda and the Cold War', *Yale Review*, 42 (September 1953), pp. 103–16.

Clark, B., 'The BBC's External Services', *International Affairs*, 35 (1959), pp. 170–80.

Clive, N., 'Labour and the Cold War', *Government and Opposition*, 28, 4 (1993), pp. 553–8.

——, 'From War to Peace in SIS', *Intelligence and National Security*, 10, 3 (1995), pp. 512–13.

Conquest, R., 'Small Terror, Few dead', *Times Literary Supplement* (31 May 1996), pp. 3–5.

——, 'In Celia's Office: Orwell and the Cold War', *Times Literary Supplement*, 21 August 1998, pp. 4–5.

Cohen, Y., 'News Media and the News Department of the Foreign and Commonwealth Office', *Review of International Studies*, 14 (April 1988), pp. 117–31.

Cook, B.W., 'First Comes the Lie: C.D. Jackson and Political Warfare', *Radical History Review*, 31 (1984), pp. 42–70.

Corke, S.J., 'Bridging the Gap: Containment, Covert Action and the Search for the Missing Link in American Cold War Policy, 1948–1953', *The Journal of Strategic Studies*, 20, 4 (1997), pp. 45–65.

Coste, B., 'Propaganda in Eastern Europe', *Public Opinion Quarterly*, 14 (1950), pp. 639–66.

Crossman, R.H.S., 'Psychological Warfare', *Journal of the Royal United Service Institution*, 97 (1952), pp. 319–32.

——, 'Psychological Warfare', *Journal of the Royal United Service Institution*, 98 (1953), pp. 351–61.

Crozier, B., 'What's Wrong with British Foreign Policy? A Time for Reconsideration', *Encounter*, 63 (July/August 1984), pp. 9–15.

Cummings, R.H., 'Balloons over East Europe: The Cold War Leaflet Campaign of Radio Free Europe', *The Falling Leaf*, 166 (1999), pp. 97–110.

Dahl, H.F., 'The Pursuit of Media History', *Media, Culture and Society*, 16, 4 (1994), pp. 551–63.

Davies, P.H.J., 'Organisational Politics and the Development of Britain's Intelligence Producer/Consumer Interface', *Intelligence and National Security*, 10, 4 (1995), pp. 113–32.

——, 'From Special Operations to Special Political Action: The "Rump SOE" and SIS Postwar Covert Action Capability 1945–1977', *Intelligence and National Security*, 15, 3 (2000), pp. 55–76.

Deery, P., 'Confronting the Cominform: George Orwell and the Cold War Offensive of the Information Research Department 1948–50', *Labour History*, 73 (1997), pp. 219–25.

——, 'Covert Propaganda and the Cold War: Britain and Australia, 1948–1955', *The Round Table*, 361 (2001), pp. 607–21.

——, 'The Dove Flies East: Whitehall, Warsaw and the 1950 World Peace Congress', *Australian Journal of Politics and History*, 48, 4 (2002), pp. 449–68.

Defty, A., ' "Close and Continuous Liaison": British Anti-Communist Propaganda and Cooperation with the United States, 1950–51', *Intelligence and National Security*, 17, 4 (2002), pp. 100–30.

——, 'Organising Security and Intelligence in the Far East: Further Fruits of the Waldegrave Initiative', *Study Group on Intelligence Newsletter*, 16 (Winter 1997/98), pp. 2–5.

DeMowbray, S., 'Soviet Deception and the Onset of the Cold War', *Encounter* (July/August 1984), pp. 16–24.

Dobson, A.P., 'Informally Special? The Churchill–Truman Talks of January 1952 and the State of Anglo-American Relations', *Review of International Studies*, 23, 1 (1997), pp. 27–47.

Dockrill, M., 'The Foreign Office, Anglo-American Relations and the Korean War, June 1950–June 1951', *International Affairs*, 62, 3 (1986), pp. 459–76.

Dravis, M.W., 'Storming Fortress Albania: American Covert Operations in Microcosm, 1949–54', *Intelligence and National Security*, 7, 4 (1992), pp. 425–42.

Ellwood, D.W., 'The 1948 Elections in Italy: A Cold War Propaganda Battle', *Historical Journal of Film, Radio and Television*, 13, 1 (1993), pp. 19–33.

Fish, M.S., 'After Stalin's Death: The Anglo-American Debate Over a New Cold War', *Diplomatic History*, 10, 4 (1986), pp. 333–55.

Fletcher, R., 'British Propaganda since World War II: A Case Study', *Media, Culture, and Society*, 4 (1982), pp. 97–109.

Flinn, A., 'National Museum of Labour History Archive and Study Centre', *Contemporary Record*, 7, 2 (1993), pp. 465–72.

Gaddis, J.L., 'The Emerging Post-Revisionist Synthesis on the Origins of the Cold War', *Diplomatic History*, 7 (1983), pp. 171–90.

——, 'Intelligence, Espionage, and Cold War Origins', *Diplomatic History*, 13, 2 (1989), pp. 191–213.

Garson, R., 'Eastern Europe in America's Containment Policy', *Journal of American Studies*, 13 (1979), pp. 73–92.

——, 'American Foreign Policy and the Limits of Power: Eastern Europe, 1946–50', *Journal of Contemporary History*, 21 (1986), pp. 347–66.

Gedye, G.E.K., 'Broadcasting and the Iron Curtain', *Contemporary Review*, 183 (April 1953), pp. 206–210.

Glaser, W., 'Semantics of the Cold War', *Public Opinion Quarterly*, 20 (Winter 1957), pp. 691–716.

Gould-Davies, N., ' "Pacifistic Blowback"? New Evidence on the Soviet Peace Campaign in the Early 1950s', *Cold War International History Project Bulletin*, 11 (Winter 1998), pp. 267–8.

Grant, M., 'Towards a Central Office of Information: Continuity and Change in British Government Information Policy 1939–51', *Journal of Contemporary History*, 34, 1 (1999), pp. 49–67.

Greenwood, S. 'Frank Roberts and the Other Long Telegram', *Journal of Contemporary History*, 25, 1 (1990), pp. 107–25.

——, 'Ernest Bevin, France and the Western Union,' *European History Quarterly*, 14 (1984), pp. 319–38.

Haight, D., 'The Papers of C.D. Jackson: A Glimpse at President Eisenhower's Psychological Warfare Expert', *Manuscripts*, 27 (1976), pp. 27–37.

Healey, D., 'The International Socialist Conference, 1946–1950', *International Affairs*, 26 (July 1950), pp. 363–73.

Hemsing, A., 'The Marshall Plan's European Film Unit, 1948–1955: A Memoir and Filmography', *Historical Journal of Film, Radio and Television*, 14, 3 (1994), pp. 269–98.

Heuser, B., 'NSC-68 and the Soviet Threat: A New Perspective on Western Threat Perception and Policy-Making', *Review of International Studies*, 17 (1991), pp. 17–40.

Hopkins, M.F., 'A British Cold War?', *Intelligence and National Security*, 7, 4 (1992), pp. 479–82.

Jacob, I., 'The British Broadcasting Corporation in Peace and War', *Journal of the Royal United Services Institution*, 94 (February–November 1947), pp. 379–89.

——, 'The Conduct of External Broadcasting', *Journal of the Royal United Service Institution* 103 (February 1958), pp. 172–83.

Jeffreys-Jones, R., 'The Perils of Propaganda in War and Peace', *Diplomatic History*, 16, 4 (1992), pp. 605–10.

Johnston, A.M., 'Mr Slessor Goes to Washington: The Influence of the British Global Strategy Paper on the Eisenhower New Look', *Diplomatic History*, 22, 3 (1998), pp. 361–98.

Jong-Jil, R., 'The Special Relationship at war: Anglo-American Relations During the Korean War', *Journal of Strategic Studies*, 7, 3 (1984), pp. 301–18.

Joshua, W., 'Soviet Manipulation of the European Peace Movement', *Strategic Review* (Winter 1983), pp. 9–18.

Jurgensen, K., 'British Occupation Policy after 1945 and the Problem of "Re-educating Germany"', *History*, 68 (1983).

Kaplan, L., 'Towards the Brussels Pact', *Prologue*, 12 (1980), pp. 73–86.

Karabell, Z. and Naftali, T., 'History Declassified: The Perils and Promise of CIA Documents', *Diplomatic History*, 18, 4 (1994), pp. 615–34.

Kennan, G.F., ' "X" article: 'The Sources of Soviet Conduct', *Foreign Affairs*, 25 (1947), pp. 560–82.

Kenyon, M., 'Black Propaganda', *After the Battle*, 72 (1992), pp. 8–31.

Kirby, D., 'Divinely Sanctioned: The Anglo-American Cold War Alliance and the Defence of Western Civilization and Christianity, 1945–48', *Journal of Contemporary History*, 35, 3 (2000), pp. 385–412.

Kisatsky, D., 'Voice of America and Iran, 1949–1953: US Liberal Developmentalism, Propaganda and the Cold War', *Intelligence and National Security*, 14, 3 (1999), pp. 160–85.

Knight, W.S., 'Labourite Britain, America's Sure Friend?: The Anglo-Soviet Treaty Issue 1947,' *Diplomatic History*, 7 (1983), pp. 267–82.

Lashmar, P., 'Covert in Glory', *New Statesman and Society* (3 March 1995), pp. 3–5.

Lasswell, H.D. 'The Theory of Political Propaganda', *American Political Science Review*, 21 (1927), pp. 627–31.

Laville, H., 'The Committee of Correspondence: CIA Funding of Women's Groups, 1952–1967', *Intelligence and National Security*, 12, 1 (1997), pp. 104–21.

Leeper, R.A., 'British Culture Abroad', *Contemporary Review*, 148 (1935), pp. 201–7.

Leffler, M.P., 'The American Conception of National Security and the Beginnings of the Cold War, 1945–1948', *American Historical Review*, 89 (1984), pp. 346–400.

Lodeesen, J., 'Radio Liberty (Munich): Foundations for a History', *Historical Journal of Film, Radio and Television*, 6, 2 (1986), pp. 197–210.

Loory, S.H., 'The CIA's Use of the Press: A "mighty" Wurlitzer', *Columbia Journalism Review* (September/October 1974), pp. 9–18.

Lucas, S., 'Campaigns of Truth: The Psychological Strategy Board and American Ideology, 1951–1953', *The International History Review*, 18, 2 (1996), pp. 279–302.

Lucas, S. and Morey, A., 'The "Hidden" Alliance: The CIA and MI6 Before and after Suez', *Intelligence and National Security*, 15, 2 (2000), pp. 95–120.

McMahon, R.J., 'Credibility and World Power: Exploring the Psychological Dimension in Postwar American Diplomacy', *Diplomatic History*, 15, 4 (1991), pp. 455–72.

Marchio, J., 'Resistance Potential and Rollback: US Intelligence and the Eisenhower Administration's Policies Toward Eastern Europe, 1953–56', *Intelligence and National Security*, 10, 2 (1995), pp. 219–41.

Martinez, C.E. and Suchman, E.A., 'Letters from America and the 1948 Elections in Italy', *Public Opinion Quarterly* 14, 1 (1950), pp. 111–25.

Mastny, V., 'Europe in US-USSR Relations: A Topical Legacy', *Problems of Communism*, 37, 1 (1988), pp. 19–29.

Mayhew, C., 'British Foreign Policy since 1945', *International Affairs* (1950), pp. 477–86.

Merrick, R., 'The Russia Committee of the British Foreign Office and the Cold War 1946–1947', *Journal of Contemporary History*, 20, 3 (1985), pp. 453–68.

Miliband, R. and Liebman, M., 'Reflections on Anti-Communism', *Socialist Register* (1984), pp. 11–12.

Miller, D., 'Aerial Combat', *New Statesman and Society* (18 November 1994), p. 24.

Miller, J.E., 'Taking Off the Gloves: The United States and the Italian Elections of 1948', *Diplomatic History*, 7 (Winter 1983), pp. 35–55.

'The Ministry of Truth', *The Leveller*, 13 (March 1978), pp. 11–13.

Nachmani, A., ' "Its a Matter of Getting the Mixture Right": British Post-War Relations with America in the Middle-East', *Journal of Contemporary History*, 18 (1983), pp. 117–40.

Needell, A.A., ' "Truth is Our Weapon": Project TROY, Political Warfare and Government–Academic Relations in the National Security State', *Diplomatic History*, 17, 3 (1993), pp. 399–420.

Oudes, B.J., 'The Great Wind Machine', *The Washington Monthly*, 2, 4 (June 1970), pp. 30–9.

Ovendale, R., 'Britain, the US and the European Cold War, 1945–1948', *History* 67 (1982), pp. 217–36.

——, 'Britain, The US and the Cold War in South East Asia, 1949–1950', *International Affairs*, 58, 3 (1982), pp. 447–64.

Parry-Giles, S., 'The Eisenhowers Administration's Conceptualization of the USIA: The Development of Overt and Covert Propaganda Stratagems', *Presidential Studies Quarterly*, 24, 2 (1994), pp. 263–77.

——, 'Propaganda, Effect, and the Cold War: Gauging the Status of America's "War of Words" ', *Political Communication*, 11, 2 (1994), pp. 203–13.

——, 'Rhetorical Experimentation and the Cold War, 1947–53: The Development of an Internationalist Approach to Propaganda', *Quarterly Journal of Speech*, 80, 4 (1994), pp. 448–67.

Parsons, A., 'Vultures and Philistines: British Attitudes to Culture and Cultural Diplomacy', *International Affairs*, 61, 1 (1985), pp. 1–8.

Platt, A.A. and Leonardi, R., 'American Foreign Policy and the Italian Left', *Political Science Quarterly*, 93, 2 (1978), pp. 197–215.

Pollard, J.A., 'Words are Cheaper than Blood: The Overseas O.W.I. and the Need for a Permanent Propaganda Agency', *Public Opinion Quarterly*, 9 (Fall 1945), pp. 283–304.

Porter, B., 'Secrets from the Edge' *Intelligence and National Security*, 9, 4 (1994), pp. 759–63.

Pronay, N. and Taylor, P.M., ' "An Improper Use of broadcasting . . . " The British Government and Clandestine Radio Operations against Germany during the Munich Crisis', *Journal of Contemporary History*, 19 (1984), pp. 357–84.

'Psychological Warfare in Korea: An Interim Report' *Public Opinion Quarterly*, 15, 1 (Spring 1951), pp. 65–75.

Rawnsley, G.D., 'Cold War Radio in Crisis: The BBC Overseas Services, the Suez Crisis and the 1956 Hungarian Uprising', *Historical Journal of Film, Radio and Television*, 16, 2 (1996), pp. 197–219.

——, 'Overt and Covert: The Voice of Britain and Black Radio Broadcasting in the Suez Crisis, 1956', *Intelligence and National Security*, 11, 3 (1996), pp. 497–522.

Reynolds, D., 'A "Special Relationship"? America, Britain and the International Order Since the Second World War', *International Affairs*, 62 (1985/6), pp. 1–20.

Rositzke, H., 'America's Secret Operations: A Perspective', *Foreign Affairs*, 53, 2 (1975), pp. 344–56.

Ross, G., 'Foreign Office Attitudes to the Soviet Union, 1941–45', *Journal of Contemporary History*, 16 (1981), pp. 521–40.

Ruane, K., ' "Containing America": Aspects of British Foreign Policy and the Cold War in South East Asia, 1951–54', *Diplomacy and Statecraft*, 6, 4 (1996), pp. 142–62.

Rudgers, D.F., 'The Origins of Covert Action', *Journal of Contemporary History*, 35, 2 (2000), pp. 249–62.

Sanders, M.L., 'Wellington House and British Propaganda during the First World War', *Historical Journal*, 18, 4 (1975), pp. 119–46.

Scott-Smith, G., ' "A Radical Democratic Political Offensive": Melvin J. Lasky, *Der Monat* and the Congress for Cultural Freedom', *Journal of Contemporary History*, 35, 2 (2000), pp. 263–80.

——, 'The "Masterpieces of the Twentieth Century" Festival and the Congress for Cultural Freedom: Origins and Consolidation 1947–52', *Intelligence and National Security*, 15, 1 (2000), pp. 121–43.

Shaw, T., 'Government Manipulation of the Press during the 1956 Suez Crisis', *Contemporary Record*, 8, 2 (1994), pp. 274–88.

——, 'Eden and the BBC During the 1956 Suez Crisis: A Myth Re-examined', *Twentieth Century British History*, 6, 3 (1995), pp. 320–43.

——, 'The British Popular Press and the Early Cold War', *History*, 83 (1998), pp. 66–85.

Shaw, T., 'The Information Research Department of the Foreign Office and the Korean War, 1950–53', *Journal of Contemporary British History*, 34, 2 (1999), pp. 263–81.

——, 'The Politics of Cold War Culture', *Journal of Cold War Studies*, 3, 3 (2001), pp. 59–76.

Smith, B.F., 'A Note on the OSS, Ultra, and World War II's Intelligence Legacy for America', *Defense Analysis*, 3, 2 (1987), pp. 184–9.

Smith, H., 'BBC Television Newsreel and the Korean War', *Historical Journal of Film, Radio and Television*, 8, 3 (1988), pp. 227–52.

Smith, L., 'Covert British Propaganda: The Information Research Department, 1947–1977', *Millennium: Journal of International Studies*, 9, 1 (1980), pp. 67–83.

Smith, R., 'A Climate of Opinion: British Official and the Development of British Soviet Policy, 1945–47', *International Affairs*, 64, 4 (1988), pp. 635–47.

Smith, R. and Zametica, J., 'The Cold Warrior: Clement Attlee Reconsidered, 1945–47', *International Affairs*, 61, 2 (1985), pp. 237–52.

Stern, S., 'A Short Account of International Student Politics and the Cold War with Particular Reference to the NSA, CIA, Etc.', *Ramparts* (March 1967), pp. 29–38.

Stone, N., 'McCarthy was Right', *The Spectator* (14 May 1994), pp. 33–4.

Taylor, P.M., 'Back to the Future? Integrating the Press and Media into the History of International Relations', *Historical Journal of Film, Radio and Television*, 14, 3 (1994), pp. 321–30.

——, 'Cultural Diplomacy and the British Council, 1934–39', *British Journal of International Studies*, 4 (1978), pp. 244–65.

——, 'The Foreign Office and British Propaganda during the First World War', *Historical Journal, 23* (1980), pp. 875–98.

Tulloch, J., 'Policing the Public Sphere: the British Machinery of News Management', *Media, Culture and Society*, 15 (1993), pp. 363–84.

Wagnleitner, R., 'The Empire of the Fun, or Talkin' Soviet Union Blues: The Sound of Freedom and US Cultural Hegemony in Europe', *Diplomatic History*, 23, 3 (1999), pp. 499–524.

Wark, W.K., 'Coming in from the Cold: British Propaganda and Red Army Defectors, 1945–1952', *International History Review*, 9, 1 (1987), pp. 48–72.

——, 'In Never-Never Land? The British Archives on Intelligence', *The Historical Journal*, 35, 1 (1992), pp. 195–203.

——, 'The Study of Espionage: Past, Present and Future?', *Intelligence and National Security*, 8, 3 (1993), pp. 1–13.

——, 'Great Investigations: The Public Debate on Intelligence in the US after 1945', *Defense Analysis*, 3, 2 (1987), pp. 119–32.

Warner, M., 'Cultural Cold War: Origins of the Congress for Cultural Freedom, 1949–50', *Studies in Intelligence*, 38, 5 (1995), pp. 89–98.

——, 'Sophisticated Spies: CIA's Links to Liberal Anti-Communists, 1949–1967', *International Journal of Intelligence and Counter-Intelligence*, 9, 4 (1996), pp. 425–33.

Watt, D.C., 'Intelligence and the Historian: A Comment on John Gaddis's "Intelligence, Espionage and Cold War Origins"', *Diplomatic History*, 14, 2 (1990), pp. 199–204.

——, 'Intelligence Studies: The Emergence of a British School', *Intelligence and National Security*, 3, 2 (1988), pp. 338–41.

——, 'The Proper Study of Propaganda', *Intelligence and National Security*, 15, 4 (2000), pp. 143–63.

Weiler, P., 'Labour and the Cold War: The Foreign Policy of the British Labour Governments, 1945–51', *Journal of British Studies*, 26 (1987), pp. 54–82.

——, 'The United States, International Labour and the Cold War: The Break Up of the World Federation of Trade Unions', *Diplomatic History*, 5 (1981), pp. 1–22.

——, 'Britain and the First Cold War: Revisionist Beginnings', *Twentieth Century British History*, 9, 1 (1998), pp. 125–38.

Welch, D. 'Citizenship and Politics: The Legacy of Wilton Park for Post-War Reconstruction', *Contemporary European History*, 6, 2 (1997), pp. 209–18.

Westerfield, H.B., 'America and the World of Intelligence Liaison', *Intelligence and National Security*, 11, 3 (1996), pp. 523–60.

Wildy, T., 'From the MOI to the COI – Publicity and Propaganda in Britain, 1945–1951: The National Health and Insurance campaigns of 1948', *Historical Journal of Film, Radio and Television*, 6, 1 (1986), pp. 3–18.

Wilford, H., 'The Information Research Department: Britain's Secret Cold War Weapon Revealed', *Review of International Studies*, 24, 3 (1998), pp. 353–69.

——, ' "Unwitting Assets?": British Intellectuals and the Congress for Cultural Freedom', *Twentieth Century British History*, 11, 1 (2000), pp. 42–60.

——, 'Playing the CIA's Tune? The *New Leader* and the Cultural Cold War', *Diplomatic History*, 27, 1 (2003), pp. 15–34.

——, 'American Labour Diplomacy and Cold War Britain', *Journal of Contemporary History*, 37, 1 (2002), pp. 45–65.

Yurechko, J., 'The Day Stalin Died: American Plans for Exploiting the Soviet Succession Crisis of 1953', *Journal of Strategic Studies*, 3, 1 (1980), pp. 44–73.

Books

Aldrich, R.J., *The Hidden Hand: Britain, America and Cold War Secret Intelligence* (London: John Murray, 2001).

—— (ed.), *British Intelligence, Strategy and the Cold War, 1945–51*, (London: Routledge, 1992).

Aldrich, R., 'Secret Intelligence for a Postwar World: Reshaping the British Intelligence Community, 1944–51,' in Aldrich (ed.), *British Intelligence Strategy and the Cold War*, pp. 15–49.

——, 'Unquiet in Death: The Special Operations Executive and British Post-War Special Operations, 1945–51', in Gorst, A., Johnmann, L. and Lucas, W.S. (eds), *Contemporary British History, 1931–1961: Politics and the Limits of Policy* (London: Pinter, 1991).

——, 'The Value of Residual Empire: Anglo-American Intelligence Cooperation in Asia after 1945', in R.J. Aldrich and M.F. Hopkins (eds), *Intelligence, Defence and Diplomacy: British Policy in the Post-War World* (London: Frank Cass, 1994), pp. 226–58.

——, 'European Integration: An American Intelligence Connection', in A. Deighton (ed.), *Building Postwar Europe: National Decision-Makers and European Institutions, 1948–63* (London: Macmillan, 1995), pp. 141–58.

Aldrich, R.J. and Hopkins, M.F. (eds), *Intelligence, Defence and Diplomacy: British Policy in the Post-War World* (London: Frank Cass, 1994).

Aldrich, R.J., Rawnsley, G. and Rawnsley M. (eds), *The Clandestine Cold War in Asia, 1945–65: Western Intelligence, Propaganda and Special Operations* (London: Frank Cass, 1999).

Alexandre, L., *The Voice of America: From Detente to the Reagan Doctrine* (Norwood, NJ: Ablex Publishing Corp., 1988).

Amis, M., *Koba the Dread: Laughter and the Twenty Million* (London: Jonathan Cape, 2002).

Andrew, C. and Gordievsky, O., *KGB: The Inside Story of its Foreign Operations from Lenin to Gorbachev* (London: Sceptre, 1991).

Andrew, C. and Mitrokhin, V., *The Mitrokhin Archive: The KGB in Europe and the West* (London: Allen Lane, 1999).

Anstey, C., 'Foreign Office Publicity, American Aid and European Unity: Mobilising Public Opinion 1947–49', in Becker and Kniping (ed.), *Power in Europe?*, pp. 373–95.

Applebaum, A., *Gulag: A History of the Soviet Camps* (London: Allen Lane, 2003).

Atherton, L., *'Never Complain, Never Explain': Records of the Foreign Office and State Paper Office 1500-c.1960* (London: PRO, 1994).

Balfour, M., *Propaganda in War, 1939–1945: Organisations, Policies, and Publics in Britain and Germany* (London: Routledge and Kegan, 1979).

Barghoorn, F.C., *Soviet Foreign Propaganda* (Princeton, NJ: Princeton University Press, 1964).

Barker, E., *The British between the Superpowers, 1945–50* (Toronto: University of Toronto Press, 1983).

Barnes, T. 'Democratic Deception: American Covert Operations in Post War Europe', in D.A. Charters and Tugwell (eds), *Deception Operations*, pp. 297–321.

Barrett, E.W., *The Truth is Our Weapon* (New York: Funk & Wagnalls Inc., 1953).

Becker, J. and Kniping, F. (eds), *Power in Europe? Great Britain, France, Italy and Germany in a Post-War World, 1945–50* (New York: W. de Gruyter, 1986).

Bell, P.M.H., *John Bull and the Bear: British Public Opinion, Foreign Policy and the Soviet Union, 1941–1945* (London: Edward Arnold, 1990).

Best, R., *Co-operation with Like-Minded Peoples: British Influence on American Security Policy* (Westport, CN: Greenwood, 1986).

Bethell, N., *The Great Betrayal: The Untold Story of Kim Philby's Biggest Coup* (London: Hodder & Stoughton, 1984).

Bloch, J. and Fitzgerald, P., *British Intelligence and Covert Action* (London: Junction, 1983).

Bourne, J. and Lucas, W.S., *The Korean War, 1950–1953*, Inter-University History Film Consortium Archive Series, no. 5 (IUHFC, 1992).

Bower, T., *The Perfect English Spy: Sir Dick White and the Secret War, 1935–90* (London: Heinemann, 1995).

Boyle, A., *The Climate of Treason* (London: Coronet, 1980).

Briggs, A., *History of Broadcasting in the UK*: vol. 4, *Sound and Vision* (Oxford: Oxford University Press, 1979).

Brown, J.A.C., *Techniques of Persuasion: From Propaganda to Brainwashing* (London: Harmondsworth Penguin, 1963).

Bullock, A., *Ernest Bevin: Foreign Secretary, 1945–51* (Oxford: Oxford University Press, 1985).

Carew, A., *Labour under the Marshall Plan: The Politics of Productivity and the Marketing of Management Science* (Manchester: Manchester University Press, 1987).

Carew-Hunt, R.N., *The Theory and Practice of Communism* (London: Penguin Books, 1963).

Carruthers, S.L., *Winning Hearts and Minds: British Governments, the Media and Colonial Counter-Insurgency* (Leicester: Leicester University Press, 1995).

Challis, R., *Shadow of a Revolution: Indonesia and the Generals* (Stroud: Sutton, 2001).

Charters, D.A. and Tugwell, M.A.J. (eds), *Deception Operations: Studies in the East-West Context* (London: Pergamon Brassey's, 1990).

Clews, J.C., *Communist Propaganda Techniques* (London: Methuen, 1964).

Coleman, P., *The Liberal Conspiracy: The Congress for Cultural Freedom and the Struggle for the Mind of Postwar Europe* (New York: The Free Press, 1989).

Conquest, R., *The Great Terror* (London: Pelican, 1971).

——, *Reflections on a Ravaged Century* (London: John Murray, 1999).

Copeland, M., *Without Cloak or Dagger: The Truth about the New Espionage* (New York: Simon & Schuster, 1974).

Crick, B., *George Orwell: A Life* (London: Penguin, 1992).

Crofts, W., *Coercion or Persuasion? Propaganda in Britain after 1945* (London: Routledge, 1989).

Crossman, R.H.S. (ed.), *The God that Failed: Six Studies in Communism* (London: Hamish Hamilton, 1950).

Cull, N.J., *Selling War: The British Propaganda Campaign Against American 'Neutrality' in World War II* (Oxford: Oxford University Press, 1995).

Cumings, B., 'Revising Post-Revisionism Revisited', in M. Hogan (ed.), *America in the World: The Historiography of American Foreign Relations since 1941* (Cambridge: Cambridge University Press, 1995).

Curtis, E., *Ireland – The Propaganda War: The British Media and 'The Battle for Hearts and Minds'* (London: Pluto, 1984).

Danchev, A., *Oliver Franks* (Oxford: Clarendon Press, 1993).

Darling, A.B., *The Central Intelligence Agency: An Instrument of Government to 1950* (University Park, PA: Pennsylvania State University Press, 1990).

Davison, P. (ed.), *Orwell and Politics*, (London: Penguin, 2000).

Daugherty, W.E. and Janowitz, M.A., *Psychological Warfare Casebook* (Baltimore, MD: John Hopkins University Press, 1958).

Deacon, R., *'C': A Biography of Sir Maurice Oldfield* (London: MacDonald, 1985).

Deighton, A. (ed.), *Britain and the First Cold War* (London: Macmillan, 1990).

Dizard, W.P., *The Strategy of Truth: The Story of the US Information Service* (Washington, DC: Public Affairs Press, 1961).

Dockrill, M. and Young, J.W., (ed.), *British Foreign Policy, 1945–56* (London: Macmillan, 1989).

Donaldson, F., *The British Council: The First Fifty Years* (London: Cape, 1984).

Doob, L.W., *Public Opinion and Propaganda* (New York: Henry Holt & Co., 1948).

Dorril, S., *MI6: Fifty Years of Special Operations* (London: Fourth Estate, 2000).

Dorril, S. and Ramsay, R., *Smear!: Wilson and the Secret State* (London: Grafton, 1992).

Elliott, G. and Shukmanm, H., *Secret Classrooms* (London: St Ermin's Press, 2002).

Ellwood, D.W., 'From Re-education to the Selling of the Marshall Plan in Italy', in N. Pronay and K. Wilson (eds), *The Political Re-education of Germany and Her Allies after World War II* (London: Croom Helm, 1985), pp. 219–239.

Ellul, J., *Propaganda: The Formation of Men's Attitudes* (New York: Knopf, 1972).

FCO Historians, *IRD: Origins and Establishment of the Foreign Office Information Research Department* History Notes, no. 9 (London: FCO/LRD, 1995).

FCO Historians, *FCO Records: Policy, Practice and Posterity, 1782–1993*, History Notes, no. 4 (London: FCO, 1992).

FCO Historians, *Changes in British and Russian Records Policy*, Occasional Papers, no. 7 (London: FCO, 1993).

Fife-Clark, T., *The Central Office of Information* (London: Allen & Unwin, 1970).

Folly, M.H., *Churchill, Whitehall and the Soviet Union, 1940–45* (London: Macmillan, 2000).

Foot, P., *Who Framed Colin Wallace?* (London: Macmillan, 1989).

Gaddis, J.L., *Strategies of Containment: A Critical Appraisal of Post-War American National Security Policy* (Oxford: Oxford University Press, 1982).

——, *The United States and the End of the Cold War: Implications, Reconsiderations, Provocations* (Oxford: Oxford University Press, 1992).

——, *We Now Know: Rethinking Cold War History* (Oxford: Oxford University Press, 1997).

——, 'The United States and the Question of a Sphere of Influence in Europe, 1945–49', in O. Riste (ed.), *Western Security: The Formative Years* (New York: Norwegian University Press, 1985).

Gallup, G.H., *The Gallup International Public Opinion Polls: Great Britain, 1937–1975*, vol. 1, 1937–1964 (New York: Random House, 1976).

Geniesse, J.F., *Freya Stark: Passionate Nomad* (London: Chatto & Windus, 1999).

Gilbert, M., *Never Despair: Winston S. Churchill, 1945–1965*, (London: Minerva, 1988).

——, *In Search of Churchill* (London: Harper Collins, 1994).

Godson, R. and Schultz, R., *Dezinformatsia: Active Measures in Soviet Strategy* (New York: Pergammon-Brassey's, 1988).

Green, F., *American Propaganda Abroad from Benjamin Franklin to Ronald Reagan* (New York: Hippocrene Books, 1988).

Grose, P., *Gentleman Spy: The Life of Allen Dulles* (London: Andre Deutsch, 1995).

——, *Operation Rollback: America's Secret War behind the Iron Curtain* (London: Andre Deutsch, 2001).

Halliday, J., 'Anti-Communism and the Korean War', in R. Miliband *et al.* (eds), *The Socialist Register* (London: Merlin Press, 1984), pp.130–63.

Harris, K., *Attlee* (London: Weidenfeld & Nicolson, 1982).

Hathaway, R.M., *Ambiguous Partnership: Britain and America, 1944–47* (New York: Columbia University Press, 1981).

Heilbrunn, O., *The Soviet Secret Services* (London: Allen & Unwin, 1956).

Henderson, J.W., *The United States Information Agency* (New York: Praeger, 1969).

Heuser, B. and O'Neill, R., *Securing the Peace in Europe, 1945–62: Thoughts for the 1990s* (London: Macmillan, 1991).

——, 'Stalin as Hitler's Successor: Western Interpretations of the Soviet Threat', in Heuser and O'Neill (eds), *Securing Peace in Europe*, pp.17–40.

——, 'Covert Action within British and American Concepts of Containment, 1948–51', in Aldrich (ed.), *British Intelligence, Strategy, and the Cold War*, pp. 65–84.

Hixson, W.L., *Parting the Curtain: Propaganda, Culture and the Cold War, 1945–61* (London: Macmillan, 1997).

Holt, R., *Radio Free Europe* (Minneapolis, MN: University of Minnesota Press, 1958).

Holt, R.T. and VandeWelde, R.W., *Strategic Psychological Operations and American Foreign Policy* (Chicago, IL: University of Chicago Press, 1960).

Hopkins, M.F., 'The Washington Embassy: The Role of an Institution in Anglo-American Relations, 1945–55', in Aldrich and Hopkins (eds), *Intelligence, Defence and Diplomacy*, pp. 79–99.

Ismay, Lord, *NATO: The First Five Years, 1949–1954* (London, Paris: NATO, 1955).

Jones, B., *The Russia Complex: The British Labour Party and the Soviet Union* (Manchester: Manchester University Press, 1977).

Kent, J., 'Bevin's Imperialism and the Idea of Euro-Africa, 1945–49', in Dockrill and Young (eds), *British Foreign Policy, 1945–56*, pp. 47–76.

Kent J. and Young, J.W., 'British Policy Overseas: The "Third Force" and the Origins of NATO – in Search of a New Perspective', in Heuser and O'Neill (eds), *Securing Peace in Europe*, pp. 41–61.

——, 'The "Western Union" Concept and British Defence Policy, 1947–8', in Aldrich (ed.), *British Intelligence, Strategy and the Cold War*, pp. 166–92.

Kerr, S., 'The Secret Hotline to Moscow: Donald Maclean and the Berlin Crisis of 1948', in Deighton (ed.), *Britain and the First Cold War*, pp. 71–87.

——, 'British Cold War Defectors: The Versatile Durable Toys of Propagandists', in Aldrich (ed.), *British Intelligence, Strategy, and the Cold War*, pp. 111–40.

Kirby, D., *Church, State and Propaganda: The Archbishop of York and International Relations – A Political Study of Cyril Forster Garbett, 1942–1955* (Hull: Hull University Press, 1999).

Koch, S., *Double Lives: Spies and Writers in the Secret Soviet War of Ideas Against the West* (New York: The Free Press, 1993).

Kotek, J., *Students and the Cold War* (London: Macmillan, 1996).

Kovrig, B., *The Myth of Liberation* (Baltimore, MD: John Hopkins University Press, 1973).

Larson, D.W., *Origins of Containment: A Psychological Explanation* (Princeton, NJ: Princeton University Press, 1985).

Lashmar, P. and Oliver, J., *Britain's Secret Propaganda War, 1948–1977* (Stroud: Sutton, 1998).

Lasswell, H.D., *Propaganda and Promotional Activities* (Minneapolis, MN: University of Minnesota Press, 1935).

Lawrenson, J. and Barber, L., *The Price of Truth: The Story of Reuters Millions* (London: Sphere Books Ltd, 1986).

Leffler, M.P., *A Preponderance of Power: National Security, the Truman Administration and the Cold War* (Stanford, CA: Stanford University Press, 1992).

Leigh, D., *The Frontiers of Secrecy: Closed Government in Britain*, (London: Junction Books, 1980).

——, *The Wilson Plot: The Intelligence Services and the Discrediting of a Prime Minister* (London: Heinemann, 1988).

Lerner, D., *Psychological Warfare Against Nazi Germany: The Sykewar Campaign, D-Day to VE-Day* (London: MIT Press, 1971).

Lewis, J., *Changing Direction: British Military Planning for Post-War Strategic Defence, 1942–1947* (London: Sherwood Press, 1988).

Lilly, E.P., 'The Psychological Strategy Board and Its Predecessors: Foreign Policy Coordination, 1938–1953', in G. Vincitorio (ed.), *Studies in Modern History* (New York: St John's University Press, 1982), pp. 337–82.

Linebarger, P.M., *Psychological Warfare* (Washington, DC: Infantry Journal Press, 1948).

Lowe, P., *Containing the Cold War in East Asia: British Policies towards Japan, China and Korea, 1948–53* (Manchester: Manchester University Press, 1997).

Louis, W.R. and Bull, H. (eds), *The Special Relationship: Anglo-American Relations Since 1945* (Oxford: Oxford University Press, 1986).

Lucas, S., *Freedom's War: The American Crusade Against the Soviet Union* (New York: New York University Press, 1999).

——, 'Beyond Diplomacy: Propaganda and the History of the Cold War', in Rawnsley (ed.), *Cold War Propaganda in the 1950s*, pp. 11–30.

Lucas, W.S. and Morris, C.J., 'A Very British Crusade: The Information Research Department and the Beginning of the Cold War', in Aldrich (ed.), *British Intelligence, Strategy and the Cold War 1945–1951*, pp. 85–110.

Mackenzie, J., *Propaganda and Empire: The Manipulation of British Public Opinion, 1880–1960* (Manchester: Manchester University Press, 1985).

Mansell, G., *Let Truth Be Told: Fifty Years of BBC External Broadcasting* (London: BBC, 1982).

Marchetti, V. and Marks, J.D., *The CIA and the Cult of Intelligence* (New York: Laurel, 1980).

May, E.R. (ed.), *American Cold War Strategy: Interpreting NSC-68* (London: Macmillan, 1993).

Medhurst, M.J., *Cold War Rhetoric: Strategy, Metaphor and Ideology* (Westport, CN: Greenwood Press, 1990).

—— (ed.), *Eisenhower's War of Words: Rhetoric and Leadership* (Detroit, MI: Michigan State University Press, 1994).

Mickelson, S., *America's Other Voice: The Story of Radio Free Europe and Radio Liberty* (New York: Praeger, 1983).

Miller, D., *Don't Mention the War: Northern Ireland, Propaganda and the Media* (London: Pluto Press, 1994).

Mitrovich, G., *Undermining the Kremlin: America's Strategy to Subvert the Soviet Bloc, 1947–1956* (Cornell University Press, 2000).

Montague, L.L., *General Walter Bedell Smith as Director of Central Intelligence October 1950–February 1953* (University Park, PA: Pennsylvania State University Press, 1992).

Morgan, K., *Labour in Power 1945–51* (Oxford: Oxford UniversityPress, 1985).

Nelson, M., *War of the Black Heavens: The Battles of Western Broadcasting in the Cold War* (London: Brassey's, 1997).

Ogilvy-Webb, M., *The Government Explains: A Study of the Information Services – A Report of the Royal Institute of Public Administration* (London: Allen & Unwin, 1965).

Oliver, J.A., 'Britain and the Covert War of Words: The Information Research Department and Sponsored Publishing', MA thesis, University of Kent, 1995.

Ollivant, S., 'Protocol "M"', in Charters and Tugwell (eds), *Deception Operations*, pp. 275–96.

Ostermann, C.F., '*The United States, the East German Uprising of 1953 and the Limits of Rollback*', Cold War International History Project Working Paper, no. 11 (Washington, DC: CWIHP, 1994).

Ovendale, R., *The English Speaking Alliance: Britain, the United States, the Dominions and the Cold War 1945–51* (London: Allen & Unwin, 1985).

——, *Anglo-American Relations in the Twentieth Century* (London: Macmillan, 1998).

—— (ed.), *The Foreign Policy of the British Labour Governments, 1945–51* (Leicester: Leicester University Press, 1984).

Page, B., Leitch, B. and Knightley, P., *Philby: The Spy Who Betrayed A Generation* (London: Penguin Books, 1969).

Parry-Giles, S.J., 'Exporting America's Cold War Message: The Debate over America's First Peacetime Propaganda Program 1947–1953', PhD thesis, Indiana University, 1992.

Partner, P., *Arab Voices: The BBC Arabic Service, 1938–1988* (London: BBC, 1989).

Pease, S.E., *Psywar: Psychological Warfare in Korea, 1950–1953* (Harrisburg, PA: Stackpole Books).

Pirsein, R.W., *The Voice of America: An History of the International Broadcasting Activities of the United States Government, 1940–1962* (New York: Arno Press, 1979).

Pisani, S., *The CIA and the Marshall Plan* (Edinburgh: Edinburgh University Press, 1991).

Porter, B., *Plots and Paranoia: A History of Political Espionage in Britain, 1790–1988* (London: Unwin Hyman, 1989).

Potter, K., 'British McCarthyism', in R. Jeffreys-Jones and A. Lownie (eds), *North American Spies: New Revisionist Essays* (Edinburgh: Edinburgh University Press, 1991), pp. 143–57.

Prados, J., *The Keepers of the Keys: A History of the National Security Council fronm Truman to Bush* (New York: William Morrow, 1991).

Puddington, A., *Broadcasting Freedom: The Cold War Triumph of Radio Free Europe and Radio Liberty* (Lexington, KY: The University Press of Kentucky, 2000).

Qualter, T., *Propaganda and Psychological Warfare* (New York: Random House, 1962).

——, *Opinion Control in Democracies* (London: Macmillan, 1985).

Ramsay, R., *The Clandestine Caucus: Anti-Socialist Campaigns and Operations in the British Labour Movement since the War*, Lobster: Special Issue (Hull: Lobster, 1996).

Ranelagh, J., *The Rise and Decline of the CIA* (New York: Simon Schuster, 1987).

Ranelagh, J., 'Through the Looking Glass: A Comparison of United States and United Kingdom Intelligence Cultures', in H. Peake and S. Halperin (eds), *In the Name of Intelligence: Essays in Honour of Walter Pforzheimer* (Washington, DC: NIBC, 1994).

Rawnsley, G.D., *Radio Diplomacy and Propaganda: The BBC, the VOA and International Politics, 1956–64* (London: Macmillan, 1996).

Rawnsley, G.D. (ed.), *Cold War Propaganda in the 1950s* (London: Macmillan, 1998).

Richardson, C., *From Churchill's Secret Circle to the BBC: The Biography of General Sir Ian Jacob* (London: Brassey's, 1991).

Richelson, J. and Ball, D., *The Ties that Bind: Intelligence Co-operation Between the UKUSA Countries* (London: Allen & Unwin, 1985).

Roberts, F.K., 'Ernest Bevin as Foreign Secretary', in Ovendale (ed.), *The Foreign Policy of the British Labour Governments, 1945–51*, pp. 21–42.

Romero, F., *The United States and the European Trade Union Movement, 1944–1951* (Chapel Hill, NC: University of North Carolina Press, 1993).

Rose, C., *The Soviet Propaganda Network: A Directory of Organisations Serving Soviet Foreign Policy* (London: Pinter, 1988).

Rositske, H., *The CIA's Secret Operations: Espionage, Counter Espionage and Special Operations* (New York: Reader's Digest Press, 1977).

Rothwell, V., *Britain and the Cold War 1941–47* (London: Cape, 1982).

Sanger, C., *Malcolm MacDonald: Bringing an End to Empire* (Liverpool: Liverpool University Press, 1996).

Saunders, F.S., *Who Paid the Piper? The CIA and the Cultural Cold War* (London: Granta, 1999).

Scott-Smith, G., *The Politics of Apolitical Culture: The Congress for Cultural Freedom and the Political Economy of American Hegemony, 1945–1955* (London: Routledge, 1991).

Seldon, A., *Churchill's Indian Summer: The Conservative Government, 1951–1955* (London: Hodder & Stoughton, 1981).

Shaw, T., *Eden, Suez and the Mass Media: Propaganda and Persuasion during the Suez Crisis* (London: I.B. Tauris, 1996).

——, *British Cinema and the Cold War: The State, Propaganda and Consensus* (London: I.B. Tauris, 2001).

Shelden, M., *Orwell: The Authorised Biography* (London: Heinemann, 1991).

Short, K.R.M. (ed.), *Western Broadcasting over the Iron Curtain* (London: Croom Helm, 1986).

Shulman, H.C., *The Voice of America: Propaganda and Democracy, 1941–1945* (Madison WI: University of Wisconsin Press, 1990).

Simpson, C., *Science of Coercion: Communication Research and Psychological Warfare, 1945–1960* (Oxford: Oxford University Press, 1994).

Sisman, A., *A.J.P. Taylor: A Biography* (London: Sinclair-Stevenson, 1994).

Smith, B.F., *The War's Long Shadow: The Second World War and Its Aftermath – China, Russia, Britain, America* (London: Andre Deutsch, 1986).

——, *The Ultra-Magic Deals and the Most Secret Special Relationship, 1940–1946* (Novato, CA: Presidio, 1993).

Stafford, D., *Churchill and the Secret Service* (London: John Murray, 1997).

Stewart-Smith, D.G., *No Vision Here: Non-Military Warfare in Britain* (Richmond: Foreign Affairs Publishing Company, 1966).

Strang, Lord, *The Foreign Office* (London: Allen & Unwin, 1955).

Summers, R.N. (ed.) *America's Weapons of Psychological Warfare* (New York: Wilson, 1951).

Taylor, P.M., *Global Communications, International Affairs and the Media since 1945* (London: Routledge, 1997).

——, *The Projection of Britain: British Overseas Publicity and Propaganda, 1919–1939* (Cambridge: Cambridge University Press, 1981).

——, *British Propaganda in the Twentieth Century: Selling Democracy* (Edinburgh: Edinburgh University Press, 1999).

——, 'Publicity and Diplomacy: The Impact of the First World War Upon Foreign Office Attitudes Towards the Press', in D. Dilks (ed.), *The Retreat From Power,* vol. 1, (London: Macmillan, 1981).

——, 'The Projection of Britain Abroad, 1945–51', in Dockrill and Young (ed.), *British Foreign Policy, 1945–1956*, pp. 9–30.

——, 'Power, Propaganda and Public Opinion: The British Information Services and the Cold War, 1945–57', in E. di Nolfo (ed.), *Power in Europe? II: Great Britain, France, Germany and Italy and the Origins of the EEC, 1952–1957* (Berlin/New York: Walter de Gruyter, 1992), pp. 445–61.

—— 'Through a Glass Darkly: The Pyschological Climate and Psychological Warfare of the Cold War', in Rawnsley (ed.), *Cold War Propaganda in the 1950s*, pp. 225–42.

Thomas, H., *Armed Truce: The Beginning of the Cold War* (London: Hamish Hamilton, 1986).

Thurlow, R., *The Secret State: British Internal Security in the Twentieth Century* (Oxford: Blackwell, 1994).

Tracey, M., *A Variety of Lives: A Biography of Sir Hugh Greene* (London: Bodley Head, 1983).

Urban, G.R., *Talking to Eastern Europe: A Collection of the Best Reading from the Broadcasts and Background Papers of Radio Free Europe* (London: Eyre and Spottiswoode, 1964).

Verrier, A., *Through the Looking Glass: British Foreign Policy in the Age of Illusions* (London: Cape, 1983).

Warner, G., 'Britain and Europe in 1948: The View from the Cabinet', in Becker and Kniping (eds), *Power in Europe?*', pp. 27–44.

Weiler, P., *British Labour and the Cold War* (Stanford, CA: Stanford University Press, 1988).

Weinstein, A. and Vassiliev, A., *The Haunted Wood: Soviet Espionage in America – the Stalin Era* (New York: Random House, 1999).

Wenden, D.J., 'Churchill, Radio and Cinema', in R. Blake and W.R. Louis (eds), *Churchill* (Oxford: Oxford University Press, 1994), pp. 215–39.

West, N., *The Friends: Britain's Post-War Secret Intelligence Operations* (London: Weidenfeld and Nicolson, 1988).

—— (ed.), *The Faber Book of Espionage* (London: Faber, 1993).

Whitfield, S.J., *The Culture of the Cold War* (Baltimore, MD: Johns Hopkins University Press, 1996).

Whitton, J.B. (ed.), *Propaganda and the Cold War: A Princeton University Symposium* (Westport, CT: Greenwood Press, 1984).

Wilford, H., *Calling the Tune? The CIA, the British Left and the Cold War* (London: Frank Cass, 2003).

Williams, A.J., *Labour and Russia: The Attitude of the Labour Party to the USSR, 1924–34* (Manchester: Manchester University Press, 1989).

Williams, G. and Reed, B., *Denis Healey and the Policies of Power* (London: Sidgwick & Jackson, 1971).

Winks, R.W., *Cloak and Gown: Scholars in the Secret War, 1939–1961* (New York: Morrow, 1987).

Wood, N.O., 'Strategic Psychological Warfare of the Truman Administration: A Study of National Psychological Warfare Aims, Objectives, and Effectiveness', PhD thesis, University of Oklahoma, 1982.

Young, J.W., *Britain, France and the Unity of Europe, 1945–51* (Leicester: Leicester University Press, 1984)

——, *Winston Churchill's Last Campaign: Britain and the Cold War, 1951–1955* (Oxford: Oxford University Press, 1996).

—— (ed.), *The Foreign Policy of Churchill's Peacetime Administration, 1951–1955* (Leicester: Leicester University Press, 1988).

Young, J.W., *The British Foreign Office and Cold War Fighting in the Early 1950s: PUSC(51)16 and the 1952 'Sore Spots' Memorandum*, University of Leicester Discussion Papers in Politics, no. P95/2 (Leicester: Leicester University, 1995).

Yurechko, J., 'From Containment to Counteroffensive' PhD thesis, Berkeley CA, 1980.

Zametica, J., 'Three Letters to Bevin', in J. Zametica (ed.), *British Officials and British Foreign Policy* (London: Pinter, 1990), pp. 39–97.

Zubok, V. and Pleshakov, C., *Inside the Kremlin's Cold War: From Stalin to Krushchev* (London: Harvard University Press, 1996).

Index

Acheson, Dean 152, 162, 163, 169, 171
Africa 236
Albania 148–9, 185, 214–15, 230, 232
Alexander, A.V. 92
Allen, Denis 109
Allen, George V. 104–5, 108
Allied Information Service 29, 47
American Committee for a United Europe 192–3
American Federation of Labor 198
American Forces Radio Service 31
Amery, Julian 232
Anglo-Iranian Oil Company 43
Asia Foundation *see* Committee for a Free Asia
Aspidistra 146–7
Attlee, Clement 27, 34, 38, 49, 66–7, 72, 92, 183–4, 247
de Auer, Paul 193

Bagot, Milicent 197
balloon leaflet operations 136, 148–9, 188, 192, 216
Barghoorn, Frederick 190–1
Barrett, Edward 121, 134, 139–40, 142, 145–9, 152, 163, 168–70, 223, 224, 226
BBC 41, 65, 66, 70, 90, 93–4, 145, 182, 240–1; cooperation with US government 47, 145; cuts in services 162–4, 190, 237; Eastern European services 53, 73, 89, 148–9, 190–1, 237; Home Services 48–9, 241; liaison with Radio Free Europe 158–60, 192; liaison with Voice of America 110, 146–7, 192; Middle East services 43, 53, 91, 237; relations with IRD 3, 6, 13, 73–4, 110, 190–1, 212, 237; Western European services 45, 90, 237; *see also* Jacob, Sir Ian
Benton, W.B. 31
Berlin Blockade 118, 248
Berlin, Isaiah 205, 211
Berlin uprising 228

Bevin, Ernest 7–8, 38, 48, 92, 114–15, 183, 192; attitude towards Soviet Union 34, 45, 50–1, 68; and the Projection of Britain 29, 40–2, 114; reaction to Czech coup 71; resistance to political warfare 7–8, 42–4, 47, 72–4, 94, 114, 160, 246; and Western Union 51–3, 64–9, 72, 74–5, 112, 118–19, 138
Blum, Robert 207
Bohlen, Chip 251
book publishing 91, 154, 165–6, 191, 211–12
Boy Scouts 192, 198
Bracken, Brendan 182
Braden, Thomas 197
Brimelow, Thomas 81
Brimmell, Jack 77
Britain: general elections 29, 33–4, 162, 182–4; official secrecy 2–4, 12–18; public opinion 5, 38–9, 48–9, 50, 164, 208–13; US propaganda in 208–13
British Council 163–4
British Information Service in US 104, 153, 159, 212–13
British Society for Cultural Freedom 204, 210–11
broadcasting *see* individual broadcasters
Brogan, Denis 212
Brotherhood of Freedom 91–2, 100
Brussels Pact 72, 75, 102–3, 113–15, 118–20, 164
Burgess, Guy 75–6, 253
Burrows, Bernard 159–60

Campaign of Truth 2, 138–43, 169–70, 251
Carew-Hunt, R.N. 165
Carr, E.H. 49, 211–12
cartoons 133, 155
Catholic Church *see* religious propaganda
Central-Eastern European Committee 192–4
Central Intelligence Group 35
Central Office of Information 27, 82, 84–5, 87, 93, 162, 182, 236–7, 246

Challis, Roland 16
Chiefs of Staff 72, 83–4
China 148, 153–5, 224, 228
Church of England *see* religious propaganda
Churchill, Winston 33, 136, 192–3, 223, 227–8, 247; attitude towards propaganda 182–3, 188–9; election October 1951 162, 182–4; hopes for a summit with the Stalin 183–5; Iron Curtain speech 34, 39; meeting with Eisenhower 228–9; meeting with Truman 183–4, 188–9
CIA 5, 14–15, 50, 141, 143, 192–3, 227, 230, 251; in Albania 148–9, 185, 232; creation of 46–7; International Organisations Division 197–8, 203–4; intervention in Italian elections 107; in Korea 153; liaison with IRD 107, 152–3, 156, 160, 204–5, 208, 232; relationship with Radio Free Europe 142, 158–9; in South-East Asia 152, 207–8
Clarke, J.B. 145
Clay, Lucius 47
Clews, John 210, 212
Cloake, John 91, 197
Colonial Information Policy Committee 83
Colonial Office 83, 166
Colville, Jock 229
Cominform 50, 68, 246
Committee for a Free Asia 207–8, 214
Commonwealth Relations Office 83, 116–18
Compton, Wilson 168, 189, 224
Congress for Cultural Freedom 198, 204–7, 210–12, 214
Congress of Industrial Organizations 198
Conquest, Robert 3, 7, 77, 205
Conservative Party 167, 180
Cooper, Duff 182, 188
Cooperative Movement 92
Crankshaw, Edward 85
Crossman, Richard 87, 154, 205, 252
Crozier, Brian 16, 166
Cudlipp, Percy 92
Cultural Relations Department 9, 49, 53, 196
Cutler, Robert 225
Czechoslovakia 5, 70–1, 89, 93, 247–8

Daily Telegraph, The 48, 78, 252
Daily Worker, The 155, 209–10
Darlington, C.D. 166
Davies, John Paton 144, 156
Diplomatic Wireless Service 146–7
Donovan, William 142
Douglas, Fred 210
Drogheda Committee 236–8, 253–4
Dulles, Allen 191, 223, 230

Dulles, John Foster 222–3, 224, 228, 229–30, 251

Eastern Europe: British propaganda in 45, 64, 71–3, 88–9, 147–9, 185–90; Soviet occupation 32–4
Eden, Anthony 184, 192, 229–30
Edwards, W.P.N. 104–5
Eisenhower, Dwight D. 142, 156, 222–4, 228–30
Encounter 204–5, 210
Essex, Aubrey 78, 87
European Movement 160, 192–4
Ewer, Norman 87, 166

Falla, Paul 161
Feather, Victor 166, 213, 236
Federal Bureau of Investigation 198
Fenoaltea, Sergio 202
film *see also* newsreels 91, 112, 154, 209–10
Finland 44
Foot, Michael 3, 71
Foreign Office: attitudes to propaganda 10, 27, 63–4, 167–8, 248
Foreign Office News Department 81, 155, 166
Foreign Office Research Department 79, 87, 99
France 44, 47, 90, 121–2, 148, 202–3, 235
Fraser, Sir Robert 27, 83, 85
Frye, W.F. 156, 157, 163
Fyvel, T.R. 204–5

Gaitskell, Hugh 163
Germany 29, 38, 45, 47, 69, 132, 192, 198, 235
Goodwin, Michael 210–11, 212
Gordon-Walker, Patrick 164, 247
Gore-Booth, Paul 15, 153, 159, 212–13, 228
Gray, Gordon 135, 157, 225, 231
Greene, Sir Hugh 6
Guardian, The (The Manchester Guardian) 4, 154, 197

Harriman, Averell 47
Healey, Denis 3, 13, 16, 50, 73, 92, 196, 248
Heyworth, J.L. 236
Hook, Sidney 207
Hough, J.A. 87, 166
Hurd, Douglas 2
Huxley, Gervase 236

India 36, 116–17, 205–6, 241
Information Policy Department 29–30, 110, 151, 158

Information Research Department:
  cooperation with Brussels Powers 112–15;
  cooperation with Commonwealth
  Governments 117–18; cooperation with
  United States 11–12, 16–17, 104–12,
  143–64, 188–94, 227–33, 241, 249–54;
  effectiveness 234; establishment 1,
  74–80; funding 78–9; historiography of
  2–12; intelligence requirements 79–80;
  and Korean War 11; liaison with Chiefs of
  Staff 83–4; liaison with COI 84–5; liaison
  with NATO 123–4, 199–203; liaison with
  Radio Free Europe 158–60, 192; liaison
  with SIS 85–6; origins 51–3, 64–74;
  output 80–2, 88–93, 109, 115, 132–3,
  154–5, 164–6; relations with BBC 3, 6,
  73–4, 190; relations with George Orwell
  3–4; release of files 2, 12–15
International Confederation of Free Trade
  Unions 207
International Information Administration
  168–9, 189
Iran 32, 42–3
Iraq 90–1, 124
Ismay, Lord 182, 201–2
Italy 41, 44, 47, 90, 106–7, 235, 250

Jackson C.D. 16–17, 134, 156, 159–60,
  192, 223–4, 225, 227, 231–3, 241, 251
Jackson Committee 224–6, 233
Jackson, William 225
Jacob, Sir Ian 43, 67, 70, 73, 160, 182
Jebb, Gladwyn 50, 75, 119–20
Joint Chiefs of Staff 34
Joint Information and Propaganda
  Committee 151, 154, 155
Joint Intelligence Committee 35, 42, 81
Josselson, Michael 204

Keep Left 48, 50, 53
Kelly, Sir David 193
Kennan, George 36–8, 46, 47, 139, 156, 251
Keyes, Roger 225
Kirkpatrick, Ivone 15, 41–5, 63, 113, 235
Kirwan, Celia 87
Koestler, Arthur 5, 87
Korean War 121, 140, 152–3, 163, 210–11,
  212, 231, 248
Kravchenko, Victor 49
Kristol, Irving 204
Kuwait 161

Labour League of Youth 198
Labour Party 8, 28–9, 34, 48, 49–53, 71,
  92–3, 183–4, 197, 249
Laski, Harold 252
Law, Richard 193

Lawther, Will 87
Leveller, The 3
Lilly, E.P. 30, 143
Litvinov, Maxim 32
Lockhart, Sir Robert Bruce 75, 96, 160,
  165, 192, 236
London Controlling Section 85–6
London Press Service 73, 84–5, 93, 236–7
Lunghi, Hugh 77

MacArthur, General Douglas 153
MacDonald, Malcolm 151, 154, 207–8
Maclachlan, Donald 236
Macmillan, Harold 160, 192
McNeill, Hector 82, 92
Makins, Roger 228
Malaya 116, 151–5, 207–8
Malcolm, Angus 151
Malenkov, Georgi 222
Marett, Robert 15
Marshall, George 114
Marshall Plan 47, 198, 209–10
Masani, Minoo 205–6
Mayhew, Christopher 2, 6, 16, 50, 51–3, 67,
  76, 92, 102, 117, 119–20, 165, 246–7
Menzies, Sir Stewart 86
MI5 14, 151, 197
MI6 *see* SIS
Michener, James A. 207
Michie, Allan 192
Middle East 36, 102, 146–7; British
  propaganda in 42–4, 64, 70, 88–9, 90–1,
  149, 160–2, 234–5, 248
de Mille, Cecil B. 142
Ministry of Education 198
Ministry of Information 27, 29, 246
Morrison, H. 29, 67, 92, 160, 162, 192, 247
Muggeridge, Malcolm 205, 210, 212
Murray, Ralph 77, 84–5, 93, 102, 108, 110,
  113–15, 123, 130, 145–8, 151, 158, 163,
  196, 199

Nadler, Si 152
National Committee for a Free Europe
  141–2, 144, 156, 158–60, 192–3
National Council for Civil Liberties 196
National Security Act (1947) 46
National Security Council 46, 191, 225–7;
  NSC-68 138, 140–3
National Student Association 198
National Union of Students 49, 196
NATO 103, 118–24, 164, 199–200, 237,
  241; Caravan of Peace 137, 202;
  Information Policy Working Group
  201–3; Information Services 122–4,
  199–201
Nehru, Jawaharlal 117, 206

newsreels 91, 154
New Statesman 211
Newton, Theodore 122–3, 202
New York Times 206, 253
Nicholls, John 162, 189–92, 198–9, 200, 222, 238–9
Nicholls Committee 234–6, 252
Norberg, Charles 230
Nye, Sir Archibald 117

Office of Intelligence Research (State Department) 108–9, 112, 143
Office of International Information (State Department) 31, 46–7, 108
Office of Policy Coordination 141, 153, 156, 158, 163
Office of Strategic Services 28, 31
Office of War Information 28, 31, 223
Operations Coordinating Board 225, 227
Orwell, George 3–4, 87, 133, 154–5, 165
Orwell, Sonia 87, 165
Owen, David 16, 253

Parrott, Cecil 15, 77
Peck, John 123, 131, 156–7, 160–1, 182, 195–6, 199, 204, 228–9, 239–40, 247, 249, 253
Permanent Under-Secretary's Department/Permanent Under-Secretary's Committee 158, 161–2, 185–8, 222
Peterson, Sir Maurice 46
Philby, Kim 149, 158, 253
Phillips, Morgan 73
Plowden Committee 254
Policy Planning Staff 37, 144, 156
Political Warfare Executive 27, 29, 72–3, 77, 246–7
Post Hostilities Planning Staff 34
Potsdam Peace Conference 34, 47
Pravda 253
Projection of Britain 28–9, 40–1, 157, 164
Project Troy 142, 157
Project Vagabond 141, 189–90
Psychological Strategy Board 143, 191, 200, 202, 225; liaison with British 156–7
Psychological Warfare Division 29, 204
public opinion: American 39, 212–13; British 5, 38–9, 48–9, 50, 164, 208–13

Radio in the American Sector 31, 228
Radio Free Asia 207–8
Radio Free Europe 136, 142, 146–7, 158–60, 171, 189–90, 192, 198, 224, 251
Radio Liberty 169, 190, 198, 227
Radio Red-White-Red 31
Radio Ring Plan 135, 140–1, 146, 160–2, 170, 186, 189, 251

Radio SEAC 91
Rayner, John 152–5, 207–8
Reagan, Ronald 254
Regional Information Office, Singapore 151–5, 207–8
religious propaganda 71, 150, 165, 167, 229
Retinger, Joseph 193
Rimington, Stella 15–16
Roberts, Frank 36–8, 48
Rockefeller, Nelson 231, 251
Rockefeller Committee 224–5
Roosevelt, Franklin D. 33, 56
Russell, Bertrand 3, 7, 87, 165–6, 252
Russia Committee 37–8, 44, 47–9, 50, 69–70, 106, 150–1, 186, 191, 230, 248
Russian Secretariat 77, 79, 81

Salisbury, Lord 228
Sandys, Duncan 192–3
Sargeant, Howland 153, 168–9, 189
Schapiro, Leonard 7, 165–6, 213, 252
Schumann, Robert 114
Sharq al-Adna 91
Sheeks, Robert 207–8
Sheffield Peace Congress 196–7, 199
Sheridan, Leslie 77
Shuckburgh, Evelyn 120–1, 228
Simpson, John 25
SIS (MI6) 14, 85–6, 151, 208, 254; in Albania 148–9, 185–6, 215; in Middle East 43, 91
Slessor, Sir John 86
Smith, Joseph Burkholder 152, 208
Smith, Lyn 6–7
Smith-Mundt Act 46, 108
Smith, Walter Bedell 46, 156, 223, 231, 233, 251
Snow, Peter 3
Soviet Monitor 76
Soviet Union 222–3, 230 occupation of Eastern Europe 32–4; propaganda 26, 35–8, 67, 194–5; as a target for British and American propaganda 72–3, 140–1, 147, 157–8, 170, 183–94, 214–15, 238–42, 253
Spaak, Paul Henri 114, 193
Special Branch 198
Special Operations Executive 27, 77, 182
Spender, Stephen 3, 204–5
Stalin, Josef 32, 184, 222, 230
Stark, Freya 100
Stassen, Howard 229
State Department: attitudes towards the use of propaganda 28, 30–1, 140, 169–70, 226; information agencies 31, 46–7, 108–9, 139–43, 168–70, 224–7; liaison with Foreign Office 30, 104–12, 143–50, 156–8, 189, 212, 250–1

State-War-Navy Coordinating Committee 46
Stewart, James L. 207
Stone, Bill 104–5, 145
Strang, William 2, 54, 163–4,
    194–5, 199
Strategic Services Unit 31
Streibert, Theodore 223, 226
Student Christian Association 198

Talbot, Milo 77
Tallents, Sir Stephen 28
Taylor, A.J.P. 252
television 210
Thatcher, Margaret 254
Thayer, Charles 109–10
Third Force propaganda 8, 51–3, 65–9,
    112–25, 247, 249
Times, The 4, 49, 68, 191
Tito 232
Tokaev, Grigori 191
Tracey, Herbert 92
Tribune 71, 204
Truman, Harry S. 135–6, 139, 224; attitude
    towards propaganda 27, 31; attitude
    towards Soviet Union 33–4, 46; meeting
    with Churchill 183–4, 188–9
TUC 8, 43, 92–3, 167, 196
Tucker, H.H. 78
Tusa, John 3
Twentieth Century, The 211

United Nations 51, 76, 240–1
USA: British propaganda in 212–13, 221;
    Congress 28, 31–2, 46, 140, 146, 169–70,
    198; disposition of wartime propaganda
    agencies 27–32; Presidential elections
    33, 212–13, 222–4; public opinion 39,
    212–13

US Information Agency 225–7
US Information Service 112, 148, 152–4,
    208–10

Voice of America 31, 109–10, 140–1,
    146–7, 154, 160–2, 171, 190–1, 208, 226,
    227, 251
Volunteer Freedom Corps 191
Vyshinsky, Andrei 184

Waddams, Herbert 165
Walmsley, Margot 205
Warburg, Frederic 165, 205, 210
Warner, Christopher 37–8, 41, 44, 69–70,
    75, 86, 104, 110, 121, 143, 145–8,
    158–9, 163
Washburn, Abbott 226
Watson, Adam 16–17, 77, 87, 110, 144–5,
    156–9, 171, 189, 198–9, 205–6, 214,
    231–3, 241, 251
Watson, Francis 166
Watts, Stephen 165
Weldon, Fay 24, 78, 192
Wilkinson, Peter 77, 153, 191
Williams, E.S. 29–30
Wisner, Frank 156, 158–9, 232–3
Wolfe, Bertram 211
Woodhouse, C.M. 165, 205
World Assembly of Youth 49, 207
World Federation of Democratic Youth 49,
    196, 203
World Federation of Trades Unions
    35, 196
World Peace Council 196
Worsthorne, Peregrine 3, 5, 16
Wyatt, Woodrow 252

Yakobson, Sergius 211